MEDIA CIRCUS

MEDIA CIRCUS

The Trouble with America's Newspapers

HOWARD KURTZ

TIMES **T** BOOKS

RANDOM HOUSE

Library of Congress Cataloging-in-Publication Data

Kurtz, Howard.
    Media circus : the trouble with America's newspapers / Howard Kurtz. 1st ed., pbk. ed.
        p.   cm.
    Includes bibliographical references and index.
    ISBN-0-8129-6356-3 (pbk.)
    1. Journalism—United States—History—20th century.
2. Journalistic ethics—United States—History—20th century.   I. Title.
[PN4867.K86   1994]
071'.3—dc20   94-1063

Book Design by Naomi Osnos and M. Kristen Bearse

Manufactured in the United States of America
9   8   7   6   5

To Judy and Bonnie,
who may have wondered why Dad was spending all
those nights in the basement

Acknowledgments

My heartfelt thanks to Paul Golob, my editor, whose incisive suggestions and gentle prodding helped enhance the manuscript time and again, and to Peter Osnos, the publisher of Times Books, for believing from the start in my vision of the book. I am also grateful to Bob Kaiser for his wise counsel, and to my editors at *The Washington Post* for the freedom and support they have given me in the delicate and sometimes awkward assignment of media reporter. I am indebted to my parents, Leonard and Marcia Kurtz, for giving me the newspaper habit. Special thanks to my wife, Mary Tallmer, whose patience and forbearance made this book possible.

Contents

MEDIA CIRCUS

Introduction to the
Paperback Edition

Late on the evening of December 23, 1992, the first edition of *The New York Times* hit the streets with a front-page exclusive.

For weeks the nation's top newspapers had been filled with breathless speculation about the new administration that President-elect Bill Clinton was slowly assembling. The *Times* had already reported that Clinton planned to name the first woman attorney general and listed four top contenders. *The Washington Post* and *Los Angeles Times* followed suit by designating one of the four, Judge Patricia Wald, as the leading candidate. Now, just before Christmas, the *Times* had the big scoop: the nominee appeared to be Brooksley Born, a Washington lawyer who had met with Clinton and, according to unnamed associates, "expected to be named attorney general."

Hours after that first edition came off the presses, Clinton introduced his choice for attorney general at a Little Rock news conference. She was Zoe Baird, an obscure corporate attorney whose name had never surfaced in the dozens of pregame accounts that so mesmerized the small group of reporters chasing the story.

This pointless exercise in crystal-ball gazing would be repeated just six weeks later. After Zoe Baird became a two-word synonym for the affluent professional who hires illegal nannies, the same newspapers were again immersed in speculation about who would head the Justice Department. On February 5, 1993, *The New York Times* anointed Judge Kimba Wood with this definitive headline: "Clinton Chooses New York Judge for Justice Post." *The Washington Post* carried a similar account

3

but backed off in later editions at the urging of White House officials. Wood abruptly withdrew the next day after belatedly acknowledging that she too had hired an illegal alien as her baby-sitter.

Despite this embarrassing pattern, the press simply could not break the habit. Throughout the spring, reporters filed a seemingly endless series of stories about the president's search for a Supreme Court nominee. Each leak was hyped into headlines by the all-consuming desire to be first, only to be overtaken by the next day's leak. In early June, the press pack touted Interior Secretary Bruce Babbitt as "a leading contender" *(New York Times)*, "the clear front-runner" *(Wall Street Journal)* and "the odds-on favorite" *(USA Today)*. Then, in the blink of a news cycle, the oddsmakers shifted their bets to Judge Stephen Breyer. On June 12, a Saturday, *The New York Times* said that "officials . . . expected Mr. Clinton to announce his selection of Judge Breyer soon, possibly Saturday." The *Los Angeles Times* agreed that Breyer's appointment "appeared imminent." On the morning of Monday, June 14, *The New York Times* boldly reported that "some top aides said Mr. Clinton would nominate Judge Breyer on Monday." That afternoon, the president named Ruth Bader Ginsburg to the high court.

The media's own blunders helped dictate the story line. Many of the White House correspondents who had gathered for the Rose Garden ceremony seemed less interested in Ginsburg's nomination than in the twists and turns that had led the press down the wrong path. When ABC's Brit Hume asked Clinton about the "zigzag quality" of the search, the president angrily ended the news conference, complaining that reporters cared only about "political process" stories.

In the broad sweep of history, it matters little that the press was wrong about Brooksley Born or Kimba Wood or Stephen Breyer. Mistakes, after all, are inevitable in a business that processes millions of words and pictures each day under constant deadline pressure. What is far more troubling is the media's obsession with the gossip and gamesmanship of political insiders and the extent to which this so-called news is increasingly remote from most readers' lives. Ordinary folks are far more worried about neighborhood crime than who might be in line to become attorney general, and they have grown disgusted with journalists who behave like members of the political elite. Reporters, society's perennial outsiders, have become the new insiders.

This cultural estrangement between establishment journalists and the consumers of news is of relatively recent vintage. The old B-movie image of the newspaper reporter—a tough-talking, hard-drinking, rum-pled-looking guy who might be found badgering the police lieutenant, rushing to the nearest phone booth or laying down a few bucks at the track—is gone. Working-class stiffs have been replaced by a new generation of yuppie reporters who prefer cappuccino to a few brews at the corner bar. Today's scribe is a well-tailored, well-educated, health-conscious baby boomer who travels with a cellular phone and Toshiba laptop and speaks the language of political image-makers. The new zeitgeist is one of cool detachment, of moving with the media mob from one mega-event to the next, scribbling down the details that CNN might miss. Passion is noticeably absent, lest it be confused with partisanship. Journalists have become part of a vast entertainment culture that seeks to amuse and titillate and shies away from the risks of old-style muckraking, as media corporations have grown wary of abusing their influence or offending their audience.

Since the first edition of this book was published the circus aspects of the media world have reached new heights of outlandishness. NBC gave the profession a black eye by first setting a General Motors truck afire to hype a newsmagazine show, and then solemnly defending such incendiary journalism. Joe McGinniss and his publisher, Simon and Schuster, made the ludicrous argument that there was nothing untoward about inventing thoughts and dialogue in a biography of Ted Kennedy. *Time* magazine published a cover story about child prostitutes in Russia and took three months to admit that a photographer had staged the photos and paid the children to pose as prostitutes. *The New Yorker* ran an unsigned piece about the trial of Erich Honecker, the former East German leader, without bothering to disclose that it was written by the wife of Honecker's defense lawyer. And of course there was the seemingly endless O.J. Simpson saga.

Newspapers also found new ways to embarrass themselves. They worked themselves into a frenzy over disputed allegations that Michael Jackson had had sex with a thirteen-year-old boy, besmirching the pop star's reputation despite the meager evidence. Michael Jordan's anger at the media when he announced his retirement stemmed in part from reckless and unfounded newspaper speculation that his father's murder might have been linked to the basketball star's gambling. And the papers took their infatuation with sex to a new level of silliness in the short-lived frenzy over Heidi Fleiss, the Hollywood Madam, not to mention Lorena Bobbitt, whose celebrated mutilation of her husband made it possible for respectable newspapers to use the word "penis."

On a more ideological level, the virus of political correctness seemed to penetrate more deeply into newsroom culture, turning editors into sensitivity cops and writers into semantic outlaws. The *Los Angeles Times* was subjected to some much-deserved national ridicule in December 1993 after someone slipped me a copy of the paper's nineteen-page "Guidelines on Ethnic, Racial, Sexual and Other Identification." In what seemed almost a parody of leftist orthodoxy, the *Times* barred or strongly discouraged such terms as "WASP" ("may be pejorative"), "co-ed" ("considered derogatory to female college students") and "Dutch treat" ("an offensive reference to sharing expenses"). Also placed off-limits were "babe," "biddy," "bra-burner," "crazy," "Eskimo," "ghetto," "gypped," "handicap," "hick," "hillbilly," "inner city," "lame," "New World," "normal," "powwow" and "welsher." One of those who mocked the new vocabulary police was *Boston Globe* columnist David Nyhan, who, in his own bout with political correctness, had been fined $1,250 by *Globe* management for jokingly using the word "pussywhipped" in a casual hallway conversation. The effect of such PC crackdowns, intentional or otherwise, was to make already skittish journalists shy away from candid writing about race, sex or other sensitive matters. Timidity and inoffensiveness were becoming the ruling principles of newsroom life.

The phenomenal rise of talk radio has underscored another troubling shortcoming of the newspaper business. Millions of folks want a chance to talk back to an arrogant media establishment, yet most editors and reporters are still conducting a one-way conversation. Much of the carping about press bias is at bottom a complaint that newspapers impose one inherently subjective version of reality each morning and pretend it is absolute truth. We must stop preaching at people and find ways to let them hear their voices in the paper, even if it means ceding some of our precious newsprint to those outside the priesthood.

Despite these mounting problems, there have also been welcome reminders that newspapers remain part of the fabric of society. *The Des Moines Register*, its power knocked out by the Mississippi River floods of 1993, managed to publish an emergency edition from a Holiday Inn and distribute it across much of Iowa. *The Miami Herald* pulled off a similar miracle in 1992 after Hurricane Andrew, even as the homes of some staff members were being destroyed. Both papers provided crucial information when their disaster-stricken communities needed it most. And in an age when some analysts argue that newspapers are destined for Jurassic Park, the New York Times Company's purchase of

The Boston Globe in June 1993 amounted to a billion-dollar vote of confidence in the industry. While every big paper in America is exploring ways of downloading the headlines by computer, Arthur Sulzberger's company clearly believes that ink-on-paper news still has a solid future.

Equally encouraging is the way that some papers have stretched the boundaries of conventional journalism. The New Orleans *Times-Picayune* published a remarkable series on race relations—including a brutally candid examination of its own racist past—that brought a torrent of reaction from readers. *The Albuquerque Tribune,* in an amazing bit of detective work, uncovered the identities of five people who were unwittingly injected with plutonium by government scientists in the 1940s—and the national media failed to pick up on the little paper's revelations until federal officials held a news conference three weeks later. *USA Today* invited reader queries on Clinton's complicated health care plan and regularly published the answers. *The New York Times* reported on the once-taboo subject of violent lyrics in black rap music. A number of foreign correspondents bravely and relentlessly reported on the carnage in Bosnia, despite public indifference around the world.

In an old-fashioned demonstration of a newspaper's power to right wrongs, *The Washington Post*'s Linda Wheeler reported on the death of James Hudson, a lowly maintenance worker at the Lincoln Memorial, whose wife and seven children were left without a pension or life insurance because of the government's refusal to extend such benefits to temporary employees. Volunteers quickly raised $80,000 for Hudson's family, and the National Park Service vowed to reexamine its benefits policy.

I am convinced that the finest newspaper stories are infused with the kind of passion that is all too often missing from an increasingly bland profession. Busy readers don't have time for the sort of dull and inconsequential reports that we mass-produce each day, but they invariably respond to journalism that is fueled by commitment. In traveling around the country, I've been struck by how strongly people feel about their local paper, even when they're in the process of denouncing it. The old, low-tech newspaper still has a weight and a permanence that television lacks, and a reservoir of trust that makes readers feel betrayed when we let them down. They sense the obvious hypocrisy among media big shots who seem to investigate everyone but themselves.

· · ·

To be a media reporter for one of the nation's biggest newspapers is to dwell in the belly of the beast.

It is virtually impossible to report honestly on the news business without also writing about the folks who pay my salary. Should I ever be tempted to forget this vital link, I'm reminded each morning when I walk to my desk, which is a few feet from the glass-enclosed office of Leonard Downie, Jr., *The Washington Post*'s executive editor.

A standing joke in the newsroom is that people get nervous when they see me coming with pen and pad. It is awkward, to say the least, to have to interview colleagues about whether they slanted a story or went easy on a source, or to question Bob Woodward or David Broder about his reporting method, or to press Ben Bradlee on why he is retiring. It is even less fun confronting my bosses with sensitive questions about plagiarism, bias, racial preference or sexual harassment. But they understand that a media reporter wouldn't have a shred of credibility if he simply ignored the Washington Post Company—even if that means granting me an unusual license to second-guess them in print. It is a built-in conflict of interest, to be sure, but one that there is no satisfactory way around.

Working for a major media company means that much of what I write is automatically viewed with suspicion. If I criticize *The New York Times,* some people think I'm simply dumping on the *Post*'s biggest rival. If I take a shot at *Time,* there are suggestions that I'm really giving a boost to *Newsweek,* which is also owned by Katharine Graham's company. And if I say a nice word about the *Post*'s coverage, I'm sure to be dismissed as a hometown booster. The only answer is to play it straight and try to develop a reputation for calling 'em as I see 'em.

The fun part of patrolling the media beat is that I get all kinds of tips and leads from my gossipy brethren. If there's a plagiarism incident in Fort Worth, a newsroom revolt in Boston or a complaint about sexism in St. Petersburg, chances are someone will drop a dime. I also get a steady torrent of unsolicited advice about people's pet peeves—in the hallway, in the elevator, in the men's room. Strangers call with breathless tips or send me scrawled letters accusing the press of shocking bias. Everyone, it seems, is a frustrated media critic.

Covering the press means constantly putting other journalists on the spot. Many are good-natured about finding themselves at the other end of the notebook, but a surprising number resort to a brusque "no comment" or "you'll have to speak to my editor." Some refuse to talk to me because of past stories or launch into tirades over some picayune point. Others nervously call back two or three times, adding detailed rebuttals, faxing me backup data or endlessly refining their quotes. It's part of a writer's genetic makeup, I suppose, that we always think of the perfect phrase after hanging up. But it's strange how often a reporter will ask for kid-gloves treatment—"Protect me on this, will you?" or "Don't make me sound too bad"—when they would huffily dismiss such suggestions from a public official. Perhaps journalists are overly cautious because they know, having sinned themselves, how words can be wrenched out of context.

I've been interviewed quite a bit since taking on this beat, either because media reporters are presumed to know a little bit about everything or because other reporters know we can't say no. I've been asked about subjects ranging from AIDS coverage to Pentagon censorship to the annual outbreak of silly summer stories. After writing a magazine piece about how television's most ubiquitous experts often have more glibness than expertise, I was, of course, invited on television to pop off on the subject. Sometimes I hear myself spewing forth opinions I didn't know I had in an effort to provide a serviceable quote. At other times reporters try to nudge me in a certain direction, fishing for the comment that will match their preconceived notion of the story. You begin to understand why politicians choose their words so carefully. Still, I can babble on with the best of them, knowing full well that my penetrating insights will be reduced to a sentence or two through the miracle of journalistic condensation.

In the end, covering the media beat properly means making people mad, an uncomfortable prospect when the targets of your darts are often friends and colleagues. It means setting yourself up as a moral authority when readers know full well you're as fallible as those you're writing about. And it means opening yourself up to special scrutiny, since people take great pleasure in convicting a media critic of the charges he is constantly leveling at others.

Especially if he has the temerity to write a book.

For a lifelong newspaperman to examine the prognosis of newspapers in the age of CNN is, in a broader sense, a conflict of interest as well. For it is in my own self-interest to believe that the bulky paper that arrives on your doorstep each morning, filled with yesterday's news, has not become obsolete.

When I got my first newspaper job in the mid-1970s, the denizens of the press were on a Watergate high, glorified by movies and television as the six-gun sheriffs who had cleaned up Washington. A decade later I watched in amazement as newspapers seemed to acquire the Midas touch, swept to profitable new heights in the golden age of the 1980s. Yet in recent years the forecast has suddenly turned grim. The newspaper world of the '90s is reeling from its worst downturn since the Depression. I have watched colleagues lose their jobs and once-healthy newspapers wither and die. The proportion of households reading a daily newspaper continues to shrink, as it has for the past thirty years. Newspapers are losing ground to C-SPAN and pay-per-view, to home computers and fax machines, to direct mail and specialty magazines and home shopping clubs and books-on-tape and a hundred other leisure pursuits. Our once-lofty prestige has sunk to new depths. We have been censored by the military during the Persian Gulf war, castigated by depositors for missing the savings-and-loan debacle, ridiculed by voters for feeding the Gennifer Flowers frenzy. We have been blamed by both blacks and whites for exacerbating racial intolerance and all but ignoring the problems that produced the Los Angeles riots. We have been reduced to fodder for late-night comics.

Even as our journalistic fortunes have plummeted, the economic fates seemed aligned against us as well. Labor strife continues to cripple some big-city papers, and noisy, dirty printing presses seem ancient in an era of satellite communications. Big chains have gobbled up independent dailies, turning them into assembly-line products with lots of shorts and graphics and four-color weather maps. The number of competitive newspaper towns has rapidly dwindled, and the only newspaper success story of the past decade has been *USA Today,* which made its name spoon-feeding McNuggets of news to the video generation. There is a deep-rooted fear, even at the biggest papers, that much of the audience has tuned out, leaving us writing for a small, self-important elite.

Newspapers, in short, have become unplugged from their readers. There is a fatal disconnection, a growing gap between editors and reporters on the one hand and consumers of news on the other. We have this fabulous franchise that, for all its limitations, provides a daily cornucopia of information and insight and opinion, and yet we have allowed it (and in some ways caused it) to become dangerously eroded. My incestuous profession has become increasingly self-absorbed, even as its practitioners wring their hands about why fewer people seem to be listening. I hear this depressing talk every day, in newsroom meetings, in casual conversations, in my colleagues' bitter jokes about toiling for a dying business.

In some ways we are the architects of our own misfortune, sacrificing our credibility for a misguided notion of what sells. Dumbing down the product has done nothing to stem the tide of newspaper closings. We have all but forfeited our watchdog function at government agencies like HUD while showcasing media manipulators like Donald Trump and Al Sharpton. And as we increasingly grapple with our own racial conflicts and ethical lapses, we seem to the outside world to be haughty and hypocritical, holding others to a standard that we ourselves could never meet.

For two decades, even as newspapers steadily lost market share, they continued to produce the equivalent of huge, clunky sedans with tail fins. They were gray, bulky products, poorly designed, poorly edited and poorly printed. Wedded to the ways of the past, the newspaper business found itself overtaken by a domestic information explosion. Demographics were also working against us as city dwellers fled to the suburbs, taking their purchasing power with them. The metropolitan newspaper seemed about as nimble as a dinosaur.

Most newspapers are afflicted with what I call "creeping incrementalism." We take a handful of stories and chew them over and over, with second-day stories and third-day stories and ninth-day stories, until they are utterly devoid of flavor. We seize on minute developments and imbue them with cosmic significance: "House Clears Way for Vote on Rights Bill." "Baker Urges Israeli Response on Talks." "Economists at Odds on Recession." "G-7 Vows to Stabilize Currencies." We delude ourselves into believing that most people are as fascinated by the inner workings of government and politics as we are. We relentlessly round up experts who are as likely to be wrong as your dimwitted neighbor down the street. We tell you what happened yesterday when you've already seen it on the tube. We drive away readers—particularly women—by immersing ourselves in the empty maneuverings of middle-aged white guys in suits. We have become bland purveyors of fact, polite packagers of bureaucratic news. No wonder people are turned off.

Still, newspapers have somehow managed to hang on. There is something about flipping through the local paper, like our parents and grandparents before us, that remains a comfortable habit. You can fold it up and take it with you on the bus. You can put aside the Metro section and read it later. It has what computer people call random access, meaning you can take what you want, from basketball scores to movie listings to supermarket ads, when you want it, not when some network programmer wants you to have it.

More important, newspapers help us make sense of the blur of televised images racing by. We provide the context, the explanations, the fine print. When it comes to finding out things that government and business leaders don't want us to know, newspapers remain the last bastion of what used to be called muckraking. From Watergate to Iran-contra to the BCCI banking fraud, it is the pencil press that has dug up the dirt. Sure, we have missed too many scandals in recent years and salivated over the exploits of too many celebrities. But we have tried to hold on to the basic mission in a way you rarely get from television.

Yet we in this business have gone a long way toward squandering our natural advantages. For too long we have published newspapers aimed at other journalists—talking to ourselves, really, and to the insiders we gossip with—and paying scant attention to readers. We console ourselves with high-minded claptrap about our responsibility to inform the masses, forgetting that you can't teach people a thing until you get them inside the tent.

Where once newspapers were at the very heart of the national conversation, they now seem remote, arrogant, part of the governing elite. Where once newspapers embodied cultural values, they now seem mired in a tabloid culture that gorges itself on sex and sleaze. Where once newspapers helped spur a crusade for civil rights, they now seem to aggravate racial tensions. Where once newspapers helped turn the country against an unjust war, they now are jeered for daring to question a wildly popular war. Where once newspapers were on the front lines in exposing official corruption, they now bring up the rear, more concerned with accommodating power than challenging it.

The paradox for those of us laboring behind the word processors is this: Newspapers in the '90s are better written and better edited than at any time in history, and yet our efforts have fallen far short of what readers demand in an information-saturated age. It seems not to matter that journalists today are better educated and more specialized, in fields ranging from medicine to the environment, than their ink-stained predecessors. Or that the profession's ethical standards, once something of a joke, have never been higher. Or that the work force, whose doors were long closed to minorities and women, has never been more diverse. Publishers and editors struggle mightily to divine the desires of their readers, yet they increasingly resemble overpaid Detroit auto executives trying to figure out why people keep buying Toyotas and Hondas.

It's not that people aren't reading—magazine circulation has climbed steadily in recent decades—but that they ain't buying what we're selling. The blunt truth is that tinkering and half-measures will no longer do the trick. There is a cancer eating away at the newspaper business—the cancer of boredom, superficiality and irrelevance—and radical surgery is needed.

This book is a media critic's attempt to examine what has gone wrong with the profession he loves, written from a vantage point inside the newsroom. It is roughly divided into four sections. The first deals with stories that the press has fumbled, bumbled or otherwise botched in recent years. The reasons range from a growing tendency toward pack journalism to a preference for glitter over substance, from an obsession with celebrities to an unwillingness to challenge expert opinion. The result has been one missed opportunity after another on the biggest scandals of the last decade.

The second group of chapters explores the rules around which newspapers have tried to organize themselves, and how amorphous and inadequate these rules seem when push comes to shove. The industry's standards have been virtually shredded by rumors and gossip, by stories about race and extramarital affairs and the outing of homosexuals, and by the ethical transgressions of our colleagues. All this has left reporters confused about where the boundaries lie, both for themselves and the people they write about.

The third section examines the incestuous interplay between press and government at the highest levels of power. It is here, in covering the military, the White House and presidential politics, that journalism makes its most indelible mark—or, as is increasingly the case, is molded and manipulated by powerful and seductive forces.

Finally, the book concludes by returning to the basic dilemma facing the newspaper business—figuring out its role in a society that can instantly access information from dozens of sources. These final chapters will look at newspapers that have died and those that are struggling to be reborn, and the values that are pushing editors and publishers along dramatically different paths.

In many ways, the newspaper business is still trying to regain its balance after the roller-coaster ride of the '80s. It was a time when the well of media profits seemed bottomless, when a booming America was an article of journalistic faith, when the feats of corporate titans were chronicled with a fervor once reserved for athletes and movie stars, while stories that affected people's pocketbooks and their confidence in government were largely overlooked. It was a time when celebrities were big news and rumors about celebrities even bigger news.

And no story of the '80s was bigger than the self-promotional saga of one man, his money and his mistress.

1

Trump: The Decade

n the fall of 1976, *The New York Times* had this to say about Donald Trump:

"He is tall, lean and blond, with dazzling white teeth, and he looks ever so much like Robert Redford. He rides around town in a chauffeured silver Cadillac with his initials, DJT, on the plates. He dates slinky fashion models, belongs to the most elegant clubs and, at only 30 years of age, estimates that he is 'worth more than $200 million.'

"Flair. It's one of Donald J. Trump's favorite words, and both he, his friends and his enemies use it when describing his way of life, as well as his business style as New York's No. 1 real estate promoter of the middle 1970s."

That feature story would serve as a model for the kind of fawning, uncritical reporting lavished upon Trump for the next fifteen years. It is a bit embarrassing to recall how wild we all went over The Donald, how eagerly we gushed over his antics, and how utterly inconsequential it all seems now. Trump set the standard for pointless excess in the press, a standard that now serves to remind us of our worst shortcomings: the relentless panting after big-name stars, the bottomless fascination with seamy gossip, the tawdry spectacle of highbrow newspapers following the tabloids into the gutter. It was the ultimate media circus. Sure, the Donald-and-Marla saga was fun, but we acted like little kids gorging ourselves on chocolate fudge. Trump had become our national playboy, a man who was famous for being famous, and reporters and editors were the co-conspirators who kept his name in lights.

The media's Trump infatuation was all the more humiliating in light of the stories we so cavalierly kissed off during those years. The homeless, the urban poor, the less fortunate were all deemed hopelessly déclassé during the 1980s.

The press corps all but ignored the Housing and Urban Development Department, which was being looted by politically connected builders and fixers while Trump's exploits were front-page news. Covering a regulatory agency, after all, was hard work, while chasing after Trump was seductively easy—so easy that we never bothered to question whether his much-ballyhooed wealth might involve a sizable dose of media hype.

There were larger forces at work here as well, for newspapers faithfully reflect the prejudices of their times. Blinded by Trump-like glitter, the press grew increasingly disconnected from the middle class, losing sight of the unglamorous work that had once defined its mission. Digging into public malfeasance and challenging those in power began to seem less important than chronicling the exploits of the fabulously wealthy. Journalists were swept along by the fashion of the hour, helping to create a cult of personality that often took the place of investigation and analysis. It was easier to lavish breathless prose on Trump Tower than to examine the government's failure to provide housing for the poor. It was easier to glorify rich developers than to scrutinize the overleveraged banks that were lending them vast sums of money. Only years later, when the party was over and the country woke up with a hangover, would the magnitude of the media's failure become clear.

When Trump first became a staple for New York gossip columnists in the early '80s, most respectable newspapers did not consider it within their purview to delve into the extramarital affairs of married business-men. But as more news organizations discovered that tales of the rich and famous could be an irresistible marketing tool, every paper in America started a personalities column and beefed up its life-style section. And editors needed juicy subjects to fill all that space.

The New York tabloids were the alchemists that turned Trump into a folk hero. Gossip-mongers like Liz Smith and Cindy Adams were becoming stars in their own right, with big salaries and television con-tracts, and Trump was their pal, eager to supply them with a steady diet of tidbits.

Since the tabloids plied their trade in the nation's media capital, the Trump legend quickly spread to the newsmagazines and to television. The Manhattan publishing world took note, and soon Trump was out with a best-selling autobiography. The phenomenon came full circle as the Trump soap opera hooked the elite press and played to a worldwide audience.

Year after year, even the best reporters were mesmerized by Trump's carefully constructed persona. They faithfully repeated Trump's claim that he didn't have a public relations agent, when in fact he employed one of New York's most prominent superflacks, Howard Rubenstein.

All editors love symbols, and Trump consciously advanced himself as the preeminent symbol of the greed decade. He shrewdly understood from the start that wealth would be worshiped in Ronald Reagan's America, that the shameless accumulation of luxury would be envied. If the press failed to discover that Trump's magical kingdom was built on a shaky mountain of debt, it was largely because no one tried. The pink-marble image was more important than the balance-sheet reality. Trump was as much a master of image-making as Michael Deaver or Roger Ailes.

When Trump was flying high, who dared say when the bubble might burst? Everyone, from Ivan Boesky to Saul Steinberg, from Michael Milken to T. Boone Pickens, was getting rich on borrowed money and getting good press to boot. Twenty-four-year-old MBAs were making $200,000 a year. Real estate was booming. Big companies were swallowing even bigger companies. The profit motive was in. Newspapers went along for the ride, rolling up 25 to 30 percent profit margins year after year with little effort. It seemed like the merry-go-round would never stop. And there was The Donald, with his 80-foot living room and his 118-room Palm Beach estate and his 282-foot *Trump Princess* yacht, the cover boy for an era of excess.

"As people are addicted to heroin and alcohol, this guy's addicted to publicity," one Trump associate says. "Someone would print a hatchet job about him and if it had a good photo, he'd love it. He would constantly want to get his name in the papers, associated with beautiful women. His philosophy was, get the name out there. That's good for business. People buy the name."

Donald Trump no longer looks ever so much like Robert Redford. In fact, he barely resembles the Trump of the mid-'80s—the supremely confident whiz kid who could add millions to a property's value merely by chiseling his name on it. But even in decline, he remains a cultural touchstone, the '80s icon who got his '90s comeuppance. Newspapers are never actually wrong, you see, they merely adjust the conventional wisdom from time to time.

Despite the fact that so many journalists were taken in for so long, we still have a seemingly insatiable appetite for Trump-o-mania. Sure, the game now is to ridicule Trump instead of glorifying him, but it's just the other side of the coin of celebrity. "He's still fascinating," says Jerry Nachman, who hyped Trump constantly as editor of the *New York Post.* "The same pack instinct that gets him up there and keeps him up there is now driven to kick him whenever he puts his head up."

It has all the trappings of a medieval ritual: First we build 'em up, then we tear 'em down.

In a news culture that runs through celebrities like Kleenex, nothing is more important than being wealthy or famous, and the media play a crucial role in marketing these larger-than-life personalities. But just as they reach mythic proportions, some cosmic turn of fate seems to ensure that we splatter them with handfuls of mud. The process seemed strangely accelerated in New York in the late 1980s as the high and mighty were dragged to the federal courthouse at Foley Square, there to be roughed up by the waiting media mob.

Bess Myerson was a glamorous former Miss America and top New York City official before she was tried (and acquitted) for allegedly fixing a divorce case involving her sewer-contractor boyfriend and his ex-wife. "The Bess Mess," the tabloids called it.

Leona Helmsley was the queen of a glitzy hotel empire and star of a thousand magazine ads before she was convicted of fraud and tax evasion. She was ridiculed as the Queen of Mean before heading off to prison.

Michael Milken was the junk-bond genius responsible for dozens of corporate takeovers before his company went belly-up and he pleaded guilty to securities fraud. The man who made $550 million in a single year wound up spending more than two years behind bars.

Imelda Marcos was a powerful first lady and the toast of Manhattan's jet set before being pilloried as the shopping-mad widow of a fallen dictator. She was acquitted of criminal charges but enshrined in history as the woman who accumulated a thousand pairs of shoes.

Donald Trump's climb to fame began more modestly. As the '70s ended, he was an ambitious young developer from Queens who wore burgundy leisure suits and was trying to make it in Manhattan. By 1982, however, the Trump name had taken on an unmistakable cachet. Trump Tower was nearing completion on the ultra-glitzy corner of Fifth Avenue and 56th Street, and Trump was clever enough not to deny a false rumor that Prince Charles was considering buying an apartment there. As he summed up his credo: "Bad publicity is sometimes better than no publicity at all. Controversy, in short, sells."

The press grew obsessed with the Trump life-style. *The Wall Street Journal,* the bible of the moneyed class, paid homage in a 1982 piece by Randall Smith: "Combining a huckster's flair for hyperbole with a shrewd business sense, he sells himself as well . . . weaving an aura of glamour and chic around his name." The Trump apartment was "replete with platforms, mirrors, chrome wall-sculptures and two dining-room tables made of goatskin hardened to a marble-like surface. . . . Mr. Trump courts such fame. He offers journalists rides in his Cadillac limousine and not-for-attribution tidbits."

The selling of Donald Trump, mogul, was in full swing. "He really took on almost mythic status," says Tony Schwartz, who covered Trump for *New York* magazine and later became his co-author. "He became larger than life. It's a blond, Aryan, young, brash, limitless, don't-play-by-anyone's-rules, do-whatever-the-fuck-you-want approach to life that seemed to work in spades. What his life was actually like was never really part of the equation."

Trump was one of the boldfaced names, showing up at the right parties with his wife, Ivana, on his arm. "I always liked him," says Liz Smith, the longtime gossip doyenne of the *Daily News,* who now plies her trade for *Newsday.* "I found him very funny. He reminded me of a big adolescent boy."

When journalists needed color for an article, Trump would take them along in his helicopter and they in turn would burnish the image. He routinely offered Liz Smith the use of his yacht or rides on his helicopter. "The quid pro quo was you would promote his gig and he was always good copy," Jerry Nachman recalls.

One of the few dissonant notes during this period was sounded by Sydney Schanberg, *The New York Times'* local columnist, who railed about Trump's efforts to force tenants out of his apartment building at 100 Central Park South so he could tear it down and build a bigger, more luxurious one. Schanberg was particularly exercised over Trump's offer to house the homeless in some of the building's vacant apartments, calling it "obscenely condescending" and a thinly veiled attempt to harass the tenants into leaving.

"Trump either had a fawning ride or a free ride all the way through with the New York press," says Schanberg, now with *New York News-day*. "They overlooked all kinds of things he did. They were just totally uncritical. I find it hard to explain why we all bought into him."

Although Trump was often involved in messy litigation, Schanberg says, "the *Times* would never cover it. People would send me documents and I would send them to the desk. I stopped. I was told it was being thrown in the wastebasket."

As Trump built one luxury tower after another, few journalists questioned, as Schanberg did, whether he had any responsibility to build housing for middle-income families. Such concerns had nearly vanished from the journalistic agenda. There was little debate at the time about the wisdom of granting huge tax breaks to rich New York developers to build soaring palaces that blocked sun and sky.

Schanberg's caustic columns about the man he referred to as "Young Donald" brought him a rebuke from Arthur Ochs Sulzberger. "The publisher got annoyed at one point about my columns on Trump and sent me a note," Schanberg says. "He didn't like the tone, said it was not *Times*-like. He said, 'I can't imagine he hasn't done anything good for the city at all.' It was the only note I ever got from him.

"I wrote back: 'The reason you don't know about all the bad things he's done is that Metro isn't covering it,' and I made a list. I was driving nails in my coffin." Sulzberger killed Schanberg's column in 1985, prompting him to quit. He had apparently upset his bosses by writing too caustically about the city's social problems.

More typical of the paper's coverage was a seven-thousand-word paean to Trump in *The New York Times Magazine*. "Donald J. Trump is the man of the hour," William Geist wrote in 1984. "Turn on the television or open a newspaper almost any day of the week and there he is. . . . He has no public relations agent. . . . Spending a day with Donald Trump is like driving a Ferrari without the windshield. It is exhilarating. . . . The Trump touch. It has set some people in New York to outright Trump worship." Indeed.

Geist did make a passing reference to "poor people . . . sleeping in the streets" while folks like Trump got richer, but quickly noted that "many urban-affairs experts view the developers as saviors of our post-industrial cities."

Nearly all traces of skepticism had vanished from Trump's press coverage. The merest suggestion that he was considering a new venture would produce big headlines. Trump would build a luxury tower in

Brazil. He would erect the world's tallest building on Manhattan's West Side. He would build a hotel in Moscow. He would buy a Hollywood studio. He would build a football stadium in Queens, help bankroll a new baseball league, start a chain of superstores to compete with Bloomingdale's. There would be Trump the board game, Trump the television game, Trump the movie, Trump the blimp, Trump the limousine. That most of these proposals died a quiet death did nothing to diminish the developer's luster.

The Donald even drew erudite words of praise from the high-toned columnist George Will: "Trump, who believes that excess can be a virtue, is as American as Manhattan's skyline. . . . He carries purposefulness in every crease of his clothes." *Manhattan inc.,* an '80s magazine that did not survive 1990, even started a "Trump Watch" column.

Trump gave interviews by the dozen, protesting all the while. "I hate to do these things, you know," he told Lois Romano of *The Washington Post*'s Style section in 1984.

Trump spun a yarn for Romano about "one of the most successful men in New York" who had a debilitating problem: "He couldn't get a table at a restaurant." Trump says he rescued the man from social humiliation by getting him a prime spot at Le Cirque.

" 'The man calls me back a week later. He wants to know the name of my public relations firm,' says Trump, who has no public relations firm. 'And I said to him, Either you have it or you don't.' "

Trump, of course, had it—the Howard Rubenstein PR firm, that is—but he didn't share this secret with Romano.

"He needs press attention in the way that most people need food," Tony Schwartz says. "He simply must have it. It's his way of feeling alive."

Trump soon learned he could make news simply by lashing out. When Paul Goldberger, the *New York Times* architecture critic, displeased him, he phoned in from the Aspen ski slopes to tell the *New York Post*'s Page Six: "He just dresses so badly. . . . Oh my God, look at his clothes." When a *Chicago Tribune* critic blasted his proposed 150-story skyscraper, Trump went a step further, filing a $500-million libel suit that generated nationwide headlines. Few noticed when a judge threw out the suit a year later.

The press loves nothing better than a good feud, and few understood this better than Trump. He started a running battle with Ed Koch, attacking him as "our idiot mayor," "a disaster waiting to explode," a "moron" and a "bully." Koch returned fire by calling Trump "greedy" and "piggy." Reporters ate it up.

Trump also became a presence on the sports pages by buying the New Jersey Generals (part of the ill-fated United States Football League), staging Atlantic City prizefights and becoming an adviser to heavyweight champion Mike Tyson.

For all his press clippings, though, Donald Trump was still primarily a New York figure. That began to change in the spring of 1986, when the developer, in a brilliant public relations stroke, took on a job that city officials had botched for years: the renovation of the Wollman ice-skating rink in Central Park.

After six years and $13 million, the Koch administration had failed to reopen the once-grand rink. Trump did the job in three and a half months for less than $3 million. Of course, as Koch was quick to point out, a private builder has certain advantages—he is not bound by cumbersome contracting laws or required to hire the lowest bidder—but such subtleties were lost in the torrent of headlines from Miami to Los Angeles.

"He would demand to have one press conference after another," Trump's associate says, recalling this period. "That's when he started to lose it a little, to take himself much too seriously. He went from being this ambitious, bright real estate guy to someone who believed his own hype."

And what hype it was. *Washington Post* columnist Haynes Johnson called Trump "a modern-day Gatsby." *Newsweek* began a cover story this way: "Donald John Trump—real estate developer, casino operator, corporate raider and perhaps future politician—is a symbol of an era. He is the man with the Midas fist. For better or worse, in the 1980s it is OK to be fiercely ambitious, staggeringly rich and utterly at ease in bragging about it. . . . Asked if he's the ultimate Yuppie, he replied, 'Yeah, maybe.' "

That issue was one of the best-sellers of 1987. "It should be; he bought ten thousand copies himself," a *Newsweek* spokeswoman sniffed.

In the fall of 1987, Trump began to encourage speculation that he might run for president. This, says one source, was part of a deliberate plan to draw attention to his forthcoming book, *Trump: The Art of the Deal*. The Trump publicity machine set out to raise his national profile by planting the farfetched notion that he might try to succeed Ronald Reagan.

Trump's first move was to spend $94,000 on full-page ads in the *New York Times, Washington Post* and *Boston Globe,* assailing the Reagan administration for in effect subsidizing Japan and Saudi Arabia by providing safe passage for Persian Gulf oil tankers. The advertisement was produced by the "Tuesday Team," the Madison Avenue admen who had handled Reagan's 1984 reelection campaign.

Just as reporters were wondering what was up, Trump accepted a speaking invitation in New Hampshire. The result was a press agent's fantasy. When Trump helicoptered to Portsmouth, New Hampshire, for the Rotary Club luncheon, the New York dailies, the Boston television stations and a team from ABC's "20/20" were all on hand.

The New York Times carried this dispatch: "Insisting that he is not a candidate for president, Donald J. Trump flew to New Hampshire, the state with the earliest presidential primary, and today delivered what sounded like an impassioned campaign speech to an enthusiastic audience. . . . Mr. Trump told the audience he was tired of the United States 'being kicked around' by allies like Japan, Saudi Arabia and Kuwait."

But as J.J. would ask her husband in Garry Trudeau's "Doonesbury" comic strip: "Oh, c'mon. A condo developer for president?" Few journalists paused to question what would happen if a rich casino owner— whose views on national issues were often glib at best—actually mounted a campaign for the White House. There was a collective suspension of disbelief. This was no mere news story; it was a cultural phenomenon, and a different set of rules seemed to apply.

Even normally cynical New York journalists had little trouble imagining Trump seeking office. "Donald Trump insisted yesterday that he would not run against Mayor Koch," the *New York Post* reported in a serious tone.

I met Trump for the first time during this publicity blitz. I had been *The Washington Post*'s New York bureau chief for just two months when the Rubenstein firm offered me a one-hour interview pegged to the publication of *The Art of the Deal.*

It was the oldest form of barter in the newspaper business. Trump got what he wanted—a long profile playing up the book in the *Post*'s Style section—and I got access to one of the city's most prominent characters. Reporters are used all the time in this fashion, often by top government officials, but more transparently by movie stars, actors and authors promoting their latest film, play or book. Such interview pieces are usually an exercise in superficiality, based on little more than a forty-five-minute chat in a hotel room.

At the appointed hour I was ushered into the twenty-sixth-floor Trump Tower office, where The Donald greeted me in his gruff style. He sounded like the guys I grew up with on the streets of Brooklyn. "When I go up to New Hampshire—I'm not running for president, by the way—I got the best crowd, the best of everything in terms of reception," he assured me without being asked. "The politicians go up and get a moderate audience. I go up and they're scalping tickets. You heard that? They're scalping tickets! Why? Because people don't want to be ripped off, and this country is being ripped off. I think if I ran, I'd win."

But Trump's New Hampshire foray may have been more than just pre-publication hype. "The guy was beginning to lose touch with reality," Trump's longtime associate says. "He'd say, 'Whaddya think? You think I should run for president?' "

Over the next two years, Trump went on an unrestrained buying spree, often flouting the rules he espoused in his own book. He bought the Plaza, the crown jewel of Manhattan hotels, for a staggering $400 million. He floated $675 million in junk bonds to take over the still-unfinished Taj Mahal, although he already owned two other casinos in Atlantic City. He bought the Eastern Shuttle for $365 million, and tried to buy American Airlines for $7 billion. He picked up Adnan Khashoggi's yacht for $29 million.

Each purchase was played in the press as a triumph. Few reporters questioned whether Trump was overpaying or becoming overextended. Most accepted his view that these were trophy properties whose value could only soar, especially once they were emblazoned with his magic name. And Trump had ways of making his investments look good. He let it be known that the sultan of Brunei had offered him $600 million for the Plaza, a "fact" duly recorded by *The Wall Street Journal*. There was no certain way to check this, so it became part of the lore.

In those boom years, when corporate raiders were dashing figures and the Japanese were snatching up Manhattan landmarks such as Rockefeller Center, no price seemed too high. The media market was so overheated that even smaller newspapers were fetching hundreds of millions of dollars. With the banks (whose day of reckoning had not yet come) lending huge sums on easy terms, who was to say what a hotel or an airline might be worth?

Still, Trump was underwriting such purchases by personally guaranteeing more than $500 million in loans, as Neil Barsky would later report in *The Wall Street Journal*. Although no one knew it at the time, Trump's neck was on the line.

For the press, however, the story was the glitz and the glitter, not the price-to-earnings ratio. Trump-watching had become a national pastime. When Donald threw himself a forty-second birthday party at Trump's Castle, complete with a flying saucer and smoke-snorting dragon, it warranted a sizable story in *The Philadelphia Inquirer* (and coverage by eight TV crews). *The Washington Post* ran a story on how Mikhail Gorbachev planned a drop-by at Trump Tower (Gorby later canceled). *The Boston Globe* ran a lengthy piece calling Donald and Ivana "the nation's royal couple. . . . They are the most talked about, most written about, most photographed, most high profile couple around. They live the 'Dynasty' life."

Ivana Trump began to receive more attention in her own right after her husband installed her at the helm of Trump's Castle and, later, the Plaza. The *Daily News* ran one piece called "Shopping with Ivana Trump" and another on her diet and exercise regimen. A long feature in the *Chicago Tribune* was titled "The Queen of Trump."

As Donald Trump soared into the media stratosphere—he was the subject of fresh cover stories in *Time* and *Newsweek* in 1989—he again began popping off on serious subjects. When a young jogger was raped and brutally beaten in Central Park by a gang of Harlem youths, Trump took out an ad calling for the revival of the death penalty. "I want to hate these muggers and murderers," he said in the ad.

Trump found he could settle old scores at will. He wrote a scathing letter to Leona Helmsley, then under indictment on tax evasion and extortion charges, and made it available to his favorite paper, the *New York Post*. The letter, prompted by a dispute over some Atlantic City property, called Helmsley a "disgrace to humanity" and said that "without the veil of Harry Helmsley, you would not be able to randomly fire and abuse people in order to make yourself happy."

When I reached Trump the next day, he happily faxed me the letter. "This is a bad woman. . . . The funny thing is, she always kisses my ass when she sees me," Trump said. He understood the game well enough to know that no reporter could resist such a slashing personal attack, and that by leaking the letter he could dictate the spin on the story.

But those in Trump's inner circle saw the emptiness behind all the media attention. As one put it, "He began to feel he should start commenting on everything: Too much investment in this country by the Japanese, harsher penalties for the guys who raped that girl in Central Park. I'd always be scratching my head and saying, people believe this shit?"

After twenty-seven years of captivity, Nelson Mandela was released from a South African prison on February 11, 1990. But the historic event was overshadowed, at least in the New York tabloids, by Liz Smith's column on the impending breakup of the Trumps' marriage.

One of the most spectacular media frenzies of the late twentieth century was quickly under way. "SPLIT!" roared the next day's *New York Post,* relegating Mandela's release to a small box in the lower left-hand corner of page one. Each legal demand, each fleeting sign of reconciliation, each twist and turn of the melodrama was breathlessly reported. Whole forests were felled to tell the world about Marla Maples, the bit-part actress and billboard model from Georgia who everyone knew was Trump's paramour, notwithstanding his coy insistence that they were "just friends."

The headline-writers went wild: "IVANA BETTER DEAL." "GIMME THE PLAZA." "DON JUAN." "TRUMPS UP THE ANTE TO $100,000,000." "LEGAL DONNY-BROOK." "THE DONALD, MARLA SETTING UP HOUSE." "NOW THE DONALD WILL SQUEEZE HIS PEACH IN PUBLIC." "MARLA'S HIDEAWAY." "IVANA IN TEARS." "IVANA SEES A SHRINK." "MARLA BLOWS HER STACK." "MOM SAYS DONALD AND MARLA WANT TO GET MARRIED."

Within days, Trump: The Divorce was the lead story in *USA Today. Time, People* and *New York* magazine ran cover stories. The *New York Post,* describing Maples as the "blonde bombshell," "busty beauty" or "curvy starlet," had the tawdry tale on page one for eight straight days, the *Daily News* for nine. Television was in hot pursuit. When the *National Enquirer* came up with an exclusive photo of Donald and Marla on a date, TV stations rushed to broadcast it.

Even *The New York Times,* while positioning itself above the fray, ran pieces on the legalities of prenuptial agreements and, of course, the excessive media coverage. The "media story" is a venerable ploy by which respectable, high-minded newspapers take note of disreputable, low-brow happenings without soiling their petticoats: Look what those wretched tabloids are up to now! But although the *Times* seemed uncomfortable with the tackiness of the Trump divorce—"It's News?" a headline asked—the paper couldn't very well ignore the story that all of haute society was chattering about.

Hell, it *was* news. I shamelessly churned out more than a dozen stories on Trump versus Trump for *The Washington Post*'s Style section, which couldn't get enough of it. One senior editor harrumphed that perhaps I was spending too much time on such tabloid trash, but others assured me they were reading every word. As Don Forst, editor of *New York Newsday,* said, "It revolves around lust, power, money, sex. . . . People just lap it up."

The carnival atmosphere was heightened by the legions of spin-control artists on each side. Each Trump communicated through a designated gossip columnist. Donald tossed tidbits to Cindy Adams of the *New York Post,* while Ivana dished dirt to Liz Smith at the *Daily News.* Smith's smiling face was plastered on the *News'* front page when she attended, and reported on, an exclusive luncheon with Ivana's pals from which the working press was barred. Even Smith complained that the story had degenerated into a "media circus" and that "I have been one of its performers."

On the second day of the escalating madness, I put in a call to Trump, hardly expecting him to talk to an out-of-town paper while his marriage was publicly disintegrating. To my surprise he returned the call, fielding the most personal questions in his rat-a-tat style. Our conversation was emblematic of how he enlisted the press in his perpetual self-promotion. As usual, he was prepared with a few succinct sound bites and got off the phone in three minutes.

His $20-million prenuptial agreement with Ivana? "Sealed in gold," Trump said. "A very, very substantial amount of money."

Ivana's contribution to his financial success? "You know me pretty well," Trump said with a tone of camaraderie. "Do you think anybody helped me build this fortune?"

The Alleged Other Woman? "Marla Maples is just a friend. They're all friends. The press is going wild. The press is having a field day. Over forty [women] have been mentioned. It's just wild."

Then came the abrupt sign-off: "I gotta go, baby. You take care. I'll read you tomorrow."

No editor could resist milking the Trump tiff, but the coverage soon careened out of control. The divorce was still front-page news two months later. To reread the clippings now is an embarrassment. The tabloids would not get so swept away by another breakup until 1992, when they would go berserk over Woody Allen and Mia Farrow. The war between the Trumps was a celebrity skirmish covered by a small army of reporters with World War III intensity.

"His fall was so spectacular it was almost like a Greek drama," Liz Smith says. "People liked to see his carcass dragged around." Such hyperbole aside, the Trump divorce saga was clearly a form of lowest-common-denominator journalism. Had the *News,* the *Post* and *Newsday* moved on to something else, the story would have faded. But the tabloids were in hog heaven, and they set the tone for the raucous New York coverage, which resounded through the media echo chamber across the land.

Perhaps, after a year in which New York had been shaken by the Central Park jogger rape, the Bensonhurst racial murder and the onset of a deep recession, a pissing match between two rich celebrities provided some much-needed comic relief. Or perhaps male editors couldn't get enough of Marla Maples. It wasn't as if there were no other news worth covering. The tabloids were so wrapped up in the divorce that first week that they paid scant attention to the bankruptcy of Michael Milken's firm, Drexel Burnham Lambert, which had fueled the junk-bond mania of the '80s—let alone the revolutionary events in South Africa.

Trump himself played a big role in keeping the story alive. Even while decrying the coverage as sensational, he kept on giving interviews. He hardly seemed displeased when the *New York Post* ran its famous "Best Sex I Ever Had" story, in which an acting-school classmate quoted Maples as hailing The Donald's bedroom prowess.

"He loved it," says Bill Hoffmann, a *Post* reporter who covered Trump. "People in his office said he wanted to frame it." Trump boasted to Cindy Adams that he had made someone a million-dollar bet that he could make Maples "the world's hottest name in three months."

But there were signs that Trump was growing tired of being portrayed as a selfish tycoon trading in his wife for a younger model. He demanded that the *News* fire Liz Smith, complaining to the *Post* that she had "disgraced the industry," was "being used" by Ivana's side and was "making up quotes." Trump said he might sue the *News* over Smith's columns.

"He just felt I was on Ivana's side," Smith says. "I really didn't have much choice because he wouldn't talk to me."

It was the soap opera that would not die. On March 22, Bill Hoffmann and Esther Pessin reported in the *Post*: "It's over! The scandalous and steamy liaison of Donald Trump and Marla Maples has come to an abrupt end. The Don bid a sad adieu to the starlet in a brief and tear-drenched phone call. She sobbed uncontrollably and begged him not to leave her." Except that it wasn't over. Soon Maples was telling Diane Sawyer, "I do love him. . . . Oh, I do," on ABC's "PrimeTime Live."

Trump had a tendency to blow hot and cold with reporters. Hoffmann says Trump viewed him as "his personal mouthpiece," and they became so friendly that they talked about cooperating on a quickie book during a limousine ride from Atlantic City. But when Hoffmann reported on Donald's dating agreement with Ivana (under the banner headline "SAFE SEX"), and how it fell apart the next day ("UNSAFE SEX"), Trump was furious. "He called and said, 'I can't believe how sleazy you are.' He didn't talk to me for two or three months."

On another occasion Trump fired off a letter to Hoffmann, calling him "a disgrace to your profession." But later on, Hoffmann says, "He called and said, 'Hey, Bill, how ya doin',' like nothing had ever happened. As long as he thinks you can do him a favor down the line, you're his best pal again."

The Marla Maples saga became intertwined with Trump's other obsession, the Trump Taj Mahal, which was scheduled to open April 5. When Trump told Cindy Adams that Maples would be at the Taj's opening-day bash, it set off a new round of tongue-wagging that, not coincidentally, also had the effect of hyping the casino. Trump eventually dropped plans to unveil his Georgia peach at the party.

I visited the Taj a few weeks before it opened, walking past the onion-domed façade and bejeweled elephants into the world's largest casino, with 3,000 slot machines and 167 gaming tables shimmering beneath hand-cut Austrian crystal chandeliers. I strolled through the fabulous penthouse suites, with their Jacuzzis and steam rooms and grand pianos and gold-leaf ceilings, a stark contrast to the dilapidated wooden shacks and debris-strewn lots a few blocks away.

When I called Trump and asked a skeptical question about the casino, he blew a fuse. "I don't know why I even talk to you," he snapped. "You've never written anything nice about me." And after all the ink I had lavished on him and Marla!

The conventional wisdom was that the Taj Mahal would be a smashing success. But for all its opulence, there were troubling questions about whether Trump's billion-dollar gamble would pay off. The Taj had to generate a million dollars a day just to cover its huge debt service. It might well draw customers from Trump's other two casinos down the boardwalk, or oversaturate the market on the eve of a recession. Marvin Roffman, an analyst with Janney, Montgomery, Scott, told me that "Donald is making a very serious mistake in owning three properties."

Two days before my story ran, Roffman was fired. He had been quoted making similar comments in *The Wall Street Journal,* and Trump complained to the firm. Roffman was canned after he refused to sign a letter praising the Taj and claiming he had been misquoted. Investment analysts are paid for their independent judgment, of course, but the company's shameful cave-in to Trump received little attention in the press. Reporters were so mesmerized by Marla and Ivana and Donald that we were missing a much bigger financial story right under our noses.

The herd instinct is one of the strongest forces in journalism. A baseball team on a hot streak is an invincible machine; lose a few games and it's a collection of overpaid malcontents. A politician can go from hero to goat in the blink of a news cycle. Miracle cures are discarded like yesterday's oat bran.

When Trump was on top, we all vied with one another to depict him as the richest, the shrewdest, the classiest, the greediest, the gauchest. Almost no one broke from the pack to question whether it was all smoke and mirrors.

That's why the *Forbes* magazine cover of May 14, 1990, came as something of a shock. "How Much Is Donald Really Worth Now?" it asked. The magazine advanced what seemed like a radical notion, that Trump was in a severe cash-flow squeeze. His debts were said to far outweigh his assets. He was worth $500 million at best, not the $1.7 billion estimated on *Forbes*'s list of the richest Americans.

At first Trump spun the story to his advantage. He denounced *Forbes* and said he was selling off some of his properties as part of a plan to make himself "king of cash" so he could snatch up bargains during the recession. "CASH KING," the *Daily News* banner announced, echoing the Trump line.

Within weeks it became clear that the emperor indeed had no

clothes. By early June, Trump was in marathon negotiations with his bankers over his $5-billion debt. The price of his casino bonds plummeted. He put the Trump Shuttle up for sale. He failed to make $45 million in debt service payments for Trump's Castle. He stopped talking to the press, issuing terse statements through his PR firm. Donald Trump, mogul, could no longer pay his bills.

Financial analysts said that Trump's backers, which included Citicorp, Chase Manhattan and Merrill Lynch, had been seduced by the Trump aura and blinded by the prospect of hefty interest payments and upfront fees. But what was the excuse of a press corps that had dozens of reporters panting after Marla Maples?

"I never felt particularly guilty because I wasn't any less prudent than the banks were," Jerry Nachman says. "Did we create the cachet around Trump that enabled him to describe his projects as trophies, that enabled him to convince the banks that the normal values were irrelevant? I guess you could argue we contributed to that."

That sounds like a rationalization for a Fourth Estate that doesn't usually place much stock in official assurances. Once Trump started buying such debt-laden properties as the Plaza, the Eastern Shuttle and the Taj, the average financial reporter could have seen what was coming. Richard Stern, coauthor of the *Forbes* article, says no one could calculate the debt of Trump's privately held companies until *Forbes* obtained some confidential documents from New Jersey casino regulators. Still, he says, "A lot of the reporters who covered Trump merely accepted whatever numbers he gave. There were people out there who could give you a cash-flow function. You call analysts, competitors. But if you asked any reporter, how do you value a property, they wouldn't have the slightest idea. He was paying world-class, Japanese prices while the bubble was breaking."

Once the blood was in the water, the press sharks started swimming in the opposite direction. Now they vied to tell the world how far the great one had fallen.

Trump avoided financial collapse when a consortium of banks granted him $65 million in emergency loans in exchange for approval of all major decisions and a half-million-a-month limit on Trump's personal spending. Ivan Boesky was in prison, Michael Milken was headed there and Donald Trump was on an allowance. The '80s were truly over.

"Do you think you could live on $450,000 a month?" Trump jokingly asked reporters. But this time no one was fooled. In fact, some journalists seemed to welcome Trump's fiery descent as a kind of poetic justice.

"At last, all of us who've so loved the game of kicking Donald Trump when he was up will have the fiendish thrill of kicking Donald Trump when he's down," said *Newsday* columnist Robert Reno. "He's a Third World nation. He's Brazil," said Stern. Even the *Times* loosened up a bit. "Almost Everybody's Playing Stomp-the-Trump," its story tittered.

Reporters began to feel the developer's sting. "You can say anything about his sexuality or who he's screwing," Bill Hoffmann says, "but the fact that he's going to lose money or lose face in the financial community—he really went nuts. His financial empire is like his manhood. You can do anything, kick him in the ass, say he's a homewrecker, but talk about how he's mismanaging his casinos and it's like castrating the guy."

Trump struck back at some of his media detractors in his second book, *Trump: Surviving at the Top,* published in August 1990. He said that Liz Smith "used to kiss my ass so much that it was downright embarrassing." He called Richard Stern "mediocre" and blamed the *Forbes* piece on a vendetta by the recently deceased Malcolm Forbes, who was described as striking back "from the grave" because Trump didn't advertise in the magazine. "It was almost as if Donald couldn't possibly be fighting with a lowly reporter, so the fight had to be among the gods," Stern says.

What Trump never acknowledged is that the *Forbes* piece was essentially correct. Over the next two years, he lost sizable chunks of his empire. He sold his personal 727. He sold the *Trump Princess* to a Boston bank. He sold the Trump Shuttle to USAir. He scrapped his idea for the world's tallest building on Manhattan's West Side. He auctioned off his sixty-three Palm Beach condos. He had to give his bankers a 49 percent share of the Plaza. And the Trump Taj Mahal, the most hyped casino in history, filed for bankruptcy, followed by Trump's two other casinos and the Plaza Hotel. Marvin Roffman had been right all along—and he collected $750,000 in a lawsuit against his former company for wrongfully dismissing him.

There was one final irony. While others focused on fluff, Neil Barsky of *The Wall Street Journal* had covered Trump's finances more aggressively than any other daily reporter. But when Barsky made a misstep, Trump pounced. In the spring of 1991, Barsky reported that Trump was so strapped for cash that he was considering borrowing money from his father. Trump called his old friend Norman Pearlstine, the *Journal*'s managing editor, denounced the story and revealed that Barsky had recently accepted three $1,000 tickets from Trump's firm for an Atlantic City prizefight. Barsky's editor had said he could take one freebie for the purpose of rubbing shoulders with Trump's aides, but was unaware that Barsky had taken additional tickets for his father and brother.

Neil Barsky was taken off the Trump beat.

"There's a general rule in journalism that if it's worth going to, it's worth paying for," says Pearlstine, who had himself accepted boxing tickets and a helicopter ride to Atlantic City from Trump several years earlier. In the furor over the Barsky affair, Pearlstine admitted that he probably should not have accepted these freebies.

Donald and Ivana's divorce became final on December 11, 1990. By this time, even the press was Trumped out, and for six months all was quiet in Trumpland. But in June 1991, the *Post* was back with another front-page exclusive. "IT'S OVER," the headline roared. "The Donald Boots Marla from his East Side Condo." *Newsday* had a similar story: "MOVE OVER, MARLA—TRUMP'S NEW PAL." The momentous scoop was that twenty-two-year-old Italian supermodel Carla Bruni had displaced Maples as the love of Donald Trump's life.

The Carla Bruni flirtation rated a juicy item (and a stunning picture) in every major newspaper and magazine in America. It was nothing more than a bit of PR bait, and the press swallowed it whole. "Trump is obviously a lunatic," Bruni later told the *London Daily Mail*. "It's all untrue. . . . I've only met him once."

But the media loved the roller-coaster romance. "MARLA'S AGONY," the *Post* bleated. Days later, however, all was forgiven. Trump announced his engagement to Maples by phone on "Live with Regis and Kathie Lee." There was a new blizzard of headlines. "MARLA GETS HER MAN," *The Washington Post* said. "TRUMP TO MARRY MARLA! (THINGS ARE SLOW IN JULY)," *The New York Times* winked. The *Daily News* ran a diagram of "Marla's Rock," a 7.45-karat engagement ring from Tiffany's.

It was just another charade. We had been sucked in for the umpteenth time. Three months later the engagement was off. "HERE WE GO AGAIN—DONALD DUMPS MARLA," the *Daily News* thundered with its "exclusive" banner headline. *USA Today* had it about right: "Who gets the ring? Who's the latest date? Who cares?"

Donald Trump's fame, which had once depended on his financial dealings, had now reached that lofty plateau where his celebrity over-shadowed all else. If he and Maples donned baseball uniforms for a charity game at Yankee Stadium, the *News* would run a picture. If Trump made a weird, multimillion-dollar offer to try to keep Mike Tyson out of prison after his rape conviction, the *Post* would run a banner headline. Marla's shoes stolen? Donald's stretch limo ripped off? Another page-one sensation! There were the inevitable Trump-Is-Back stories. Trump was like Mick Jagger or Elizabeth Taylor: He made news merely by showing up.

Trump still got angry when he felt the press had mistreated him. In 1991, he announced that he would sue the *New York Post,* his formerly favorite paper, for $250 million. The tabloid's offense: running a wire-service story that said a number of key executives were leaving Trump's employment. "The purpose of this alleged lawsuit is for Mr. Trump to get some more news coverage," Jerry Nachman declared. "He apparently will succeed." There were, indeed, plenty of headlines. But Trump never filed the suit.

The whole shebang would be recycled yet again just when the press had finally grown bored with Trump's sex life. In the spring of 1993, six months after a Cindy Adams "exclusive" declaring that "Donald and Marla are calling it quits for good," the *Daily News* bannered its own monster scoop: "MOMMA MARLA." Maples was pregnant, Trump was the father, and a circus atmosphere prevailed once again. There were endless pictures of Maples in bathing suits and speculation about what the *Post* called "Donald Trump's love child."

On July 1, the *News* boldly predicted that Trump would wed Maples that weekend. He didn't. Rather than run a correction, the paper taunted Trump with a banner headline—"CHICKEN!"—when he said he was afraid of getting married.

In October, reporters and photographers from around the world gathered in Palm Beach for the birth of what the *Post* dubbed "the world's tiniest media celebrity"—Donald and Marla's baby, Tiffany. But that was a mere ripple compared to the tidal wave of coverage that enveloped the much-delayed Trump wedding on December 20.

The press and The Donald had finally come full circle. Four years after the big breakup with Ivana, the scandalous mistress, the financial debacle, the screaming headlines, reporters could now fixate on a new, younger Mrs. Trump, complete with her own collection of maternity wear. There was no longer a pretense that anything more than sheer stargazing was involved, and no more snooty condescension from the elite press. While the tabloids provided the breathless buildup—"Marla to Wear White at Wedding," "Marla Will Take Hubby's Name"—the extravaganza at the Plaza was also touted on the front page of *The New York Times*.

The preferred pose was to strike a tone of ironic detachment, even while lapping up each detail of the mega-marriage. "BIG DEAL," sneered the *New York Post*. "They Do, They Do Already!" shouted *The Washington Post*. "Tacky. Overblown. Depraved in its conception," scoffed *Daily News* columnist Amy Pagnozzi. Yet they all showed up, along with more than one thousand of the glitterati, from Liz Smith (who had patched things up with the bridegroom) to Bianca Jagger to Howard Stern. Trump was nothing less than "our P. T. Barnum," declared one guest, *Vanity Fair* editor Graydon Carter, who promptly plastered the newlyweds on the magazine's cover. The press went wild over Marla's $2-million diamond tiara, the Carolina Herrera gown, the five-tiered butter-cream cake, the $60,000 worth of caviar. It was an '80s wedding for the sober '90s, one last self-indulgent fling for a press corps that had feasted for too long on the empty calories of celebrity journalism.

2

The Agency Nobody Covered

I had one clear advantage when I asked my editors if I could cover the Department of Housing and Urban Development. No one else wanted the job.

Just a few years earlier, in the late '70s, HUD had been one of the "hot" Washington beats. Newspapers, like much of the political world, were still actively grappling with the dark underbelly of urban decay. Jimmy Carter had created a popular program called UDAG, or Urban Development Action Grants, and mayors around the country were flooding HUD with proposals for shiny new Hyatt hotels and convention centers and waterside developments like Baltimore's Harborplace. There was a sense of excitement not seen since LBJ's Great Society gave birth to the agency a month after the Watts riots.

But now, in the fall of 1982, poverty was passé. Ronald Reagan had a mandate to shrink the size of government, and nowhere did the budget knife slice deeper than into HUD's costly, do-gooder programs. The problems of big cities seemed intractable, and if federal housing programs appeared mainly to benefit blacks and Hispanics, well, their concerns had nearly vanished from the political radar screen. Trendy publications were filled with tales of Nancy Reagan and Betsy Bloomingdale and their Palm Springs buddies. Newspapers were running upbeat profiles of canny corporate leaders and takeover artists. It was OK to be rich in America; there was no need to feel guilty about the poor. And the press, increasingly disconnected from its downscale readers, went along for the ride.

It was hardly surprising, then, that the urban affairs beat at *The Washington Post* was vacant. Most editors and reporters viewed HUD as a sleepy backwater. The real action was at places like the Pentagon, where untold billions were being poured into new missiles and jet fighters and submarines. HUD's headquarters, a massive, V-shaped concrete fortress in Southwest Washington, was far removed from the capital's nerve center.

If Reagan wanted someone to preside quietly over the agency's dismantling, he could hardly have found a more suitable candidate than Samuel Pierce, Jr., a laconic New York lawyer whose demeanor quickly earned him the sobriquet "Silent Sam." Pierce's profile was so low that Reagan, at a White House reception, once mistook him for a visiting mayor. Pierce was uncomfortable with reporters and almost never made news. HUD became the forgotten agency.

Beneath the placid surface, the Reaganites were proclaiming a new, business-oriented approach at HUD. Nearly eight years later, this would explode into a huge national scandal, but the evidence was there all along for any reporter willing to take a look.

I poked around in a seemingly bottomless pit of HUD scandals during Reagan's first term. My point in recounting them here is not to inflate my role, for any diligent reporter could have found these stories, or others like them, by talking to people at HUD. The more interesting question is why the stories never caught on with the press, the political community or the public. Many journalists have found themselves in situations where they got the goods on some scam, only to discover that no one gives a damn. The great irony of HUD is that the media descended with a vengeance only after the stables had been unlocked and the horses were long gone.

My first brush with the new regime came in early 1982, when I was working for Bob Woodward's investigative unit, known within the *Post* as the SWAT team. I got a tip that top HUD officials were selling off seven housing projects in New York, New Jersey and Connecticut without competitive bidding. Such "sole-source" deals, in government jargon, were often a sign that something unusual was going on.

A little digging showed that the buyers included two Republican insiders who had opened the right doors at HUD. Edward Weidenfeld had been the lawyer for Ronald Reagan's 1980 campaign and still handled legal matters for the Reagan-Bush committee. His wife, Sheila Rabb Weidenfeld, had been press secretary to first lady Betty Ford and had served on a Reagan transition team dealing with housing issues. The company that included the Weidenfelds had arranged to buy the properties for $11 million in a deal that included tax breaks and a below-market mortgage. The plan was approved by Assistant Secretary Philip

Winn, a former developer, and by Sam Pierce. Sheila Weidenfeld called it "a pretty straight business deal" but added: "I can understand why people would raise eyebrows."

After sharp criticism by Democrats in Congress, HUD dropped the idea, and the company had to buy the properties at auction. Still, it was clear that the men running the agency were playing by a different set of rules.

Only a handful of reporters were assigned to keep an eye on HUD, and most covered the agency only part-time. Some also roamed the urban landscape and kept tabs on the nation's mayors and governors. Others were primarily political reporters or specialized in minority affairs, dropping in on HUD now and then. The agency didn't generate many headlines.

Covering a regulatory agency is tedious work. Getting beyond the rhetoric means delving into documents and deciphering jargon. It takes a year or two to master the intricacies of federal housing programs and develop sources in the bureaucracy. By then, most ambitious reporters have moved on to greener pastures.

"The material is too technical for the average reporter to want to tackle," says Joseph Haas of *Housing and Development Reporter,* a trade publication. "HUD really is not something you see on the front page very often. Let's face it: Newspapers are in the business of selling papers and advertising. A lot of HUD is boring."

Albert Hunt, Washington bureau chief of *The Wall Street Journal,* says the agency is "frankly not a place where you put a lot of resources. We just didn't pay that much attention to HUD. It wasn't considered hot; it wasn't considered important."

In government, as in any private company, the ethical tone is set at the top. Sam Pierce and his aides saw no need to keep their distance from the industries they regulated. The cozy arrangement was clear from the agency's travel records. Groups of builders and bankers had picked up the tab for Pierce's visits to New Orleans, San Francisco, Philadelphia and Colorado Springs. Such groups also paid for Undersecretary Donald Hovde to visit Puerto Rico and Italy. (Hovde later had to repay $2,800 for using a HUD car and driver for personal errands.) Federal housing commissioner Philip Abrams went to Las Vegas and Martha's Vineyard at the expense of industry groups. Even media organizations got into the act, trying to boost their prestige by inviting top officials to fancy retreats. Time Inc. paid Pierce's way to the Bahamas for a housing conference. Pierce's executive assistant, Lance Wilson, also visited the Bahamas, courtesy of a real estate group. No one at HUD seemed embarrassed by all this junketing, and few in the press thought it was a big deal.

One of the bright young stars at HUD in the early 1980s was an assistant secretary named Emanuel Savas. A former Columbia University professor, Savas was a chief architect of the Reagan administration's policy of slashing aid to the cities. He had helped write a draft report for Reagan that outraged the nation's mayors by calling them "wily stalkers of federal funds."

As it turned out, Savas was no slouch at stalking the Treasury himself. All told, Savas had billed the taxpayers more than $14,000 for one year's travel, including two visits to Paris, two to London and one to Athens—and this at a time when poverty programs were being pruned in the name of austerity.

A more telling irony came later. Savas had published a book called *Privatizing the Public Sector—How to Shrink Government.* It was fascinating to learn, therefore, that two lower-level HUD employees had been ordered to type and proofread Savas's manuscript on government time. I tracked down the two women, who confirmed it. Savas said he had been unaware of their work, but he was contradicted by a former assistant, Joseph Esposito, who said Savas had told him to use the HUD employees to prepare the manuscript.

HUD's veteran inspector general, Charles Dempsey, began an investigation of the book affair. He referred the case to the Justice Department, which declined to prosecute but sent HUD a stinging letter saying Savas had "abused his office." Savas resigned under pressure, saying the charges were "frivolous" and that he had been "exonerated."

The Savas case barely caused a ripple in official Washington, which was preoccupied with the Nicaraguan contras, MX missiles, the 1982–83 recession and other grand concerns. But a pattern was starting to develop at HUD. Some midlevel employees wanted it known that things were far worse at the agency than anyone had imagined. My phone started to ring more often.

Every administration has its hacks, and Ronald Reagan's was no exception. After the 1980 election, thousands of Republican loyalists descended on the White House, résumés in hand. Reagan's personnel office needed a place for many of these retreads and ideologues, and HUD seemed the ideal spot. How much harm could a few hacks do at an agency that was being slowly taken apart? "The White House used HUD as a dumping ground for the dregs," one department official says. "We just had a lot of slimy people."

One of the most ideological appointees at HUD was Baker Armstrong Smith. He had worked for a Virginia group called the Center on National Labor Policy, whose goal, according to a brochure, was to provide "free legal aid to the victims of union power." HUD had the perfect job for him: director of labor relations.

Smith's main task was to oversee federal wage laws on government construction projects. The agency's records showed that Smith had waived 100 of the 133 fines proposed by his staff for companies that had failed to pay workers minimum wages or overtime, or had submitted false payroll records. He had all but taken the agency out of the enforcement business, writing comments such as "this is bull" on staff memos proposing hefty fines.

Smith had other problems. He had fired or transferred a number of HUD employees with union backgrounds, and a government inquiry attributed two of the firings to Smith's "anti-union animus." His secretary told investigators she had to type and proofread his master's thesis on government time. That had a familiar ring.

Smith said his actions had been "100 percent correct," but he resigned after the *Post* reported the allegations. All the stories ran inside the paper. HUD was still not front-page news.

Some of the agency's shenanigans took place in its ten regional offices, which the Washington press corps considered beneath its notice. Bill Sloan, a former director of the California Republican party, was installed in the San Francisco office. Sloan wound up having to repay the government $6,800 in improper charges for trips to such places as Las Vegas, Beverly Hills and a GOP fund-raiser at Disneyland. In one year, Sloan also charged the taxpayers $1,026 for meals while staying at his home in Fresno. He told investigators—and this was a classic—that he usually ate in restaurants because "my wife doesn't like to cook." Sloan resigned after the Justice Department declined to prosecute.

Sloan's assistant, Wayne Tangye, also liked to travel. Tangye had to repay $8,027 in questionable travel expenses, some of it for trips to his Arizona ranch. Tangye followed Sloan out the door.

Dick Eudaly, head of the Dallas office, also quit after allegations that he had demoted or transferred subordinates who questioned his efforts to manipulate a HUD grant program. The Chicago administrator, James Cummings, was transferred after he rented an apartment at bargain rates from a friend who did business with HUD.

The deputy undersecretary, Gordon Walker, a former Utah broker and developer, had an interesting sideline. While working at HUD, he earned $145,000 speaking and writing for a Salt Lake City firm that sold books and cassettes on how to make money in real estate. The cassettes and Walker's book, *Develop Your Way to Success,* sold for up to $59.95 apiece. "Six National Real Estate Experts Show YOU How to Create Wealth," a typical package said. What's more, Walker promoted these products at paid seminars while he was on official HUD trips.

The *Post* ran my story about Walker's moonlighting on page 8. Walker resigned after prosecutors declined to bring charges, saying that "the Justice Department has cleared me of any wrongdoing." Blowing the whistle on guys like Walker made for interesting reading, but it turned out to be like a dog whistle. Human beings, at least in official Washington, couldn't hear it.

Whenever the latest HUD nonentity bit the dust, my colleagues would joke that I had reeled in another little fish. After each episode someone would give me a small picture of a fish, which I tacked to the bulletin board above my desk. The truth was, while I enjoyed digging out scandals, I never felt great about causing people to lose their jobs. Each miscreant, after all, probably had a wife, two kids and a dog.

But the "little fish" ritual masked an inequity that nagged at me. While I was knee-deep in the HUD cesspool, it was the reporters covering the White House, the Hill, the Pentagon and national politics who dominated the front page day after day. My stories were often relegated to the *Post*'s Federal Page, a collection of bureaucratic news that appears on the last page before the editorials. It wasn't until a colleague and I began investigating Deputy Defense Secretary Paul Thayer—who resigned and pleaded guilty to obstructing justice and giving false testimony in an insider-trading case—that someone went out and bought me a real, large, somewhat malodorous fish. But then it was back to the guppy pond at HUD.

It didn't take a brain surgeon to recognize what was going on. Newspapers love stories about big names. I once wrote a magazine piece about an organization that got lots of federal money because the

Georgian who ran it had ties to President Carter and his wife. The story drew nationwide publicity because the outfit raking in the federal bucks had hired Carter's son Chip. It's a reliable rule of thumb: The closer to the White House, the better the play. Substance is secondary.

HUD was light-years from Pennsylvania Avenue, but it was handing out billions of dollars for programs that touch every city and county, from mortgage insurance for middle-class homes to subsidies for squalid public housing projects. These programs were riddled with fraud and mismanagement. Documenting such abuses was as simple as picking up the latest batch of audits from Chuck Dempsey's office and making a few phone calls. Yet none of the articles generated much interest. It was still morning in Reagan's America. The stories seemed to disappear into a journalistic black hole.

Inside HUD's concrete fortress on 7th Street Southwest, many employees believed that decisions on grants and contracts were routinely being fixed at the highest levels of the agency. This was hard to prove, of course, for Congress had created certain "discretionary" programs that gave top officials lots of leeway in handing out federal money. Yet the door at HUD swung open most often for those with the right Republican connections. That became clear from the way some developers in Manchester, New Hampshire, won a $7-million UDAG award.

HUD staff members had rejected the proposal as too risky and expensive, but the developers had other cards to play. One partner in the venture was Daniel Hughes, who had resigned as HUD's deputy undersecretary the year before. The other was a longtime business partner of Philip Abrams, a former Boston developer who was now HUD's number-two official. They lobbied Pierce's executive assistant, Lance Wilson, who was often the contact person for developers seeking help. The project also got a boost from Senator Gordon Humphrey, a New Hampshire Republican, who took up the matter with Pierce. HUD investigators later found "an appearance of preferential treatment" in the way the award was made.

The message was unmistakable. Developers and local officials who couldn't get their phone calls returned were increasingly turning to GOP consultants and former HUD officials to grease the skids for them. There was even a going rate: a thousand dollars per apartment. But the national press corps could not have cared less.

The magnitude of abuse never quite sank in because housing scandals are inherently local news. In Boston, precinct captains made sure that HUD grants were handed out to folks who did political work for city hall. In Memphis, housing officials used HUD money to speculate in the volatile bond market, buying and selling more than $1 billion worth of bonds in 1,700 transactions.

In Camden, New Jersey, *The Philadelphia Inquirer* discovered that real estate speculators had repeatedly falsified federal mortgage applications to sell houses to welfare recipients. The developers bought dilapidated shells from HUD, then flipped them for as much as twenty times the original cost, thanks to HUD's federally insured mortgages. HUD officials were so out to lunch that they even approved a mortgage for a four-year-old girl. When the welfare recipients defaulted, the homes wound up back in the government's inventory, and the federal government was stuck with the bill. A number of brokers were convicted for defrauding HUD's "bulk sales" program. Yet this sordid episode received little national publicity.

While crooks and fast-buck artists were feasting on HUD, the budget cuts were taking their toll. By the end of the Reagan years, HUD's staff would be cut from 16,000 to 11,000, and subsidized housing outlays from $26 billion to $8 billion. Carter's popular UDAG program was abolished. Many of the employees who understood the technical programs quit or were laid off. Audit after audit—public documents available to any reporter or congressman who bothered to ask—painted a picture of mounting chaos.

"The whole system just collapsed," says Gerald McMurray, a longtime congressional housing expert. "They couldn't even pay the bills."

Why didn't the HUD scandal catch on sooner? One reason is that it was too abstract for television, which relies so heavily on visuals. A series of complicated ripoffs by anonymous Joe Blows is not exactly compelling material for the evening news. If a TV reporter can't explain it in twenty seconds, forget it. And that limited the story to the local papers. No scandal can reach national proportions without the networks, which remain the primary source of news for most Americans. Only three newspapers (*The New York Times, The Wall Street Journal* and *USA Today*) have coast-to-coast circulations; they cannot set the national agenda unless their reports are amplified by television. A page-one story in the *Chicago Tribune* or *San Francisco Chronicle* has little resonance elsewhere until it becomes part of the electronic conversation.

Local officials and advocacy groups were in no position to point the finger at HUD because they were at the mercy of those holding the purse strings. The inspector general's office issued plenty of reports, but failed to interview Pierce about the allegations until his last day in office. Both Chuck Dempsey and his successor, Paul Adams, say they warned Pierce about the lack of financial controls. Some critics say Adams should have gone public in more dramatic fashion, rather than putting out bland reports.

Adams responds that "we could have screamed all day long . . . [but] Congress itself bears a substantial responsibility. They're just like the media. They merchandise what sells, and it's sensational things, things with personalities. Congress doesn't want to hold hearings on boring things."

Many lawmakers were silent coconspirators in the sleazy deal-making that permeated HUD. They too were making phone calls to high-level officials, trying to shake loose a grant for their hometown or steer a contract to a big contributor. When lobbyists and former officials do it, it's called influence peddling. When Congress does it, it's called constituent service.

In such an environment, the press was effectively neutralized. Reporters, after all, are part of the political process, a conduit for official leaks and grievances. No series of newspaper articles can accomplish much without official reaction. We need something else to "drive" the story--congressional hearings, outraged interest groups, resignations, subpoenas, indictments, some colorful drama that will command public attention. Even the Watergate scandal dragged on for months without arousing much interest, at least until the criminal case of the burglars, an activist judge and an FBI investigation produced enough fireworks to warrant Senate hearings and a special prosecutor.

To a greater degree than we would like to admit, editors and reporters also bend with the prevailing political winds. When the public tires of hearing about Ronald Reagan's gaffes or the Iran-contra affair, we can flog the story for a few more weeks or months, but eventually we have to drop it. Donald Trump's free-spending ways were big news during this period, and HUD, which represented the other end of the income scale, was non-news. The contrast is hard to miss: We were pumping up the story that didn't mean much and turning our backs on what would become one of the decade's most notorious scandals.

Such news judgments were not made in a political vacuum. By the mid-'80s many media people, perhaps subconsciously, had adopted the

Reagan line: that programs like those at HUD were a colossal ripoff, that corruption was endemic, that poor people had to do more for themselves. Each new mini-scandal served only to reinforce that perception.

In some ways the press was no match for the Reagan magic. During the 1984 campaign, the president went to Buffalo to dedicate the opening of Santa Maria Towers. He called it a "wonderful project for senior citizens and the handicapped." What Reagan didn't mention was that he had tried to cut the budget for such projects almost in half. Several news accounts pointed this out, but Reagan got the television pictures he wanted, and by the next day the campaign, and the press, had moved on to other issues.

What made the media myopia even more dramatic was that HUD's failure was evident on the streets of every city in America. The homeless, a class of people who barely existed five years earlier, were by the mid-'80s a pervasive and depressing problem for communities everywhere, an unsightly reminder of society's failure. They filled the train stations, crammed the soup kitchens, begged at store entrances, slept on heating grates.

To be sure, the reasons for homelessness were complex, ranging from alcoholism and drug addiction to the emptying of state mental hospitals. But the Reagan administration's abrupt withdrawal from the subsidized-housing business played a significant role. HUD officials were fundamentally dishonest about this, and the press was lax in calling them to account.

In 1984, HUD put out a report saying there were 250,000 to 350,000 homeless people in the United States, a fraction of the two to three million estimated by some advocacy organizations. Although the advocates' figures were probably inflated, HUD's estimate was ludicrously low, an attempt to wish away the problem by statistical fiat. Yet Pierce used the bogus study to dismiss all descriptions of homelessness as a national crisis. In a city like New York, he said, "You are hardly talking about anything."

Pierce insisted that the country was not suffering from a shortage of affordable housing, except perhaps in isolated areas. In fact, he claimed that some parts of the country had more subsidized housing than poor people who needed it. After one such claim, Representative Barney Frank of Massachusetts asked the agency to prove it. HUD produced a list of sixty-four "surplus" housing projects, but Frank's staff discovered that some of them had long waiting lists. Embarrassed HUD officials had to whittle down the list—first to fourteen projects, then to just four—and apologize at a hearing. So much for the housing surplus.

The argument was important because Pierce's all-purpose solution to the housing crunch was something called housing vouchers—government subsidies that low-income people could use to rent existing apartments. The catch was they had to find the apartments themselves. If there were few affordable apartments out there, the experimental program was doomed to failure. Pierce neglected to mention that as many as half the vouchers were being returned in cities like Boston because recipients could not find apartments with low enough rents. It was little more than a shell game.

In this debate, as in so many others, the press was a captive of he said/she said journalism. Trapped by the conventions of objectivity, most newspapers would simply quote both sides—Pierce Says Housing Shortage Nonexistent, Critics Disagree—even though one version was demonstrably false.

The media's lack of interest was in part a product of Sam Pierce's personality. For better or worse, the man at the top is the story in American journalism. When James Watt took over the Interior Department, his combative brand of conservatism made him a lightning rod for controversy. When Watt resigned and was replaced by the low-key Donald Hodel, the coverage faded, although Interior pursued many of the same pro-industry policies.

Pierce had often been the "first Negro" in this or that post—Cornell Law School; congressional aide; a Manhattan judge appointed by Nelson Rockefeller; the Treasury Department's general counsel under Richard Nixon; a $280,000-a-year partner in Battle, Pierce, Fowler and Kheel, a blue-chip Manhattan law firm; and a director of such corporations as General Electric and Prudential Insurance. A private man thrust by white politicians into important public roles, Pierce did his work quietly and never made waves.

But journalists thrive on conflict, and Sam Pierce's aloof style—he would spend part of the afternoon watching soap operas in his tenth-floor office—kept him out of the news. The one time I was granted an interview, Pierce read stiffly from a set of talking points for nearly fifty minutes. I had never seen a public official more ill at ease.

As criticism of his tenure at HUD grew louder, Pierce became more absorbed with the perks of office. He spent more and more of his time on the road, flying first-class to China, Japan, Hong Kong, Egypt, Singapore, Kenya, France, Austria, Germany, Denmark and Sweden, along with five trips to the Soviet Union. He delegated much of the daily decision making to his young special assistant, Deborah Gore Dean.

When I left the HUD beat in 1985 to cover the Justice Department, *The Washington Post* assigned no one to replace me. In this respect the *Post* was no different from most major papers. The real estate section still covered housing issues, but the national staff had bigger fish to fry.

We had no one on the case, therefore, when the White House nominated Debbie Dean as assistant secretary for community planning and development in 1987. A striking woman with a large mane of blond hair, Dean, thirty-three, had tended bar at a couple of Georgetown night spots and had started a short-lived magazine. She wound up in the Reagan administration after former attorney general John Mitchell, who lived with her mother, called an old friend from his Nixon days.

Dean's nomination was held up by Senator William Proxmire, who said she was totally unqualified to run a division that controlled $3.4 billion a year in federal grants. A *Post* reporter, Bill McAllister, suggested that he cover Dean's confirmation hearing, but his editors weren't interested. We duly recorded the news when Dean's nomination was dropped. What we didn't know, because no one was watching, was that this lowly special assistant was all but running the Department of Housing and Urban Development.

In the summer of 1988, Andre Shashaty, a free-lancer for the trade publication *Multi-Housing News,* started checking out rumors of favoritism at HUD. He filed a Freedom of Information request and spent weeks poring over the records of HUD's Section 8 "mod rehab" program, which provided the funds to renovate subsidized housing.

Shashaty's story said that "some funding decisions were made on the basis of politics and personal loyalties." It spoke of "large fees earned by former HUD officials—the same people who helped cut federal spending on housing when they were in the Reagan administration." And it focused on Debbie Dean's influence over funding decisions.

HUD officials braced for a barrage of media inquiries; no one called. Shashaty sent his story to ten large newspapers, but it was ignored. The story was missing one thing: names. None of the consultants or former HUD officials were identified. More work was needed.

It was a busy political season. The Democrats were about to nominate Michael Dukakis for president, and Attorney General Edwin Meese III, the subject of an independent counsel's investigation, was on the verge of resigning. The press had other things to worry about.

. . .

In April 1989, Paul Adams released a seventy-page inspector general's report about a bevy of consultants cashing in on the "mod rehab" grants, part of a housing program the Reaganites had tried to kill. Within days, the story was a full-fledged media sensation. And the reason can be summarized in two words: James Watt.

A sharp-tongued conservative from the West, Watt had made a career of denouncing federal poverty programs. Now he was playing the Beltway bandit game, taking $169,000 from a developer to speak to Pierce, Dean and other top HUD officials about a Maryland housing project.

One intoxicating whiff of hypocrisy was all it took to boost the story into the journalistic stratosphere. Other prominent Republicans were cashing in on the program—former Massachusetts senator Edward Brooke, who made $183,000; GOP fund-raiser Frederick Bush, who made $260,000; John Mitchell, who made $75,000; former Kentucky governor Louis Nunn, who made $375,000; and Reagan and Bush campaign consultant Paul Manafort, whose firm handled twenty-one HUD projects and who would later admit that what he did was "influence peddling." Former Pierce aide Joseph Strauss, who had joined HUD in 1981 at the age of twenty-four, later made $1.3 million lobbying his old agency.

Watt's presence was like waving raw hamburger before a pack of hungry dogs. This, after all, was the man who once condemned those who are "lured by the crumbs of subsidies, entitlements and give-aways." Suddenly the story was catapulted onto the front page of *The New York Times, The Washington Post* and other big papers. "After Years of Obscurity, HUD Emerges in Scandal," a *Post* headline said. Television got interested. The media finally had the angle they needed.

Representative Tom Lantos, a previously obscure California Democrat who held hearings on the scandal, says the uproar was fueled by "the whole notion that a former secretary of the interior, whose only previous housing experience was making Bambi homeless, should get hundreds of thousands of dollars for a couple of phone calls."

Watt, who made $120,000 on two other HUD projects, said he had been hired to cut through a "paralyzed" bureaucracy. He defended his conduct as "moral, ethical and effective." He was nothing if not effective. "Thanks!" he wrote Pierce in 1986 after winning a $28-million grant for the Maryland project. "You are a man of your word." Watt then invited Pierce and his wife to visit him at his new home in Wyoming. (Watt later pled guilty to a misdemeanor.)

The press was also captivated by a human interest story. Marilyn Harrell, a HUD escrow agent in Maryland, admitted she had embezzled more than $5 million from the agency, claiming she donated it to the poor. While prosecutors insisted Harrell kept most of the cash, the media dubbed her "Robin HUD."

More important, the political climate had changed, and the press's attitude along with it. George Bush was now in the Oval Office, and he was talking up the need for higher ethical standards in government. There was a growing consensus among the pundit class that too many domestic problems had piled up on America's doorstep, that Reagan's feel-good government had been asleep at the switch. And the new HUD secretary was the ever-quotable Jack Kemp, who tried to get out in front of the scandal.

Now everyone was leaping on the bandwagon. Members of Congress were shocked—shocked!—to learn that HUD officials had been manipulating the programs. Lantos's hearings were carried on C-SPAN and received plenty of network coverage. HUD was finally ready for prime time.

"Before the national media were involved, Mr. Lantos didn't have time to hold hearings," Shashaty says. "The minute *The New York Times* and *The Washington Post* decided it was news, he couldn't hold hearings fast enough. If the press deems it to be news, Congress deems it to be a horrible scandal."

Editors couldn't get enough of the HUD mess. Major papers put a half-dozen reporters on the case; smaller papers sniffed out local angles. While *The New York Times* ran nothing on the Adams audit for the first two days, it published 134 stories on HUD over the next six months, sometimes running three pieces a day.

"I've kicked myself a hundred times for our failure to come up with something as important as this," says Bill Kovach, who ran the *Times'* Washington bureau for most of the '80s. "We dismissed Sam Pierce out of hand from the beginning as someone who was just not important. . . . So we and the rest of the Washington press corps dismantled our coverage."

In the overheated atmosphere that followed, the key to unraveling the story was all those boring audits that Chuck Dempsey's office had churned out during the early '80s. HUD officials were deluged by so many Freedom of Information requests that they had to open the office on weekends. As many as fifty reporters would crowd into a room and wait their turn at the copying machine—all to get their hands on the same reports that I had had trouble getting anyone excited about a few years earlier.

"What we learned was that a lot of that stuff was on paper," says Gwen Ifill, who covered the scandal for the *Post*. "We weren't breaking this stuff on our own. It was who beat who to the audits that were published five years before."

The competition was fierce. One day, Ifill says, "I set aside a stack of documents I had copied. I left the room, and when I came back they were gone." She later learned that a rival reporter had taken them.

Many of the stories were remarkably similar to the abuses of the early Reagan years, and in some cases they were the same stories. I watched with amazement as the 1984 tale of Manchester's UDAG grant turned up on the front page of *The Boston Globe*. "A lot of it was written as current events, but it was really history at that point," Paul Adams says.

Many of the main characters were familiar faces. There was Phil Abrams, the former undersecretary, and Phil Winn, the former assistant secretary, who won HUD contracts for 1,347 housing units. Winn later pleaded guilty to conspiracy.

There was Lance Wilson, Pierce's former executive assistant, who obtained an interest in five developments that received $92 million in HUD subsidies and helped his new employer, Paine Webber, win a million-dollar HUD contract. Wilson was later convicted of providing an illegal gratuity to a government employee, but acquitted of more serious charges.

There was Debbie Dean, who helped approve millions of dollars in grants to people who wined and dined her and sent her chocolates. Dean invoked the Fifth Amendment before the Lantos subcommittee. In October 1993, Dean was convicted of funneling housing grants to Republican insiders, friends and her common-law stepfather, John Mitchell. She was also convicted of lying to Congress and accepting a $4,000 loan from an Atlanta consultant while he was asking her help in obtaining HUD business. Not one major newspaper covered the trial.

And there was Sam Pierce himself, who at times was less detached than people had thought. According to HUD records, Pierce helped friends, former aides and prominent Republicans—including his old Manhattan law firm—obtain housing funds. And in one case, according to DuBois Gilliam, a former aide who pleaded guilty in another scam,

Pierce made sure his harshest critic did not obtain HUD money. Henry Gonzalez, a Democratic congressman who had once called Pierce a "Stepin Fetchit," was seeking approval for a project in San Antonio. Gilliam says Pierce told him: "Does Gonzalez want the project? Well, Gonzalez don't got the project," and hung up.

Pierce told the Lantos panel he had been betrayed by his top aides. In a second appearance he took the Fifth, the first Cabinet member to do so in sixty-six years. An independent counsel, while criticizing Pierce's conduct, declined to bring charges against the man who now deserved the name Silent Sam.

The HUD story finally played itself out in the fall of 1989. Reporters drifted back to their regular assignments; the stories moved further inside the paper. Jack Kemp and his agency drifted out of the limelight, ignored by the White House and the press—until two and a half years later, when the Los Angeles riots created a surge of interest in Kemp's agenda and the major newspapers, still lacking urban-affairs reporters, rushed into print with Kemp profiles.

"The great failure to me is that after the scandal faded, no one went back to see whether Kemp's reforms worked or whether they were just PR," Gwen Ifill says.

In March 1993, a page-one *Washington Post* story touted "a confidential report compiled by the Clinton administration" as revealing that "critical management failures" were putting more than $1 trillion in HUD programs at risk. "Another HUD scandal is a distinct possibility," *The New York Times* agreed. But buried in the *Post* story was an acknowledgment that the Clinton study "drew heavily for its findings on HUD reports filed, and in many cases made public, during the Kemp years." In other words, newspapers could have published the same information years earlier had they focused less on public relations and more on how Jack Kemp was running the agency. The press did pay more attention to the HUD mess after Henry Cisneros took over, largely because a Democratic administration had put urban problems back on the political radar screen.

It would be comforting to believe that the HUD fiasco was an unfortunate oversight, a one-time screwup by an otherwise vigilant press corps. But a disturbing pattern of shortsightedness was beginning to emerge. In the months that followed, many of the same weaknesses would become apparent as reporters realized they had napped through the biggest financial scandal of the twentieth century.

3

Bank Job

Picking over the journalistic remains of the savings-and-loan scandal is a bit like embarking on an archaeological dig. From the early part of the era are scattered pieces and artifacts, useless by themselves but important clues to the overall picture. Here is a yellowed clip about a Texas thrift that went belly-up. There is a tattered remnant about congressmen getting campaign cash from wealthy bankers. Over here is a carbon-dated piece in which Danny Wall says the whole mess can be cleaned up for a few billion dollars.

The clues were staring us in the face for years, yet almost no one in the press managed to piece them together. It was the ultimate study in creeping incrementalism. We chronicled each twist and turn of the story, each bill, each bailout, each quarterly report, drowning in details while the crisis reached disaster proportions. Even in retrospect, it is startling to contemplate how badly the press performed.

Our collective failure would be easier to dismiss if the S&L collapse had been an intelligence scandal that could not have been cracked without some well-placed Deep Throat. But unlike HUD, an obscure federal agency all but ignored by the press, the savings-and-loan industry never suffered from a lack of coverage. Most reporters simply did not grasp the magnitude of the mess on their hands. The evidence was hidden in plain view.

"This thing was not happening in secret," says William Greider, who wrote about the S&Ls for *Rolling Stone.* "It was happening in fucking broad daylight in the Congress. This stuff was all available. In the 1980s, most reporters and most editors, for whatever psychic reasons, didn't want to challenge the government on a lot of fundamental stuff. It's easier—you're protected—if the authorities say there's no problem, until events blow up in your face. Nobody goes back to *The Washington Post* and *The New York Times* and says, how come you didn't do this?"

As usual, we all traveled in a pack, no one daring to suggest that the problem might be more than a few billion dollars worse than everyone else was saying. We were trapped by the conventions of objective journalism, the insistence on quoting experts, when what was needed was some old-fashioned crusading. Conditioned by decades of restraint not to cause panic among depositors, we were afraid to shout fire in a crowded theater. The problem was, the theater was burning down while we quibbled about the intricacies of the fire code.

Ask journalists what went wrong and you get a whole lot of lame excuses. The problems of S&Ls were too dull, too arcane, too complicated for the broad-gauged machinery of daily newspapers. No responsible official predicted the collapse. It wasn't a hot political issue. No one really cared because most depositors were insured. Democrats and Republicans joined in the cover-up because both parties had a hand in the mess.

Yet there was something more. To fully understand how the press botched the story requires a brief lesson in the culture of the newsroom. A basic fact of newspaper life is that political reporters work on one side of the room and financial reporters on the other. They inhabit vastly different worlds. Political reporters are obsessed with campaign strategy and consultants, polls and negative ads, fund-raising and focus groups. Financial reporters worry about the market, interest rates, deficits, unemployment, corporate profits and government regulation.

While it may seem like a single entity to outsiders, a big-city newspaper is actually a collection of medieval fiefdoms. They compete for space, money and bragging rights. They fight over juicy stories rather than teaming up, sometimes producing different versions for the sake of ego. One desk editor may not tell another what his troops are doing for fear that a good project might be stolen. Each afternoon, when the section editors assemble for the front-page meeting, the business editor or the sports editor may belittle the national desk's stories in hopes of making room for his own.

Every paper has its own pecking order. The Metro staff is generally the heart of the newsroom, with sports, features and business in secondary roles. On a handful of larger papers, the national and foreign staffs are preeminent. A reporter may spend years at city hall before he gets a crack at the Washington bureau or a posting in Moscow or Tokyo. The paper's top editors tend to be drawn from the national and foreign staffs, and their interests naturally incline toward politics and diplomacy.

Until the early '80s, the business desk was a backwater at most newspapers. It was seen as a haven for hacks content to rewrite corporate press releases and chronicle upticks in the stock market. Few newspaper people knew or cared much about the strange language of municipal bonds and pension funds. But business staffs began expanding as editors came to understand that economics played a fundamental role in almost everything they covered, from airlines and autos to Hollywood and high tech.

Still, the political beat remained the pulse of daily journalism. Politics ran on the front page, financial stories near the stock tables. Political reporters concerned themselves with business stories only when they forced their way onto the political agenda, as when the jobless rate topped 10 percent just before the 1982 midterm elections.

"A lot of reporters don't know anything about economics," says Jerry Knight, who covers banking for *The Washington Post*. "One of the great failings of this newspaper is that people at the top don't care about business and economic issues. The track to the top here is politics and government. None of the political reporters understood the S&L story. Political reporters specialize in process, not substance. They would go out and write these mood-of-America pieces. Banks and S&Ls never hit the charts."

Even financial reporters, however, were not immune to the strain of corporate boosterism that infected the media during the Reagan era. The press, which had looked down its nose at businessmen during the '70s, was treating corporate entrepreneurs as the new heroes. Freed from the shackles of government regulation, they would make deals and raise capital and stimulate the economy.

Savings and loans, as in the old Frank Capra film, had been staid institutions that quietly offered home mortgages on the 3-6-3 formula— you paid depositors 3 percent, loaned money at 6 percent and hit the golf course at 3. Now the new S&L kings were wheeling and dealing like Las Vegas gamblers, pouring money into shaky real estate ventures and peddling high-interest junk bonds. Reagan had succeeded in making government the issue, and regulators who questioned these high rollers were seen as meddlesome bureaucrats. The press essentially bought into the underlying assumptions of the go-go years. The Dow was headed for 3,000, Michael Milken was considered a visionary and the economy—along with media profits—was booming.

"I've kicked myself for not doing more. If anybody should have been suspicious, it's *The Wall Street Journal,*" says Brooks Jackson, a former *Journal* reporter who specializes in financial investigations.

"Everyone you talked to said it was this huge mess, that it was only going to get worse and it was going to cost the taxpayers billions of dollars," says John Yang, a former *Journal* reporter who covered banking. "You would relay this to your editors, but because it was banking regulation, their eyes would glaze over."

"We nibbled at it," admits Albert Hunt, the *Journal*'s Washington bureau chief. "We should have been covering it more in '86 and '87. It was elusive. It was a Texas story. It was a Michigan story. It was a Maryland story. It was a California story. But no one put it together."

Actually, a handful of writers sounded the alarm, but it fell on deaf ears. The story needed some spark, some act of spontaneous combustion, to propel it onto the nation's front pages and evening newscasts. On the surface, at least, the S&L debacle was tailor-made for newspapers. It was far too abstract to make good television, a medium that relies on colorful visuals and ninety-second summaries. Only major newspapers had the resources and investigative know-how to tackle a story like this. Unfortunately, with the political reporters exploring grand themes and the business reporters immersed in regulatory details, they were like blind men feeling different parts of the elephant.

The outlines of the beast were visible as early as 1980, when the *Journal* quoted one thrift president as saying that S&Ls hadn't seen such bad financial results "since the Depression." The following year the *Journal* declared that the S&Ls were "hemorrhaging," raising the specter of "an onslaught of insolvencies." By the mid-'80s it was clear that the Federal Savings and Loan Insurance Corporation (FSLIC), the fund that insured depositors for $100,000 per account, was essentially broke. No brilliant inspiration was needed to follow up on these articles:

"Throughout the country there are more than 400 insolvent S&Ls. . . . Hundreds more are on the brink of insolvency," a *Washington Post* editorial warned in July 1985 after reports by four government economists.

"Looming insolvencies among the most troubled third of the thrifts will bankrupt FSLIC," consultant Bert Ely wrote in the *Journal* in July 1986.

"The failure rate for savings and loans is now greater than during the Great Depression. . . . Congress won't own up to the real cost," *Forbes* magazine said in May 1987.

"Disposing of the carcass is going to be very expensive for the federal government—and ultimately for the taxpayers," Bill Greider wrote in *Rolling Stone* in August 1988. "It will add tens of billions of dollars to a federal budget that's already deep in red ink."

But the slow suicide of the thrift industry remained consigned to the business pages until the end of the greed decade. To the extent that political reporters thought about the economy at all, they tended to focus on what Washington was doing about the big-picture stuff: inflation, unemployment and the budget deficit. Ronald Reagan essentially ignored the S&Ls, and the hordes of reporters who covered him were unable, or unwilling, to call him to account. What the story desperately needed was someone to personalize it, someone to symbolize the era of excess, someone whose very name would evoke outrage. That someone turned out to be Charles Keating.

Mike Binstein is the first to admit he was not part of the fraternity.

It was the fall of 1986, and Binstein had been a leg man for Jack Anderson for three years. He was twenty-nine years old. A few years earlier Binstein had been running his own gardening business in Washington and was fired by George Will for allegedly killing his lawn. A large, hulking man with a quick sense of humor, Binstein was trying to develop an economics specialty for the Anderson column.

"I was not a pedigreed financial reporter," says Binstein, now the column's coauthor. "At first that caused me to have an insecurity complex. What I ultimately learned is that this wasn't a financial story, it was a political story."

While the daily beat reporters had to worry about staying on good terms with their sources, Binstein had no regular deadlines and no constituency to protect. Just as Watergate was broken not by the White House press corps but by two local reporters, Binstein managed to barrel his way past the heavyweights from the *New York Times* and *Wall Street Journal*.

His first chunk of the story involved Charles Keating, the chairman of Lincoln Savings & Loan. Keating was a high-flying Phoenix businessman who lived in a million-dollar mansion and had a lavish spread in the

Bahamas and three private jets, one with gold-plated bathroom fixtures. Although Keating had once been accused of improper financial conduct by the Securities and Exchange Commission, he had a star-studded résumé. He had chaired John Connally's 1980 presidential campaign. He was a national crusader against pornography.

Keating had bought Lincoln two years earlier with $51 million in junk bonds floated by Michael Milken at Drexel Burnham. Now the Irvine, California, thrift was showing a healthy profit, and Keating was winning kudos for donating a million dollars to Mother Teresa.

Keating's chief nemesis was Edwin Gray, the chairman of the Federal Home Loan Bank Board. Gray was an affable PR man who had been Ronald Reagan's press secretary when he was governor of California, as well as an executive at a big California S&L. Reagan had rewarded him for his loyal service with the bank board job. But Gray had become an increasingly vocal critic of the industry. He was locked in a bitter feud with Keating over a long-running bank board audit of Lincoln. Keating wanted Ed Gray off his back.

Mike Binstein wrote a column saying that Keating had offered Gray a lucrative job to lure him from the bank board, and when that failed, had lobbied for Gray's ouster. But Binstein had a problem. Libel insurance premiums had skyrocketed, and Jack Anderson, who had a habit of getting sued, could no longer afford the bills. Anderson's libel lawyer, David Branson, was reviewing his columns on a pro bono basis. Branson was a hero to Anderson's young staffers, and Anderson gave him a de facto veto over each column before it appeared.

"I finally had to turn to an attorney and give him the last word," Anderson says. "If he said our exposure was too great, I wouldn't use it. Drew Pearson [Anderson's late partner] would turn over in his grave if he knew this. Financially, I couldn't fight all these lawsuits."

Branson, it turned out, worked for a law firm that had a far more profitable client: Charles Keating.

"Branson sees this column and he goes berserk," Binstein says.

Branson says he merely told Binstein the story sounded "totally implausible" and that Keating, whom he had never met, was represented by other attorneys in the firm of Kaye, Scholer, Fierman, Hays & Handler. "All I knew was that Charles Keating was litigious," Branson says. He says he warned Anderson that if Keating sued, he, Branson, could not handle the case because of the potential conflict. "All I told him was, this was the problem if you get sued."

The Keating column ran, but the warning that Keating was litigious persuaded Anderson not to publish any more such columns. He now says he is "appalled" at Branson's conduct. "We did not break the big stuff because we were represented by Keating's lawyer," Anderson says.

Branson, however, says he was willing to review stories about Keating and that Anderson always could have taken the columns to another attorney. Besides, he resigned as Anderson's lawyer in early 1988 to avoid further difficulties. "For Jack to say there was some story he couldn't publish because I wouldn't review it is utter rubbish," Branson says.

Even Anderson concedes that his primary fear was a Keating lawsuit: "My rule was, if someone is litigious and it will lead to a costly lawsuit, we won't run the stories. I hated every minute of it. . . . This has grieved me more than anything that has happened in my whole career."

Keating, meanwhile, was faring reasonably well with the press. *The New York Times* said that while his methods were controversial, "Mr. Keating has transformed Lincoln from a money loser into a profitable institution."

Mike Binstein was convinced that Lincoln was cooking the books. But with Keating off limits at the Anderson column, Binstein found himself "a reporter without a country." He shopped the story around, but most editors were skeptical. "Unfortunately," a colleague says, "Mike comes across as a gunslinger type."

Binstein soon hooked up with Bill Regardie, a cigar-smoking publisher who owned a glossy Washington magazine called, modestly enough, *Regardie's*. It was a classic '80s magazine, thick with ads for new office towers and housing developments, and it was building a reputation for taking on sacred cows.

Binstein's 1987 article for *Regardie's* ripped into Lincoln. Quoting from confidential bank board documents, it said that Lincoln had no credit reports on many of its borrowers. That Keating had made "threats" in "a crude attempt to intimidate" bank examiners. That the bank board had concluded that "Lincoln is unsafe."

Keating was outraged; it was a crime for anyone to leak such confidential documents. He sued the bank board in U.S. District Court in Washington, seeking to bar the board from further leaks. The lawsuit was signed by David Branson. Binstein, who felt he had spoken freely to Branson, was livid. Branson, however, says his firm decided it was no conflict for him, as the only litigation partner in Washington, to review and sign the lawsuit. "I worked for Jack Anderson, not for *Regardie's,* not for Michael Binstein," he says.

A magazine called *Arizona Trend* reprinted a version of Binstein's story for $1,000. Keating promptly hit the magazine with a $35-million libel suit.

A vice president from *Arizona Trend*'s parent company came to Washington and took Binstein to breakfast at the swank Jefferson Hotel. Binstein asked how much the case would cost. "He looked up very dryly and said, 'Not including this breakfast, $50,000.' " The suit wound up costing the magazine $150,000.

"That's the terror of the libel suit," Binstein says. "They can make you bleed. The message gets telegraphed to people who cover the S&L industry: If you want to write about Charlie Keating and Lincoln, it'll cost you $150,000. That's the admission price."

Binstein obtained more confidential bank board documents and tried to peddle S&L stories to *The New York Times* and the *Los Angeles Times,* among others. He was turned down.

"I had hundreds of pages of documents from '86 on that spoke to how big the problem was, who was going to fail, by name, and how much it was going to cost," Binstein says. "It was rejected by the General Motors and IBMs of our business."

Charles Bowden, the editor of *City Magazine* in Tucson, was interested in printing Binstein's material. But Bowden says he got a letter from Branson's law firm, saying the audits "were illegally obtained confidential documents, full of unnamed errors, and that if we printed them, all hell would break loose." After that, he says, "the magazine's major investor lost interest in freedom of the press and heroic journalism, and the story died."

Mike Binstein was getting frustrated. "Intimidation was really the byword here," he says. "There was a yellow streak running through journalism. Once the libel suit came down, I had AIDS as far as everyone in the business was concerned."

When a government program is in trouble, the facts are usually well known to a small circle of politicians, journalists, lobbyists and other insiders. But as was the case at HUD, it takes some event, some metaphor, to arouse public concern and spur the press into action.

"One of the things that makes a story is a big name," says Brooks Jackson, now with CNN. "If you have a George Bush or a Lee Iacocca or a Donald Trump, any minor peccadillo you catch these guys in can be a big story. If you don't have a big name, it's harder to sell the story. It's someone you never heard of doing something."

The seeds of the S&L scandal had been sown in the final months of Jimmy Carter's presidency. Congress boosted the level of deposits that the FSLIC would insure from $40,000 to $100,000, thus guaranteeing that the government would get stuck with a far bigger tab if a thrift went under.

In 1982 the Reagan administration, with help from Jake Garn, the Republican chairman of the Senate Banking Committee, and Fernand St Germain, the Democratic chairman of the House Banking Committee, pushed through a law that loosened the regulatory reins on S&Ls. The industry was in a cash squeeze, and the new law encouraged thrifts to expand from stable home mortgages into more profitable—and risky—commercial and real estate loans. Reagan's Home Loan Bank Board, meanwhile, eased the accounting rules for S&Ls and lowered the amount of cash they had to keep on hand to cover bad loans.

The new age of wheeler-dealer S&L men had dawned, and the aroma of sleaze was not far behind. The most dramatic collapse of the early '80s involved Empire Savings & Loan of Mesquite, Texas, which claimed to be the fastest-growing thrift in the nation. Its owner, Spencer Blain, Jr., had a taste for Rolls-Royces and $5,000 Rolexes. Empire was financing construction of thousands of apartments and condos, many of them poorly built. Federal examiners were finding serious problems with Empire's books.

In 1983 Allen Pusey, a reporter for *The Dallas Morning News,* began digging into Empire. "The whole mind-set was we can't say anything to undermine people's faith in financial institutions," says Pusey. "That's a mind-set that grows out of the '30s. It's sort of like real estate—everything's hunky-dory all the time."

Soon the fraud became too massive to ignore. In 1984 the bank board voted to shut down Empire. It was the largest insolvency in the board's history. Federal investigators charged that Empire had artificially inflated the price of its real estate as partners sold the tracts back and forth. Congress held hearings. More than one hundred people were convicted of fraud. But it remained largely a Texas story, despite pieces in *Forbes* and on "60 Minutes." Pusey couldn't understand it. "A lot of people viewed what happened at Empire as a singular event, a group full of crooks that found an innovative way of stealing money," he says. "The national press took its cue from the regulators, who were downplaying the whole thing."

But while S&Ls were big news in Texas, they barely registered on Washington's radar screen. "It was the absolute bottom beat in the financial section," says Jerry Knight, then the *Post*'s deputy business editor. "It was too boring, too unsexy. S&Ls were mom-and-pop businesses that did nothing. . . . I'll take the blame for not having moved on it."

In 1985, the media got a dramatic reminder that the possibility of widespread S&L failures was more than just economic theory. In March, Ohio shut down its state-chartered S&Ls for several weeks to stem a multimillion-dollar run on deposits after the collapse of Home State Savings Bank. In May, Maryland limited withdrawals at its privately insured S&Ls after a Baltimore *Sun* story triggered a run on Old Court Savings and Loan, whose owners had used depositors' money to buy racehorses and oceanfront condos. The Maryland insurance fund proved to be a mirage, and some depositors would not recover their money for years.

"We really bear a lot of the responsibility for Maryland," Knight says. "We were timid. We were extremely nervous about terrifying depositors and starting runs on banks. We really should have started some bank runs. If the press did a better job of starting bank runs, the system would be a lot healthier."

Despite the crises in Columbus and Annapolis, few believed that federal thrifts—backed by the full faith and credit of the U.S. government—were in danger. A handful of critics warned that the thrift industry was a house of cards. But it was like the endless hand-wringing about Reagan's $200-billion budget deficits. The country was still riding a tide of prosperity in the mid-'80s, and the press largely dismissed the doomsayers.

"People in the press don't want to hear this, but it's true: Most reporters and editors defer to authority," Greider says. "That's a chilling way to put it, but that's what it comes down to. Most reporters will call up Regulator X or Senator Y and say, 'We hear this, is that true?' And they'll say, 'No, there's no problem. There's a few crazies out there saying the whole thing is going to blow up, but that's not how we see it.' And most reporters will stop at that point."

Bert Ely, the financial consultant, was frequently quoted as warning of an impending disaster. But he was usually thrown in as a token dissenter to balance the optimistic chorus of official Washington. "The question was, who the hell is Bert Ely? Where does this guy come from?" Ely says. "I was still an unproven quantity."

Henry Gonzalez, the populist San Antonio congressman who had taken on Sam Pierce, also preached the gospel of gloom and doom. In 1986, Gonzalez says, "The only thing I could do was have a press conference. Who came to the press conference? Only some Texas newspapers. I was warning that there was a big bubble that eventually would have to burst. I have a jillion speeches I made. Even back home, I just got a little snippet."

When congressional auditors said the S&L bailout would cost $23 billion, Gonzalez says, "I said it would take that amount of money in Texas alone. Nobody paid any attention. I had another press conference. Hardly anyone came. I was embarrassed." The prevailing attitude was, "Who is this guy? What does he know about banking? And the lobbyists would help with that image."

Gonzalez's problem was that he was a somewhat comic figure. He favored electric-blue polyester suits, kept calling for Reagan's impeachment and delivered interminable, late-night speeches to an empty House chamber. "A lot of people thought he was a kook," says Kathleen Day, a *Washington Post* banking reporter.

The most important man warning of a taxpayer bailout was Ed Gray, Reagan's bank board chairman. Jerry Knight recalls one of his reporters taking him to meet Gray:

"He sat in his office for about an hour and told us how the industry was gone, that it was falling apart and the administration didn't care, that it was going to be a disaster. I came back and tried to tell people, but nobody was interested. People just couldn't get excited about it."

Ed Gray also had a credibility problem, and I had played a minor role in that, my one brief footnote in the S&L affair. In 1984, less than a year after Gray took office, I reported that the FBI was investigating allegations that he had improperly used a special entertainment fund and had failed to fully account for a $47,000 redecoration of his office and reception area. The piece suggested that Ed Gray had a taste for high living at other people's expense, a perception reinforced by my colleague Kathleen Day, who later reported that Gray had accepted thousands of dollars from the S&L industry for limousines, booze,

Wimbledon tickets, cruises, expensive Paris restaurants and $650 hotel suites as he traveled around the world. Gray's message—that Keating and the rest of the industry were in big trouble—was obscured by the little mini-scandals that newspapers love to chase.

If ever there was a time when the disparate cultures of political and business journalism might have come together, it was during the 1988 presidential campaign.

Everyone—the press, the lawmakers, the candidates' handlers— knew that members of Congress had papered over the S&L crisis with an $8.5-billion bailout designed solely to get them past the election. But campaign reporters let the issue slide, more interested in Willie Horton than Charlie Keating. And business reporters were more concerned with the aftershocks from Black Monday, the 500-point plunge in the stock market the previous fall. The ailing thrifts remained the great invisible issue of the campaign, which was fought over the Pledge of Allegiance and other trivialities while the one crisis that would touch every American taxpayer was ignored.

"The press did not ask the question, period," says David Hoffman, who covered the 1988 Bush campaign for the *Post*. He says the reporters traveling with Bush were reduced to "shouting questions at picture-taking opportunities. How can you discuss a complicated issue like S&Ls in three seconds? We had no access to Bush for days on end, none. We had very little leverage to force him to respond."

Michael Dukakis was partly to blame for Bush's free ride. He raised the S&L issue exactly once, accusing the vice president of having "walked away from a ticking time bomb" that "will cost tens of billions of dollars," but quickly dropped it. Dukakis was undoubtedly worried about Democratic vulnerability to the issue. The Democratic Congress had gone along with deregulation. House Speaker Jim Wright was under investigation by the ethics committee for pressuring Ed Gray not to move against thrifts in his home state of Texas, and would resign the following spring. Freddy St Germain, the House Banking chairman, had come under Justice Department investigation for failing to report meals and entertainment from S&L lobbyists, and although he was not prosecuted, he would lose his seat that fall. Clearly, the Democrats had their own skeletons in the S&L closet.

Early in the year a *Wall Street Journal* article warned of a "federal fiasco" covered up by "voodoo accounting," but the *Journal* pressed the issue just once during the campaign. "The sad shape of U.S. savings institutions is such a complicated and alarming topic—and the solutions so unpleasant—that neither George Bush nor Michael Dukakis has wanted to seriously discuss it in the presidential campaign," the paper said two weeks before Election Day.

"That was one story," Al Hunt says. "It wasn't rat-a-tat-tat. We don't like complexity in campaigns. It's the horse race and who's going to win Michigan and what's the major flap of the day."

Since federal deposit insurance was cushioning the blows, Hunt says, "There was a lag time before it affected people, so you didn't have victims. At that stage you didn't have anyone who was getting hurt. We tended not to place enough credence in what some of those doomsayers were saying. To some extent we are victims of the experts."

The Wall Street Journal, more than any other paper, might have been expected to blow the whistle on the thrift scandal. But while the *Journal* remained the businessman's bible during the '80s, it abandoned its strict focus on bonds and pork-belly futures in favor of a broader, more feature-oriented approach. Norman Pearlstine, then the managing editor, added two daily sections that covered everything from lawyers to fast-food restaurants to Madison Avenue.

"It was a time when Norm was looking for a lot of glitz and glamour for page one," John Yang says. Yang got one story about the deteriorating condition of S&Ls on the front page in 1987, but only because it had a sexy lead: "The Day of the Living Dead is upon the Federal Home Loan Bank Board."

By 1988 Yang was off covering the Hill; *Journal* reporters rarely stayed on the banking beat more than a year or two. At most newspapers, covering business was just a step on the corporate ladder until one could reach the loftier terrain of national politics, to which most reporters aspired.

Says Pearlstine: "If I had told you in the mid-'70s that the sexiest stories of the late '80s and early '90s at *The Wall Street Journal* would be insurance, real estate, S&Ls and banks, you'd have looked at me like I was crazy. These were boring, backwater beats. . . . We're all better at writing about rotten apples than rotten barrels. When a Keating emerged, it was easier for all of us to jump on—crooks in limos, and fancy food. But the crooks in the S&L case were not the Keatings of the world, they were the White House and Congress. That is a harder story for publications to sensationalize."

With no prominent villain to follow, the press remained afflicted with creeping incrementalism, seemingly intent on burying the reader with numbers. A sampling of *New York Times* stories from the summer of 1988: "Federal Home Loan Bank Board more than doubles its projection of the cost of shutting down or merging more than 100 Texas S&Ls. . . . Reagan administration rejects any suggestion that taxpayer money be used to rescue nation's S&Ls. . . . FDIC chairman says $50 billion will be needed to rescue S&Ls. . . . FHLBB announces sale of 12 insolvent S&Ls. . . . FHLBB consolidates eight insolvent Texas S&Ls into one, its most expensive rescue package yet. . . . FHLBB arranges to merge nine more insolvent savings institutions. . . . FHLBB chairman Wall says no more than $16 billion in promissory notes will be issued to guarantee assets of insolvent savings institutions." Lots of trees and no forest.

M. Danny Wall, who had succeeded Ed Gray as chairman of the bank board, played a key role in lulling the press. A longtime aide to Jake Garn on the Senate Banking Committee, Wall had essentially written the 1982 Garn–St Germain law that turned the thrifts loose. Now he had to deal with the wreckage. Wall kept reassuring the world that no taxpayer bailout would be needed.

Nathaniel Nash, who covered S&Ls for *The New York Times*, tried to convince his editors to run more S&L stories on the front page, but "there was a fear that kind of story would move the markets," as one source at the *Times* reported. Nash's reporting was thus guarded in tone. In a 1988 article, Nash wrote: "Many in the industry applaud Mr. Wall's day-to-day management. . . . Despite the criticism, with a little luck on his side, Mr. Wall could still wind up a hero of the thrift industry, supporters say." The headline: "Staying Calm—Maybe Too Calm—in the Midst of a Crisis."

Creeping incrementalism was made worse by another bureaucratic fact of newspaper life: The operation is geared toward getting tomorrow's paper out. Beat reporters are busy chasing day-to-day developments. The big stories at the time were the booming real estate market and the record low unemployment in some parts of the country; S&Ls were just a blip on the horizon. The only way a newspaper could have plumbed the depths of the S&L crisis was to break off a couple of reporters from their daily duties. "No one thought it was that big a deal," Kathleen Day says. "I remember saying, 'Let's go to Texas, let's do this, let's do that.' I had to beg and beg and push to get them to do an investigation of St Germain," which fizzled.

Everyone in Washington knew that St Germain was too close to the industry (he would later become an S&L lobbyist). But few reporters thought that such respected senators as Alan Cranston of California, John Glenn of Ohio or Donald Riegle of Michigan might be worthy subjects for investigation.

"Those who the press considered the good guys in Congress were in some ways the most enmeshed in the problems," says Jim Leach, a Republican congressman from Iowa and an early S&L critic. "This was disproportionately a liberal Democratic problem in Congress. It's also a Republican regulator problem and a Reagan philosophical problem. But legislatively, it was a Democratic problem."

A couple of publications woke up during the 1988 campaign. *Business Week* did a cover story on "The S&L Mess." James O'Shea of the *Chicago Tribune* did a huge front-page series, quoting one critic as saying the situation was a "big, big, black bottomless pit" and predicting that a taxpayer bailout could top $100 billion. O'Shea also had an unforgettable quote from Don Dixon, a Texas S&L owner who had charged the thrift to take an entourage on a $22,000 eating tour of Europe. "You think it's easy eating in three-star restaurants twice a day, six days a week?" Dixon asked.

The idea for the series came from Leach, whom O'Shea knew from his days at *The Des Moines Register*. O'Shea had just come onto the economics beat after covering the Pentagon and was looking for a good project.

"Everyone else saw it as a story that wasn't new," O'Shea says. "It just pissed me off and I decided the S&Ls shouldn't get away with that shit. One of the problems is that no one had drawn it all together. We were out on a limb, no question about it."

But the *Tribune* series did little to change the debate. "A paper like the *Tribune* is a large newspaper, but because it's not read in Washington, it simply doesn't have the influence the *New York Times* and *Washington Post* have," O'Shea says. "It just doesn't set the agenda. If that had been on the front page of *The New York Times,* it would have had a lot more impact."

In the final weeks of 1988—with the election safely past—the lame-duck Reagan administration launched a fire sale of bankrupt S&Ls. More than two hundred insolvent thrifts were sold off to billionaires and big banks, the deals greased by more than $50 billion in government subsidies.

"Where I would say I fell down as a reporter was when all those multibillion-dollar deals came down twice a week ," says Nathaniel Nash. "I didn't say, 'Wait a minute, let's sit down and analyze these things.' That's where we failed as a press corps. Never in the history of regulation has so much money been obligated so quickly by people whose authority was at least questionable."

Or as Jerry Knight put it: "A lot of taxpayers' money was being given away to zillionaires, but it was complicated and hard to write in English."

A few weeks after George Bush took office, he confronted the issue he had ducked throughout the campaign. The bailout estimates were growing larger. What had been an abstract, boring story began to make occasional appearances on the front page.

"S&L Rescue Could Cost Average Taxpayer $450," the *Los Angeles Times* declared. And *The Wall Street Journal* finally adopted a more alarming tone: "Brace yourself, taxpayers. One of the most colossal blunders in regulatory history is about to cost each and every one of you about $500."

As public resentment began to rise, Kathleen Day asked the *Post* if she could write a big wrap-up piece. People were finally paying attention, she felt, and needed to understand how the calamity had come to pass. Day's editors weren't interested, so she did the story for *The New Republic* in early 1989.

Day's piece became a stinging cover story called "S&L Hell." In the headlines, Danny Wall and Freddy St Germain were described as "stooges," and the speaker of the House was Jim "Money Talks" Wright. Wall's performance, Day wrote, "might be enough to condemn him to S&L hell."

Top *Post* editors were "furious," Day says. Peter Behr, then the assistant managing editor for financial news, "was irritated because it told the truth. He wished we'd had it."

Behr sees it differently: "She did things in that piece that were wonderful, powerful stuff, but not newspaper journalism. The opinions she offered about people and their motives . . . were absolutely not appropriate." Behr briefly questioned whether Day could continue to cover banking after writing such an opinionated piece, but decided to keep her on the beat. Ironically, she had finally done what so many reporters had failed to do within the constraints of daily journalism: to scream out loud that this was an outrage and to finger the villains.

What had been a regional story for so long was finally going national. In the spring of 1989, two *Post* reporters, David Maraniss and Rick Atkinson, produced a six-part epic on the collapse of Texas S&Ls. Written in sweeping, novelistic style, it recounted Ed Gray's battles against the Texas billionaires, the spectacular failure of Empire Savings and Loan, the arrogance of Don Dixon's $22,000 dining spree across Europe. Allen Pusey of *The Dallas Morning News* couldn't help but notice that he had plowed the same ground six years earlier.

"It was sort of a vindication, but it hurt a little bit," he says. "It's a little hard to watch your work be taken by *The Washington Post* and made into a series. . . . The Eastern seaboard press is very parochial in its own way. They're good at catching on to the big picture and working their way backwards."

The saga of Charles Keating took years to penetrate the national consciousness. Our archaeological dig would turn up all sorts of articles in the mid-'80s about Keating's battles with federal regulators, his sale of risky junk bonds to thousands of hapless investors, his prodigious use of campaign cash. But no one could nail the full story.

In the fall of 1986, Gregory Gordon of United Press International reported that Charles Pashayan, a Republican congressman from California, had offered legislation to aid Lincoln Savings & Loan in its battle with the bank board—and received $26,000 in campaign contributions from Keating, his relatives and employees.

A week later, Gordon reported that several other members of Congress had helped Keating in his face-off with Ed Gray. Among those receiving money from Keating and others at Lincoln were Arizona Representative (and later senator) John McCain ($55,000), Senator Alan Cranston ($19,000) and Senator John Glenn ($14,000). But the UPI stories were largely ignored outside the lawmakers' home states. Political reporters had no reason to notice what seemed like a minor business story.

In the spring of 1987, Mike Binstein obtained the confidential minutes of an extraordinary meeting between five United States senators

—Cranston, Glenn, McCain, Riegle and Arizona's Dennis DeConcini—and the San Francisco bank examiners who were investigating Lincoln. Binstein describes the documents as "the Pentagon Papers of the S&L crisis." There was Glenn saying, "To be blunt, you should charge them or get off their backs." There was Riegle saying, "Where's the smoking gun? Where are the losses?" There was a regulator calling Lincoln a "ticking time bomb."

The meeting had taken place in DeConcini's office just a few weeks earlier. But Keating was still a forbidden subject for the Anderson column, and Binstein couldn't find anyone to publish the story.

That fall, *National Thrift News* reported the meeting, with substantial detail about what the paper called "an unprecedented display of senatorial effort on behalf of a thrift institution." But the article drew little attention, perhaps reflecting the mainstream media's lack of respect for trade publications, which often scoop them on regulatory matters.

In early 1988, two *Detroit News* reporters, Michael Clements and Roger Martin, discovered that Riegle had received at least $66,000 from Lincoln executives and their spouses. "That puzzled us, because Keating was a big conservative Republican," Clements says. The reporters, who had missed the *Thrift News* piece, soon learned of the meeting in DeConcini's office. After their story ran, Riegle quickly returned $78,000 in Lincoln contributions. But the article caused few ripples outside Michigan.

That spring, Binstein began meeting with Peter Behr to try to persuade *The Washington Post* to publish the minutes of the meeting. Like most papers, the *Post* almost never accepted investigative stories from free-lancers; the risk was simply too great. But Behr was intrigued. He retraced Binstein's steps, even accompanying him to interviews with DeConcini and McCain.

"He kept saying, 'Are you sure? I've got kids going to school and a mortgage to pay,' " Binstein recalls. "It was a gutsy call." The *Post* ran Binstein's story in the business section, but failed to follow up.

"What I really feel bad about is, once that story ran, why the hell didn't we go?" Behr says. "So many of our people work on beats, it's hard to suddenly throw good people at a big story that wasn't on anybody's radar screen." The political reporters and the business reporters were still at opposite ends of the newsroom, going their separate ways.

Danny Wall took the San Francisco examiners off the case and transferred authority for Lincoln to the bank board's Washington head-quarters. It was an audacious move, one that clearly signaled that bankers unhappy with aggressive federal regulation could shop around for a venue more to their liking. The same pattern had surfaced at HUD, where top officials ignored findings by their regional offices when they wanted to award grants to politically connected recipients.

But the press barely noticed Keating's victory. *The Wall Street Journal* ran the story on page 38, *The Washington Post* in its business section. *The New York Times* had no story. "In the space of a news story," says Brooks Jackson, "you couldn't prove Charlie Keating is a bad guy."

But the proof wasn't far off. Eleven months later, in the spring of 1989, the Federal Home Loan Bank Board declared Lincoln Savings & Loan insolvent. The bailout of Lincoln cost the taxpayers $2.6 billion, the most expensive failure in S&L history. Danny Wall's delay of the shutdown had added hundreds of millions of dollars to the final cost.

Even then—after Lincoln's collapse, after Ed Gray's warnings proved correct, after Wall's delay and the pressure from the five senators was well known—Charles Keating was still not a major news story. Not even at *The Washington Post*, which thrives on politics and scandal. Most political reporters were busy chronicling the early stages of George Bush's presidency.

In July 1989, Charles Babcock, a *Post* reporter who specializes in campaign finance, wrote that Alan Cranston had successfully solicited $850,000 from Keating for three voter-registration groups he helped found. One was run by the senator's son. The story, which first appeared in the Los Angeles *Daily News,* ran on page A-21.

Two days later, Babcock reported that Keating had given John Glenn's political action committee $200,000 in undisclosed corporate donations. Glenn's disclosure, prompted by questions from Ohio reporters, made it to page A-5 of the *Post*.

In October, Babcock, following up on a report in *The Arizona Republic,* wrote that John McCain had repaid Keating $13,433 for nine corporate jet flights he and his family had taken. The senator had never disclosed the flights, which included vacation trips to Keating's home in the Bahamas. The story ran on page A-8.

It finally took Henry Gonzalez, the eccentric congressman who had endured so many snickers, to turn "the Keating Five" into a shorthand phrase for Washington influence peddling. Gonzalez, who had become the House Banking chairman after St Germain's defeat, held more than fifty hours of hearings into Lincoln's collapse. Although the hearings covered familiar ground, they made front-page news and all the networks. Now there was some drama: Gonzalez demanded Danny Wall's scalp and raised questions about the five senators whose campaigns and causes had received $1.3 million from Keating. When Keating was asked whether he had given money to politicians to influence them to go to bat for him, he replied, "I want to say in the most forceful way I can: I certainly hope so."

Wall resigned under pressure the following month. The FBI began investigating the Keating Five. Since the basic outlines of the case had been known for two years, this simply reinforced the notion that law enforcement agencies are sensitive to what runs on the front page.

While Don Riegle was being pilloried by the press, he punched back by highlighting a bit of hypocrisy back home. In a letter to the editor of the *Detroit Free Press,* Riegle outlined how the chief executive officer of Knight-Ridder, the paper's corporate owner, had asked him to help win government approval of its plan for a joint operating agreement with Gannett's *Detroit News.* Everyone lobbies senators, he argued, even newspapers. Riegle had a point, of course. While news organizations tend to wrap their requests in the garb of the First Amendment, they are as capable of special pleading as the greediest bank executive. The difference is that Knight-Ridder, unlike Keating, didn't give money to Riegle's campaign.

In the weeks following the Gonzalez hearings, the media couldn't get enough of the story. The Bush administration raised its estimate of the S&L bailout to $164 billion. Neil Bush, a director of a Denver S&L that had handed out millions in loans to insiders, was blamed in part by federal regulators for its $1.6 billion collapse. Now the headline-writers had another symbol to go with the numbers—the president's son, caught up in the greed decade. Taxpayers were fuming over a bailout that was soon estimated to cost more than $500 billion.

"It peaked when people finally decided to publish the $500-billion number," Nathaniel Nash says. "Then it was feeding-frenzy time."

In the fall of 1990, Charles Keating was indicted for defrauding 22,000 investors of more than $250 million. He was later convicted of seventeen counts of fraud and, in 1992, sentenced to ten years in prison. Keating was also convicted in 1993 in a billion-dollar civil racketeering suit by the government. The lawsuit also named Keating's brother, Bill, the chairman of *The Cincinnati Enquirer,* a development the paper did not see fit to mention until the 14th paragraph of a story that began on page C-4. Editor George Blake said he considered his boss "a friend" who would never do anything illegal. Bill Keating, who had been a director of Lincoln's parent firm, was later dismissed from the suit.

Four of the Keating Five got off easy, with mild criticism from the Senate ethics committee for their "poor judgment." Only Alan Cranston was reprimanded for "repugnant" conduct.

In 1992, federal regulators sued David Branson's law firm, Kaye, Scholer (Branson's conduct was not at issue). The government froze the firm's assets, charging that it withheld crucial information about Keating's crumbling empire. The firm paid $41 million to settle the lawsuit and another $20 million in suits brought by bondholders who charged they were ripped off by Keating. "It would've been cheaper if they had kept me as a client," Jack Anderson says.

The S&L debacle was a crashing finale to the excesses of the '80s, but it was a humbling experience for the press as well. Chastened journalists vowed not to be caught asleep at the switch again. In 1991, when the first signs of the global fraud at the Bank of Commerce and Credit International became public, most major papers assigned teams of reporters to chase (and in some cases hype) the story. When there were signs that the banking crisis might spread to hundreds of commercial banks, newspapers were quick to depict the warnings as serious, rather than bury them with the housing starts and durable-goods orders.

But some things haven't changed. We still have a compelling need to personalize financial stories whose multibillion-dollar abstractions are hard for readers, and especially television viewers, to grasp. BCCI didn't become a full-fledged media sensation until it was linked to Clark Clifford, an elder statesman of the Democratic Party. Clifford was chairman of a Washington bank that investigators—with help from *Regardie's* and *The Washington Post*—charged was a BCCI front. The grand-old-man-gone-wrong angle proved much more colorful than the convoluted paper trail of BCCI's Arab investors.

Political reporters and business reporters still inhabit different worlds. Occasionally these worlds converge, as they did in 1991 when federal regulators charged Arizona governor Fife Symington in the collapse of a Phoenix savings and loan of which he had been a director. But while business reporters continued to sift through the vast wreckage of the banking world, political reporters in 1992 concerned themselves with such trivial pursuits as the check-kiting congressmen who abused the House Bank.

News organizations still place far too much faith in financial "experts," even when their upbeat pronouncements consistently prove false. On December 19, 1991, the *New York Times, Washington Post, Los Angeles Times, Boston Globe* and *USA Today* all gave front-page play to congressional testimony by Alan Greenspan, chairman of the Federal Reserve. Greenspan announced that the economy appeared to be "faltering." This shocking declaration came after a year-long recession that had thrown millions of people out of work and had sent thousands of businesses into bankruptcy. Who the hell cared whether Alan Greenspan was finally confirming the obvious? It was almost as inane as all those earlier stories quoting experts on whether the country was in a "recession," a "slowdown," a "lull" or, in Greenspan's words, a "meaningful downturn." Such semantic nonsense made the press seem hopelessly out of touch with the real world.

Besides, news organizations no longer needed experts to tell them how bad things had gotten. In previous recessions, expense-account journalists would fly into the Rust Belt to interview laid-off autoworkers, but they never felt personally threatened; they were as disconnected from the pain and suffering as some well-heeled correspondent in a Third World country. But the recession of 1991–92 was a disaster for the professional classes. Thousands of reporters and editors lost their jobs as media profits plummeted and some newspapers shut their doors. The economic story had hit home. It was almost as if a perverse fate were punishing them for their giddy coverage of the decade symbolized by Donald Trump.

4

The Fire This Time

When violence erupted in the streets of Los Angeles on April 29, 1992, the press pounced on the story with single-minded intensity. There were vivid front-line reports on the burnings and beatings, some of them filed by reporters who themselves had been assaulted or shot at. There were stories about Korean merchants who lost their shops and about black mothers who joined in the looting to secure diapers and orange juice for their children. Even more disturbing were the stories about the legacy of police brutality, about white victims who were murdered at random, about black gang members who used the verdicts in the Rodney King case as a pretext for crime. While live television captured the horror of a black mob beating truck driver Reginald Denny, newspapers provided the context, the history, the agonizing search for answers.

After fifty-one people had been killed and ten thousand businesses burned, the press plunged into a nonstop orgy of racial analysis, expert hand-wringing and urban sociology. There was a front-page series on racial problems in the *Chicago Tribune,* a two-part examination of segregated communities in *The New York Times,* a big spread on race in the workplace in *The Wall Street Journal,* a week of special riot sections in the *Los Angeles Times.* The *Times'* superb coverage even included front-page commentaries by some of its staffers.

"Los Angeles, you broke my heart," reporter George Ramos wrote. "And I'm not sure I'll love you again. That's not an easy thing for me to say. I know—reporters are supposed to be detached observers of the routine and the unusual. Notebooks in hand, we are historians on the run, asking the obvious, repeating the answers and wondering—after the story is done—if we really understood what it was all about. . . ." Conventional journalism could not do justice to the senselessness of the riots, so the paper wisely opted for a more personal approach.

Still, one had to ask: Where had the press been all along? Why was the anguish of big-city poverty and the ugliness of racial hatred suddenly page-one news? The despair of urban America had been the media's S&L issue of 1992, hidden in plain view until it exploded.

Most news organizations had discounted the possibility that an all-white jury in Simi Valley might not convict four white officers whose brutal beating of King had been replayed on television thousands of times. And like the Los Angeles Police Department, they were completely unprepared for the violence that followed. But the failure was far, far larger than that. The mainstream press had totally underestimated the depth of the anger, frustration and sense of hopelessness in communities like South-Central L.A., whose eruption exceeded the deadly fury of the Watts riots a quarter-century earlier.

A new generation of affluent reporters, who drove in from the suburbs and did much of their reporting by phone and fax, was increasingly cut off from what was happening on the meanest streets. The press corps that had stopped covering HUD during the 1980s was still largely uninterested in the abandonment of the central cities. Most blacks in slum neighborhoods simply did not make news—did not exist in the media universe—except by committing violence. Thus it was hardly surprising that many reporters, their dangling press cards identifying them as members of the political establishment, were singled out for attack during the rioting. And it was utterly predictable that the killing and looting would produce an avalanche of stories about the country's racial wounds, and that these headlines would fade within weeks as the political world lost interest.

For years, most newspapers had been more concerned with courting suburban readers than plumbing the painful depths of the inner cities. Andrea Ford, a black reporter at the *Los Angeles Times* whose teenage sons had been harassed by police, says her white editors "did not take police brutality in the black community seriously; they have no experience like that." *Times* editors dispute this, of course. Yet at the time of the riots, the *Times* published separate community news sections for all the sprawling suburbs from Orange County to Ventura County, but had no such section for South-Central L.A., and no bureau in the central city.

Newspapers have always had trouble coming to grips with racial animosity. It is the subject everyone talks about and few write candidly about. It fascinates and frightens us at the same time. Take any issue—crime, urban decay, housing, hiring, politics, schools—and race is the backdrop, the steaming mixture bubbling just beneath the surface. A black-white conflict can pump up any news story until it is twisted out of shape.

While a handful of journalists have done sophisticated reporting on race relations in recent years, the only blacks consistently covered by the press seem to be basketball stars, cocaine dealers and welfare mothers. White-owned news organizations have been particularly deficient in seeking out a wider range of spokesmen for the black community, particularly its younger, more disaffected members, whom we barely understand at all. Instead, we distort the picture by training our blinding spotlight on an assortment of kooks, crazies and crackpots whose mission is to divide and polarize. And no one understands that process better than the Reverend Al Sharpton.

For the New York press in particular, Sharpton's antics have been one of the great journalistic soap operas, a guaranteed source of entertaining headlines. Racial strife is such a painful subject that we need a colorful figure to simplify, to personalize, to reduce the story to a running clash between an outspoken militant and the establishment. The Sharptons of the world, who purport to package black resentment in easily digestible sound bites, fill the bill quite nicely.

For all our focus on Sharpton's racial ambulance-chasing, it is clear in retrospect that most white editors and reporters missed the point of what he was saying. Time and again, Sharpton warned that the ghettos were ready to explode, that the rage among young blacks was so great that any spark could trigger an eruption. Most middle-class journalists dismissed this as Sharpton running off at the mouth, but the L.A. riots proved that he was right. Other danger signals, such as the violent, racially charged images that pervaded rap music, also fell on deaf ears. The mainstream press was, once again, tuned to the wrong frequency.

The plain fact is that newspapers reflect the mood and values of white, middle-class society, and that society, by the early '90s, had simply grown tired of the intractable problems of the urban underclass. Bombastic spokesmen like Sharpton were tolerated as harmless buffoons, and indeed Sharpton exploited his media celebrity by playing to the stereotype of a pork-chop preacher. But in our fascination with

Sharpton's brand of street theater, our periodic obsession with spectacular racial crimes, our blind belief that riots were a relic of the 1960s, we missed the larger story. We glossed over the hatred. But the warning signs were there all along.

There is no shortage of angry prejudice on both sides, as I learned in the late 1980s walking the streets of Howard Beach and Bensonhurst, and of Harlem and East New York. Newspapers rarely send reporters to these communities, except in the aftermath of violence.

"They don't know anything about those neighborhoods," Jimmy Breslin told me in the summer of 1991, the morning after he had been pulled from a cab and beaten by a group of blacks in the Crown Heights section of Brooklyn. "Nobody goes into those neighborhoods, no editor. These fucking editors don't even know the joint exists. . . . The overriding story is the hatred. Nobody wants to face the truth."

New York is particularly vulnerable to such racial frenzies because it is a tabloid town. Tabloid standards—overheated drama, high-pitched rhetoric, screaming headlines—set the tone as the rest of the media feast upon the turmoil. It is journalism reduced to its lowest common denominator.

It's not hard to understand why many blacks view the press as part of the white establishment. When the Watts riots broke out in 1965, major metropolitan newspapers had almost no black reporters. The *Los Angeles Times* had to use a black advertising salesman to cover the violence. By the early '70s, the relative handful of black reporters in the business were suing *The New York Times, The Washington Post* and other papers for discrimination. Only in the mid-'80s did a few blacks migrate into the senior management ranks of some papers. Even today, just one major newspaper, the *Oakland Tribune,* is run by a black editor. Just over 10 percent of all newspaper editors and reporters are minorities. Half the nation's newsrooms have no minority employees.

But many whites, I have come to understand, are equally suspicious of the press. They see it as part of a self-appointed liberal elite, catering to black pressure groups and crusading for such solutions as busing and integration that wreak havoc on working-class communities. In their view, white people are regularly beaten or killed by blacks with little public fuss, while black victims of white attacks are treated as front-page news.

This was driven home to me on a cold day in Queens in December 1987. The night before, a jury had convicted three white teenagers of manslaughter in the death of twenty-one-year-old Michael Griffith.

The Howard Beach racial attack a year earlier had reverberated throughout the country. Three black men, stranded in that neighborhood after their car broke down, found themselves being chased by a mob of bat-wielding teenagers shouting "Niggers, get the fuck out of the neighborhood!" The white youths chased Griffith onto the Belt Parkway, where he was struck and killed by a car.

As I spoke to people amid the clam bars and pizza parlors of Howard Beach, I was stunned by the lack of sympathy for Griffith's death and the stubborn insistence that any blacks with the temerity to enter their white enclave after dark must have been up to no good. "The only reason they got manslaughter was because the black people raised a lot of hell," said Elizabeth, thirty, one of many Howard Beach residents who refused to give their last name. Each community, viewing the world through a racial prism, saw the press as loyal to the other side.

The palpable rise in racial tensions in New York, Washington, Boston, Los Angeles and other cities since 1986 has coincided with the crack epidemic. Crack cocaine ushered in a massive surge in homicides and street crime. As whites watched the nightly televised parade of black hoodlums being led into precinct houses, their attitudes toward the underclass hardened. Even many liberals had no more patience for experts who prattled on about the "root causes" of crime. Each new headline seemed to many readers to be a journalistic code for minority criminals.

"What gets missed in all this is the vast numbers of blacks who live lives like everyone else," says Joe Klein, a *Newsweek* columnist who has written extensively about race. "It's gotten to the point where it's news to learn there are black men who take care of their children and go to work every day."

I always had trouble understanding why the press lavished so much attention on a 285-pound college dropout. Al Sharpton was an unabashed media hound, a professional rabble-rouser, a minister without a congregation. He seemed to represent no one but a few busloads of angry young blacks who turned out for his demonstrations—and we later learned he had often paid them five dollars apiece to show up.

To classify Sharpton's career is an exercise in futility. He hung out on the fringes of the boxing and entertainment world with Don King, sometimes landing contracts to promote black singing groups. He had dealt with such reputed organized-crime figures as Michael Franzese. He had spent years as a Justice Department informant, secretly recording phone conversations with his associates. He had been indicted (and acquitted) for fraud in connection with his antidrug organization, the National Youth Movement.

Yet each new revelation seemed only to enhance Sharpton's standing among his followers. He would visit the studios of WLIB, a black radio station, and denounce the white media for criticizing him. A sizable chunk of the black community relied on a form of samizdat, using separate channels of communication, and regarded the fact-laden accounts in the white press as lies.

In one conflict after another, it was the same old tired act, crying racism in front of the television cameras. Even after editors started cropping him out of photographs, Sharpton found ways to keep himself in the news.

When Nelson Mandela visited New York in the summer of 1990, Sharpton briefly upstaged the visit by demanding to be jailed on a two-year-old protest charge. He posed for a behind-bars picture that the *New York Post* splashed on its front page.

When Washington mayor Marion Barry was being tried on cocaine charges, Sharpton, who had spent a lifetime denouncing drug use, showed up and declared that Barry was the victim of racially motivated prosecutors.

Sharpton even got himself arrested at the Miss America pageant in Atlantic City, ostensibly to protest the city's lack of opportunity for minorities. More and more he took his show on the road: Sharpton goes to Los Angeles after the Rodney King beating. Sharpton goes to London. Sharpton goes to Israel. Sharpton goes to Haiti after a military coup. And the press invariably followed. "If he is the monster, then we are the Dr. Frankensteins who created him," says Jerry Nachman, the former *New York Post* editor.

Only gradually did I come to understand that Sharpton was a shrewd tactician who fulfilled the media's need to reduce complex issues to personalities. And he made no attempt to hide his headline-hunting role. "People get paid a lot of money on Madison Avenue to do what I do in the ghetto for nothing," he once told me.

Beyond the hype, beyond the processed hair, the jogging suits and the gold medallion, Sharpton taps into a vein of black discontent with white society so deep that its very existence makes white reporters and editors uncomfortable. To be sure, much of the black middle class finds Sharpton an embarrassment, but that isn't his constituency. He plays to a different audience.

Once known as the "boy preacher," Sharpton, whose father abandoned the family when he was ten, grew up attaching himself to a series of father figures, from Adam Clayton Powell to Jesse Jackson to James Brown. He became a minor-league celebrity who once painted red Xs on crack houses to draw press coverage.

All that changed after Howard Beach. Sharpton and his extremist allies, attorneys Alton Maddox and C. Vernon Mason, urged the black victims not to cooperate with the Queens district attorney. This tactic prompted Governor Mario Cuomo to name a special prosecutor, Charles Hynes, who won convictions in the case. The politics of confrontation had worked.

Sharpton, then thirty-three, realized that the city's polite black leadership had left a vacuum on racial issues, which he was all too happy to fill. He was building a media myth, one that would grow so large that the tabloids started running stories on his hairdresser.

When Tawana Brawley crawled out of a garbage bag, covered with feces, the words "nigger" and "KKK" scrawled in charcoal on her body, it was a spectacle made to order for Sharpton's brand of demagoguery. Here was a fifteen-year-old cheerleader from Wappingers Falls, New York, who claimed to have been abducted and sexually assaulted by six white men over Thanksgiving weekend in 1987. Yet the case, shocking as it was, received scant media coverage. *The New York Times* ran a single story by a black reporter-trainee and made no attempt to follow up.

To some it was just another violent crime. "One of the dilemmas of New York journalism is that a murder is not a news story ipso facto," Nachman says. "In Milwaukee, Pittsburgh, Washington, every murder probably gets at least a short in the Metro section. We have six homicides a day. Most don't make the paper at all. There are tests: Is the victim prominent? Were the means of death baroque? Did you chop someone up and put them in the freezer and make soup out of them?"

From the outset, it was obvious there were sizable holes in Brawley's story. But she was a powerful symbol of racial injustice, and no white journalist dared go out on a limb by questioning the attack. Sharpton, Maddox and Mason again demanded a special prosecutor, but when Cuomo turned over the case to his attorney general, Robert Abrams, the trio refused to cooperate.

It was an acute dilemma for the press: Many reporters privately regarded Sharpton as a clown, yet they kept on reporting his bizarre claims. Here he was blaming the kidnapping on a "racist cult," with links to the Irish Republican Army, run out of the Dutchess County sheriff's office. Sharpton even likened Abrams, who is Jewish, to Adolf Hitler. Maddox accused Abrams of masturbating to seminude hospital photos of Brawley. But as outlandish as the charges were, few editors could restrain themselves. To ignore the self-appointed spokesman for the nation's most prominent black victim was simply not part of their chemistry. Anything Sharpton did was news.

"I get nervous about censoring people's statements," says Don Forst, the *New York Newsday* editor. "I know sometimes they can be incendiary. We've always leaned toward the side of giving people their say, as long as you try to get the other side."

But merely getting the other side is an abdication of journalistic responsibility when libelous charges are hurled without proof. It is a throwback to the worst days of McCarthyism, when the press would ruin people's careers simply by reporting someone's blanket assertion that they were Communists.

While the tabloids went wild, the *Times* sent six reporters to Dutchess County for some old-fashioned door-knocking. E. R. Shipp, one of the two black members of the team, worried about being part of a white cover-up. "We had some concerns," she says, "about whether we were blowing it again on a racial story, and whether we, the black reporters, were being used by our paper. We didn't know what our colleagues were up to, if they were buying the police line."

Such racial questions made the white members of the team uncomfortable. "One thing that got under our skin was this idea that we had to be policed, that the black reporters had to keep us in line," says reporter Craig Wolff. "A black reporter can go into a black neighborhood and do just as bad a job as anyone else."

The reporters uncovered numerous contradictions in Brawley's account, and the *Times* published their findings in an extraordinary, 6,700-word story on February 29, 1988. The piece strongly suggested that Brawley had returned to her family's former apartment during her four-day disappearance. It also explored her stormy relationship with her stepfather, Ralph King, who had served time in prison for killing his wife. Still, the *Times* editors were cautious—too cautious—about drawing conclusions.

The tabloids, meanwhile, sank to new depths. Sharpton, Maddox and Mason called a news conference on March 13 and, without a shred of evidence, named Dutchess County prosecutor Steven Pagones as one of Brawley's attackers. After obtaining the obligatory denial from Pagones's lawyer, every news organization in New York trumpeted the allegation.

The story had become so overheated, so racially polarizing, that the normal rules of journalism were suspended. What editor could hold back when everyone else was printing this crap? I wrote some of it myself, usually in the context of how Sharpton and his colleagues were manipulating the media.

The racial element was undeniable. After all, it's hard to imagine newspapers mindlessly repeating baseless charges by white attorneys that a black prosecutor had committed rape. But Sharpton, Maddox and Mason knew what buttons to press. They cleverly framed their case as a crusade against a racist criminal justice system, and editors, who knew the system was flawed, did not want to be appear to be defending it.

"We did get suckered," says *Newsday*'s Sydney Schanberg. "Why we kept covering Maddox and Mason, I don't know. It was seen as good copy. . . . Everyone's afraid of Sharpton. They're afraid the blacks will think we're disrespecting their leaders."

Even Andrew Cooper, the publisher of the *City Sun,* a black weekly in Brooklyn that championed Brawley's cause, says Sharpton and his allies "didn't help things by not coming forth with anything but accusations and rhetoric. They've got their own axes to grind. That not only tends to overshadow the event, but it gives the media an excuse to come down on them. They are the bad guys."

The first time I met Sharpton, a large, beefy man with a Fu Manchu mustache, he boasted about how he had pulled the wool over reporters' eyes, his booming bass voice reverberating in the tiny basement office of the Brownsville church where we met.

Some weeks earlier, the tabloids had run front-page pictures of Sharpton escorting Brawley from her uncle's house in Monticello, New

York. He had announced to the waiting crowd of reporters that he was moving Brawley to an undisclosed location to keep the media from harassing her. Tawana in hiding! Another big story.

Sharpton told me what really happened: "We packed the suitcase, we came outside, we put the suitcase in the trunk, they're snapping pictures. Tawana gets in the car with me. We ride around the corner and get ice cream. We come back through the back door, where she climbed through the basement window of her uncle's house. Tawana never left Monticello." It was more smoke and mirrors, like the Brawley case itself.

Despite the mounting discrepancies in Brawley's account, the *Times'* E. R. Shipp kept the lines of communication open. "Even the ones who thought Sharpton, Maddox and Mason were the scum of the earth and liars, there was always a fear that we would wake up the next day and Tawana would have told her story," she says.

The Sharpton trio missed no opportunity to play to the press. After a judge ordered Glenda Brawley, Tawana's mother, jailed for thirty days for ignoring a grand jury subpoena, the story took on an Alice in Wonderland quality. Sharpton sheltered her in the basement of a Brooklyn church, where they staged an appearance on "Donahue." Shipp finally concluded that the Brawley tale was "a joke. They kept finding ways to avoid answering the questions. There was nothing there."

When the *Times* published a leaked version of the grand jury findings on September 27, 1988, Brawley's story was finally exposed as an elaborate hoax, aided by her mother, apparently out of fear that the girl's stepfather would punish her for past misbehavior. Tawana had smeared the feces on herself and written the racial slurs on her body.

"It brought out the worst in us," says Jerry Nachman, one of the few editors not shy about criticizing his own role in the media circus. "The system entrapped us, Sharpton exploited us, and we abetted the worst exploitation of the system. We were coconspirators." To be sure, the racial cauldron stirred up by Sharpton fed the tabloids' bottomless appetite for conflict, drama and outrage. They live off people plunking down their quarters at newsstands, and screaming headlines don't grab readers when there is little to scream about.

Still, what is accepted as truth in the mainstream press is viewed more darkly in minority neighborhoods. Many blacks saw the grand jury report as just another effort to discredit their man Sharpton. "They don't trust white people," Andy Cooper says. He still believes something did happen to Brawley.

Six months later came a real gang rape, an attack so brutal that it stunned even hardened New Yorkers. This time, however, Sharpton and the other black activists who so passionately demanded justice for Tawana Brawley had little to say about the woman known as the Central Park jogger, a white investment banker who lived on the Upper East Side.

Instead, the activists defended the black and Hispanic kids from Harlem who had allegedly taken turns raping her, smashed her head with a rock and left her to die. Why weren't the teenagers out on bail, they demanded? Why had the media labeled them a "wolfpack"? It was hard to avoid the conclusion that their sympathies depended solely on skin color. Maddox even suggested the case might be a hoax. "What are we going to do, accept some white person's word?" he asked.

But there was no denying one criticism voiced by the black community. The attack on the jogger touched off a media frenzy so intense it was easy to forget that blacks are raped and killed with depressing regularity in New York's worst neighborhoods, often rating just a few paragraphs in the paper. A few days before the Central Park attack, a twenty-nine-year-old Harlem woman was raped by two gun-wielding men atop a housing project, then pushed off the roof. She grabbed onto some cable wires as she fell and was pulled to safety through a seventeenth-floor window. It was treated as a one-day story. One can only wonder how much attention the victim of this attack would have received had she been a white investment banker.

To be sure, the drama of the young jogger clinging to life struck a deep chord with millions of people. But it is also true that white middle-class journalists and white middle-class readers tend to identify with people like themselves. Things are not nearly as bad as thirty years ago, when editors routinely treated the murder of any "Negro" as a one-paragraph brief, but we are still wrestling with unconscious bias, which inflates the news value of events affecting those who live nearest us and look most like us.

In the summer of 1989, Al Sharpton took center stage once more when sixteen-year-old Yusuf Hawkins was shot and killed after a white mob cornered him in Bensonhurst, a white, working-class neighborhood in Brooklyn. Never shy about exploiting a tragedy, Sharpton led busloads of protesters on marches through the heart of Bensonhurst. Editors who had vowed to ignore Sharpton quickly forgot about the Brawley hoax. Sharpton cut off press access to the Hawkins family and became the official spokesman; once again, he was stage-managing the hottest story in town.

When the first two Bensonhurst defendants, Joey Fama and Keith Mondello, went on trial for murder the following spring, Sharpton issued a dire warning. Unless the two men were found guilty, he said, "You are lighting a match to the end of a powder keg and telling us to burn the town down." The press supplied the gunpowder; the *New York Post* carried Sharpton's words in a red-ink headline on page one. "CITY ON THE EDGE," warned the cover of *New York Newsday,* with a burning match set against the Manhattan skyline.

Fama was convicted of murder charges, but when a second jury acquitted Mondello of murder, Sharpton announced another march into Bensonhurst. There was a festive air on 20th Avenue in Brooklyn the following afternoon. Hundreds of neighborhood folks lined the streets, chatting amiably and awaiting the day's entertainment. On some corners there were almost as many reporters as onlookers. As if on cue, the racial invective started flying when Sharpton and his five hundred pro-testors arrived, flanked on either side by lines of riot-helmeted police-men. Young men in T-shirts and gold chains shouted "Nigger!" and "Get a job!," knowing from past experience that this would get them on television. A seventeen-year-old boy held up a watermelon emblazoned with the words "Reverend Al, You Fat Bastard." Hawkins's brother, Amir, was hit by a half-filled beer bottle, and a photographer was splat-tered with mud. But it was a made-for-television sort of racism: forty-five minutes later, the Sharpton contingent left and the crowd quietly dispersed. The closeup shots of white people shouting at black marchers looked much more ominous on TV that night. What you couldn't see was that the march never occupied more than a couple of blocks.

Sharpton knew that his very presence would bring out the water-melon-waving elements, and that the press, needing a second-day story after the verdicts, would not be able to stay away. He scored a clean media sweep, even making the front page of the Sunday *New York Times.* Sharpton had become a certified celebrity, a tabloid caricature. Like Donald and Marla, he was always good for a feature on a slow day.

The press seemed far less interested in Sharpton's fraud trial that spring. There was evidence that most of the antidrug activities for which Sharpton was raising money had come to naught. There was testimony that Sharpton had used the staff of his National Youth Movement to urge radio stations to play records he was promoting through his for-profit corporation, Hitbound. A former aide, asked why Sharpton had paid black kids five dollars to appear at his rallies, testified: "Because Reverend Sharpton had no followers."

None of this got burn-down-the-town treatment on the front page. Although Sharpton was acquitted of fraud, the press had missed a prime opportunity to paint a more complete portrait of him as a part-time hustler.

Six months later, Sharpton was stabbed in the chest by a Bensonhurst man· as he led yet another protest march through the Italian neighborhood. Even as he recovered in the hospital, there were reassessments in the press. The *Times* ran a piece called " 'New' Sharpton: Maturing of a Maverick."

But the reverend always kept his can of gasoline in reserve, ready to start pouring when the racial sparks flew. In the summer of 1991, when blacks and Hasidic Jews rioted in Crown Heights after Gavin Cato, a black child, was struck and killed by a car in the Lubavitcher rabbi's motorcade, Sharpton, Maddox and Mason were again on the scene, again crying cover-up, again demanding a special prosecutor. Sharpton vowed to march on the rabbi's temple on the Jewish holiday of Succoth and personally serve him with court papers. When that plan fizzled, Sharpton flew to Israel in a comic attempt to serve papers on the car's Hasidic driver, only to find the country shut down for Yom Kippur. The press couldn't get enough of this absurd spectacle. "EL AL," a *Post* headline scoffed.

This time the town really was burning and the "new" Sharpton was fanning the flames, not unlike the old Sharpton, who had never admitted that Tawana Brawley had lied. Sharpton decried the accidental death of the black child but had nothing to say about Yankel Rosenbaum, the young Jewish scholar who was killed by blacks in Crown Heights in apparent retaliation. The same columnists attacked the Sharpton trio, who in turn denounced the white media.

One might reasonably wonder how Al Sharpton, a man who holds no public office and ministers to no congregation, keeps himself in the headlines year after year. The answer is that he understands one of journalism's dirty little secrets: its dependence on "spokesmen" who can supply succinct sound bites on deadline. A reporter who needs a comment from a civil rights group can always call the NAACP. But who speaks for poor blacks in the New York ghettos, where Jimmy Breslin says that journalists fear to tread? Sharpton is always available, always dressed for the part, always willing to supply the inflammatory quote that will perk up a story. And if that makes him into a larger-than-life figure that white readers love to hate, so much the better.

Al Sharpton has mastered one other skill that most politicians can only dream of: the ability to perpetually reinvent himself. In 1992, while still under indictment on income-tax charges, to which he would later plead guilty, he mounted a campaign for the Senate. Although Sharpton raised little money, he shrewdly moderated his tone and won new respect from his old adversaries in the press, finishing third in a four-person primary. *The New York Times* went so far as to dub him "a poor-person's Ross Perot."

In a 1993 jailhouse interview with the reverend, who was serving time for blocking the Brooklyn Bridge five years earlier, the *New York Post* marveled at how "the election transformed Sharpton's image. Now, Bill Clinton nods hello. Mayor Dinkins calls all the time. Even Cardinal O'Connor picks up the phone to say hello. Sharpton is on the cover of *The New York Times Sunday Magazine*. He's featured on '60 Minutes.' "

"I haven't changed," Sharpton says. "I think what has changed is the mainstream of America. . . . After Rodney King and L.A., after such blatant acts, people say, 'Well, maybe Sharpton is not crazy—maybe there is something wrong in the justice system.' "

The coverage of the Los Angeles riots was fueled by a sense of injustice. Yes, it was understandable that blacks would be shocked by the obvious travesty of justice for Rodney King, for most journalists were shocked as well. Yes, the rage in South-Central L.A. had to be viewed against a tableau of poverty and discrimination. For the most part, journalists played a constructive role in illuminating the grievances on all sides.

But the King case was an aberration in one key respect: Had an amateur filmmaker named George Holliday not captured the beating on videotape, the claims of a black man who had led police on a wild car chase would have been dismissed, rating a few paragraphs in the paper at best. In most clashes involving police officers and minority residents, the press tends to give great weight to the law enforcement version of events, a version instinctively distrusted by many black readers.

Urban violence is often preceded by a tense period in which a community teeters on the edge of disorder. The press can be at its worst in such situations, too quick to fan the flames of intolerance with huge headlines. Perhaps there is no more compelling example than the murder case that prompted Boston's newspapers to whip the city into an unprecedented frenzy.

In the late 1980s a sense of racial anxiety hung over Boston. Many white residents were angry about a federal attempt to move black families into the public housing projects of South Boston, an Irish enclave that had been the stronghold of antibusing forces in the early '70s. At the same time, many blacks in the decaying neighborhoods of Roxbury, Mattapan and Jamaica Plain were embracing a plan to secede from Boston and form their own city. While the newspapers were filled with upbeat stories about the Massachusetts Miracle, the ghetto communities felt, with some justification, that they had been left behind.

The Irish and Brahmin ruling class was reflected in the staffs of the two local papers. Most of the top editors at *The Boston Globe* and the *Boston Herald* were white. The big-name columnists—Mike Barnicle, Howie Carr, David Nyhan—were white. From city hall to the statehouse to the media, blacks were not a major factor in the power structure.

Mayor Ray Flynn, once one of the most vociferous antibusing crusaders, had begun preaching the gospel of racial harmony after his 1983 election. But Flynn's sermons were increasingly drowned out by the furor over crime and drugs. The Massachusetts Miracle may have propelled Michael Dukakis to the Democratic presidential nomination, but it was Willie Horton who caused the governor's campaign to crash and burn.

On the evening of October 23, 1989, a twenty-nine-year-old man named Charles Stuart called 911 from his car phone in the inner-city neighborhood known as Mission Hill. He had been shot, as had his pregnant wife, Carol. A black man in a jogging suit had forced his way into their car at an intersection, shot them both and made off with their jewelry. The Stuarts had been on their way home from childbirth class.

A CBS camera crew from the program "Rescue 911" happened to be in the ambulance that raced to the Stuart car. Dan Rather aired the dramatic footage the following night. The next morning, the *Boston Herald* ran a graphic, front-page photo of the bloodied couple slumped in their car.

Carol DiMaiti Stuart, shot in the head, was dead. Her baby, delivered by cesarean section, would die seventeen days later. Chuck Stuart, shot in the stomach, was saved on the operating table. The thirteen-minute tape of the 911 call was played over and over.

The *Herald,* a scrappy tabloid owned by Rupert Murdoch, christened them the Camelot couple. "Christmas Birth of Baby Was to Cap an Idyllic Life," one *Herald* headline said. The *Globe,* with its more dignified tone, described their relationship as so loving "it even warmed those at its edge." It was a tale of yuppies from suburbia, ambushed by inner-city tragedy. Younger white editors and reporters seemed to identify with the Stuarts. Chuck Stuart managed a fashionable fur boutique; Carol was an attorney. The city grew obsessed with the case. The Boston police launched a manhunt across Mission Hill, stopping and frisking more than one hundred blacks with no more evidence than the color of their skin. The killer was at large. Any black man was a suspect.

By the time the dust settled, the press would be assailed for being all too willing to believe that the culprit in such a cold-blooded murder must be black. But journalism, like life, is often more complicated than that.

Michelle Caruso, a police reporter for the *Boston Herald,* was immediately drawn to the Stuart case. It was her kind of story. A dark-haired Gilda Radner look-alike who swore like the cops she covered, Caruso was thirty-four years old and already on her third marriage. She had learned the business from the bottom up in the hill towns of western Massachusetts, selling stories to the Greenfield *Recorder* for ten dollars apiece.

Once, when a policeman showed her the shirt of a man who had been killed by a woman he met in a bar, Caruso noticed a pink smudge on the collar. "I was thinking, 'Man, this is what reporting is about—a bloody shirt and a lipstick stain.' That really whetted my appetite."

After she joined the *Herald* in 1986, Caruso's reputation soared in law enforcement circles. She cracked a homicide case, the poisoning of two Roxbury children, after police concluded they had died from natural causes. She exposed a bogus rape charge by a woman named Mary Beth Lenane—whom the *Herald* had supported in a front-page editorial —by finding the evidence that saved two innocent men from conviction. "Everyone, including my own paper, was blowing her on the front page, 'the poor victim,' " Caruso says.

The hype surrounding the Stuart case troubled Caruso from the start. "I disagreed with my paper playing the murder as big as it did," she says. "They were overreacting. That birthing class angle—a lot of people are real sentimental about pregnancy and babies. Most of the murders in Boston are black guys killing black guys."

Even more troubling was Stuart's account of the murder. Would someone really shoot two people in a car just to steal some jewelry? What assailant would shoot the woman first? Why didn't Stuart call to passersby for help? Why did he never mention his wife's name or try to comfort her? Every rookie reporter knows the first suspect is always the spouse.

Caruso went to the scene of the shooting and concluded that dozens of cars and pedestrians must have passed by. She listened to the 911 tape over and over. She drew up a list of thirty-eight discrepancies. She worked her sources in the district attorney's office. But investigators gave Caruso no sign that she might be on to something.

"Nobody in Boston would say that something wasn't right for political reasons," Caruso says. "Nobody wanted even to hint at calling Chuck Stuart a liar. That was the sorest point in my relations with my editors here. I was pretty frenzied up. I figured I've got this guy. We were sitting here making jokes about Chuck Stuart and how he offed her [mimicking:] 'I've been shot, my wife's been shot.'"

In Michelle Caruso's mind, it was a replay of the phony rape case. She had done the legwork and poked holes in the victim's story. But Herald editors would not run a piece raising questions about Stuart's account, not without some official confirmation.

"Shit, what would have happened if we had done that speculative story?" Caruso asks. "We would've had a massive number of readers canceling subscriptions and saying, 'How dare you?' There would've been a real backlash against the paper for irresponsible journalism, with nothing to back it up other than the suspicions of a reporter. Pointing the finger of blame at the so-called victim with not one hook to hang it on."

Across town at the *Globe,* reporters were also digging into theories about Charles Stuart's role, even while writing articles that continued to portray him as the victim of a black man's gun. This was hardly unusual, for newsrooms are always filled with speculation that never makes its way into print.

"There's a difference between what you can talk about and what you can put in the paper," says Jack Driscoll, then the *Globe*'s editor. "We looked really hard at Stuart and, frankly, came up empty. We could never quite come up with the smoking gun. The violation was murder —you've got to be really careful about pointing fingers."

At times like these, the media can either have a calming influence or fuel the hysteria. Readers are hungry for any shred of news. The temptation is to glorify the victims and vilify the suspects. Unsubstantiated rumors find their way into print.

Boston reporters lived in fear of being scooped. Even without an Al Sharpton inflaming passions, the pressure seemed to grow more intense each day. The sheer volume of coverage began to magnify the case, creating a city-under-siege mood that exacerbated the fear of crime.

Reporters began hearing that police were investigating a Roxbury man named Willie Bennett. Bennett, thirty-nine, was a career criminal who had gotten out of prison a year earlier. He had once shot a legless cabdriver in a robbery. He had shot and wounded a police officer. Michelle Caruso prepared a profile of Bennett, just in case he was charged, but argued against naming him in print.

"I told the editor this is chickenshit," Caruso says. "This is too simple. They can't really think it's this guy. A guy with a record like him —there's no need to jump in a couple's car and perform two murders to get a little bit of jewelry. I know how the robbers in Boston work. It's a lot easier than that. You don't have to hurt anyone. All you have to do is stand in front of a fancy Boston restaurant and pull a knife and snatch a purse."

In the early-morning hours of November 11, the police arrested Willie Bennett. A *Herald* photographer was on hand to record the action.

"It was so big there was no way we could not print the name," Caruso says. "They tore apart Willie Bennett's mother's house, his sister's house, his girlfriend's house. They nabbed Willie Bennett from bed in the middle of the night and were holding him on a feeble motor-vehicle violation charge." Bennett's mother told a *Herald* reporter that her son was wanted for questioning in the Stuart case.

The *Herald* gave the arrest a huge front-page splash in the Sunday paper: "Police Nab #1 Suspect in Stuart-Killing Case." The *Globe* had missed the Saturday-morning raid and had to catch up by confirming the story Saturday night and rewriting it for later editions. The police quickly charged Bennett with holding up a video store. "Prime Suspect in Stuart Shooting Arraigned on Store Robbery Charges," the *Globe* headline said. *Prime suspect.* Caution had been tossed out the window. The clear impression was that Bennett was guilty.

Driscoll regrets the spate of "prime suspect" stories. "We had the name for several days," he says. "The fact of the matter was, there was an arrest. It was partly competitive. We normally wouldn't have leaped that fast. There was a genuine belief on the part of some top police investigators that Bennett was the man. The public's heightened interest was such that you really had to give them every little detail."

Michelle Caruso was torn about the Willie Bennett arrest, even as she spent her days investigating him. "I would feel better if we had believed it," she says. "The foolish competitive instincts were carried to the highest degree I've ever seen. It wasn't as if we were sitting here saying, 'Yeah, Bennett did it.' It was worse than that. We had to do it to remain competitive."

Soon it was the *Globe*'s turn to score an exclusive. The paper reported that investigators had shown Stuart photographs of suspects and that he had said Bennett's picture looked "most like" the murderer. It was pretty thin stuff, but the *Globe* played it on page one.

"Our editor was like a madman: 'If we're not on top of the cops twenty-four hours a day, we're gonna wake up and read it in the *Globe*,' " Caruso says. "You're in mortal fear. It became this nightmarish thing where you're trying to call up every freaking cop in the universe you know. You were getting second- and thirdhand scraps because these are the only guys who will talk. The guys who are doing the investigation won't talk."

The scramble for information pointed up a basic fact of journalistic life. Reporters have no subpoena power; they can't conduct ballistics tests or force people to talk. In 99 percent of crime stories, they get their information from police and prosecutors, who generally provide their own "spin" on a not-for-attribution basis. This produces an inherent bias toward the law enforcement version of events. In this case, however, Caruso went a step further. She went to Mission Hill to search for witnesses.

"It wasn't just that we sat back and took it from the cops," Caruso says. "Then you could say, that's why we got fucked on that story. We were chasing around the projects for weeks, where nobody has a last name. We found the witnesses, and they implicated Bennett up the wazoo."

One source was Toni Jackson, a twenty-one-year-old welfare mother. Jackson, in tears, told Caruso that Bennett had confessed to the shooting, that he had said that the bullet was meant for Chuck Stuart, not his wife.

"I must have asked that woman fifteen times if she was pressured, bribed or coerced," Caruso says. Jackson denied it. A police source told Caruso that Toni Jackson had given authorities the same account. "We went with it, page one," Caruso says.

Just after Christmas, both papers reported that Stuart had identified Willie Bennett in a police lineup. The authorities were leaking like mad.

But the worst was yet to come. On January 4, 1990, Charles Stuart jumped off the Tobin Bridge into the Mystic River.

There are times when a story is so hot, a community so aroused, editors so anxious, reporters so fired up, that all semblance of journalistic restraint falls by the wayside. Such an episode can quickly turn into a feeding frenzy. You print first, ask questions later.

The Stuart frenzy began with the avalanche of stories that followed the suicide: "Stuart Probe Eyes Cash Plot." "Probers Link Stuart, Woman." "Stuart Sent Kin to Hide Wife's Insurance Money." "Police 'Gestapo' Search Tactics Assailed." "Blacks Assail Handling of Case."

The same officials who were close to seeking an indictment of Willie Bennett were now saying they believed Chuck Stuart had killed his wife, then wounded himself, albeit more seriously than he had intended. There had been no black gunman. It was all a hoax. Police said Stuart's brother, Matthew, told them Stuart had tossed him a bag with the gun and his wife's jewelry to make the incident look like a robbery.

The press, which had all but canonized the Stuarts, looked absurd. As in the Brawley case, editors and reporters had whipped up public sympathy for a victim who turned out to be a liar. But here it was even worse, since Charles Stuart might also be a murderer. The Boston press doubled and tripled its efforts, as if somehow that might erase its earlier failure.

The *Globe* reported that Stuart had received a $480,000 insurance check on a policy the couple took out on Carol Stuart's life weeks before the shooting. The inevitable "other woman" surfaced; the *Globe* said police were investigating Stuart's relationship with a "striking blonde" graduate student at his fur shop. Other allegations came fast and furious: Stuart had gambling debts. He wanted the insurance money to start a new career as a restaurateur.

"There was no way a reader could tell what the hell was going on," says Mark Jurkowitz, media critic for the *Boston Phoenix*. "Every piece of innuendo, gossip, theory, speculation made it into the newspapers. Anything that could be put in was put in. It was the equivalent of FBI files. It was a brutal sense of catch-up, hyper competition between the two newspapers. Everyone was fair game."

Not everyone joined in the orgy of recriminations against the police. Mike Barnicle, a *Globe* columnist who specialized in mean-streets prose, rose to the cops' defense. Though he lived in a posh suburb, earned $200,000 a year and drove a black BMW with cellular phone, the forty-eight-year-old Barnicle was well acquainted with the town's seedier precincts. His brother Paul was a Boston homicide detective, and Barnicle's columns often "appeared to have been reported from the passenger seat of a police cruiser," as Christopher Lydon put it in the *Washington Journalism Review*.

During his seventeen years as the city's most popular columnist, Barnicle was occasionally accused of embellishing his yarns or making things up, but the charges never seemed to stick. It was Barnicle who broke the disputed story about the $480,000 life insurance policy on Carol Stuart.

After Chuck Stuart's leap into history, Barnicle wrote that the homicide cops had "covered themselves with glory" by refraining from charging Willie Bennett, even though they had sworn statements implicating Bennett from the teenagers in Mission Hill. Such an argument conveniently overlooks the fact that the cops framed Bennett by pressuring the teenagers. Nor was this the only case in which the Boston police were accused of manufacturing evidence to lock up black suspects.

But Barnicle bemoaned the "wail of a black community demanding apologies for the fact that a black man was arrested." No one, he wrote, should feel sorry for Willie Bennett, who had been labeled a "mental defective" decades earlier. "The man's pathetic, violent history is so much a part of the unyielding issues of race, crime and drugs tearing daily at America that it is amazing how any black minister or black politician could ever stand up and howl in public that his arrest was a product of police bigotry."

Mike Barnicle is convinced he had it right. "Our business today is populated by many younger people who have no idea of what the function of the police happens to be," he says. "Vast numbers of reporters never leave the fucking building and have no idea what reality is all about. They don't go out and talk to poor kids who live in the shitty areas of town. They don't have clue one as to what life is actually about in a project like the one in Mission Hill.

"The police did not call the Stuarts the Camelot couple. The police did not run endless fucking reams of articles about how these two people loved each other. It was a classic case of the white media thinking they had the great white victim and going absolutely fucking overboard on that murder. They were embarrassed. They've got to fuck someone around.

"*The Boston Globe* isn't going to write an editorial saying, 'Boy, did we fuck up when we wrote about what a great couple they were.' So we say, why didn't the fucking cops figure out it was the husband? They're a convenient punching bag. I don't understand how we can blame the police when we are as culpable as we have been."

After all, Barnicle says in his deadpan delivery, "The woman is shot. She's dead at the scene. The husband appears to be dying. He is capable of talking briefly to the police. He says, 'A black man shot my wife.' He gives them a vivid description. Where the fuck are the police supposed to go? Are they supposed to say, 'We don't believe you, you maggot'? They have to take his word for it."

Barnicle is right in castigating the media, but his apologia for the Boston police was embarrassing, and it brought him much ridicule from his journalistic brethren. To say that the cops covered themselves with glory after they came close to framing an innocent man is to completely miss the point. No one blames the police for investigating Stuart's claims, but they essentially manufactured a case against a convenient black defendant, albeit with lots of help from the press.

The witnesses who implicated Willie Bennett, including Caruso's source, later insisted the cops had pressured them. Here, too, Barnicle echoed the police line by dismissing the witnesses' accounts. "Once the newspapers publish the names of the people who were brought in by the police and gave them information about Willie Bennett, in that environment, these people are fucking dead," he says. "They cooperated with the police. Of course they're gonna say, 'They beat me, they threatened me.' Of course they're going to say, 'Fuck no, I didn't cooperate.'

"Willie Bennett," he says, "is a fucking evil guy. I first wrote about

Willie Bennett in 1973 when he robbed a record shop." Barnicle still believes Bennett had some involvement in the Stuart case.

Even the outrage in the black community, Barnicle says, was overblown by the press: "Anyone can say they're a black leader and we'll write it: 'Joe Shithead, black community leader, said yesterday Willie Bennett is the victim of white racist injustice.' " On that score, crudeness aside, he has a point.

While Barnicle was doggedly defending his police buddies, the *Herald* ran more than one story describing Michelle Caruso's doubts and her earlier attempts to crack the case. "That's Monday-morning quarterbacking; it doesn't count," Mark Jurkowitz says. Drawing an analogy with the error that caused the Red Sox to lose the 1986 World Series, he says: "It's like John McNamara saying, 'I meant to take Bill Buckner out in the top of the ninth.' "

A poll showed that most people, black and white, blamed the media for mishandling the case. "We didn't get a search warrant for Willie Bennett," says Greg Moore, the *Globe*'s deputy managing editor. "We didn't arrest him and take him to the grand jury. Now, in hindsight, you say, boy, they really did everything they could to frame Willie Bennett. But those kinds of things were reported in the newspaper. People were able to see that this police work was really shoddy. We came up with his girlfriend before the police did."

The tragedy soon assumed a made-for-Hollywood flavor. Boston reporters were inundated with offers from book publishers and Hollywood producers. The Carol Stuart murder would become a TV movie within a year.

Michelle Caruso turned down several such offers. She was busy reconstructing what had gone wrong. She learned that authorities had interviewed a truck driver who said Chuck Stuart had spoken of murder weeks before the shooting. "The trucker told them Chuck had asked, Did he know someone who could whack his wife? That's what really fucking frosts my ass. They knew that the whole time."

Willie Bennett was cleared of the Stuart murder, but was sentenced to twenty-five years in prison for the video store robbery. The U.S. attorney's office later reported that the Boston police had used "coercion and intimidation . . . through the use of actual or implied threats of arrest, imprisonment and physical beatings." When one witness balked, the report said, Detective Peter O'Malley gestured to Officer Billy Dunn and threatened to put the witness in a small, dark room with Dunn.

Most journalists have made their peace with the Stuart case. "We did almost everything humanly possible," Moore says. "Every once in a while you come up against stories that can't be broken."

We all engage in this sort of rationalization from time to time: It was the banks that loaned Trump the money. It was Congress that failed to discover the abuses at HUD. Don't blame us. But the press's great failure in Boston was not, as in the S&L debacle, the failure to crack a difficult case. It was the headlong rush to print every leak from police and prosecutors. In other situations—when covering the mayor, the governor or the White House—reporters are justifiably skeptical of what those in power have to say. There is no excuse for tossing aside this skepticism when the sources happen to be cops investigating a high-profile crime.

Michelle Caruso still agonizes over each twist and turn. "You can't imagine what it feels like to know you had it in the palm of your hand and if you'd had one break—one cop, one DA who said 'You're right, we're looking into that'—we would've had it made."

A year and a half later, all but unnoticed by the Boston press, there was a brief footnote to the Willie Bennett case.

One night in August 1991, a black man was beating a black woman on the roof of a Mission Hill housing project. The woman had a broken jaw, several teeth missing and was bleeding profusely. Four cops charged up to the roof and grabbed the assailant. The victim was Linda Bennett, Willie Bennett's sister. Among the cops who rescued her was Billy Dunn, one of the officers accused of coercing witnesses in the Stuart case. The assailant was charged with assault and attempted rape. The savage beating of Linda Bennett was not a big story in the Boston papers. Only Mike Barnicle wrote about it.

"Nobody gives a fuck about these people unless something big goes down involving white people," Barnicle says.

The lingering issue for big-city newspapers is whether they can cover black neighborhoods with more than brief bursts of journalistic fire about the latest homicide or drug bust. It is a difficult task, for the culture of poverty remains foreign to most middle-class reporters, black as well as white.

"There hasn't been any serious, ongoing coverage of communities like Dorchester, Mattapan and Roxbury by mainstream journalists," Mark Jurkowitz says. "The Stuart scenario fit with the prevailing sense that these neighborhoods were getting out of control. It was 'Look out, all hell has broken loose, it's time we caged these animals.' "

Greg Moore, who is black, says he is aware of the *Globe*'s short-comings. "A lot of what gets covered in the black community is pathology, crisis-oriented stuff," he says. "Our sources of information are not good. Newspapers tend to cover power centers, and there ain't a lot of power in communities of color. We just don't know a lot of people there. If a reporter has a choice of covering the statehouse or covering Roxbury, there's no percentage in choosing to cover Roxbury." Or Bed-Stuy, or Liberty City, or South-Central L.A.

Our attention span is severely limited. A few weeks after the Los Angeles riots, the press again reverted to business as usual. The urban "crisis" degenerated into political finger-pointing—it was Reagan's fault, Bush's fault, the Great Society's fault—and the brief renewal of media interest in HUD's programs faded. There had to be a post-riot story every day, so each blast of hot air from Washington became news. A front-page *New York Times* story reported that "the White House and congressional leaders today announced broad agreement to enact measures they said would bring relief to American cities." The following day a *Times* headline said: "Bush and Congress Return to Urban Politics As Usual." Days later it was "Compromise on Urban Aid Package Reported Near," "Bush May Veto Urban Aid Bill," "Squabbling Stalls Urban Aid." Six months later, when Bush finally vetoed an aid package that Congress had loaded up with tax breaks, the press had lost interest.

And the press was not yet through with Los Angeles. Having been blind to the potential for violence after the first Rodney King beating trial, the media wildly overcompensated a year later, when the four police officers were tried on federal civil rights charges. A small army of journalists descended on the city in the spring of 1993, reporting so feverishly on official preparations for another riot that their very presence seemed incendiary. The frightening tone of the coverage was epitomized by a front-page *USA Today* photo of five angry-looking black men posing with pistols, a rifle and an ammunition belt. "Gangs Put L.A. on Edge," the headline said.

But the picture, it turned out, had been staged. The five young blacks were in fact turning in their guns, and had been assembled for *USA Today* by a community activist seeking to launch a guns-for-jobs program. When the youths showed up without guns, the reporter, Richard Price, drove one of them to his mother's house to retrieve his weapon. *USA Today* kissed off the incident with a one-sentence "clarification," but ran a fuller account thirteen days later after the activist, a man named CaShears, threatened to sue. Joseph Bates, one of the young blacks, said of the paper, "They wrote what they wanted, what would get more papers sold . . . They portrayed us as hard-core criminal gang members who are ready to incite a riot."

Editor Peter Prichard said he would not have run the photograph had he known the circumstances under which it was taken. Price argued that he was being unfairly blamed for a misunderstanding, saying he thought the picture would be properly labeled and that CaShears had made most of the arrangements. But Prichard suspended Price for one month, demoted him and cut his salary by $15,000.

Local television, blaring such headlines as "Civil War" and "Will It Happen Again?," was even more inflammatory than the newspapers. Reporters were shown donning bulletproof vests and asking local residents what they would do if rioting broke out—actions that bordered on irresponsibility. "The media are actually planting the seeds for another riot," said Bill Press, the California Democratic chairman. Strangely enough, when the city remained calm after two of the policemen were convicted, there was almost a sense of disappointment among some journalists. There was no murder, no looting, no mayhem; the big story they had come to cover had fizzled out. There was nothing but poverty and despair as usual in South-Central L.A., and that, of course, was not news.

The journalistic scars run deep to this day. Linda Williams, a black editor at the *Los Angeles Times,* complained that during the riots her paper was "busing minority journalists into the city to use as cannon fodder because the management felt the white reporters would be in danger." *Times* editors vehemently denied the charge, but it was clear that the riots had brought to the surface years of racial resentment.

Unlike most institutions, the press can be judged each day by its outpouring of words and images. Our failure to adequately cover the black community, our tendency to promote inflammatory spokesmen, our willingness to convict a black suspect with little evidence, is painfully apparent to most readers. What is far less visible are the racially charged struggles that erupt within the inner sanctum of the newsroom.

5

A House Divided

Two stories in the morning paper caught Donald Kimelman's eye. One involved a report from a black research organization, which found that half the nation's black children were living in poverty, usually with single mothers on welfare. The other noted that the Food and Drug Administration had approved a new contraceptive called Norplant, in which small capsules are implanted in a woman's arm.

Kimelman, forty-three, was deputy editorial page editor of *The Philadelphia Inquirer*. The son of a former U.S. ambassador to Haiti, he had graduated from an exclusive New Jersey prep school and had come of age as a '60s liberal. He had been a VISTA volunteer and worked for George McGovern's presidential campaign. But as he approached middle age, Kimelman had grown more skeptical of government solutions. He was increasingly troubled by the problems of the underclass and felt the country needed a new approach to poverty, one that transcended the old liberal-conservative arguments.

Now, on the morning of December 11, 1990, he kept thinking about Norplant. He mentioned the idea to his boss, David Boldt, who agreed he should write an editorial. Kimelman sat down at his computer terminal.

The juxtaposition of the two articles intrigued him. "Dare we mention them in the same breath?" he typed. "To do so might be considered deplorably insensitive, perhaps raising the specter of eugenics."

Kimelman pressed on. While no one should be forced to use Norplant, perhaps "welfare mothers" could be offered "incentives" to do so. At the very least, the contraceptive "should be made available for free to poor women."

"All right, the subject makes us uncomfortable, too," he concluded. "But we're made even more uncomfortable by the impoverishment of black America and its effect on the nation's future. Think about it."

People in the *Inquirer* newsroom didn't need to think about it very long. When the editorial—"Poverty and Norplant: Can Contraception Reduce the Underclass?"—appeared the next day, it sparked a furor that shook the newspaper to its foundations.

If communities are often upset at the way the press handles racial issues, the backlash can be equally strong in the newsroom itself. All the nagging questions about bias, favoritism and negative stereotypes resonate with special force in offices that are dedicated to something resembling the daily pursuit of truth.

It is easy to underestimate the importance of a newspaper's internal culture to the gathering, writing and processing of news. If the dominant world view is white and middle class, that shapes the way a Central Park jogger story might be framed, or a Bensonhurst racial murder, or any story touching on race.

When black journalists are a significant force on a newspaper, that tends to broaden the approach to news, while also producing clashes over what is acceptable in covering the black community. Some blacks contend that their newspapers have sensationalized allegations involving black public officials and depicted minority neighborhoods as populated mainly by criminals and lowlifes. Such arguments form the invisible backdrop for much of what readers see in the paper on racial subjects.

In the space of two years, the major newspapers in Philadelphia, Boston and Washington, all of them liberal voices, found themselves torn by bruising racial controversies. In each case black and white staffers viewed the same events through a very different lens, and even black colleagues found themselves sharply divided.

Newspapers have devoted millions of column inches to the emotional debate over affirmative action programs, which have drawn strong support from liberal editorial pages. What has gone largely unreported, however, is the growing white resentment toward such programs at the newspapers themselves, where some staffers see them as rigid quotas. This sort of backlash might be deemed politically incorrect on the op-ed pages, but it may more accurately reflect the racial strains in American society than much of what appears in print.

Twenty years ago, newspapers were largely white, middle-class bastions. A concerted push to hire more minorities began in earnest in the late '70s, complete with numerical goals, special internships and the other paraphernalia of affirmative action. These laudable efforts have produced more diverse newsrooms, which in turn have demanded more sensitivity to the problems of a multilayered culture.

Yet this very diversity has stoked internal tensions and contributed to racial resentment. These feelings were muted during the boom years of the '80s, when there always seemed to be enough jobs to go around. But in the early '90s, as the recession put the newspaper business into a deep freeze, jobs became scarce. Competition for each new vacancy or promotion was intense. Journalists found themselves fighting over slivers of a shrinking pie.

"In tough economic times, race comes into play," says Peggy Hernandez, a Hispanic reporter at *The Boston Globe* during the tense period that followed the Stuart case. "We thought we were immune. We thought we were above it. And we weren't. Suddenly it dawned on us that there were some people who looked at us as minorities first."

A respected journalist with thirty years' experience told me how he had shopped his résumé at some of the country's top newspapers, only to be told they had no openings for a white man. One paper said it had used up its quota by hiring a few white sportswriters. "The hypocrisy in this business is unbelievable," the reporter said. "They all write editorials opposing quotas, and every one of them has a quota. The fact that you're a middle-aged white man is death."

These internal frictions, mirrored by a new sensitivity to community reaction, have set the parameters on how far newspapers can go in covering race-related stories. In some ways that can be positive. Few newspapers today would run a front-page headline dripping with racial innuendo "Marauders from Inner City Prey on L.A.'s Suburbs"—as the *Los Angeles Times* did in 1981. But there is a chilling effect as well. Even the bravest journalists have learned in recent years that race and strong opinions are an explosive mixture. In an era when a few ill-chosen words can touch off an organized boycott by some offended faction, even a little bit of candor can be dangerous. The result is a new skittishness in the press, a powerful urge to skirt sensitive subjects and airbrush the ugliest realities.

If plenty of readers find newspapers too bland for their taste, it is in part because so many Norplant-like matters have been declared off-limits, fit for private whispers but not for publication. Editors have learned to walk on eggshells, often buying themselves protective cover by assigning black reporters to inner-city beats.

They are, in a sense, under siege. Some black politicians are all too willing to cry racism when white-owned news organizations dig up the kind of dirt on them that they have been printing about white officeholders for decades. White reporters are easily stung by such rhetoric. And black journalists who report aggressively on the black community are equally vulnerable to the charge that they are gutless Uncle Toms betraying their brethren.

"I think there are issues the media just can't discuss," says Richard Cohen, a *Washington Post* columnist who has been the target of black protests. "No one knows how to deal with charges that you're a racist, that you're an anti-Semite. It's easier not to do these stories than to do the stories and face the consequences."

To be sure, there are times when racial violence forces the press to look such issues squarely in the eye. But more often race is dealt with in superficial ways—the government report on housing discrimination, the hearing on affirmative action. Privately, many reporters say that black politicians are often held to a lesser standard because white newspapers, in an unconscious form of racism, feel the need to bend way over backward.

Touchiness about race is hardly a new phenomenon. In 1965, when Daniel Patrick Moynihan wrote his report on the breakdown of the black family, 26 percent of nonwhite children were born out of wedlock. The uproar that greeted Moynihan's findings chilled discussion of the issue for a generation. Now the out-of-wedlock figure for minorities is 61 percent, and we still have trouble talking about it.

The silence is more ominous in the '90s because the stakes are so much higher. The seemingly intractable culture of poverty has inflicted on society problems ranging from crack babies to teenage drug dealers blowing each other away with semiautomatic weapons. Yet even sympathetic liberals who dare raise the question of personal responsibility for such behavior are assailed for blame-the-victim views.

During New York's 1989 mayoral campaign, Joe Klein says, "I would ask, 'How do we as a society address the fifteen-year-old mother on welfare? What do we owe her, and what does she owe us?' That was generally seen as a racist question. I was once hissed at the 92nd Street Y when I asked this at a mayoral forum."

In his five years as a *New York* magazine columnist, Klein wrote about "the core issues that are never discussed: the disintegration of the black family and the growth of a violent, anarchic, alienated, welfare-dependent underclass over the past quarter-century. This is the pathology at the heart of the city's agony."

Newspapers tend to shy away from such gut-wrenching stuff because they are worried—too worried, perhaps—about offending readers. Increasingly, local papers are filled with such yuppie subjects as day care, traffic, the Mommy track, home-equity loans and personal computers. The mere mention of race raises a red flag that sets editors on edge.

When a 1991 fire at a chicken-processing plant in North Carolina killed twenty-five people, virtually all of them black, editors at *The Washington Post* deleted the racial identification from a story by Paul Taylor. There was concern that the focus on race would seem gratuitous in such a tragedy. But the relevance was beyond dispute: As Taylor pointed out in a follow-up story, it was poor black women who took these low-wage jobs in the rural South, and therefore were most likely to be killed when white owners locked the doors to an unsafe factory.

In 1989, a *Post* editor asked me to write about the apparent belief among some blacks that drug abuse, and even AIDS, are the result of a deliberate white conspiracy to destroy the black community. The idea, espoused by the likes of the Reverend Louis Farrakhan, seemed so ludicrous on its face that it was hard for me to take it seriously. But as I interviewed blacks from different walks of life, I was struck by how many found credence in such theories, or at least believed that white authorities had acted with criminal indifference in allowing the drug scourge to devastate black America. I noted that of course there was "no concrete evidence" for such conspiracies; it was a question of what people persisted in believing, rational or not.

The Washington Monthly attacked my story as "bizarre." "Not one fact about the conspiracy—not even the name of a single conspirator— is revealed in the story," Scott Shuger wrote. "This is news?" Shuger complained that I had no polling data to back up my findings, as if simply interviewing people was far too unscientific. The following year, a *New York Times*/CBS poll found that 25 percent of blacks believe that the government "deliberately makes sure that drugs are easily available in poor black neighborhoods." Another 35 percent said this was possibly true.

Daring to mention the unmentionable is even riskier for black journalists, whose role is misunderstood by many in the black community. To be sure, black writers are acutely aware of their heritage. If not for a generation of protests and sit-ins, most of them would not have jobs in white-owned news organizations.

At the same time, the best black journalists believe that their role is to tell it like it is, not to gloss over the problems of the ghettos or serve as propagandists for whichever black leader is popular at the moment. After all, no one expects all Jewish journalists to have identical views on Israel, or all Hispanic journalists to embrace Hispanic candidates. Yet black reporters who take controversial stands are often assailed as traitors.

One such target is Juan Williams, a *Washington Post* reporter whose heresies include disparaging Spike Lee's movies and criticizing Jesse Jackson. Williams has built a national reputation by zigging when other blacks are zagging, an approach that has also boosted his career as a television commentator.

"Nothing wears more on my soul than people who criticize me as a writer not so much for the content of what I wrote, but for the fact that I'm willing to challenge and debate some decree from a black leader," Williams says. "There's a whole notion that to really be a black person, you have to have certain political views, otherwise you're 'not really black.' There's a tremendous instinct toward censorship. That's what it boils down to. It's very dangerous. It's limiting, both intellectually and politically. It invites demagoguery."

Williams says he is tired of hearing "that the reason you're making the case is to please your white masters. That you have no integrity. That you are a captive of white America. There's simply a reluctance to understand that black people can have different opinions.

"I don't like being the bad guy," he says. "I don't like getting beat up constantly. The easy way to be the good guy is to say certain things. That's a high price to pay."

A few days after the Norplant editorial appeared, dozens of *Inquirer* staff members, black and white, vented their rage at an emotional meeting with Don Kimelman and David Boldt. Garry Howard, a black sports editor and one of six children raised by a welfare mother in a South Bronx project, said the thrust of the editorial was "that I shouldn't have been born." Chuck Stone, a veteran black columnist for *The Philadelphia Daily News,* accused Kimelman of "Nordic arrogance" and said that "Hitler could have written the same editorial." A fringe group with ties to Lyndon LaRouche demonstrated outside the newspaper, handing out fliers that said, "Inquirer Pushes Nazi Eugenics . . . to REDUCE THE NUMBER OF BLACK CHILDREN THAT ARE BORN!"

Black reporters circulated a petition calling for Boldt's removal as editorial page editor. The paper's top Metro columnist, Steve Lopez, wrote a piece likening Kimelman and Boldt to David Duke, the former Ku Klux Klansman. "What we have, basically," Lopez wrote, "is the *Inquirer* brain trust looking down from its ivory tower and wondering if black people should be paid to stop having so many damn kids."

"I feel bad about it," Kimelman told me the day after the Lopez column appeared. "Certain things as a white man you just don't see. I still believe what I wrote, but . . ." His voice trailed off. "I felt very bad that every single black reporter and editor I know, from the most radical to the most reasonable, hated this editorial."

That Saturday, Don Kimelman walked into David Boldt's office. He hadn't been able to sleep for two nights. Kimelman had already posted an apology on the office bulletin board, but he was worried that the staff Christmas party at his home would be ruined. He was weighing a public apology on the editorial page.

It would be an extraordinary reversal, and not one that Kimelman suggested lightly, for both he and Boldt believed there was nothing duller than mushy, conventional-wisdom editorials. But the Norplant editorial seemed "to have touched some exposed nerve," as Boldt put it.

Boldt had been "shell-shocked" by the "McCarthyite tone" of the staff meeting, at which some of his old writings had been read back to him in an accusatory tone. He suggested that they wait until things calmed down. Kimelman disagreed.

"I still think we were right," Boldt says of the editorial. "Dancing in the back of my mind was the thought that if we apologize, it would become an even bigger story. . . . The mob howling at the door may possibly have had a peripheral effect on our deliberations."

Kimelman's apologia was turned over to a black editorial writer, Lorraine Branham, for editing. She strengthened the piece, making it more "abject" and "groveling," Boldt says. It ran two days before Christmas.

The *Inquirer* received hundreds of letters, far more than the original editorial had generated. Most letter-writers were appalled that the *Inquirer,* having dared to advance the notion that poor people shouldn't have so many children, had backed down from a courageous stance. One writer called the paper's staff "spineless scum." There was a buzz among some staffers that the *Inquirer* had caved in to the left-liberal "thought police."

"There were a lot of readers who were angry about that apology— basically white readers, not black readers," Don Kimelman recalls. "It keeps getting played back to us: 'You backed down to blacks. You don't back down to anyone else. When the blacks complain you apologize.' "

The three black editorial board members saw the matter in a different light. Their views on race and poverty had long been ignored, they said, and one of them, Claude Lewis, had stopped attending meetings in protest. He said that Kimelman "suffers from the notion of class and cultural superiority." Another black member, Acel Moore, had complained before the editorial ran that Kimelman was turning Norplant into "a race thing," but Kimelman made only minor wording changes in response.

"When the right loses, then they charge that it's the thought police," Moore says. "I just don't see it." Had blacks been more fully consulted about the Norplant piece, he says, "It wouldn't have been as snide and as insulting."

Oddly enough, Kimelman had written about Norplant a few weeks earlier. His first editorial urged that Norplant be promoted for "impoverished, unmarried young women" who were having "too many babies." No one noticed. It was only when he mentioned race that the issue exploded.

"Whenever they talk about the urban poor or the inner-city poor, it just gets painted all black," says Vanessa Williams, a black reporter. "You come away with a feeling, 'If only we could do something about those black people.' "

Don Kimelman did not shrink when colleagues compared him to David Duke. "Does this make me ashamed?" he asked in an internal memo. "No. It helps explain to me why David Duke, in his post-Klan incarnation, is getting so many votes. He talks publicly about stuff that the rest of us only reserve for our private conversations."

After the apology, Boldt worried that the editorial board would become excessively cautious. "Every pressure on me is pulling me is that direction," Boldt says. "No one will punish me if I become bland and boring."

New rules were established. Any controversial editorial had to be fully discussed in advance by the full thirteen-member board; a majority vote would no longer suffice. On racial issues, Kimelman says, "The three black members of the board have what amounts to an effective veto. There's been a shying away from certain subjects where we know there's going to be a knock-down-drag-out fight."

The black journalists can hardly be blamed for pressing their point of view, any more than one would fault the white liberals who denounced the Norplant editorial as racist. But the inevitable result of such a polarized atmosphere is for everyone concerned to tiptoe around explosive subjects, hoping to avoid stepping on another land mine. And that is a surefire prescription for more of the bland mush that plagues so many editorial pages.

The *Boston Globe* newsroom has always been somewhat stratified, like the city it covers. At its core the paper was a pillar of the WASP establishment, "journalism's equivalent of the *Mayflower*," as Mike Barnicle put it. There was the august Taylor family, who had owned the place for four generations, and other Brahmins like former editor Thomas Winship and Metro editor Ben Bradlee, Jr. There was the sizable Irish contingent, led by editor Jack Driscoll, Barnicle, and countless others. There was a minority caucus, a Jewish caucus, a women's caucus. "The fucking place is like Beirut," says one Boston journalist.

Women often felt shunted aside on a paper whose stars tended to be men who spoke the locker-room language of politics and sports. There were complaints that Bradlee, the editor with the famous name, was "running a macho newsroom," as reporter Muriel Cohen put it. Bradlee said he was simply trying to shake things up and create a meritocracy, but the women were upset that Bradlee and the guys were leaving the office two afternoons a week to play basketball. The women believed that juicy assignments were being awarded on the court.

Tempers grew particularly short in the fall of 1991 because the union contract had expired a year earlier and almost no one had gotten a raise. There had been some grumbling a year earlier when a black business reporter, who was being lured by *The Washington Post*, got a raise and a transfer to the prestigious statehouse beat. Now another black reporter, Renee Graham, had gotten a big raise and a transfer to the Living/Arts section after being courted by *The New York Times*. Graham was not universally admired by her colleagues, and some white staffers saw the move as an outrage. Almost no one in the newspaper business was hiring, but somehow black journalists kept getting lucrative offers from other papers trying to meet their hiring targets.

"The middle-sized papers rob the little ones and the *New York Times* and *Washington Post* rob everyone else," says Frank Grundstrom, a *Globe* vice president.

In a larger sense, the strains of fifteen years of affirmative action were starting to show. A generation of white reporters had grown weary of being told in interviews that they could not even be considered because the next slot had to go to a minority. At the same time, many black reporters regarded the pace of integration as pathetically inadequate. No matter how hard they worked, they saw the best assignments and promotions being handed to white colleagues in what looked very much like a good-old-boy network.

Most major newspapers had special personnel directors whose job was to roam the country in search of minority journalists. Nearly everyone was playing the numbers game. At the *Times,* the goal—what Max Frankel calls "an unofficial little quota system"—was to hire one minority reporter for each new white hire. At the *Post,* editors set a target that one of every four hires be a minority. At the *Globe,* which had signed an affirmative action pact with the city's minority community in the early '80s, the hiring goal was also 25 percent.

The sniping over Renee Graham's raise would never have reached the outside world had it not been for a fateful fax. One white staffer faxed word of the controversy to *Boston Herald* columnist Howie Carr, who never tired of ridiculing the "bow-tied bumkissers" at *"El Globo."* Carr wrote that *Globe* staffers were "up in arms" and "disgusted" about Graham's raise. " 'Her byline appears about as often as Halley's Comet,' " he quoted "one ink-stained wretch" as saying. Another staffer told Carr, "If she were white, would they have made this effort to keep her?"

Carr somehow failed to mention that the *Herald* did not have a single black news reporter at the time. It was an appalling situation for a big-city paper, but Carr would not let such petty details spoil his fun.

Minority reporters at the *Globe* were furious at the leak. They circulated an open letter signed by forty-eight staffers. "We won't stand for this kind of racism," it said. "To inject race into this in such a vengeful way is reprehensible." The staffers said the anonymous criticism "mirrors the kind of bigotry that propelled David Duke's campaign in Louisiana."

The *Globe*'s response was somewhat curious for a newspaper that depends on daily leaks. Management officials started checking the phone logs at each fax machine in an effort to nab the mystery leaker. As the fax police closed in, Peter Howe, a Harvard graduate and scion of a wealthy WASP family, confessed to being Carr's source.

In a letter to his colleagues, Howe, a statehouse reporter, apologized to Renee Graham "for the enormous grief I have helped cause her." But he also assailed the paper for conducting "a witch hunt," calling it "a move straight out of the Nixon White House." Howe said he was no racist, but believed that "hard work" and "performance" should be rewarded. The *Globe,* he said, must "be forced to confront the issue of an alleged double standard."

Renee Graham refused to accept Howe's apology, calling his letter "smug" and "rife with arrogance." She said that "in some ways I don't think we'll ever heal. . . . This was the worst racial incident of my life, second to none."

Globe officials noted that white reporters had also gotten raises by using job offers as leverage. But in a meeting with the staff, Jack Driscoll admitted he had erred by not denouncing the leak to Carr at the outset. He suspended Peter Howe for two weeks without pay, further angering some white staffers.

"The *Globe*'s management is kowtowing to what is essentially a special-interest group and placating them by going on this hunt, much like the CIA would," a top white reporter said. "If they want to keep her because she's black and they need to keep black reporters, fine. But they should say that."

Minority staffers, however, thought Howe got off lightly. "For me, race was the issue," said reporter Peggy Hernandez. "This was just intolerable. We got slapped in the face."

It is a measure of the raw feelings about race that a single raise could produce such a maelstrom of emotion. But it was hardly unique. The *Inquirer* had experienced much the same sort of eruption earlier in the year.

A few weeks after the Norplant flap died down, the *Inquirer* unveiled its new "pluralism" program. A pluralism committee, required for all Knight-Ridder newspapers, had begun its work under Gene Roberts, the brilliant editor who had transformed the *Inquirer* from a second-rate rag into a nationally respected newspaper. Now it fell to Maxwell King, who had recently succeeded Roberts as editor, to explain the new policy to the staff.

Fifty percent of all new hires would be minorities, King said, and 50 percent would be women. The numerical targets—King did not shy away from the word "quotas"—would remain in place for five years. The paper would also launch such initiatives as "sensitivity" seminars on racial and ethnic matters.

The staff meeting quickly turned contentious. A number of white reporters declared that the *Inquirer* newsroom had always been a meritocracy. It was a place where a reporter could be covering the Bucks County school board one year and, by dint of talent and enterprise and long hours, find himself in New Delhi the next. "I got where I am through hard work," said health reporter Gilbert Gaul. "I worked at a lot of small newspapers before I was able to get to this level. Some of this gets lost in the otherwise admirable goal of trying to make newsrooms more diverse."

Ralph Cipriano, a copy editor, expressed his views in a memo, identifying himself as "one of those white guys people are complaining about." He said he felt angry about being "stereotyped" and resented the suggestion that "we white males are all identical slices from the same loaf of Wonder Bread."

White folks were teed off, to put it mildly. But many black staffers were equally passionate in their belief that an aggressive hiring plan was long overdue. "We've always had quotas in America," Claude Lewis said. "It's just that the quotas were 95 or 96 percent in favor of whites." He also bristled at talk that the policy might lead to the hiring of unqualified blacks. "We never hear the word 'qualified' when we talk about whites," he said. "It's only brought into the discussion when we talk about blacks. . . . There's an assumption that whites are qualified."

The divisions cut across racial lines. Some blacks were flatly opposed to quotas. Others viewed affirmative action as "a double-edged sword," as business reporter Glenn Burkins put it, a policy that stigmatized those it purported to help by stamping them as second-class citizens. At the same time, many whites thought the *Inquirer* plan put too little emphasis on journalistic merit. "We recently hired a Vietnam veteran," a senior editor said. "He's a very different white man than I am in terms of background. But he doesn't represent diversity, whereas if we hired Bryant Gumbel's younger brother, it would be diversity."

Inquirer management insisted the issue was being exaggerated by a handful of critics. The idea, King and other editors said, was simply to be more aggressive in diversifying a staff that was one-third women and

13 percent minority—a particularly important goal in a city that is 40 percent black. "It was never regarded as a quota that would be met come hell or high water," said managing editor James Naughton. "The standards will not change."

Anger over the quota issue continues to flare in many newsrooms. At *USA Today,* some harmless banter in an internal computer newsletter turned ugly in 1992 when automotive writer James Healey said that perhaps the paper should hire David Duke as an editor to counter "our eagerness to make quotas more important than merit. . . . White men have rights, too." This prompted a torrent of messages from furious staffers, including reporter Blair Walker: "Call me an overly sensitive black man who sees bigotry lurking behind every bush, but a proposal that we name an avowed racist and Nazi sympathizer as our next DME [deputy managing editor] doesn't strike me as humorous, not even a little bit."

One problem for big-city papers is that most of their openings are in the suburbs, where they are chasing upscale readers and advertising dollars. Some black reporters have little interest in covering white-bread suburbia, and editors tend to deploy their best black staffers on inner-city beats. This can be a form of ghettoization, confining black reporters to "black" stories. In one three-week stretch in 1992, *The New York Times* ran major pieces on Spike Lee's *Malcolm X* by Lena Williams, Sheila Rule, Felicia Lee and Isabel Wilkerson—all black women. "We have become so pathetically politically correct that it's beyond the pale not to have a black write these things," one *Times* person says.

Still, it seems clear that minority reporters can unlock doors that remain closed to white journalists, who are often viewed with suspicion or hostility in slum neighborhoods. At *The Washington Post,* for example, Athelia Knight penetrated the subculture of Lorton Prison in Virginia by riding on vans that ferried black women to visits with their imprisoned husbands and boyfriends. Knight wrote a compelling series about drug smuggling at the prison. Leon Dash, another black *Post* reporter, wrote movingly about teenage pregnancy after living in an impoverished neighborhood for several months. By contrast, when frustrated Hispanics sparked a riot in the Mount Pleasant section of Washington in 1991, the Metro staff was hampered by the fact that it had only four Hispanic reporters.

Minorities are woefully underrepresented in the senior management ranks of most newspapers. Until *The New York Times* promoted Gerald Boyd to assistant managing editor in 1993, the paper had never had a black at that level, and it had no regular black op-ed columnist until Bob Herbert was hired that year. The *Los Angeles Times* "is still an overwhelmingly white institution, especially at the upper levels," says David Shaw, the paper's media critic. The editor, managing editor, senior editor, national editor, foreign editor, metro editor, city editor and business editor are all white males.

Minority staffers often serve their papers as internal ombudsmen, puncturing stereotypes and suggesting story angles that might not occur to middle-class whites. Yet there are still too many papers with no black or Hispanic columnists, art critics, foreign correspondents or senior editors. The industry's record is improving, but not nearly fast enough.

While most newspapers are fixated on hiring percentages, they pay far less attention to developing minority talents once the reporters are on board. Black and Hispanic reporters often grow frustrated and jump to other papers. Rather than expanding the pool of talent, editors spend too much time chasing after the same small group of experienced black reporters, who are constantly romanced with promises of better pay and assignments. This merry-go-round is a game that inflates the market value of mediocre reporters and causes whispers about the better ones.

When Gwen Ifill was the only black reporter at the *Boston Herald* in the late '70s, someone left her a note that said "Nigger go home." But the talented Ifill accumulated enough experience to move to the Baltimore *Sun.* Four years later she was hired away by *The Washington Post,* where she became a national political reporter, and she later joined *The New York Times* and then NBC.

"Big newspapers aren't interested in training young black reporters," Ifill says. "They're interested in raiding. . . . Frequently, newspapers are so proud of themselves for having recruited black people that they don't take the necessary effort to see that they succeed once they get there."

Ifill recalls one editor who took a yellow pad and listed every black reporter who had left the paper. "He proceeded to explain how each one of these people was inadequate and how each one couldn't cut it," she says. "It was one of the most insulting exchanges I've ever had."

Expectations have become an important factor in keeping talented blacks. Michel McQueen spent several years as a Maryland reporter for

The Washington Post. But when the paper failed to promote her as rapidly as she had hoped, she moved to *The Wall Street Journal,* which made her a White House correspondent. (McQueen left for ABC News in 1992 and was replaced by Michael Frisby, a black reporter from *The Boston Globe.*) At times, McQueen says, "You feel like your ideas aren't respected. I remember an editor asking if I felt I could be objective covering black people. No one asked that question of white reporters. I was very hurt by that."

In the end, it takes more than a set of affirmative action numbers to build and maintain a diversified news staff. *The Seattle Times* has quadrupled its minority representation from 4 percent to 18 percent—without numerical goals through aggressive recruiting, scholarships, urban workshops and mentor programs.

Alex McCloud, the *Times'* managing editor, says the use of quotas "carries too many negatives. If you say we're going to hire a minority for this job, it tends to categorize the job as a minority job."

A moment later, however, McCloud admitted that when he needed an assistant managing editor for news, "I made it real clear that my highest goal was to find a person of color for that job." He hired Carol Carmichael, a black woman from the *Inquirer.* "I thought it was so important to the organization that it have a minority at that level," McCloud says.

Once *The Philadelphia Inquirer* contracted a case of the racial jitters, no part of the paper was safe. Not even that fortress of literary freedom, the book review.

In the spring of 1991, Art Carey, a writer for the paper's Sunday magazine, was asked to review *Illiberal Education,* Dinesh D'Souza's polemical assault against affirmative action and multicultural programs on college campuses. Carey's views on the subject were hardly a secret. He had been a prominent critic of the *Inquirer's* pluralism plan, publicly assailing the sensitivity seminars as "a reeducation camp" and "a form of thought control and ideological totalitarianism" by "the Sensitivity Gestapo." He was also finishing his own book on the scourge of political correctness. Still, the *Inquirer's* book editor, Mike Leary, was surprised at the vehemence of Carey's review.

"The 'victims' are, narrowly, blacks and women," Carey wrote, "and, more broadly, just about anybody with a claim to having been oppressed or exploited—that is, just about anybody with a gripe other than white males, who, as we all know, are totally responsible for all the world's woes." He even worked in a familiar dig, saying that political correctness was "enforced by a prissy, morally smug Sensitivity Gestapo composed of the pathologically humorless and chronically malcontent."

Other editors raised objections, and Leary took the piece to Max King. King asked that a second review, taking the opposite view, be ordered up to run alongside the Carey review. Carey's piece was held while a suitable liberal was located.

The basic concept of an independent book review, of course, is that the newspaper defers to the reviewer's judgment, right or wrong. But the *Inquirer,* perhaps anticipating a Norplant-style protest, put its thumb on the scales. Leary assigned the second review to Fasaha Traylor of the William Penn Foundation, who, as expected, dismissed D'Souza as "a militant conservative" whose "language is calculated to incite, not solve."

Leary insisted the paper was not trying to enforce any ideological line. "I don't think anybody is going to stifle a strong opinion," he said. "We're just going to have more than one." The twin reviews ran side by side, a study in political symmetry.

Carey, naturally, was upset. "This is an example of what the book is about," he says. "This book endorses a view that is at odds with the left-liberal orthodoxy of this newspaper. It seems to me a decision has been made not to suppress it, but to muffle it or alloy it by running a counter-review. It seems to me a double standard is at work here."

In the predawn darkness on January 22, 1990, two black *Washington Post* reporters were staked out in front of the Southeast Washington home of Marion Barry, mayor of the District of Columbia and accused cocaine user. It was three days after Barry had been busted in an FBI sting for smoking crack at the Vista International Hotel, and the *Post* was keeping a twenty-four-hour watch on the mayor in case he happened to make news.

Barry was scheduled to speak at a church near his home that Sunday morning. Shortly before Barry emerged, Steve Twomey, an ace feature writer who made his name at *The Philadelphia Inquirer,* arrived on the scene to write the main feature story about Barry's day. Twomey, who is white, had been given the assignment by the city editor, who was also white. Jill Nelson, one of the black reporters, called Phillip Dixon, a black assistant city editor, at home to complain.

"What is this shit?" Dixon recalls Nelson saying. "How come we're doing all the slave labor and when the story gets good, the great white hopes come in and take the story?"

If the lengthy investigation, arrest and trial of Marion Barry divided the city of Washington along racial lines, nowhere were the tensions more visible than in the *Washington Post* newsroom. The paper had been trying for years to verify the rumors that Barry was using drugs, and there had been stormy arguments about what could be published and whether the *Post* was holding a black mayor to a lesser standard

For journalists, the Barry case was like a racial Rorschach test— some saw a crooked, coked-up pol finally getting his comeuppance, while others saw an up-from-the-streets black leader being harassed by white authorities. Like the Norplant editorial or the uproar over Renee Graham's raise, Barry's arrest was the galvanizing event that deepened the racial fault lines at the *Post,* dividing black journalists from one another as well as from whites.

For a white-owned newspaper in a city that is two-thirds black, there is no more sensitive task than covering a confrontational black mayor. The natural tension that develops between aggressive reporters and city hall can turn ugly when a black official is the target. Suddenly, black readers tend to see any press criticism as racially motivated, to dismiss corruption headlines as part of a white conspiracy.

These feelings were particularly acute in Washington, which had long been ruled by arrogant Southern congressmen before District residents were finally granted the right of self-government. Barry kept the pot boiling with his patented us-against-them tactics, accusing the white media of joining an effort to "lynch" him and speaking exclusively to black newspapers at key intervals in the case. "It was a drama in this town that was just laced throughout with race," says Milton Coleman, the assistant managing editor for local news and the senior black editor at the *Post.* "It was impossible for those diverging racial views not to be played out in the newsroom."

The *Post* had a complicated relationship with Marion Barry, who came to prominence as a dashiki-clad activist during the civil rights struggles of the '60s. The paper essentially made Barry the city's second elected mayor by endorsing him in a tight three-way race in 1978, embracing him as the best hope for reviving a paralyzed bureaucracy. The *Post* supported Barry for reelection in 1982 and again in 1986, and he won easily with strong black support. By his third campaign, however, nearly all Barry's white support had vanished as his administration became a cesspool of corruption and he was dogged by allegations of cocaine use and philandering. While the *Post* aggressively reported many of these stories, there was a feeling in the newsroom that no white mayor with such a shabby record would have won the paper's endorsement three times. Juan Williams, who spent time on the editorial page, said the paper's view was "that black politics were in their infancy and it would be unfair to hold them to the same standard."

Williams says the *Post* was not receptive when he wrote stories that criticized Barry or blamed him for decaying city services. "They didn't want to hear that shit," he says. "I just kept getting the red-light signal. People at the paper started saying, 'Hey Juan, you're going too hard on this guy.' I was being rapidly isolated. I was tainted material. Instead of reading what the fuck I was writing, they would say, 'You know Juan. He's always complaining about Barry.'"

Williams grew so disgusted that in 1986 he wrote a piece for *The Washington Monthly* called "A Black Mayor Betrays the Faith." As in the case of Kathleen Day's decision to write about "S&L Hell" for *The New Republic,* Williams felt he could not say what needed to be said about Barry in his own newspaper. The *Post,* he said, had "a strong sense of defensiveness and liberal guilt that came with being a white newspaper in a black town."

The Washington Post had a long history of paternalism toward the black community. In 1949, it agreed to play down news of a race riot (reported in part by Ben Bradlee) in exchange for a short-lived promise by authorities to integrate the city's swimming pools. Those were the days when the women's pages were reserved for "white" social events and news of black engagements and weddings was not printed. During the '60s the paper often played down what were called "near misses," or racial incidents that might spark violence. When the 1968 riots broke out, there was a shouting match in the newsroom over whether to run an inflammatory picture of three white merchants with shotguns, guarding their store against black looters. Ben Bradlee made sure the photo ran on page one. The *Post* finally won its long crusade for home rule in

1975, when a locally elected black government took power for the first time.

Then came the "Jimmy" story. In 1980, when the *Post* published Janet Cooke's piece about an eight-year-old heroin addict, many people were outraged that a reporter would watch a young boy shoot up and do nothing to help him. The police chief ordered a citywide search for Jimmy. Milton Coleman, who was the *Post*'s city editor, assembled an eleven-person reporting team to follow the case. But Mayor Barry insisted the story simply wasn't plausible. Long after the piece was exposed as a hoax and the *Post* had returned Cooke's Pulitzer Prize, many blacks would remember the paper's insistence that "Jimmy" was real.

In the spring of 1984, Milton Coleman and the *Post* were in the news again. Coleman reported that Jesse Jackson had referred to Jews as "Hymies," and New York City as "Hymietown" in private conversations with reporters. Jackson, who was running for president, had used the ethnic slurs after telling Coleman, "Let's talk black talk." This was Jackson's lingo for talking on "background," which generally means the information can be used without attribution. Coleman passed the "Hymie" story to another *Post* reporter—it appeared in the thirty-seventh and thirty-eighth paragraphs of a long article—after confirming that Jackson had used the language with other reporters. It caused a huge uproar, and many blacks denounced Coleman as a traitor. Louis Farrakhan made threats against Coleman's life.

The question, Coleman wrote later, was: "Are you black first or are you a reporter first? Which side are you on?" Coleman's answer was that whatever racial kinship he might feel with Jackson, his first duty was as a journalist.

The two incidents would haunt Coleman for years. "For the rest of my life," he says, "I will always be known as Milton Coleman, comma, who was Janet Cooke's editor and who betrayed Jesse Jackson."

In the fall of 1986, the *Post* found itself in the eye of another racial storm. In a column for the Sunday magazine, Richard Cohen wrote about white merchants who bar young blacks from their stores because they see the blacks as potential shoplifters:

"I'm with the store owners, although I was not at first. . . . White assailants are rather hard to find in urban America. Especially in cities like Washington and New York, the menace comes from young black males. Both blacks and whites believe those young black males are the ones most likely to bop them over the head. . . . We are all wary of behavior that would bring a charge of racism. But the mere recognition of race as a factor—especially if those of the same race recognize the same factor—is not in itself racism."

The column seemed more an exploration of racial fears than redneck-style racism. But Washington's black community exploded in outrage. Cohen had the misfortune to write the column for the first issue of the *Post*'s redesigned Sunday magazine, which had been heavily promoted. The cover story was a profile of black New York rap singer Joseph ("Just Ice") Williams, who had been charged with the murder of a Washington drug dealer. The dual selections, approved by white editors, were obviously less than sensitive in a majority black city. "It is difficult to explain why it didn't hit me over the head like a pipe at the time," said Leonard Downie, then the paper's managing editor.

Some black leaders formed the Washington Post Recall Committee, which held regular Sunday demonstrations at the paper to protest the way blacks were depicted in the *Post*. Despite a written apology by Ben Bradlee, more than 250,000 copies of the magazine were dumped on the *Post*'s front steps over the next three months. The protests ended when the publisher, Donald Graham, agreed to appear regularly on a black radio talk show hosted by Cathy Hughes, a leader of the recall committee.

"I felt besieged," Cohen says. "I was the target of a campaign. . . . It was an emotional reaction in which the people who screamed and yelled the loudest became the spokesmen. It is, in the end, intimidation."

Soon afterward, during a two-week period, the *Post* ran five upbeat stories about blacks on the front of the Style section, including pieces on local families gathering to watch "The Cosby Show," actress Esther Rolle and the National Council of Negro Women honoring Dorothy Height. Some white staffers believed the paper was trying too hard to appease the black community.

"The problem with the paper is there aren't enough people there who know black people as ordinary human beings, who know what their interests are, what their culture is, what their life-style is," says Tom Sherwood, a former *Post* reporter. "The paper gets so wrapped up in, 'Are we going to be sensitive?' that they get discombobulated. The paper is very uncomfortable when dealing with racial issues."

· · ·

If *Post* reporters could not prove that Marion Barry was doing dope, it was not for lack of trying. They searched for him when he vanished on mysterious "vacations." They flew to Caribbean islands where the mayor was said to have snorted coke. Reporter Michael York even had a source in Barry's car who kept a *Post* cellular phone hidden in his bag, calling York whenever the mayor went somewhere so the paper could track his movements.

Several stories produced clashes with Milton Coleman, a strong-willed man whose soft voice and easygoing manner belied a stubborn streak. Coleman would insist on more evidence or would tone down the writing. Tom Sherwood once took his name off a story about a city contract involving a Barry crony. "I announced in a loud voice, 'Milton, you're not editing that story, you're gutting it!' "

Such clashes led to an emotional staff meeting at which reporters complained that Coleman was watering down controversial stories. Coleman recalls observing that everyone else at the conference table was white.

It was not difficult to believe that Coleman was sympathetic to Barry. He had covered Barry as a reporter and had encouraged the mayor to move to his predominantly black neighborhood in Southeast Washington. Coleman knew many Barry administration figures from the black student movement and saw the mayor as a much more complex figure than the way he was portrayed in the *Post*—in his words, as "an arrogant, probable drug addict running an incompetent bureaucracy."

"I felt that some of the reporting I was looking at was not sharp enough," Coleman says. "I thought our threshold for what could get in the paper was too low. A number of those stories had to do with blacks and the Barry crowd and contracting. My raising of those questions was taken as my being soft on a story. Then this racial element comes in: 'Are you saying that because you don't want a hard story on blacks?' . . . It's harder for me to make a point because of my race."

Some white staffers thought Coleman's concerns were well founded. "Milton set a high standard for these stories," Michael York says. "He didn't want circumstantial-evidence stories. There had been rumors about Barry doing drugs forever. I thought we hurt our own credibility if we ran stories about unnamed people saying Barry did drugs."

But a black reporter says that "Milton became the official black in the eyes of *The Washington Post*," a "gatekeeper" who had to approve every racially sensitive story. "It's a racist view: All blacks think alike."

The mayor, meanwhile, did his best to keep the *Post* on the defensive. In the fall of 1988, amid rumors that he was in a drug clinic, Barry eluded the press and retreated to a Catskill Mountains spa. He said he was tired of "abusive" and "intrusive" behavior by the media, "particularly *The Washington Post.*" When he did grant an interview, it was to Dorothy Gilliam, a black *Post* columnist. Barry particularly seemed to enjoy confronting white reporters. "One time he got drunk and called me from out of state," says *Post* reporter Sharon LaFraniere. "He said, 'You'll never find two people who will tell you that I used drugs.' He was almost sort of taunting me."

The *Post*'s investigation of Barry reached a new level of intensity when police busted a friend of Barry's for cocaine use shortly after the mayor had visited his hotel room. Barry lashed out at his chief tormentor: "We love this city . . . and we're not going to let *The Washington Post* through innuendo, through rumors, do what they have done for the last ten years."

While many *Post* reporters were openly disgusted by Barry's behavior, some black staffers thought the paper was going overboard. "All bets were off when it came to Marion Barry," says Phil Dixon, now the *Post*'s city editor. "The paper wasn't playing by the rules. In the minds of some of my colleagues, Marion Barry was fair game. It was open season. A lot of people in this newsroom had their minds made up that this guy was shit, a dope addict. I thought folks had crossed the line."

Even minor stories produced arguments. Dixon recalls one sarcastic piece about Barry escaping the winter cold at a conference at a Florida resort. The message was that "this stupid fucking mayor is down here again wasting our time and money and he shouldn't be here. He was socializing—isn't that what people do at these things?"

But Michael York says that even Barry considered it "a bullshit conference of black leadership," and that "I just figured he was up to no good." Besides, he had to follow Barry because there were rumors of a possible FBI sting.

By now the notion of a racial double standard was being openly discussed in the press. "Color Barry white and he would, as he should, be swiftly gone," Richard Cohen wrote.

The denouement came on January 18, 1990, when Barry went to see Rasheeda Moore, an old girlfriend, in Room 727 at the Vista, around the corner from the *Post*'s offices. In what would become one of the most famous grainy, black-and-white scenes of the video age, an FBI camera captured Barry taking several long tokes on a crack pipe before agents burst in and arrested him.

The *Post* urged Barry to resign, citing "an especially hypocritical and cynical history of denying personal drug use and urging others to join in the fight against crime." Barry had finally been exposed as a drug abuser and a liar, and it was all on videotape.

But the city remained deeply divided. A poll showed that 42 percent of blacks, but only 14 percent of whites, believed prosecutors had targeted Barry for racial reasons. To many blacks the bust was blatant entrapment, using sex as the lure. The *Afro-American,* a black newspaper, urged the mayor to "hang in there," running such headlines as "Barry: Back, Brave and Better." The *Capital Spotlight,* another black paper, ran a piece called "Willie Horton and Mayor Barry," saying white prosecutors had used the same racist tactics as Bush's campaign team. Rasheeda Moore was assailed as the "bitch" who set Barry up.

Reporters, who are trained to put aside their biases when interviewing others, found this was one story where they could not. "Talking with whites was easy because I was white," Steve Twomey says. "It was so clear Barry had done wrong and should be punished. Blacks were far more torn. They knew he'd done wrong, but they'd hate to give you an inch. They knew you, a white person, would take delight in that. They would say, 'I think they're out to get black people,' but then they would say they had been deeply disappointed by Barry. As a reporter, I was seeking logic where there was none.

"The whites tended to see this strictly as the Barry case. Blacks tended to see it as a whole series of concentric circles—the black experience, the role of the federal government, the role of this newspaper. There was a lot of black anger."

The values of objective journalism meant little in such a polarized atmosphere. Barry's allies proclaimed that the feds had spent $42 million investigating him, and although there was nothing to back this up—the actual figure was about $2 million—the black newspapers carried it and black leaders endlessly repeated it. Facts were irrelevant. You were either for Barry or against him.

"White people in this room, and some black people, had a hard time understanding why there was anybody in the world who could still say 'I like Marion Barry' after the arrest," Phil Dixon says. "Marion Barry had been here a long time. He had touched a great many people. He had put a lot of people on the fucking payroll. And that meant something special that couldn't just be wished away. Rather than trying to understand it, we dismissed it as crazy."

But even Dixon was disheartened by the mayor: "When I saw him hit that pipe like an old pro, I said, this fucker is guilty."

The Barry trial proved as divisive for the *Post* as it was for the city. Black staffers complained that most of the paper's courtroom passes had been given to white reporters. "I didn't want to put anyone on the story purely to have a black face on the story," Coleman says. "You don't build good news machines that way."

On August 10, 1990, a jury convicted Marion Barry of one count of cocaine possession, acquitted him of a second charge and deadlocked on twelve others. White reporters saw the compromise verdict as a victory. But Jill Nelson saw her newspaper as part of a "conspiracy" against Barry. Her feature story the next morning spoke loudly, almost defiantly, about the gap in perceptions. "It was a black thing at the bar at Faces last night, and other people might not understand," Nelson wrote. People at the bar were "laughing and celebrating" at "the mayor's vindication." Nelson later quit the *Post*, calling it a "weird journalistic purgatory" for blacks.

Time has a way of healing wounds, even among grudge-happy journalists. Don Kimelman is still turning out editorials at *The Philadelphia Inquirer*. Renee Graham is still writing features for *The Boston Globe*, and her fax-machine critic, Peter Howe, is back on the statehouse beat. Milton Coleman is still running the local staff at *The Washington Post*. And Marion Barry emerged from prison to win a council seat in the city's poorest ward, and in 1994, despite the paper's opposition, he again reclaimed the mayor's office.

But the racial tensions that boiled over at the three papers are still simmering beneath the surface of many American newsrooms. As newspaper staffs become more diverse, they are finally beginning to bring more sophistication to the immensely difficult challenge of covering minority communities. But they are also struggling with the frictions and resentments that inevitably accompany racial change, a behind-the-scenes drama that rarely makes the news.

6

The Glass House Gang

On July 11, 1991, there were more than a few snickers in newsrooms around the country. *The New York Times* had run one of its famous clarifications.

This one was so delicious it was hard to believe. The unlikely chain of events had begun when H. Joachim Maitre, dean of Boston University's School of Communications, delivered his spring commencement address. *The Boston Globe* reported on July 2 that Maitre had plagiarized the speech, nearly word for word, from an article by PBS film critic Michael Medved.

The *Times* had chased the Maitre story with a piece the following day by Boston correspondent Fox Butterfield. But now, in stilted *Times*ian language, the paper was saying that Butterfield's story was "improperly dependent on the *Globe* account." Five paragraphs "closely resembled" five *Globe* paragraphs. In other words, a *New York Times* reporter had plagiarized part of a story about plagiarism!

For example, the *Globe* said: "In the article, Medved suggests there is a 'war on standards' in film and television today in which ugliness and violence are glorified, and religion and traditional family values are attacked or ignored."

Butterfield's story said: "In Mr. Medved's article, 'Popular Culture and the War Against Standards,' the author says there is a 'war on standards' in film and television in which ugliness and violence are glorified, and religion and traditional family values are shunned."

It seemed less an intentional heist than an act of sloppiness. Butterfield had credited the *Globe* for breaking the story, and he easily could have gotten a videotape of Maitre's speech from the university and done his own comparison. But the embarrassment was unmistakable, and I wrote a story about it. The copy desk thought the episode was such a hoot that it unearthed an old chestnut for the headline: "What's Black and White and Red All Over?"

Little did I realize that the story would become the opening chapter of a saga that would include the firing of one of my colleagues and a string of similar incidents across the country. No one was laughing by the time it was over.

The range of ethical problems encountered by a media reporter is somewhat startling. There are conflicts of interests, freebies, junkets, intellectual theft, deception, carelessness, kowtowing to advertisers, use of dubious evidence and outright bias. It's striking how often we in the news business fail to live up to the high-minded standards that we prescribe for everyone else.

To be sure, the situation is a far cry from thirty years ago, when free bottles of booze filled the nation's newsrooms at Christmastime and some reporters did PR work on the side. It's exceedingly rare that a journalist is actually on the take, like R. Foster Winans, who sold his trader buddies advance information from his *Wall Street Journal* columns in the early '80s. Winans was convicted of securities fraud in 1985.

But it's worth noting that even Winans had convinced himself he was doing nothing wrong. He worked long hours for $30,000 a year, while his Wall Street pals earned six-figure sums for shuffling other people's money. Winans wanted a piece of the action. "I knew what I was doing was technically unethical for a journalist," he wrote later. "But since I knew that I wasn't letting my investment alter my judgment at work in any way, the ethical question was purely one of appearances."

The principals netted $690,000 on twenty-seven separate transactions, kicking back $31,000 to Winans and his roommate. That Winans could dismiss such a nefarious scheme as a matter of "appearances" says much about the prevailing ethic on Wall Street. But the *Journal*'s editors also got a little mud on their shoes. Not only were they paying an inexperienced reporter $530 a week to write a column that affected millions of dollars in stock values, but they failed to check Winans's references and never learned that he had lost his job at the Trenton *Times* for misquoting a public official.

No newspaper can erect an airtight defense against a lying reporter, as *The Washington Post* learned during the Janet Cooke affair. But the *Post*'s editors might have approached Cooke's fabricated tale about an eight-year-old heroin addict with a higher degree of skepticism. Cooke's deceit grew out of the paper's hunger for exposés—what Bob Woodward (then running the paper's Metro staff) called "holy shit" stories.

"There's a mythology hanging in the air or the newsroom," Bill Green, the paper's ombudsman, wrote in a lengthy postmortem in 1981. "Sometimes it acts like a disease. Young reporters come onto the staff expecting to find another Watergate under every third rock they kick over."

Many papers have since tightened their rules on anonymous sources and financial disclosure. Still, even expensive gifts are not a thing of the past. While working on a fashion story, Carrie Donovan, a deputy style editor at *The New York Times Magazine,* accepted three necklaces (one of them worth $1,300) and some original drawings from designer Karl Lagerfeld. Donovan then departed Lagerfeld's Paris studio with "air kisses all around," as a *Vanity Fair* piece put it. She later wrote in the *Times* that Lagerfeld "has clearly established himself as the leader of Parisian fashion." Max Frankel, the *Times* executive editor, ordered Donovan to return the jewelry. But she was let off with a slap on the wrist for what many newspapers would have considered a firing offense.

Perhaps critics are held to a different standard. In 1991, *New York Times* art critic John Russell wrote a rave review of the Ringling Museum of Art in Sarasota, Florida, calling it a "triumph" and "in a class of its own." During the same trip, the museum paid Russell's wife, art lecturer Rosamund Bernier, $8,000 to speak to a gathering there. This is about as blatant a journalistic conflict as one can imagine, and presumably would not have been tolerated had a financial reporter been writing about a bank that had hired his wife. But Russell dismissed such criticism as "total nonsense," saying he had planned to visit the museum even before his wife's invitation. And the *Times*'s culture czar, Warren Hoge, defended Russell as "a Renaissance man" whose "great integrity" could not possibly be compromised.

What makes ethical transgressions by the media harder to swallow is our holier-than-thou attitude toward the rest of the world. Many of those who demand answers for a living turn out to be pretty thin-skinned when the questions are pointed in their direction. I've had top editors send me outraged letters over articles a fraction as harsh as they run every day. I've seen major newspapers hide behind corporate spokesmen, take days to admit error and refuse to disclose how many people they are laying off. None of this is surprising—why should media conglomerates behave differently from other Fortune 500 companies?—but somehow it's still disappointing.

Journalists inhabit a morally ambiguous universe filled with murky gray zones. There is no universal code of ethics and few hard-and-fast rules. Should a reporter who owns a home be forbidden from writing about the home mortgage deduction? Can he serve on the local school board as long as he doesn't cover the town? Should he be allowed to write about city politics if his wife works for the mayor? Should he pass on information to the CIA, as Joseph Alsop and other journalists have acknowledged doing? Should he leave the State Department and then write about diplomacy for *The New York Times,* as Leslie Gelb has done?

There is no clear consensus even on the most basic questions, such as whether a reporter must identify himself as such at all times. Over the years, journalists have posed as detectives, ambulance drivers, Medicaid patients, social workers, prison inmates, migrant workers and illegal aliens. They have justified deceptions large and small for the greater goal of exposing injustice. "I posed as everything," says Mike Royko, the *Chicago Tribune* columnist, who once carried a police badge. "I posed as a deputy coroner. I once posed as a female high school principal, in a falsetto voice over the phone." In 1977 the *Chicago Sun-Times* opened a bar called the Mirage, with reporters and photographers secretly snapping pictures of inspectors soliciting bribes.

Most papers, including the *Sun-Times,* have long since banned the old practice of reporters impersonating people (although television still does it), and a newspaper today would be denounced for running a bar, even in Chicago. But what about reporters who, while using their real names, take a job in a questionable business or check into a welfare hotel? Or, as I once did, apply for apartment vacancies to see if landlords are practicing racial discrimination? Does that require an affirmative declaration of journalistic intent? Some critics believe we must wear our press cards around our necks at all times. My own view is that it's all right to do things an ordinary citizen would do—without lying or trespassing or impersonating anyone—as long as you later call the subjects of the story, identify yourself and get their side.

While reporters are expected to be cleaner than the proverbial hound's tooth, publishers have enjoyed something of a double standard. Warren Harding owned the *Marion* (Ohio) *Star* when he was elected president in 1920, defeating another Ohio publisher and three-term governor, James Cox. More recently, William Hobby remained president of the Houston Post Company while serving as lieutenant governor of Texas. When Philip Graham owned *The Washington Post,* he helped broker Lyndon Johnson's 1960 selection as vice president. "Phil had gotten, in the world we live in today, too close to Johnson," says Katharine Graham, who succeeded her late husband as chairman of the Post Company. "He was helping him in his campaign. That's not a role a publisher should play."

Other conflicts are more indirect but no less insidious. When Punch Sulzberger was publisher of *The New York Times,* he was also chairman of the board of the Metropolitan Museum of Art and a trustee of Columbia University, two major institutions covered by his newspaper. When Stanton Cook was publisher of the *Chicago Tribune* (which owns the Chicago Cubs, a team its sportswriters are expected to cover objectively), he was also chairman of the board of the Federal Reserve Bank of Chicago. Such dual roles inevitably lead to whispered accusations of favoritism. While publishers like Sulzberger and Cook are generally not involved in the daily operation of the newsroom, their minions may feel unspoken pressure to pull punches when the boss's favorite cause is involved.

Some ethical questions are more subtle. We all cultivate sources who use us even as we try to use them. Friendships often flourish. If occasional lunches (the reporter must pay, of course) turn into regular racquetball games and home cooked dinners, have you gotten too close to the source to be objective? When you go to a party on Saturday night, is everything the guests say off the record? Or are you always working, even when you're not taking notes?

Reporters sometimes trade information with law enforcement officials, or hold off writing a story until an arrest has been made, or withhold the name of an undercover agent whose life might be in jeopardy. At what point do such deals amount to being coopted by the authorities? Any journalistic practice must be able to pass the smell test, but one editor's inoffensive odor is another man's stench.

As noted earlier, the *Journal*'s Neil Barsky was taken off the Donald Trump beat after accepting three $1,000 boxing tickets from the Trump Organization. But Barsky was simply doing what many reporters do, getting to know sources in social settings. His own boss had flown to Atlantic City on The Donald's helicopter. If the Trump folks had taken Barsky to a seven-dollar movie, no one would have cared. But the high price of the ringside seats—and the fact that Barksy grabbed two extra tickets for relatives—seemed to cross some invisible line.

Romance often creates special complications for journalists. Laura

Foreman, a *Philadelphia Inquirer* reporter, admitted in 1977 that she had written about a local pol, Henry "Buddy" Cianfrani, while they were having an affair, and that he had bought her more than $10,000 in gifts. Foreman, who by then was working for *The New York Times,* was forced to resign. The two were married after Cianfrani finished serving a prison term for fraud and racketeering.

But sexual sins are not always so clear-cut. When Ray Hanania, a *Chicago Sun-Times* reporter, started dating the city treasurer, Miriam Santos, he told his bosses and was transferred from city politics to another beat. Santos later got embroiled in a feud with Mayor Richard Daley, and rumors started flying that Hanania was secretly advising her behind the scenes. Hanania says he was just giving a friend informal advice, such as "don't let reporters put words in your mouth." But when *Sun-Times* editor Dennis Britton learned that Hanania had also suggested press aides for Santos to hire, he told the reporter he had damaged the paper's credibility. Hanania resigned under pressure and filed a $2-million wrongful-discharge suit against the *Sun-Times,* which was later dismissed.

Decisions about when to credit another writer's work can be especially tricky. The nature of newspapering is that reporters are handed an unfamiliar subject, told to "pull the clips" and expected to patch together a reasonably coherent piece within a few hours. We all recycle words for a living. We lift material from wire-service reports about events that we have no time or inclination to attend—a Senate hearing, a press conference by the governor. We boil complex matters down to a couple of phrases, often based on someone else's summary. We regurgitate old interviews by reporters we've never met. In the computer age, you can punch up stories from a dozen far-flung publications in seconds, then move paragraphs onto the very screen on which you are writing. With so much raw material available at the touch of a button, it was probably inevitable that plagiarism would become a growth industry.

Standards have also stiffened. Tom Goldstein, dean of the journalism school at the University of California at Berkeley, says that in the '60s he routinely fabricated stories as a young reporter for *The Buffalo Evening News,* having learned the practice from veteran colleagues.

In a 1984 series, David Shaw of the *Los Angeles Times* described how reporters for the Cleveland *Plain Dealer, Chicago Tribune, Newsday, Miami News* and his own paper had lifted quotes and passages from other publications without credit. The sources plagiarized were as diverse as Art Buchwald, J. D. Salinger and *Rolling Stone.* The worst offenders were fired, but others were merely reprimanded.

One 1982 incident received national publicity. *The New York Times Magazine* published a story by free-lancer Christopher Jones about his travels with the Khmer Rouge guerrillas in Cambodia. After *The Village Voice* discovered that one passage had been lifted from an André Malraux novel, Jones admitted that he had never visited Cambodia and had fabricated the piece.

While reporters of the past rarely got in trouble unless they engaged in wholesale theft, one can now be prosecuted for shoplifting a couple of paragraphs. Some writers plagiarize because they're sloppy or lazy. Others fail to see anything wrong with it. Still others succumb to deadline pressure. It is extremely easy for a writer to sidestep this ethical minefield by simply changing the language and tossing in a couple of attributions. Yet careers continue to be ruined by copycat charges.

Jonathan Kandell, a veteran foreign correspondent, was fired by *The Wall Street Journal* in 1990 after writing a front-page story on three Eastern European entrepreneurs. There was no question about Kandell's research; he had interviewed the three men and had traveled to Prague, Budapest and Moscow. But Kandell acknowledged that he had met John Kiser III, the author of a book about the three businessmen, and had read his book before writing the article. Kiser complained about similarities to his book in Kandell's wording and said he should have been credited. Kandell sued the *Journal* for $12 million over his dismissal, saying he was the victim of a "paranoid atmosphere" caused by the Winans affair. The suit was later dismissed.

Reporters had great fun kicking Joe Biden around for stealing part of a speech from Britain's Neil Kinnock. But any charge hurled against politicians can easily boomerang against the press. No matter where plagiarism takes place, it's a safe bet that some sharp-eyed reader, somewhere in the world, will discover it and blow the whistle. The *Times* was alerted to the Fox Butterfield incident by a letter-writer who thoughtfully included a paragraph-by-paragraph comparison of Butterfield's story and the *Globe*'s.

Thus it was that an anonymous reader once sent me a copy of a *Newsweek* story by Eleanor Clift. She was writing about how Senator Robert Byrd of West Virginia had arranged the move of several federal agencies from Washington to his home state. "It was done in broad daylight," Clift's story began.

Attached to the letter was a story that had run a week earlier in the

Cleveland *Plain Dealer*. That story began by calling Byrd's machinations "a heist in broad daylight." It was by Thomas Brazaitis, the paper's Washington bureau chief and, unbeknownst to me, Eleanor Clift's husband.

There were other similarities:

Clift: "No one disputes that West Virginia, one of the nation's poorest states, is deserving of federal help."

Brazaitis: "No one disputes that West Virginia, one of the nation's poorest states, deserves federal help."

Clift: "His heavy-handed approach might be called blackmail."

Brazaitis: "It is not stretching a point too far to describe Byrd's tactics as blackmail."

It turned out that Clift had written her piece first, but *Newsweek* killed it for space reasons. The two had discussed the issue, so Brazaitis decided to use it for his column. Then *Newsweek* resurrected Clift's story the following week. "In effect, I profited from her reporting and her opinions on the subject," Brazaitis said. "We both viewed the topic in a similar way, which obviously came across," Clift said.

It was a minor embarrassment, as indeed the Fox Butterfield incident appeared to be. But the morning after the *Times* clarification appeared, I heard that *The Washington Post*'s top editors were looking into plagiarism charges against Laura Parker, our Miami bureau chief.

Parker's downfall, ironically enough, involved a lighthearted piece called "Letter from the Mosquito Peninsula." It contained colorful quotes about mosquito infestation from county nature worker Roger Hammer, homeowner Sheila Mainwaring and hay farmer William Kingdom. The problem was, Parker didn't talk to any of them. She had lifted the quotes, without attribution, from articles in *The Miami Herald*. While the wording was her own, most of Parker's facts appeared to have been taken from the *Herald* and an AP story. A *Herald* photographer happened to mention the similarities to a *Post* photographer, who passed the comment on to a *Post* editor, who decided to investigate.

Parker returned to Washington for a day of meetings with editors away from the office. Late in the day, Len Downie told me that the *Post* would run a clarification about her piece the next day and that he had apologized to the *Herald*. Downie also said Parker was no longer employed by the paper. He would not say whether she had been fired.

It was a hard story to write; I knew Laura Parker and I liked her.

When I reached her the next day, all she would say for publication was that she deeply regretted her mistake but felt she had been "very harshly punished."

No one at *The Washington Post* defended what Parker did. But many wondered whether suspending her and recalling her from Miami might have been a sufficient penalty. It was, after all, one mistake in a sixteen-year career, and the firing made it difficult for her to get another job.

My story on the firing included a quote from John Pancake, the *Herald*'s state editor, who said: "I wish I could tell you this never happened at *The Miami Herald,* but I suspect it has." When the *Herald* reprinted my story from the *Post*'s wire service, it excised Pancake's comments. So much for full disclosure.

A *Times* spokeswoman said the following week that Butterfield had been disciplined, but refused to say what action had been taken against him. It was, you see, an internal personnel matter. Can you imagine a *Times* reporter calmly accepting that explanation from a flack for Salomon Brothers or General Dynamics? Newsroom sources quickly confirmed that Butterfield, whose misstep was judged less serious than Parker's, had been suspended for a week.

Such charges multiplied with the speed of a computer virus. Gregg Easterbrook, a contributing editor at *Newsweek,* called to say that Richard Pascale, a Stanford University business instructor, had lifted more than a dozen passages from him for a book on corporate management. Pascale's book, *Managing on the Edge,* even reproduced dialogue from a day on which Easterbrook had taken a factory tour with the chairman of Ford Motors. There was no mention of Easterbrook, except in some footnotes.

Easterbrook's article, which appeared in *The Washington Monthly* in 1986, began: "On a very dark day in 1980, Donald Petersen, newly chosen president of Ford Motors, visited the company's design studios. Ford was in the process of losing $2.2 billion, the largest single-year corporate loss in U.S history."

One Pascale chapter began: "On a dark day in 1980, Donald Petersen, the newly chosen President of Ford Motor Company, visited the company's Detroit design studio. That year, Ford would lose $2.2 billion, the largest loss in a single year in U.S. corporate history."

It was a dark day indeed. Pascale was nabbed after another author, Robert Levering, noticed the similar language and wrote to Stanford. "I made a major, major mistake. . . . In hindsight, 20/20, it was not the right thing," Pascale said.

Yet another shoe dropped at the *Fort Worth Star-Telegram*. Katie Sherrod, a liberal columnist who had been at the paper for twenty-two years, was stung by an insect story, in this case a colony of ants that had beheaded its queen.

In December 1990, *Washington Post* science reporter William Booth began a story thus: "There has been an accident, a terrible accident at the National Zoo. The caretakers in the Invertebrate House are in shock. It seems the ants that live in a glass-fronted display case in the Invertebrate House got excited."

Sherrod's column, six months later, began: "Last year, there was an accident, a terrible accident, at the National Zoo in Washington, D.C. The ants who live in a big glass display case in the Invertebrate House beheaded their queen." There were other similarities, although Sherrod's piece went on to make some broader sociological points. A California reporter saw a reprint of Sherrod's column in the *San Francisco Chronicle* and sent a copy to Booth, who told his editor. The *Star-Telegram* fired Katie Sherrod.

But Sherrod did not go quietly. She hotly disputed the charges, proclaiming that she had been to the zoo herself and that she had engaged in "fair use under the copyright laws," missing the point that her alleged theft was an ethical matter, not a legal one. More important, she declared that the plagiarism flap was "a pretext designed to cover up the fact that I have been discharged in retaliation for opposing sexually discriminatory practices at the *Star-Telegram*." The paper's publisher, Richard Connor, called the accusation "completely without foundation."

You might think that Sherrod's colleagues would start bending over backward to give proper credit, but in the following months, two other *Star-Telegram* staffers fell into the same trap. Editorial writer Bill Youngblood drew a week's suspension for stealing a paragraph from a *New York Times* column. Unfortunately for Youngblood, his paper reprinted the *Times* column on a facing page the same day his editorial ran. Political reporter James Walker was forced to resign for lifting several quotes about David Duke from the *New Orleans Times-Picayune* and a Louisiana TV station. This was particularly puzzling because Walker was covering the governor's race in Louisiana, where quotes about Duke were a dime a dozen.

Just to give the plagiarism outbreak a global flavor, Japan's Kyodo

News Service discovered that fifty-one medical articles by one of its senior writers were almost identical to a series that had been published in a Japanese paper seventeen years earlier. No American-style shilly-shallying here: Kyodo's president, Shiju Sakai, took personal responsibility for the affair by resigning.

Readers who turned to the Evans and Novak column on December 12, 1990, saw a discussion of what was dubbed a "free lunch" tax proposal by the Republican Party. What they didn't know was that Robert Novak had just had something of a free lunch himself.

The column was based on Novak's reporting at a Republican Governors Association conference in Pinehurst, North Carolina. The GOP gathering paid for a joint appearance by Novak and *New Republic* writer Morton Kondracke, including their air fare and accommodations at the Pinehurst Hotel and Country Club. (Kondracke's fee was $4,000; Novak described his only as "a pretty good sum.") Novak's working-stiff colleagues were particularly surprised when they saw a state trooper carrying Novak's luggage.

"Should I have done it gratis or for pay? The prudent answer is not to do it at all," Novak said later. "Of the two choices, getting paid was more of an arm's-length arrangement than doing it as a contribution."

Shouldn't Novak have told his readers he was a paid speaker at the very conference he was covering? "Maybe that should have been put in," he said.

Bob Novak is part of the journalistic star culture of the '90s. He is a regular on lots of talk shows, including a weekly CNN program that he and partner Rowland Evans host. The duo churns out no fewer than three newsletters (one of which offered subscribers a sweepstakes, with the winner getting a free trip to Washington for two and "limousine transportation to an exclusive dinner with Robert Novak"). They invite their news sources, such as James Baker, Ted Kennedy and Bob Dole, to "off the record" seminars at which guests are charged $350 a head.

In a way that would have seemed unimaginable a generation ago, some print journalists have become bigger celebrities than the politicians they cover. They are fixtures on television. They write best-selling books that are often excerpted by their newspapers. They pull in lecture fees that can range from $500 for a low-profile reporter to as much as $7,500 for *The Washington Post*'s David Broder and $20,000 for *The*

New York Times' William Safire. David Gergen made more than $1 million from speeches and punditry in the seventeen months before he joined the Clinton White House. The commercial aspect has become increasingly blatant: Kondracke and *The New Republic*'s Fred Barnes have appeared at a $75-a-plate dinner for American Express Platinum Card holders. "The McLaughlin Group" has made commercials for the National Basketball Association. Commentator William Schneider has spoken at an *Atlantic* magazine forum designed to hawk the new Toyota Camry. American Express cardholders who run up 300,000 frequent-flyer miles get to meet with Safire.

I've appeared on a few television shows myself, and one quickly discovers the seductions and fleeting fame of popping off under the klieg lights. Many opinion-mongers seem to spend less time reporting and more time merchandising themselves. The entire journalistic gestalt has shifted, with succinct, provocative, made-for-television comments more valued than the nuance and comprehension of the careful writer. It's thumbs up or thumbs down, who's a hero and who's a goat, now let's pause for a commercial message. The *Chicago Tribune* has used a TV coach to help its scribblers get themselves on the tube. Even *The New York Times*, which long looked down its corporate nose at television, has hired a PR firm to help turn its reporters into TV stars.

Some journalists, like James Kilpatrick, have railed against speaking fees for congressmen while refusing to disclose their own. Others believe the gradual absorption of big-city journalists into the upper middle class has twisted our news values. "I don't think reporters should make a lot of money," says Molly Ivins, a columnist for the *Fort Worth Star-Telegram.* "That leads to thousand-word articles on the return of place cards at dinner parties. If you're only making what a public school teacher makes, you've got a real serious interest in exposing mechanics who rip you off when they fix your car."

Without endorsing the notion that journalists should take a vow of poverty, I would agree that many of us have come to identify more closely with policymakers than with plumbers. Too many pundits make the mistake of seeing themselves as part of the political elite, in the haughty Walter Lippmann tradition, rather than as surrogates for the public. James Reston was the most celebrated journalist of his era, but his cozy relationship with Washington officialdom—he once advised Senator Arthur Vandenberg on a major foreign policy speech—would be deemed scandalous today. Proximity to the seat of power can be intoxicating. Just ask columnist George Will, who secretly coached Ronald Reagan before the 1980 presidential debate, then went on television and hailed Reagan as the victor.

Even lesser lights enjoy a glittering array of benefits and opportunities that set them apart from ordinary folk. Reporters in New York get special license plates that enable them to park in restricted zones. Reporters on Capitol Hill park for free, eat in members' dining rooms, get cheap haircuts in congressional barbershops and have free work space in the press galleries, where congressional employees take their phone messages. Movie and theater critics get free tickets. Sportswriters get free game passes. Reviewers are flooded with free books.

When I worked in the *Post*'s New York bureau, I was inundated with mail dangling the prospect of freebies. Hill and Knowlton offered me a free stay at Atlantic City's Golden Nugget, where I would be entertained by Frank Sinatra. A Mexican town promoting a tennis festival invited me to Maxim's, where I could discuss my backhand with John McEnroe and Tracey Austin. BVD asked me to lunch for the unveiling of its new underwear campaign, where reporters were given free packages of briefs.

At one point I decided to accept a couple of these invitations (solely for research purposes, of course). Cunard Lines had me aboard the *Queen Elizabeth II,* where I pigged out on prawns, prosciutto and pastrami at the most spectacular buffet I have ever seen. Westin Hotels had me to "An Afternoon in Paradise," where more than one hundred journalists, looking silly as undulating Hawaiian hula dancers placed leis around our necks, were plied with champagne and mousse with rum sauce. Three lucky reporters won a drawing for free vacations in Hawaii and Asia; the rest of us got the consolation prize, two free nights at Westin's newest San Francisco hotel. The idea is obviously to buy a bit of favorable coverage, and while most major newspapers have policies against accepting such largesse, the practice is fairly widespread among magazines and smaller papers.

In the multimedia age, the web of potential conflicts of interest is increasingly sticky. Consider the following column by Ken Jackson, book editor of the *Tulsa World.* Jackson began by noting that the paper's artist "has created his first book-jacket art. It's for a mainstream novel, *Carry Up My Bones* (Council Oak, $14.95). . . ."

Jackson quoted a local bookstore owner as saying the book "deserves and is destined to become a Southwestern and Southern classic.

It is that insightful, faithful and powerful . . . as wonderful and delightful as *To Kill a Mockingbird.*"

Another critic, he said, gushed that "the characters live and breathe on these pages." And a third: "I'm stunned by the introspection, feelings, sense of place and time, the sheer emotion depicted."

In the last paragraph, Jackson revealed: "I wrote *Carry Up My Bones.*"

("At least I kept the self-serving part down to the last paragraph or two," Jackson later explained.)

Roger Cohen, while covering the publishing beat for *The New York Times,* found himself in an awkward spot when writing about General Norman Schwarzkopf's $6-million dollar deal with Bantam Books for an autobiography. Cohen speculated about the book's chances of success, although he had just coauthored a quickie bio of Schwarzkopf for Farrar, Straus & Giroux. "There are a lot of inherent conflicts of interest" in covering the media, said Cohen, who disclosed his book in a second piece on Schwarzkopf. "You work according to your conscience. So many journalists have written books, or are living with someone who's written a book, or have some connection to people writing books. It's very hard to avoid."

Sometimes journalists make inexplicably dumb mistakes, almost as if they have blinders on. The *San Antonio Express-News* fired reporter Jerome Curry over his purchase of a 1983 Ford Econoline van, which Curry used to drive his kids to soccer games. The problem was that Curry bought the van from a local bingo operator, Eddie Garcia, who was the target of a federal investigation. Curry, who saw the $1,300 purchase as just "an appearance problem," had written a number of stories about the Garcia probe. The van deal was disclosed by the rival *San Antonio Light*; in a one-newspaper town, it never would have been revealed.

Robert Terry, a veteran police reporter for *The Philadelphia Inquirer,* is so close to the cops he has covered for thirty years that he borrowed money from the city's police commissioner and other police officials so he could gamble in Atlantic City. The paper suspended Terry with pay and asked him to enroll in a program for gambling addiction.

At other times conflicts can arise from charitable impulses. Al Hunt of *The Wall Street Journal* learned this the hard way when he raised money for the Spina Bifida Association. Hunt, whose son was born with the disease, solicited a number of lobbyists—including those representing Ford, Searle Pharmaceuticals, Gannett and CBS—to buy $10,000 tables at a fund-raising "roast" of Bob Novak. He also arranged for Vice President Quayle, Senate Minority Leader Bob Dole, House Speaker Tom Foley and others—all of whom are covered by his paper—to speak at the dinner.

The roast was to be televised live on C-SPAN, but the network's cameras were still trained on Representative Robert Dornan, who was making a late-night speech on the House floor. Hunt called the House cloakroom to ask what was holding things up, and Dornan agreed to cut short his speech. Several *Journal* reporters later complained to Hunt about the episode.

"It's something that embarrassed the bureau and shouldn't be done and I won't do it again," Hunt says. "It was done with the best of intentions and innocence."

Mixing journalism and business dealings is often a recipe for indigestion. Financial columnist Terry Savage seems to have forgotten this when she agreed to become a director of McDonald's Corporation, a post that pays $24,000 a year plus $2,000 for each meeting attended. Savage saw no conflict in a columnist joining the board of one of America's largest corporations, but some newspaper editors were more skeptical. "Is she a financial journalist," asked Dennis Britton, "or is she a businesswoman who's writing a column?"

The well-oiled revolving door between the news business and the political world enables reporters to become press secretaries and political hacks to be reborn as enlightened pundits. But serving two masters at once can be tricky. The Portland *Oregonian* put itself in a bind by hiring Gerald Frank, the top aide to Oregon Senator Mark Hatfield, to write a weekly column for $22,000 a year. Both sides insisted there was no problem because Frank did not write about Hatfield (although Frank did plug a New York travel guide he publishes on the side).

During Hatfield's 1990 reelection campaign, a Portland television station reported that Frank was for twenty-five years a director of an Oregon S&L that had collapsed at a cost to the taxpayers of $113 million. The station, KATU, also raised questions about Frank's official travel. The *Oregonian* ignored both stories, prompting charges of favoritism from Hatfield's Democratic opponent. Frank, insisting he did the column "as a public service," dropped it for the rest of the campaign.

To be sure, a preoccupation with potential conflicts can be carried too far. In 1990, the *St. Petersburg Times* fired reporter James Greiff, who was covering Florida banks, for short-selling about $2,000 worth of stock he owned in a California bank. Business reporters are generally discouraged from such highly speculative transactions. But Greiff promptly pointed the finger at his boss, business editor Leonard Apcar.

Apcar's sin was that his Individual Retirement Account had invested in a mutual fund that held a tiny percentage of its stock in Banc One Corp. of Ohio. He had been involved in two stories the previous year that mentioned Banc One, along with other banks. Apcar estimated the value of his mutual fund holding at $42. "I had no control over the investment. . . . I thought I was being conscientious," he said. Apcar was dismissed two days later, but was quickly snapped up by *The New York Times.*

Some newspapers seem to have only a passing acquaintance with the First Amendment. Dennis Washburn, a veteran columnist for the *Birmingham News,* spoke candidly with the *Washington Journalism Review* for an article on how auto dealers pressure newspapers into providing favorable coverage. Washburn, who edited the paper's weekly Wheels section, said it was "designed to sell cars" and that the newsroom "would be extra careful about doing an exposé. . . . They probably would not jeopardize such a substantial portion of our advertisers unless it was something major."

The day after the article appeared, Washburn was fired. "Maybe they thought this took away from their image," he said. "Whatever I said in that story was the truth." The *News'* editor, James Jacobson, refused to discuss the firing.

The Portland *Oregonian* has likewise displayed an unusual sensitivity to advertisers. It once destroyed thousands of copies of a Sunday edition after one of its salesmen objected to a story advising readers on how to sell a home without a real estate broker. The editor who approved the piece was demoted.

Some unethical journalism is done by deception, some by intentional hype and some by accident. The *Chicago Tribune* fell into the sucker category during the Persian Gulf war when reporter Laurie Goering interviewed an Army sergeant who said he had been secretly airlifted behind enemy lines in Kuwait. George Kakaletris also told her that his left knee was shattered by a rifle shot, his left eye damaged by a grenade and that he had been cut by Iraqis with knives and bayonets.

The *Tribune* rushed the story into print because Kakaletris had already told his tale on two local television stations. But the Army soon announced that the man had been discharged in 1987 and hadn't been in the service since. The *Tribune* admitted in a front-page piece that it had made no attempt to independently confirm the story.

"The local City News bureau here has a slogan: 'If your mother says she loves you, check it out,' " Goering said. "That's now hanging over my desk."

The New York Times was equally embarrassed by a story involving the Tribune Company, then the owner of the New York *Daily News*. During the five-month-long strike at the *News* in 1990–91, *Times* reporter David Pitt quoted an unnamed Tribune official as saying that the company had killed a proposed settlement. *News* publisher James Hoge assailed the story as "a total fabrication." Pitt later admitted to his bosses that his source was "an anonymous caller" and that he never knew the man's name. The *Times* apologized to Hoge and acknowledged the error in an editor's note. Pitt, who had flunked "Journalism 101," as metropolitan editor Gerald Boyd put it, was transferred to a noneditorial job.

The most farfetched event can take on a life of its own when the press pack pounces. In the summer of 1991, a New York horror story quickly made national headlines: A man had raped a three-year-old girl on a grassy knoll near a crowded Manhattan highway while at least twenty motorists stopped to watch. It was a Kitty Genovese tale, an uncaring city turning its back on an unspeakable crime.

"SHAME ON THE CITY—Shocking Story of New York at Its Worst," the *New York Post* wailed in a banner headline, describing the incident as "a chilling mix of apathy and voyeurism." All the New York papers and TV stations went wild over the yarn, which also generated front-page stories in the Baltimore *Sun* and *The Washington Times*.

The only problem was that it wasn't true. A tow-truck driver who stopped at the scene to help (and later bragged about his role on "Larry King Live") had told a police officer that traffic came to a halt as rubberneckers watched the rape. A spokesman for the Manhattan district attorney's office repeated the man's story to reporters. But other eyewitness accounts surfaced days later. A second motorist described how he and two other men had helped pursue the alleged rapist. Traffic had stalled behind the abandoned cars, he said, and most drivers never saw the attack.

"We just sort of used it as a metaphor. . . . If this is true, how low have we sunk?" said John Cotter, then the *Post*'s metropolitan editor.

But the *Post* never ran a follow-up story correcting its "SHAME" head-line. Perhaps crafting a metaphor is much easier than admitting a mistake.

If any author ever had a heavenly topic beyond reproach, it was Phil Donahue, writing a heartfelt essay about a nun who had touched his life. Donahue's syndicated article took the form of a letter to the late Sister Mary Andrew, a nun he had known during his Catholic school days in Cleveland in the 1940s. *The Washington Post* carried it under the head-line "Confessions of a Fallen Schoolboy."

"Dear Sister Mary Andrew," it began. "The other day someone told me you died. Imagine my guilt. . . . From my fifth year to my thirteenth you were the chalk, I was the slate—the tabula rasa on which you wrote so profoundly, so beautifully. The guilt I feel for not having thanked you looms large in my chest today."

But Donahue quickly found himself in moral purgatory over the piece. Days after it ran, a Catholic News Service reporter called the Cleveland school and found out there was no Sister Mary Andrew. The talk show host told me that while the nun was real, he had invented a fictitious name for her. He said he had been told through a friend that the nun's family did not want publicity about her death from breast cancer. He had also changed the name of another nun in the piece.

Donahue, who has put so many guests on the spot with probing questions, seemed genuinely puzzled at what the fuss was about. "I really don't think I deceived anyone . . . I'd like to know how the piece has less value if the name has been changed," he said.

There was more. The article was illustrated by what was described as a reproduction of a 1953 inscription from Sister Mary Andrew in a leather-bound prayer book she had given young Phil. But Donahue admitted he had asked a woman at a Catholic organization to write the inscription—which he reconstructed from memory—and, using the Palmer handwriting method taught in parochial schools, to sign it "Sister Mary Andrew."

This seemed a fairly blatant bit of consumer fraud. "I suppose you could argue it is," Donahue said. "I think if you're going to be exact about it. . . . Do the men on the comic strips draw every frame by themselves? How far do you want to go here? It didn't occur to me that this was some sort of moral decision." (Nearly a year later, Donahue found the actual 1953 inscription—from the woman whose real name was Sister Mary Patrick—and sent me a copy.)

Many news organizations insist on defending their brethren in court, no matter how reckless or shoddy their behavior. When psychoanalyst Jeffrey Masson accused Janet Malcolm and *The New Yorker* of fabricating quotations attributed to him, there was a great hue and cry from the media about how the courts should not concern themselves with the accuracy of quotes. Despite evidence that would prompt a jury to find that Malcolm had indeed invented some of the quotes (although the case ended in a mistrial), the American Society of Newspaper Editors, Time Warner, the Society of Professional Journalists and others took her side in briefs filed with the Supreme Court. Even if Malcolm had invented the quotes, the media lawyers argued, that was not proper grounds for a libel suit. The high court disagreed, saying writers may be sued for deliberately putting damaging words in their subjects' mouths if the misquotations are significant.

In another 1991 ruling, the court said that the Minneapolis *Star Tribune* and *St. Paul Pioneer Press Dispatch* had violated a pledge to keep a source's identity secret. A *Star Tribune* reporter had promised confidentiality to the source, Dan Cohen, when Cohen leaked him information about the criminal record of a candidate for lieutenant governor. But David Hall, the paper's editor, overruled the reporter and insisted on naming Cohen, who was promptly fired from his advertising agency job. Such behavior is reprehensible and should have been denounced by journalists everywhere. Yet *The New York Times,* Times Mirror, AP and Gannett filed legal briefs siding with the Minnesota papers. Such First Amendment absolutism in defense of stupid conduct makes us all look foolish and reinforces our reputation for arrogance.

Almost all media controversies, like those discussed above, involve mistakes and exaggerations. For a newspaper to retract a story when it has the facts right clearly belongs in the man-bites-dog category. Yet that's what happened at the Santa Fe *New Mexican* after the paper dared to take on Los Alamos National Laboratory, the area's largest employer.

The New Mexican ran a six-day, thirty-two-part series, based on thousands of pages of government documents, that detailed safety and environmental problems at the nuclear lab. But the paper's owner and publisher, Robert McKinney, went ballistic over the series. A former U.S. representative to the International Atomic Energy Commission, McKinney declared in a signed editorial that the series "presented the case for the prosecution" and that "the dangers of atomic energy are often misunderstood and overstated." He called Los Alamos "a distinguished neighbor of which we should be proud."

McKinney didn't stop there. After meeting with the director of Los Alamos, he printed and distributed, as a free insert, a twenty-seven-page government booklet that downplayed any safety hazards at the lab. He fired David Mitchell, the managing editor who assigned the series. He ordered that the series not be entered for any journalism prizes and temporarily barred the staff from covering Los Alamos. One reporter on the series, Kelly Richmond, quit in disgust; the other, Thom Cole, was fired some months later.

"To have your own paper fold on you was disheartening," Richmond says of the meltdown. "Everyone at the paper loved the series except the publisher. He's a big atomic-energy booster."

Six months later, Los Alamos released a 308-page internal evaluation that was highly critical of its failure to comply with safety and environmental rules, essentially confirming what had been in the series.

When I called the new executive editor, Walter Friedenberg, to ask about the controversy, he snapped, "I am busy trying to put out *The New Mexican.*" Then he hung up.

Any reporter who's ever been a guest on a call-in TV or radio show quickly comes to understand that a whole lot of folks out there fervently believe the press is biased. Not just sloppy or insensitive or inaccurate, but deliberately prejudiced. Some believe the media are controlled by a small, left-wing cabal that makes all its decisions in a dimly lit back room. Others are certain that reporters write stories in lockstep conformity with their paper's editorial policy.

Any time we run, or don't run, a controversial story, the conspiracy theorists come out of the woodwork. One often hears claims that the press is "protecting" Mr. Jones or "out to get" Mr. Smith or "sucking up" to some power broker. Or that *The New York Times* suppressed a story because so-and-so is a friend of Punch Sulzberger. When Bob Woodward and David Broder wrote a seven-part series that was sympathetic to Dan Quayle, some readers insisted that *The Washington Post* was cozying up to the Republicans. But Richard Nixon reached a different conclusion: that Woodward must be building up Quayle for the 1996 presidential nomination in the belief that the Democrats could most easily defeat him. In another outlandish case, a whistle-blower once complained that the *Post* had refused to do a story on the Wackenhut Corporation because the company provided the security guards in our building. Maybe he thought they'd arrest us if we got out of line.

The truth is that the "media" have no unified agenda because they are, in the words of *The Washington Post*'s Richard Harwood, "an amorphous amalgamation of thousands of enterprises, embracing everything from *The Christian Science Monitor* to *Screw* magazine." The notion that newspapers deliberately slant certain stories because they are anti-Israel, pro-Israel, pro-abortion, pro–gun control or anti-administration is equally absurd. We ain't that organized.

Many of these complaints come from readers whose real beef is that we don't share their strong opinions on the subject at hand. The National Right to Life Committee, with considerable overstatement, claimed in a 1992 fund-raising letter: "A dozen abortion marchers will get more coverage on the 'CBS Evening News,' or space in *The Washington Post* or *The New York Times,* than ten thousand pro-lifers." Bashing the media keeps the cash registers ringing for many lobbying groups.

In some ways we are haunted by the legacy of the past. From the first days of the republic, most newspapers were blatantly partisan vehicles that twisted the news in all sorts of ways. After World War II, the ethic of objectivity firmly took hold at all but a few papers. These days, though few people believe it, the editorial page and the newsroom maintain a church and-state separation. *The Wall Street Journal* is the classic example. While its reporters regularly savaged Michael Milken in the late '80s, its editorialists defended him as the victim of overzealous prosecutors long after Milken had pleaded guilty. Norm Pearlstine jokes that the *Journal* is a bargain because you get two papers for the price of one.

Sometimes newspapers investigate people because an anonymous letter came in the mail, or somebody's cousin passed on a tip to a copy aide. Some stories don't get written because the beat reporter was on vacation, or an editor screwed up, or there was too much else going on that day. News organizations are simply too diverse and idiosyncratic to hew to a single policy line.

A handful of newspapers do tend to wage ideological warfare in their news columns. The *Sacramento Union* once banned the word "gays" in favor of "homosexuals," insisted on calling NOW a "radical feminist group" and, after one anti-abortion protest, ran the headline "16,600

Stand Proud Against Abortion." The Manchester *Union Leader* crusades for its favorite politicians (it once ran a front-page analysis called "God Has Chosen Reagan to Lead the Country") and ridicules the rest. But most editors generally keep their thumb off the journalistic scales.

Does this mean that most reporters are similarly conservative? Of course not. Didn't lots of journalists detest Richard Nixon and find Ronald Reagan a boob? Sure. Journalists have plenty of opinions. But the profession is based on the idea that they can keep those opinions out of their stories. Sometimes we do a less than perfect job of it. Sometimes our personal feelings about the participants intrude into our writing. But most journalists handed damaging evidence about some liberal champion wouldn't hesitate to jump on the story.

Our real bias is a bad-news bias. We love conflict, emotion, charges and countercharges. A reporter who spends months chasing allegations of wrongdoing sometimes finds his vision clouded by the thrill of the chase. One who spends too much time hanging out with cops and prosecutors may wind up thinking the same way, sometimes overlooking reckless conduct by his law enforcement buddies. A city councilman who keeps feeding a reporter inside dope is less likely to become the object of harsh scrutiny. But such tendencies have more to do with mind-set than ideology.

Still, the news business has a problem with what I call cultural bias. As we saw on stories ranging from the Carol Stuart murder to the Marion Barry bust, white, middle-class, college-educated reporters tend to view the world through a particular prism. Their backgrounds shape their views not only on racial matters but on such subjects as religion and abortion. That was painfully evident from a February 1993 *Washington Post* story that described followers of televangelists as "largely poor, uneducated and easy to command"—and was quickly followed by an embarrassing correction.

Two major surveys have shown that 80 to 90 percent of reporters favor the right to abortion. David Shaw has written persuasively that much reporting on abortion is biased "either in content, tone, choice of language or prominence of play."

But even Shaw concedes that most reporters do not allow their personal views on abortion to influence their writing. Many bend over backward to be fair to opponents of abortion. The problem is that most journalists know few if any people who are part of the pro-life movement. It is not part of their world. And that can lead to lapses in news judgment.

When pro-life groups held a major rally at the Washington Monument in April 1990, the *New York Times, Los Angeles Times, Boston Globe* and other major papers gave it front-page coverage. But *The Washington Post* ran a relatively short story on the front of its Metro section.

It wasn't that the *Post* was deliberately trying to muffle an opposing point of view, as many pro-life activists concluded. It was simply that the editors, knowing no one who felt passionately about the march, kissed it off as just another protest. Len Downie said he was "embarrassed" at how the paper had blown it.

That episode contrasted sharply with another demonstration in the spring of 1989, when 300,000 people marched in Washington for abortion rights. As Shaw has recounted, the *Post* ran five stories in five days leading up to the event, plus a map showing the route of the march. The paper devoted five stories and three pictures to the march itself, with the main story splashed across the front page. "We all got quite energized. We heard about it from our friends and colleagues," Downie said.

The demonstration turned into a journalistic watershed because the marchers included a number of reporters and editors from the *New York Times, Washington Post* and other news organizations. One was Linda Greenhouse, who covers the Supreme Court for the *Times.*

Greenhouse openly discussed her participation in the march. She told her boss, Howell Raines, about it at a party and he saw no problem. The day after the march, however, Raines had the paper's conflict-of-interest policy faxed to him and realized that Greenhouse had run afoul of the rules. Executive editor Max Frankel also got involved. The editors told Greenhouse that she had violated *New York Times* policy and that staffers should refrain from such activities in the future. When a *Washington Post* reporter started calling *Times* editors for a story about Greenhouse's role, the paper suddenly had a PR problem. The *Times* published its own story on the matter the day after the *Post* account appeared.

"She now acknowledges that this was a mistake and accepts the policy," the *Times* quoted Raines as saying. Greenhouse was not asked for comment.

Greenhouse was not punished and continues to cover the court. She says the protest had no effect on her coverage of abortion, which is widely seen as balanced.

Linda Greenhouse's views were no secret at the *Times.* After the United Way dropped Planned Parenthood from its list of approved charities, Greenhouse posted a letter on the newsroom bulletin board each year during the United Way fund-raising drive. She urged colleagues to boycott United Way and join her in donating money to Planned Parenthood instead. "I was rather aggressively and publicly pro-choice within the paper," she says. "I wasn't the slightest bit subtle about it."

Greenhouse sees a double standard at work: "Was the civil rights situation covered objectively by a bunch of liberal northern reporters who basically preferred Martin Luther King to Bull Connor? Was the collapse of communism in Eastern Europe covered objectively by a bunch of dyed-in-the-wool believers in democracy who wanted a free Poland? Only on the abortion issue do people raise their eyebrows that reporters might have a point of view.

"The standards for how to look at this issue are basically set by men. It's not viewed as a given that reproductive freedom should be a right in a civilized society. I guess it was naïve in retrospect, but I wasn't trying to make a public statement. My participation in the march was meant to be a totally anonymous act, like voting. I was with some college friends. I wasn't marching under some banner of *New York Times* Reporters for Choice." (Some abortion disputes are not as easily resolved as the Greenhouse matter. After the *Fairfield* [Iowa] *Ledger* fired two editors for anti-abortion activities in 1990, the employees sued for religious discrimination and won a $35,000 out-of-court settlement.)

At *The Washington Post,* Downie and Ben Bradlee told the staff in a memo: "It is unprofessional for you . . . to take part in political or issue demonstrations, no matter on which side or how seemingly worthy the cause. It is the choice we make when we choose to work in this business and for this newspaper." Downie, who feels so strongly about outside political activity that he refrains from voting, asked those who joined the march to disqualify themselves from writing about abortion.

Boyce Rensberger, then the paper's science editor, challenged Downie's view in his own memo. "How can the *Post* permit reporters and editors to express their opinions on events in the news through op-ed pieces, news analyses and regular columns," he asked, "but prohibit the same people from expressing their opinions through the right of peaceable assembly?"

The thorny issue would surface again in the spring of 1993 during the largest gay rights demonstration ever held in Washington. This time many newspapers waived their normal restrictions on participating in political events, perhaps believing that a gay march was somehow different or that it would be politically incorrect to ban attendance. Dozens of gay journalists from the *New York Times, Wall Street Journal, Los Angeles Times, Miami Herald* and other papers proudly joined the demonstration. Only reporters who wrote about gay issues were asked to refrain from marching.

At *The Washington Post,* however, Downie issued a memo barring newsroom staffers, even those who covered sports or entertainment, from joining the march. He said that such participation "calls into question the whole newspaper's approach to coverage . . . whether or not we approach stories with bias."

Some gay reporters agreed with Downie, but others were livid. "For people who grew up disguising a very crucial central fact about themselves, to fail to participate is an act of denial," one *Post* staffer said. "I make no secret that I have an opinion about gay rights. Whether I march or not, those opinions are there. I feel I'm being told your job is in conflict with your life." Some gay journalists told me that they planned to march in defiance of official edicts and hoped that their bosses would not find out.

The bottom line is that appearances matter. It is one thing for a reporter to argue vehemently, within the newsroom, that the right to abortion must be sacrosanct. It is another to march in a demonstration on Sunday and write about the issue on Monday. Reporters in the '60s may have sympathized with Martin Luther King or written favorable stories about King, but they certainly couldn't march with him. That crosses the line into advocacy.

Fairly or unfairly, those who join the news business give up certain rights. Matters that are routine for most citizens, such as signing petitions or contributing to political candidates, ought to be out of bounds for members of the press. We need to avoid the mere appearance of conflict, the same standard to which we so righteously hold public officials. No one should pretend that we are opinion-free, but parading those opinions in public is the first step on a very slippery slope.

In the end, most of these questions—crediting someone else's work, turning down freebies, avoiding business relationships with sources, staying out of demonstrations—are not all that complicated.

But the way we in the press have handled matters has alienated too many of our readers, adding to a sense that we are a privileged group of hypocrites that somehow get to play by different rules. This has deflected the debate away from the greatest ethical quandary facing journalists: the daily task of deciding what to publish and how far to intrude into people's private lives.

7

Fit to Print?

Nothing in the media business spreads faster than a hot rumor. And nothing creates more headaches for editors and reporters. The line between news and thirdhand gossip has become badly blurred in recent years, and our moral compass increasingly erratic.

The most titillating rumors often involve sex and public officials, which only adds to the growing sense of unease in the nation's newsrooms. We don't like to be thought of as character cops, pecking into people's bedrooms and deciding what dirt is fit to dish. Yet our standards have become so amorphous that we are increasingly thrust into the role of moral gatekeeper.

The plain truth is that there are no rules anymore, no corner of human behavior into which prying reporters won't poke. All of the media, from the prestige press to the sensationalist rags, have been infected by a tabloid culture that celebrates sleaze. Everyone is grist for the celebrity mill. Anyone deemed to be a "public figure"—that is, anyone who was ever famous for anything at any time—is fair game for journalistic inquisition. Even false rumors, if the names are big enough and the whispering grows loud enough, float into print on the flimsy rationale that they are "out there" and therefore must be dissected and analyzed by the press.

For years it was all so easy. We knew the juicy secrets—who the mayor was having an affair with, which senator was drunk at noon, which conservative bluenose was homosexual—and we didn't tell you. Part of it reflected social mores; unless a politician was dumb enough to get himself arrested or entangled in a messy divorce, such things rarely became public. In 1940, the press corps knew that Republican presidential candidate Wendell Willkie was having an affair with Irita Van

Doren, literary editor of the *New York Herald Tribune*. She even helped edit his speeches. But no one wrote about it, although reporters sometimes called Willkie at Van Doren's apartment at night if they needed a quote for the next day's paper.

Even in the late 1960s, the press's protective instincts were so well developed that when *New York Times* reporter Eileen Shanahan filed a story saying that Russell Long was visibly drunk during a Senate debate, her paper refused to print it. (When pressed for proof, Shanahan told her editors, "I called him off the floor and was standing six feet from him and his breath almost knocked me flat.") Exposing the public inebriation of an important committee chairman was somehow less important than observing the polite rules of Washington society. A *Times* profile later said Long was often seen in "high spirits" on the Senate floor, which Shanahan described as "one of these chickenshit things that journalists do that only inform those who are already informed."

The boys on the bus generally winked at shenanigans by male politicos. If President Kennedy had a few flings on the side, it was no one's business; some of the campaign scribes were also less than faithful. But as more women infiltrated the press corps, this boys-will-be-boys arrangement became hopelessly dated.

The media have gradually broadened the definition of what voters need to know to evaluate a person's fitness for public office. A man who abuses women is not exactly showing deep respect for half his constituency. Thus, the argument goes, he is fair game for a rabid press corps. When all else fails, we invoke the hazy issue of "character," which of course can be trotted out whenever anyone does something we find faintly disreputable.

The press acts as "mother superior, party boss, neighborhood snoop and cop on the beat," as *Time* reporter Margaret Carlson put it. We are not quite comfortable with our new power and often deny it, even to ourselves. But now that we have whetted the public's appetite for the seamy stuff, the forces of capitalism have prevailed: If one outlet doesn't provide it, someone else will, making it impossible for everyone else to ignore. It is part of the new pandering, of our desperate attempts to "connect" with readers, even if that means shredding our standards in the process.

Why has there been such a booming market in sleaze journalism in recent years? One answer is that the culture has changed. Divorce was once deemed a major liability for candidates such as Adlai Stevenson and

Nelson Rockefeller. But in the '70s, when Maryland Governor Marvin Mandel left his wife, Bootsie, in the state mansion and moved in with his girlfriend, the press treated it as an entertaining soap opera. Ronald Reagan, our first divorced president, preached the values of family, yet he was barely acquainted with some of his grandchildren.

A generation after Ingrid Bergman was ostracized for having a baby out of wedlock, young actresses blab about it in *People* magazine, while Murphy Brown becomes an unwed mother on TV. Public figures from Betty Ford and Kitty Dukakis to Carrie Fisher write tell-all books about their struggles with booze or drugs, then hawk them on television. Oprah Winfrey and Roseanne Arnold share horrid tales of child abuse with the world. When the president of the National Organization for Women, Patricia Ireland, reveals that she is living a double life—she has been married to a Miami man for a quarter-century but also has a female companion in Washington—it is treated as a one-day story. Yawn. Next confession, please.

The tabloidization of the American media has created a thriving market for such gossip. The voyeuristic talk shows of the early '80s have spawned such sensational programs as "A Current Affair," "Hard Copy," "Inside Edition" and "Geraldo," which have a seemingly insatiable need for slimy stories and are willing to pay big bucks to get them. The lowlife values of such programs quickly spread through the media food chain.

In such an atmosphere, it is increasingly difficult for "respectable" publications to ignore the antics of their swamp-dwelling colleagues. Gossip becomes news, if news is what people are talking about. "MADONNA & AIDS—The Material Girl . . . fights rumors she's HIV positive," blares the cover of *Entertainment Weekly*. Readers come to expect their newspaper to keep them up to speed on who's doing what to whom, and editors, who can ill afford to lose more readers, try to oblige with gossip columns and people pages. Standards of proof fall by the wayside. The elite papers enjoy the best of both worlds, professing their devotion to high-minded principles while passing on the latest junk from trash TV or the tabloids—all in the name of sociological observation, of course.

In an era when candidates are packaged in thirty-second ads, it was probably inevitable that the mores of celebrity journalism would spread to the world of politics and business. Marla Maples appears on "PrimeTime Live." Maples and Donna Rice get big contracts from No

Excuses jeans. Jessica Hahn appears nude in *Playboy* and becomes a regular on the Howard Stern show. Al Sharpton gets decked by Roy Innis on Morton Downey, Jr.'s, show. G. Gordon Liddy gets his own radio program. Ollie North writes a book and does the talk show circuit. After each scandal a dozen media outlets are salivating for the inside story. For newspaper editors to look the other way is to ignore reality.

Still, the public is often appalled at our insensitivity in trampling people's privacy. Even many journalists were upset about the way in which Arthur Ashe was forced to reveal that he had AIDS in the spring of 1992. Some have described it as a "medical outing." Doug Smith, a *USA Today* reporter who had known Ashe since high school and had coauthored a book with him, asked the former tennis star about a source's tip that Ashe had AIDS. Ashe would not confirm or deny it, and *USA Today*, which does not publish information from anonymous sources, did not run the story. But when the managing editor for sports, Gene Policinski, told Ashe the paper would continue to pursue the subject, Ashe called a press conference the next day.

"I didn't commit any crimes and I'm not running for public office," said Ashe, who died nine months later. "I should be able to reserve the right to keep things like that private." Policinski's response was that Ashe, the first black man to win Wimbledon, was "one of the most famous athletes of the twentieth century" and that "any time a public figure is ill, it's news. . . . We have no special zone of treatment for AIDS. It's a disease." Of course, the fact that it was this particular disease, with its ever-present questions about how the virus was contracted, made it a far bigger story than would have been the case had Ashe had an inoperable brain tumor.

While I sympathized with Ashe and his family, I was even more troubled by what can only be termed a conspiracy of silence about his disease. It turned out that dozens of journalists, from *Newsweek* sportswriter Frank Deford to "Today" show host Bryant Gumbel, knew for years that Ashe had AIDS but kept the information from the public, citing either friendship or a concern for Ashe's privacy. This serves to reinforce people's worst suspicions about the press, that we keep secrets because we have grown too close to the people we cover.

"As rough and unruly and uncomfortable as it is, this is what we're supposed to be doing," says Geneva Overholser, editor of *The Des Moines Register*. "If you think about the things that are most difficult for people—rape victims' names or Arthur Ashe's AIDS—this is how society makes change. Our role is not to suppress difficult information. We've got to be willing to offend people."

In the political world, there's simply no way to keep private tribulations out of the public arena. There are too many magazines, too many cable stations, too many talk shows. Mud gets slung at election time by opposing candidates, personal enemies, disgruntled ex-girlfriends. A tabloid runs a screaming headline or someone shouts it on TV and suddenly everyone is joining the pack. An official denial merely makes it more likely that the story will meet the definition of news: "Candidate Smith denied today that he was a vicious wife-abuser. . . ."

My own view is that people who run for office give up any reasonable expectation of privacy. If they don't want their dirty laundry aired they should probably choose another profession. Besides, readers are more sophisticated than some editors believe. Most people can judge for themselves whether salacious allegations are germane or garbage.

The current era of media morality began in 1974, when Representative Wilbur Mills was caught carousing with stripper Fanne Foxe at the Tidal Basin. Two years later, *The Washington Post* discovered that another powerful congressman, Wayne Hays, had placed on the House payroll Elizabeth Ray, a non-typing secretary whose chief qualification was servicing Hays.

Those stories met the standard that prevailed from the mid-'70s until the spring of 1987: The private life of a politician is fair game only if it affects his public performance. But sexual gossip somehow became fit to print when Gary Hart was gearing up to run for president. Hart was "haunted by rumors of womanizing," as *Newsweek* put it a month before he launched his campaign. He was constantly asked about the rumors on the campaign trail, and his denials provided the justification for still more stories about whether he could keep his pants on. "HART: I'M NO WOMANIZER," shouted the *New York Post*. No one had demonstrated how this was connected to Hart's public performance; it was, in the new lingo, a question of character.

The rules changed, probably forever, when five *Miami Herald* reporters staked out Hart's Washington town house and saw Donna Rice emerge in the early-morning hours. The press offered plenty of rationales for its behavior: Hart was running for president. He had a pattern of compulsive womanizing. He had dared reporters to put a tail on him. Once the Donna Rice saga broke, the tabloids swooped in for the kill. Rice's friend, Lynn Armandt, sold the notorious *Monkey Business* photos of Hart and Rice to the *National Enquirer* for a reported $100,000, and later peddled the story to *People.*

The former Colorado senator denied the affair, prompting *Washington Post* reporter Paul Taylor's famous question: "Have you ever committed adultery?" Hart withdrew from the race the morning after Taylor told a top campaign aide of the *Post*'s evidence about Hart's long-term involvement with a Washington woman. Hart complained of "character assassination," but his conduct, in the blinding glare of a presidential campaign, was little short of reckless. Would it have been better if the country had learned of that reckless streak after he was in the White House?

Suddenly, it seemed, all bets were off. A month after Hart was driven from the race, the Cleveland *Plain Dealer* reported that Ohio Governor Richard Celeste had had three extramarital affairs. The paper's editor, William Woestendiek, justified the story by saying that Celeste had lied at a news conference about having "a Gary Hart–type problem" and that this was "another case of someone arrogantiy trying to deceive the public."

In 1988, San Antonio newspapers reported that the city's mayor, Henry Cisneros, was having an extramarital affair with Linda Medlar, the estranged wife of a prominent local jeweler. Cisneros, who would later become President Clinton's HUD secretary, had admitted the affair in off-the-record conversations with local editors and reporters and asked them to keep it out of the papers. His final term as mayor would expire the following year, and no future campaign was hanging in the balance.

Linda O'Connell, then the editor of the weekly *San Antonio Current,* says she was "astonished" that the city's two dailies, the *Light* and the *Express-News,* didn't publish the news until she did. She says readers constantly asked about the affair. "I went to a rehearsal of the Methodist Church choir and was buttonholed in the robing room by a couple of members who asked, 'When are you going to write the story about Henry Cisneros?' "

When the mayor posed for the cover of *Texas Monthly* in a bed with his new baby, O'Connell says, "I felt like he was starting to ask for it. If he was willing to use his personal life as political currency, then I felt that keeping his personal life out of the news coverage was inappropriate."

Sometimes gossip becomes news even if nobody prints it. In 1988 the political world was filled with speculation that various news organizations were about to publish the rumor that George Bush once had an affair with a woman on his vice presidential staff, whose name was known to every political reporter in Washington. On October 19, 1988, the stock market dropped forty points in one hour on a rumor that *The Washington Post* was about to go with the Bush rumor. Ben Bradlee took the unusual step of announcing publicly that the *Post* had no plans to run such a story, and the market calmed down. It would take another four years for this particular rumor to explode into print.

In 1990, Republican Jon Grunseth was within striking distance of winning the Minnesota governorship when the Minneapolis *Star Tribune* helped knock him out of the race. Three weeks before the election, the paper reported allegations by two women that Grunseth swam nude with them at a party nine years earlier, when they were thirteen and fourteen. Another woman, Tamara Taylor, said she had had a nine-year affair with Grunseth (who admitted the relationship but said it had occurred between his first and second marriages). Grunseth insisted the skinny-dipping allegation was untrue, but the damage had been done.

Grunseth says the *Star Tribune* and its reporter, Allen Short, were "out of control." But Short says, "I didn't judge Jon Grunseth. I reported some allegations. . . . The voters judged Mr. Grunseth." Of course, for a journalist to say that he simply "reported some allegations" is to sidestep responsibility for the power of headlines to damage careers. Disgruntled people make allegations all the time; it is the press's duty to sift and evaluate them before giving them currency. The Grunseth story may well have been justified, but it remained unclear why the women involved had waited nine years to exact their revenge. What is perfectly clear is that newspapers are often used as conduits for personal and political vendettas.

The debate erupted again in 1992 when *The Seattle Times* ended Senator Brock Adams's reelection bid with a devastating report on how he had fondled and harassed eight young women in incidents dating to the early '70s. One woman charged that Adams had drugged and raped her. What made the story wildly controversial is that none of the women would allow their names to be used.

Some esteemed commentators (mostly male) harrumphed at the flinging of such serious charges by nameless accusers. Adams's press secretary, Pamela McKinney, condemned the story as "journalistic terrorism." In truth, however, it was not a close call.

Four years earlier, a longtime family friend, Kari Tupper, had accused Adams of drugging and molesting her at his home, which the senator denied. Several women later contacted *The Seattle Times* to say they had had similar experiences with the Democratic senator, and *Times* reporters later found others. The paper pursued the story for three and a half years and amassed a convincing amount of detail.

Editor Michael Fancher decided to publish the story after most of the women signed statements and agreed to testify if Adams sued the paper. It was a gutsy call of the kind that few editors would have made a decade earlier, when sexual harassment was not taken all that seriously.

Most sex stories fall into a murkier gray zone, often turning on one person's word against another's. In countless seminars and op-ed pieces, editors insist they have well-developed standards on when it is appropriate to intrude on the private lives of public figures. But they don't, really. If the name is big enough, the story titillating enough, the gossip loud enough, the whispers invariably find their way into print. We stagger from one sordid episode to the next, making up the rules as we go along.

Perhaps no single event better dramatized the new, no-holds-barred attitude than the publication of Kitty Kelley's catty biography of Nancy Reagan in the spring of 1991. Hundreds of newspapers and magazines trumpeted Kelley's thinly documented allegations, and not one knew whether they were true. It was a book, and the mere fact that it was between hard covers gave the editors enough of a fig leaf to get the stuff into print. Besides, the target was the Wicked Witch of the East Wing, and most editors were willing to believe the worst.

Under the banner headline "SEX AND LIES," the New York *Daily News* breathlessly announced: "Nancy Reagan was sexually promiscuous, lied about her age and may have used pregnancy to trap Ronald Reagan into marriage—all in an iron willed pursuit of status and Hollywood stardom, an explosive new book alleges." The *News* followed with a second banner, "BEDTIME FOR RONZO," while the *New York Post* dished up five stories on Nancy's supposed exploits.

Matthew Storin, then the *News'* managing editor, says the book was "like lighting a match in a room full of dynamite. . . . I think readers understand it is being presented as a book and not as something the paper went out and reported. She obviously is picking up a lot of material from secondhand sources and people who have axes to grind."

Such behavior was hardly out of character for the *Daily News*. But the journalistic world was stunned to see *The New York Times* acting the same way. The *Times* splashed Kelley's innuendo-laden account on its Sunday front page with an almost total lack of skepticism. It was hard to imagine the *Times* of old treating the biography as fit to print, let alone giving page-one display to the juiciest bits. But in the five years since Max Frankel became executive editor, the *Times* had been trying to take a more freewheeling approach to the news.

Maureen Dowd, a gifted stylist assigned to the White House, wrote that the Kelley book "could shatter forever" the Reagan myth through "allegations of scandalous sexual behavior" by the woman who "ruled the White House with a Gucci-clad fist." Kelley, she added, had a "reputation as a giant-killer."

Dowd recounted Kelley's assertions—that Nancy Reagan had an affair with Frank Sinatra, that Ronald Reagan slept with an eighteen-year-old girl while he was governor of California, that the Reagans once smoked marijuana, that the former president loved anti-gay and racist humor—without addressing the question of proof. By contrast, *USA Today* questioned how the onetime "trash queen" knew of "the supposed affair" between Nancy and Frank. *The Washington Post* described the book as the "revenge" of Nancy Reagan's enemies, "plus some hazily substantiated gossip and free-floating bits of innuendo."

The *Times'* handling of the book was almost a comedy of errors. Dowd, who was traveling with President Bush in California, was called back to Washington to write the piece; she arrived home at midnight and worked all night to meet a noon deadline. Dowd says she believed another reporter was writing an accompanying profile of Kelley that would raise the obvious questions about her reputation, but the other piece was canceled.

The *Times* had taken a gamble. Unlike those of most newspapers, its editors had refused to sign an embargo agreement with Kelley's publisher, Simon and Schuster, in exchange for an advance copy. When the publisher nevertheless slipped a *Times* editor a bootlegged copy, the paper was free to publish twenty-four hours before the embargo— but was also forced into a rush job.

"You can either have it for a week and check it out, or feel high-minded and not sign any embargo and not be able to check it out to any real degree," Dowd says. "They wanted to treat it as news and beat everyone else."

There was also confusion about what kind of piece the editors wanted. "I was told specifically not to do an analysis, or a book review, or a light piece," Dowd says. "If I had known there would be no profile of her, I certainly would have done the story completely differently." But Dowd dismisses the resulting criticism as "much too sanctimonious. Our readers know who Kitty Kelley is. Everyone knows Kitty Kelley writes trashy biographies."

Though several top editors read the piece before publication, no one thought to add the obvious caveats about Kelley's reputation, and management was embarrassed by the critical reaction. Max Frankel later told his staff that the Kitty Kelley piece was a "mistake" that "did not live up to our standards." Dowd was furious when she heard this, and managing editor Joseph Lelyveld had to send her flowers as a peace offering.

If tabloid values can tarnish an august publication like the *Times,* tabloid television can be equally powerful in propelling a lurid story onto the front pages. That's what happened with the tale of Senator Charles Robb, a former beauty queen and a nude encounter in a hotel room—a story that *The Washington Post* initially refused to publish. That reluctance quickly vanished, however, when the *Post* found itself competing with a flashy NBC show called "Exposé."

Chuck Robb had been the subject of a spate of stories about his personal life during his 1988 Senate campaign. They involved allegations that Robb, while governor of Virginia, had attended numerous beach parties where cocaine was used. Ten people with whom Robb had socialized were later indicted on drug charges. One of the frequent partygoers was Tai Collins, a former Miss Virginia/USA.

In 1990, Collins met with two *Post* reporters, Donald Baker and Thomas Heath, over a period of months. She said she had had an affair with Robb, and that she was revealing the relationship in an effort to end what she described as intimidation by Robb's aides and attorneys.

In an interview with the *Post,* the senator acknowledged the rendezvous with Collins, which had occurred in 1984 in a New York hotel room. They had shared a bottle of wine, and she had given him a massage after he had disrobed. Robb denied that they had had sex, but admitted placing himself in an "essentially compromising position" and said, "I know the whole thing looks bad."

Robb's acknowledgment might have been grounds for a story, at least by post–Gary Hart standards. Ever since he married Lyndon John-son's daughter, Robb had always presented himself to the public as a jut-jawed, milk-drinking, ex-Marine family man. His assignation with Tai Collins went straight to the character issue. There was also the question of credibility. Was anyone really supposed to believe that Robb got a nude back rub from a stunning blonde model and quietly departed?

The reporters had other information—Collins's charge that Robb's staff was pressuring her to keep quiet, and a private investigator's evidence about the Virginia Beach drug parties. But the heart of the story was the alleged affair. Although the reporters had been told that the sex story would be printed if they could nail it down, their editors had second thoughts. Ben Bradlee was particularly uncomfortable with the Tai Collins tale.

"Ben's position was that Robb wasn't going anywhere, he was just one of a hundred senators, but if he ever ran for president, we'd use that story," says one staffer. This person says Bradlee even communi-cated that message to Robb through an intermediary. (This would have been consistent with Bradlee's decision not to publish the story on Hart's other paramour after the senator withdrew from the '88 presiden-tial race.) Bradlee denies sending a message to Robb, saying, "The problem that story presented me with was, What was the news? It was just someone who said he smoked a lot of dope and had a girlfriend. I don't think we're in the business of publishing things that we can't prove one way or another."

Managing editor Len Downie, meanwhile, was seeking a higher moral purpose. "The thing Len was interested in was the abuse of power," the source says. "He wanted to be able to say that Chuck Robb was fucking this beauty queen while his state police stood guard outside. The second paragraph would say, 'While we don't think there's anything wrong with his fucking the beauty queen, this is an outrageous use of government gasoline.' " A story to that effect was drafted, but it didn't fly.

"It was a classic one-source situation," Downie says. "There were questions about veracity." But even "assuming everything she said was accurate, when does a public person's private life become newsworthy? Most of the time, it is only if it involves misuse of public office, affects their public performance, breaks the law, or involves their veracity or their character in a way that voters need to know." The last point, of course, is inherently subjective.

Baker and Heath argued that if the *Post* didn't break the story, someone else would and they would wind up chasing it. Still, after a five-month investigation, the editors decided not to publish anything.

The reporters' fears were justified. Their key source, private investigator Billy Franklin, shared his material with NBC. Four months later, in the spring of 1991, "Exposé" was ready to broadcast the allegations. Robb, in one of the great public relations blunders of all time, tried to discredit the NBC program before it aired, hiring libel lawyers and releasing a tough letter he had sent to Tom Brokaw. That gave the *Post*, which did not want to be beaten in its own backyard, a hook to rush its earlier material into print.

Robb compounded the error the next day when his aides released a two-and-a-half-hour videotape of his interview with NBC producer Marion Goldin. All kinds of gossip that never made it onto the program—such as allegations that Robb had shared a hot tub with two prostitutes—were now served up for media consumption.

The original story simply "did not meet our standards," Downie says. But the NBC report "created a news peg that we felt we shouldn't ignore."

NBC did come up with some new revelations. One witness said he saw a woman snort cocaine at a party while kneeling in front of Robb, who has denied any knowledge of drug use. NBC played a tape of Robb's chief of staff predicting that Billy Franklin, the man digging into Robb's personal life, would have problems with the IRS and the Justice Department. Collins had given the *Post* a copy of the tape, but it was garbled; NBC used audio-enhancing equipment to decipher it. The new details (plus the airing of some cheesecake photos of Collins) gave national prominence to what had been a local story.

Tai Collins later took the bimbo route pioneered by Jessica Hahn, former congressional wife Rita Jenrette and others. She posed nude for *Playboy* and, while promoting the pictorial, came up with one of those conspiracy theories frequently hurled at newspapers. Collins declared on "Larry King Live" that she'd "heard" that Katharine Graham had killed the original *Post* story after getting a call from an old friend, Lady Bird Johnson, the senator's mother-in-law.

The chairman of the Washington Post Company was upset. There had been no such call, Graham said. She had never discussed the Robb story with the editors, had never interfered with any story in her twenty-eight years at the paper's helm. She called a Larry King producer to complain. Hey, lady, she was told, this is live television. People can say whatever they want. "OK," Graham replied, "I'll write an op-ed piece saying that anybody can lie about someone on TV and no one can do anything about it."

Larry King quickly called Katharine Graham. He agreed to read a statement from her on the air that night, calling Tai Collins's account untrue. But Graham declined to appear on the show to discuss the controversy. "Can you imagine?" she asked friends in her high-toned accent. "Me and that Collins woman?"

Ten days after the Kitty Kelley fiasco, *The New York Times* published the most vilified story in its 140-year history

The frenzy had been building since Easter weekend, when William Kennedy Smith was accused of raping a young woman he had met at a Palm Beach night spot called Au Bar. It was the quintessential tabloid tale, featuring sex, violence and the Kennedys. There was the unsightly spectacle of Ted Kennedy waking his son and his nephew around midnight to go bar-hopping. The allegations that the senator had ducked the police. The account of Michele Cassone, a friend of the accuser, who said Kennedy had walked around the Palm Beach estate in his nightshirt and nothing else.

"TEDDY'S SEXY ROMP," the *New York Post* roared.

But in the end it was the stately *Times* that soiled its petticoats with a vile, almost leering profile of Patricia Bowman, the twenty-nine-year-old woman who accused Willie Smith of raping her. Bowman had asked the press not to identify her, but this was a case in which the normal rules of journalistic behavior were checked at the Palm Beach airport. The public's right to know became a fig leaf for the press's right to titillate.

It was hard for reporters to remain aloof in a supercharged atmosphere in which tabloid television producers were brandishing big bucks for interviews. "A Current Affair" paid Cassone $1,000 and later filmed her cursing and biting correspondent Steve Dunleavy after he produced some pictures of her performing oral sex. Next the program paid $40,000 for an interview with Anne Mercer, a friend of Bowman. It was a stunning display of checkbook journalism that would later help Smith's lawyers discredit Mercer's testimony. *The Star,* a supermarket tabloid, offered Bowman $100,000 for her story. Paramount Pictures, which owns the program "Hard Copy," dangled $500,000 for the film rights.

From the beginning, the klieg-light intensity surrounding the case promised to sorely test the media's long-standing practice of not identifying rape victims without their consent. There were sound reasons for this policy. Rape was perhaps the most traumatic and personal of all crimes, and the most underreported. Many more women would undoubtedly refuse to tell authorities they were raped if they knew their names would be in the local paper and their ordeal made known to friends and family. And rape was the only crime where such personal questions—what the woman was wearing, whether she was being provocative, how many men she had slept with—were directed at the victim.

To be sure, there was a growing debate in press circles about whether this approach was outdated. Perhaps, the argument went, the media were adding to the stigma surrounding rape by withholding the names of the victims. But virtually all news organizations had stuck with the policy.

The argument had been rekindled by the 1989 attack on the Central Park jogger, the most intensely publicized rape case in New York City history. Every reporter in town knew the jogger's name, and any citizen could have gone to State Supreme Court in Manhattan and looked it up in case file 4762/89.

But middle-class journalists identified with the woman, who had certainly not asked to become a public figure. She was from a devout Catholic family in Upper St. Clair, Pennsylvania, had graduated Phi Beta Kappa from Wellesley College, earned a master's degree at Yale and worked for the corporate finance department at Salomon Brothers. The press chose to protect what was left of her privacy. Only the *Amsterdam News,* a black Manhattan newspaper, published the jogger's name in a bizarre bit of racial gamesmanship. Many blacks were angry that the white media were shielding the jogger's identity while the teenage suspects from Harlem were decried as a "wolfpack," although they had been convicted of nothing. Still, these kids had been arrested and charged by police. Suspects in a serious crime cannot be afforded the same privacy rights as a woman who is nearly beaten to death.

The debate flared anew the following year when *The Des Moines Register,* in a series that would win the Pulitzer Prize for public service, graphically detailed the ordeal of Nancy Ziegenmeyer, a rape victim from Grinnell, Iowa. Ziegenmeyer contacted the *Register* after reading a column about rape by Geneva Overholser, one of the few women running a major newspaper.

Overholser overruled male editors when they tried to remove some of the starkest details of the attack on Ziegenmeyer, such as changing "after he had ejaculated" to "when he had finished." Unlike other rape victims, however, Ziegenmeyer had voluntarily stepped into the media spotlight, which led to the inevitable "Donahue" appearance and TV movie contract. Even Geneva Overholser doesn't publish the names of Iowa rape victims without their consent.

The Willie Smith case brought forth a torrent of First Amendment hogwash from editors who had never bothered to agonize about naming rape victims before. Now that the suspect was a Kennedy, they were suddenly mesmerized by the issue. They didn't dare identify victims in their own towns, but perhaps it would be all right to name this faraway woman because "everyone in Palm Beach" supposedly knew who she was. In fact, plenty of local residents did not know Patricia Bowman's name, and publication would end any chance that she could move to another community and start a new life.

"If she wants to drive into Miami and buy a blouse," said Jerry Nachman of the *New York Post,* "I don't think it's fair that she hands the sales clerk a credit card and is asked what it was like to be allegedly raped by a Kennedy."

But the coverage quickly sank to its lowest common denominator. First the *Sunday Mirror,* a London tabloid owned by Robert Maxwell, published Bowman's name. Then she was named by the *Globe,* a supermarket tabloid based in Boca Raton. The *Globe* was run by Wendy Henry, who had been fired two years earlier as editor of *The People,* a British tabloid, after publishing pictures of a cancer-ravaged Sammy Davis, Jr., and of eight-year-old Prince William relieving himself in a park. Yet it was Wendy Henry who would set the tone for the American media by naming Bowman and running her high school yearbook picture.

"Kennedy Rape Gal Exposed," the *Globe* headline said. The tabloid was charged with violating a Florida law against naming rape victims, but a state judge would rule the law unconstitutional.

The outing of the "rape gal" didn't take long to reach the loftier heights of the news business. NBC, using the *Globe*'s action as a weak excuse, decided to broadcast Bowman's name to millions of viewers.

I spoke to Michael Gartner, the president of NBC News, half an hour before Tom Brokaw went on the air. Gartner had debated the rape issue for years and had plenty of journalistic rationales. "My first real duty is to inform my viewers. . . . Who she is is material in this," Gartner said. "This has become a national story. You try to give viewers as many facts as you can and let them make up their minds. I worry that some people will say, 'You did this to hype your show.' That's the last reason I'm doing it. I expect others will not believe that."

Gartner was right on this last point. NBC's report added nothing to anyone's understanding of the case. It was simply a story about the name controversy, with no reporting about Bowman or her allegations. But it was certain to touch off a chain reaction. I fully expected the *New York Post* or the *Daily News* to use the broadcast as an excuse to name Bowman, but their editors insisted they would not. When I called *The New York Times,* however, assistant managing editor Allan Siegal told me the paper would publish Bowman's name the next morning. Half an hour later, he called back to say it was still up in the air. An hour after that, he said the *Times* would indeed use the name.

"There's no decision left for us to make when that point is moot," Siegal said. "Once her name has become a household word, then however we may feel about her privacy, it's no longer in our hands." The *Times* editors were blaming it all on NBC, rather than offering any defense of their decision.

The April 17, 1991, edition of *The New York Times* contained more than just a story naming Patty Bowman. The front-page piece, by Fox Butterfield and Mary Tabor, was a scurrilous portrait of a woman with "a little wild streak," as one of her acquaintances put it. The article was filled with anonymous accusers, dripping with innuendo. The unspoken message throughout: She asked for it.

Bowman "gave birth to a daughter by a local man she did not marry," the story said. She "received seventeen tickets for speeding, careless driving or being involved in an accident between 1982 and 1990." She "moved sharply up the economic scale ten years ago after her divorced mother married a wealthy industrialist" following an extramarital affair. She had "a poor academic record" in high school. A friend said that "she and her friends liked to drive fast cars, go to parties and skip classes. . . . During the 1980s the woman also frequented Palm Beach's expensive bars and nightclubs." An acquaintance "who frequents some of the same nightclubs as Ms. Bowman" said that "she liked to drink and have fun with the ne'er-do-wells in cafe society."

To top it off, a bit of peeping-tom journalism: "Her own house in Jupiter appears empty, with the blinds drawn, except in her daughter's room. There, on a shelf, are children's books, including a copy of 'Babar's Anniversary Album' and 'Two Minute Bible Stories.' "

In the thunderous condemnation that followed, perhaps no comment spoke louder than that of Dan Schwartz, editor of the *National Enquirer,* which had refused to print Bowman's name. "I think we took a more ethical stand than they did," he declared.

It was a breathtaking lack of news judgment. Jerry Nachman said the *Times* story carried "the implication of 'she's a really bad girl, and her mom was virtually a slut.' " Anna Quindlen, a *Times* columnist who criticized the story in print, told me the piece was "really deplorable" and contrasted the paper's naming of Bowman with its earlier decision to shield the Wellesley-educated Central Park jogger.

"If you're raped by a bunch of black teenagers, you get protected, and if you're raped by someone who is rich and powerful, you get taken to the cleaners," Quindlen said.

Even some *Times* editors were appalled. Howell Raines, then the Washington bureau chief, said the story was "badly thought out, badly written and badly edited." Abe Rosenthal, the former executive editor, wrote that "it is sexual harassment to send reporters peering into the windows of a woman charging rape."

Most newspapers, including *The Washington Post,* did not publish Bowman's name. But a few—including the *Des Moines Register, Detroit Free Press, Detroit News, Louisville Courier-Journal* and *Denver Post*—played follow-the-leader by reprinting the *Times* story from its news service. Irene Nolan, managing editor of the *Courier-Journal,* said she used Bowman's name because "the Palm Beach case has reached tremendous public proportions. . . . I would do the same thing locally if there was a good case." But what makes a "good" case? The celebrity of the alleged assailant? What woman would report an assault by someone rich and powerful if she knew the result was that every facet of her life, from her high school grades to her mother's sexual activities, would be splashed on the front page?

Despite the global reach of television, NBC's broadcast of Patty Bowman's name was ephemeral, lasting only a few seconds. But a *New York Times* story had permanence; it was there in black and white, recorded for posterity in the archives, on microfilm and in computer data bases.

Fox Butterfield says he didn't identify Bowman in the story he filed and that "if it had been up to me, we wouldn't have printed her name." Still, he defends the tone of the article. "Nothing in the story we wrote was ever shown to be inaccurate," he says. "It's hard to apologize for a story that was accurate. I felt she had legitimately opened herself up for that story because she had sought publicity about herself. She hired two high-priced lawyers to handle the press, and they were making her case on the talk shows. That made it into a different story than if she was simply a rape victim. My wife, Elizabeth Mehren, wrote one of the earliest pieces about date rape because she was a victim of it. In this family we are sensitive to the question."

Senior editors at the *Times* did not understand what all the fuss was about. Soma Golden, the national editor, said the piece was "not about a wild woman drinking, driving fast and jumping into bed with men. It's as thorough a portrait as we could put together of a woman in the news."

Two days after the story appeared, more than three hundred *Times* staffers packed a ninth-floor auditorium to denounce the story in a meeting with management. Speaker after speaker accused the editors of insensitivity. One woman reporter talked about her own rape. Golden infuriated the staff when she said that some readers had seen negative connotations that weren't there, adding: "I can't account for every weird mind that reads *The New York Times*."

"The ones with weird minds are the ones who thought that was journalism," one reporter said afterward. (Golden later said she hadn't meant to dismiss all the story's critics.)

"They didn't get it," a female staffer said. "They don't understand they set it up to look like the slut asked for it. We came here because we didn't want to work for people who would run stories like that."

Nine days after the Bowman profile, the *Times* published a clarification: "The article drew no conclusions about the truth of her complaint to the police. But many readers inferred that its very publication, including her name and detailed biographical material about her and her family, suggested that The Times was challenging her account. No such challenge was intended, and The Times regrets that some parts of the article reinforced such inferences. The article should have explicitly asserted that nothing in the woman's known background could resolve the disputed testimony about her encounter with Mr. Smith."

In an accompanying news story, Max Frankel was quoted as saying: "This is a crisis because many people feel The Times betrayed its standards."

Frankel, who had not spoken to the press for two weeks, refused to discuss the story in a telephone interview. The executive editor of *The New York Times,* whose reporters demand answers from the world every day, was retreating behind a no-comment stance. And although the *Times* stopped printing the woman's name in subsequent stories, the editors refused to admit that they had backed away from their earlier decision. It would take another seven months for them to acknowledge that they had bowed to the public outcry and stopped naming Bowman.

As the uproar continued, Golden promised that the *Times* would produce a profile of Willie Smith just as thorough as the one of Bowman. But reporters digging into Smith's background ran into a major problem. They found women who said they had been sexually assaulted by Smith, but would not allow their names to be used. Editors would not publish such serious charges without attribution. The dilemma was whether to run a favorable profile of Willie Smith, even while knowing there was another side to the story.

The *Times* piece, which ran inside the paper on a Saturday in May, was largely laudatory. "For many friends and acquaintances, Mr. Smith is a man of gentleness and humor . . . a calm and easygoing young man . . . a good listener and a thoughtful conversationalist," Felicity Barringer and Michael Wines wrote.

They mentioned the existence of "rumors and gossip column items that ask whether the Palm Beach incident was part of a pattern of aggressiveness toward women in private. But all efforts by reporters for The New York Times to trace such rumors to their sources ended in vague and unverifiable accusation, hearsay or inconclusive silence." A far cry from the vague accusations about Bowman and her wild streak.

"It was the worst assignment of my career, bar none," Barringer says. "The people who were likely to know something were women he had dated or was in close proximity to, and they were the least likely to talk. You're asking a whole series of questions and you both know you're leading up to asking, 'Did you sleep with the guy?' and 'What was it like?' It's torture."

Washington Post reporter Mary Jordan took a similar tack, quoting friends who described Smith as "charming," "sweet" and "unassuming . . . soft-spoken, caring, a good listener . . . a quiet, gentle, considerate man." But Jordan also hinted at a darker side: "Others say that when Smith drinks, he often drinks heavily, and his personality can change from quiet and thoughtful to aggressive and difficult." She cited "a former girlfriend who said she broke up with Smith because of his behavior when he drank."

Three women told the *Post* that Smith had tried to rape them, but they wouldn't allow their names to be used or agree to come forward in case of a lawsuit. Len Downie would not allow their accounts to be published. It was, he says, a matter of "elementary fairness and libel. It raises real difficult questions about the paper's liability. What if they're not telling the truth? How do we prove it if we get sued?" At the same time, Downie says, "We made clear there were women who raised questions about his behavior."

Florida prosecutors later released affidavits from three women who said they had been sexually assaulted by Smith. Barringer and Jordan had each talked to one of the women. All were later barred from testifying at Smith's trial.

One of the women, a Georgetown University graduate student, had given her account to the *National Enquirer,* another indication of how the supermarket tabloids had taken over the story ("Second Woman's Startling Claim: I Was Raped by the Same Kennedy Kid"). It was the *Enquirer,* which had granted the woman anonymity, that put prosecutors in touch with her. In her affidavit, the woman alleged that Smith had raped her after a party: "I really thought he would hurt me. . . . I could see it in his face . . . he [had] such a . . . ferocious . . . almost animal-like kind of look to him." It was a far different portrait than the *Times* and the *Post* had painted.

"I was not surprised when the depositions came out," Felicity Barringer says. "If someone is not willing to go on the record, I wouldn't go with it. The business of anonymous accusations is a very difficult thing. I did not have a problem with the paper's decision on that.

"I'm a woman," she says. "Having seen what women in general go through when they bring rape charges, do I have any right to ask them to put themselves on the line? For what, my story? The greater god of truth? It's a very individual decision."

Smith's trial turned into a three-ring media circus, a sort of national exercise in voyeurism. Five hundred reporters descended on Palm Beach, where the courtroom was so small that all but a handful had to watch the proceedings on the tube like everyone else. During the trial, carried live on CNN, Bowman's face was barely hidden by an electronic blue blob. Her name occasionally slipped through the censor's delayed bleep. The press was having it both ways, proclaiming its honor while peeking through the judicial blinds.

Outside the courtroom, some reporters dropped the last semblances of restraint. "A Current Affair" staged a reenactment of the alleged crime and assembled a mock jury to score the proceedings. *USA Today* ran as many as eight stories a day. The tabloids went wild.

Once the judge barred the testimony of the other women, it was Smith's word against Bowman's. And Bowman's story had some obvious inconsistencies, such as why she had taken off her panty hose to walk on the beach at 3:00 A.M. with a man she had met less than two hours earlier. Smith was acquitted in seventy-seven minutes. The *New York Post* served up this suitably leering postscript: "QUICKIE FOR WILLIE."

The week after the verdict, the woman who had fought so long to preserve her anonymity succumbed to the lure of television. Patty Bowman agreed to shed her blue blob and appear with Diane Sawyer on "PrimeTime Live," just as Marla Maples had done during the height of the Trump affair. Freed from the need to shield her identity, every newspaper in America printed Bowman's name and picture the morning before the broadcast.

During the interview, Sawyer asked Bowman about the *Times* article that listed the titles on her daughter's bookshelf.

"Wonderful little paper," Bowman said sarcastically. "The nation's most reputable paper, who stands outside a two-year-old's bedroom window. . . . Now that's news that's fit to print."

Time after time, the press is assailed for being too quick to publish sleazy information, especially at election time. In the fall of 1992, however, *The Washington Post* was criticized for exercising restraint on just such a story.

Rumors had circulated for years that Senator Bob Packwood of Oregon was making improper advances toward women who worked with him, but *The Oregonian,* the state's largest newspaper, proved almost comically inept in pursuing them. In March 1992, former Packwood aide Julie Williamson told an *Oregonian* columnist, Steve Duin, that the senator had kissed her and tried to pull off her clothes more than twenty years earlier. But Williamson would not allow her name to be used, and when Duin wrote about the incident, he described Packwood only as a "Northwest politician." Three weeks later, Packwood abruptly kissed Roberta Ulrich, the paper's sixty-four-year-old Washington correspondent, after a routine interview about the Endangered Species Act. Ulrich was mortified and told two of her bosses, but the paper's top editor was never notified. Another *Oregonian* reporter assigned to look into the harassment rumors soon gave up. The paper's chief political reporter was busy with the daily warfare of Packwood's reelection campaign. *The Oregonian* endorsed Packwood for a fifth term.

Florence Graves, a free-lance investigative journalist, was pursuing the same rumors on assignment for *Vanity Fair,* but they parted company in June when the magazine refused to guarantee in writing that it would cover her legal bills in the event of a libel suit. In September, Graves approached the *Post* with her evidence—much as Mike Binstein had with the Keating Five story—and this time the paper was more receptive to joining forces with an outsider. Graves and Charles Shepard, an investigative reporter recently hired from the *Charlotte Observer,* found several more women who said Packwood had made unwanted advances toward them. The reporters kept pressing them to go on the record; they knew an election-eve story based on statements by anonymous accusers would lack credibility, and that Packwood might refuse to respond.

When Graves and Shepard asked to interview Packwood on October 23, the senator, locked in a tight race, stalled for six crucial days. The chess game was on. A mere denial was unlikely to derail the story at that point; Packwood needed to mount an offensive that would run out the clock until Election Day. In the days before the interview, six of the women agreed to have their names given to Packwood; four, including Julie Williamson, would be identified in print.

On October 29, five days before the election, Packwood made his move. He lied to the *Post,* denying that he had made advances toward any of the women. The reporters said they needed his final comments by the next day, but Packwood demanded more time to investigate the women, saying he didn't even remember some of them. Two days later he began sending the paper statements attacking the credibility and sexual history of three of the women. Two Packwood aides called Len Downie with further dirt on one accuser, claiming she was sexually promiscuous. This seamy counterattack presented the reporters with new allegations that had to be checked out, and the clock was ticking.

The editors had decided that the story could run no later than Sunday, November 1, for it would be unfair to level charges of this magnitude the day before the election. The *Post,* which obviously wanted to publish before the election, faced a classic dilemma. Graves and Shepard argued that the paper owed it to the voters of Oregon, and to the women involved, to try its hardest to finish the piece before the campaign ended. On October 30, the two reporters, in adjoining rooms in a Portland hotel, rose at 4:00 A.M. and spent all day revising the story and checking out Packwood's last-minute smears. But the following morning, Downie and the reporters agreed that the piece was not fit to print; too much reporting, editing, and lawyering still had to be done. Some of the women involved were angry. They had risked their reputations by allowing their names to be given to Packwood, and they felt betrayed.

When the *Post*'s story was finally published on November 22, three weeks after Packwood's reelection, it touched off a firestorm in Oregon. Although Packwood withdrew his denials, apologized for his conduct, and checked into an alcohol treatment center, many voters felt they had been cheated. Some were furious at the *Post* for holding up the story. The inevitable conspiracy charge surfaced, with critics saying that *Post* editors had delayed the piece because they liked Packwood and his moderate brand of Republicanism—neatly ignoring the fact that the paper had just plunged its "friend" into a career-threatening crisis. "Our decision was based on the fact that we were far from ready," Downie told *The Oregonian*. Packwood held on for three more years until finally resigning in 1995 in the face of certain expulsion.

One has to wonder whether the decision might have been different had the subject been Marion Barry, rather than a lawmaker three thousand miles away. Or whether the paper would have been quite so cautious if the allegations had not been sexual in nature. Sex remains the supercharged subject that drives editors batty, the tricky topic for which we always seem to be making up new rules as we go along. When it comes to reporting on sex and public officials, the *Post* discovered, even caution can be controversial.

8

Out of the Closet

The toughest decision I've ever faced on whether to write a story involved homosexuality. The issue was the outing of a senior Pentagon official. I tried to steer a middle course—to write about the orchestrated campaign in the gay community to discredit the man and how news organizations were wrestling with the dilemma. I never planned to use his name.

The problem with doing such a story, of course, is that you feed the rumor mill, touching off a guessing game among readers about who the person is. But the alternative is a head-in-the-sand approach that ignores a highly public controversy by pretending it doesn't exist.

I will not name the former official here, although anyone with access to a library or computerized data base could look it up in the Jack Anderson column that was distributed to six hundred newspapers. Or by finding stories that used the man's name in the *Detroit News, Philadelphia Inquirer, Oakland Tribune, Village Voice* or New York *Daily News.* Or by tracking down the August 27, 1991, edition of the *Advocate,* the national gay magazine that was the vehicle for this particular outing.

The increasingly aggressive tactics employed by gay rights groups have badly split the homosexual community. Randy Shilts, a gay reporter for the *San Francisco Chronicle* and the author of *And the Band Played On,* a best-selling book on AIDS, described outing as "lavender fascism."

"It makes gay leaders look like a bunch of bitchy queens: 'We're going to tell on you,' " said Shilts, who died from AIDS in early 1994. "It's basically punishing people by bludgeoning them with the very prejudice you say you're against."

Outing, even more than reporting on politicians' extramarital affairs, confronts the press with an insoluble dilemma. It is, without question, a hateful invasion of privacy, an attempt to manipulate journalists into "exposing" innocent people for blatant political reasons. On the other hand, if news turns on controversy, then outing may well be news—particularly if, as is usually charged, the person in the closet is hypocritical about gay rights.

Implicit in such stories is the notion that being gay is some terrible secret that must be protected at all costs. If newspapers routinely identified people as gay, some critics say, homosexuality would lose its special stigma. But that amounts to blaming the press for the lack of tolerance in American society. As long as the society imposes heavy penalties on acknowledged homosexuals—discrimination, ostracism, expulsion from the military—some men and women will continue to hide their sexual preference in ways that make them vulnerable to the terrorist tactic of outing.

Homosexuality has long been fraught with particular complexity for the press. As late as 1978, a *Tulsa World* headline would say that an Oklahoma politician who denied being gay had been accused of "Abnormal Sexuality." For years, homosexuals barely existed in the pages of family newspapers, or were discussed, with thinly disguised hostility, as "perverts." In an echo of their long institutional bias against blacks, whose affairs were barely deemed fit to print, newspapers faithfully reflected the prejudices of their times. When the federal government routinely fired gay employees in the '50s and '60s, the press paid no attention. In 1963, the front page of *The New York Times* felt compelled to warn: "Growth of Overt Homosexuality in City Provokes Wide Concern."

But the gay pride movement of the late '60s and '70s brought many people, including journalists, out of the closet. AIDS, of course, raised the stakes dramatically in the '80s. The initial failure of the government and the mainstream press to treat the epidemic as a national emergency gave rise to militant groups like ACT UP and Queer Nation, which eagerly harassed public figures in the name of homosexual rights. It also made gay journalists more aggressive, a development that by the early '90s would alter attitudes in newsrooms across America.

The attempted outing at the Pentagon was not the first time the subject had come up at *The Washington Post*. I had faced a similar dilemma a few weeks earlier. Michael Petrelis, a gay activist with Queer Nation, had staged an incident designed to out Representative Steve Gunderson of Wisconsin. Petrelis went to a gay bar in Alexandria, Virginia, and threw a drink in Gunderson's face, then called news organizations to generate coverage of the "incident."

First a Milwaukee weekly, the *Shepherd Express,* ran a story that named the politician. It was picked up by *The Capital Times* in Madison and, for one edition, *The Milwaukee Journal. The Washington Times* also ran an item on it. At that point I decided to write about the controversy without using Gunderson's name. He had a mixed voting record on gay rights, and the outing seemed to have no redeeming value beyond Petrelis's staged incident.

Gunderson later told a Wisconsin paper that members of Queer Nation are "absolute psychos" who "are willing to use every form of intimidation and threats in the book." He said the incident had taken a "major psychological toll" on him.

My concern about the guessing-game problem was heightened the day my story appeared. A reporter who sits near the *Post* library told me that an unusual number of people strolled by to look up *The Washington Times* story. Still, I thought we had handled the matter responsibly.

The distant rumblings of the Pentagon outing could already be heard around town. Petrelis had called a press conference to name the Bush administration official—waving posters with the man's picture and the words "ABSOLUTELY QUEER"—but none of the reporters who attended wrote a word. An *Advocate* flack called to peddle the forthcoming article. I sort of hoped the whole thing would go away.

Suddenly the campaign broke into the mainstream media. Jack Anderson and Dale Van Atta wrote a column naming the official, based on the *Advocate* article and their baseless speculation that he might resign. A New York television station, WPIX, broadcast his name. I started getting calls from ABC and other news organizations, asking whether *The Washington Post* planned to use the name, so they could prepare to follow. The media were, as Jerry Nachman put it, "in a headlong plunge to see who could be first to be second."

This snowballing coverage raised what I call the critical-mass question. If a supermarket tabloid writes that Senator So-and-So is gay, it's easy enough for newspapers to ignore. If a few small papers and alternative weeklies run with the story, it's a bit more difficult. If *Time, Newsweek* and the three major networks join in, it reaches a point where further resistance is silly; chances are your readers have already seen the news somewhere else.

What makes all this particularly confusing is that most editors have no real policy on outing. They instinctively dislike it, but they're willing to make exceptions. It's like reporting on politicians' love affairs—we don't do it, except when we do, and then we find a reason to justify it. It's a crazy-quilt approach that no one fully understands.

In 1990, ACT UP pasted some slogans on the campaign billboards of a well-known Oregon politician. "Closeted Gay. Living a Lie—Voting to Oppress," one said. The highway billboards were seen by thousands of commuters in downtown Portland; what was the point of suppressing the news? The *Seattle Post-Intelligencer,* two Portland TV stations and *Willamette Week,* an alternative weekly, reported the incident, using the officeholder's name. But the Portland *Oregonian* did not.

The *San Francisco Chronicle,* which generally opposes outing, reprinted the names of a rock star's daughter and a fashion designer as examples of people who have been outing targets. Editors said the names were already widely known to the public.

Hundreds of newspapers ran stories after the death of Malcolm Forbes, saying he had led a private life as a homosexual. The papers, which took their lead from a piece in *Outweek* magazine, were clearly more willing to go along because the subject was (a) famous, and (b) dead, which among other things insulated them from a libel suit.

There was a new outbreak of outing incidents in 1992. First, Queer Nation announced that the conservative head of a federal grant–making agency was a lesbian, news that was picked up by *The Philadelphia Inquirer, Los Angeles Times* and *New York Post.* (A *Post* editorial assailed the "homosexual thought police," days after the paper had abetted the outing.) Then the *Advocate* charged that Representative Jim Mc-Crery, a conservative Republican from Louisiana, was homosexual, an allegation prominently displayed by the *Shreveport Times.* McCrery strongly denied being gay, despite an affidavit from a man who claimed to be a former lover. Another gay magazine, *QW,* outed John Schlafly, whose sole claim to public attention was that he was the son of conservative activist Phyllis Schlafly. John Schlafly confirmed his homosexuality to the *San Francisco Examiner,* defending his mother and accusing some gays of "hysteria." Once a nuclear weapon of last resort, outing was becoming a commonplace tool of harassment, although its effectiveness depended on media complicity.

The *Advocate* had long opposed outing—that is, until gay author Michelangelo Signorile, who wrote the Malcolm Forbes piece, proposed the story on the Pentagon official. The article quoted two unnamed gay men as saying they had had sex with the official, and others who had seen him in a gay bar.

"It is a hateful thing to do to somebody because it disrupts their life," says Richard Rouilard, then the *Advocate*'s editor. "I do feel sympathy for him as a closeted gay man. We are about the same age. Unfortunately, the gay community cannot always be nice. We have to think of the larger issues."

The larger issue in this case was the Pentagon's virulently anti-gay policy. The Department of Defense had a long-standing policy of discharging any soldier found to be gay or lesbian on the grounds that homosexuality undermines the cohesion and morale of units whose members must live and work in close quarters.

That situation didn't apply to the Pentagon official, since he was then a civilian on the staff of Defense Secretary Dick Cheney. But the Pentagon sometimes denies security clearances to homosexuals—not because they're homosexual, of course, but because they could be subject to blackmail. This official had a security clearance.

Lots of defense reporters knew the guy was gay. But he had never publicly defended the military's anti-gay policies, always deflecting questions to others. It wasn't a question of personal hypocrisy but one of silence. Some gays saw the man's refusal to speak out as a crime that justified forcing him out of the closet.

"We commit ourselves to this singular instance of outing in the name of the 12,966 lesbian and gay soldiers who have been outed by the military since 1982," Rouilard wrote in an editorial.

Others in the gay community were critical. "The *Advocate* was against outing until they found someone really big to out," said Randy Shilts. "The *Advocate* just did it for crass commercial reasons—here was a big fish and they would get a huge amount of publicity."

I spoke with the Pentagon official, making clear I didn't plan to use his name. He found the outing attempt offensive and was clearly tempted to say so, but restrained himself. "My position is I get paid to talk about Department of Defense policy," he said. "I don't get paid to talk about my personal life. I'm not going to change my opinion based on how hard any radical group wants to yell about it."

Len Downie, the *Post*'s managing editor, had already decided to kill the Anderson column. He asked to see a draft of my story before deciding whether to run it.

I called some of the journalists involved. Jack Anderson said he found such stories "repugnant" and would "rather not run them." He generally has "a rule that a person's private life is his private business unless it affects his public conduct," and he did not contend that was the case here. Anderson simply said that "the story was out" and "it had reached the point of becoming national news."

John Robert Starr, managing editor of the *Arkansas Democrat,* which was about to run the Anderson column, said: "I think the people who are doing the outing are despicable, but once it comes out, it comes out."

The day before I finished my story, Barney Frank, one of the two openly gay members of Congress, got a chance at a House subcommittee hearing to question Cheney about the military's policy of discharging gay soldiers. Cheney said he had "inherited" the policy and found it "a bit of an old chestnut," but did not say he would change it. Everyone in the room knew there was an unspoken issue hanging in the air.

"When you have someone who is engaged in the persecution of other people for being gay, the issue is not privacy at all, it's hypocrisy," Frank told me. "If you found out that the leader of Operation Rescue had an abortion, would you print that? What if Sarah Brady [the leader of Handgun Control] kept a loaded .45 under her pillow? Is that news? Why, of all the possible hypocritical things, should people who are gay and hypocritical get a pass that nobody else gets?"

But who is to define the appropriate level of hypocrisy? What about a congressman who generally supports gay rights but opposes a particular bill? What about a bureaucrat who remains silent on the issue to protect his job—not giving aid and comfort to gay-bashers, but simply not speaking out? At what point does outing become an authoritarian insistence on political purity?

I went back and forth. Why should the guy be punished, just because he happened to work for the Pentagon instead of the Commerce Department? I didn't want to be even an indirect accomplice to outing. But I thought the media attention had reached the point where we had to write something, however circumspect.

I put together a story about the journalistic controversy that began: "The effort by some gay activists at 'outing' public figures escalated sharply this week as columnist Jack Anderson and a New York television station reported allegations that a national-security official is homosexual."

Karen DeYoung, the assistant managing editor for national news, didn't want to run it. She said it didn't meet her "threshold" for a news story; the controversy was not all that great. Downie agreed. We had no proof the official was homosexual (although he hadn't denied it), and the story added nothing to our understanding of the outing phenomenon. I didn't see how it differed from the case of the Wisconsin politician, but the decision was out of my hands. The piece was killed.

Two days later I left on a family vacation. That Sunday, DeYoung called me at my parents' house. Sam Donaldson had just asked Cheney about his homosexual aide on "This Week with David Brinkley." Now the story met her "threshold." It was exactly what I had feared; it wasn't a story for the *Post* until somebody bigger did it, and then suddenly it was a story.

But cooler heads prevailed by day's end. The reporter on duty, Curt Suplee, wrote a short story about Cheney's televised comments and briefly mentioned the Anderson column. It would have been the perfect opportunity to include my material on the journalistic controversy—Suplee's story was more specific in describing the Pentagon official than I had been—but the editors chose not to.

"To bring the hypocrisy to an even more baroque level," *Village Voice* media critic James Ledbetter wrote later, "Monday's *WashPost* account of the Brinkley show said that the subject . . . came up because of a 'controversy reported last week in a column by Jack Anderson'—without noting that the *Post* itself had killed the column!"

Downie says the paper had already run stories on the practice of outing and that "the only question was, are we going to name any of the people? We've never seen evidence that [the Pentagon official] is gay. There's no independent evidence that he is. The relevance isn't clear. I didn't see how it met any test." The *Post* ran a limited story after the Brinkley show because "it was discussed by Cheney in a public forum," Downie says.

In the days and weeks that followed, *Newsday, The Miami Herald,* the *San Francisco Examiner, Time, Newsweek* and *The Washington Times* all ran pieces that explored the outing controversy without naming the official. These stories served up a smorgasbord of views:

"To my mind, this doesn't seem the compelling case one would want before doing this kind of invasive journalism," said Howell Raines of *The New York Times.*

"Unfortunately, once it's out of the bag in the *Advocate,* it becomes public knowledge," said Robert Giles, editor of the *Detroit News.*

"What is the relevance here?" said Richard Harwood, then *The Washington Post*'s ombudsman. "This is basically in effect a smear campaign by a group of people angry with Pentagon policies toward homosexuals in the armed forces."

"Born in rage and hatred, directed exclusively at gay people, outing is gay-bashing at its sickest," said C. Carr, a *Village Voice* reporter and a lesbian.

Two weeks later, the *Post* ran a lengthy front-page story on the military's policy of discharging gay and lesbian soldiers. The paper probably would not have run that piece at that time had it not been for the outing campaign.

"On the one hand, the media said the *Advocate* was doing something awful," Richard Rouilard says. "Then they all wrote articles about how awful it is to exclude gays and lesbians from military service."

But the gay community was badly split. Rouilard's magazine received a torrent of angry letters and calls, including some death threats, from gays who objected to the outing.

"The media's criticism of outing is hypocritical—they're always invading people's privacy," Randy Shilts said. "Just about everyone who is open about being gay, like me, believes that morally you should be open about it and that most people who are not are being cowardly. But I don't feel I should use my role as a journalist to force others to make the moral choices I've made."

Some gay activists castigated Shilts for refusing to report on the Pentagon official. "The gay press went after me like crazy—the usual stuff about being an Uncle Tom and part of the establishment," he said. "The gay attack is that you have internalized homophobia. It's like, if you're against settlements on the West Bank, you're a self-hating Jew. The early black reporters faced it. When you're in a minority group, the members of the group, your compadres, want you to be their voice in the newspaper rather than being a journalist. They really want you to be an activist, and they hate you twice as much if you're not.

"Criticism from your community does hurt a lot more. It's horrible. It's very painful. It's made my life miserable."

When Robert Bauman, a Republican congressman from Maryland who crusaded against gay rights, was arrested in 1980 for soliciting a sixteen-year-old boy, publishing the story was hardly a tough call. A congressman's arrest is always news, and the spectacle of a secretly gay lawmaker who denounced gay rights legislation clearly made Bauman fair game. Few in the press agonized over his downfall; exposing Bauman somehow felt like performing a public service.

A similar fate befell Terry Dolan, founder of the National Conservative Political Action Committee, or NCPAC, who died of AIDS complications in 1986. *The Washington Post* later ran a lengthy article about Dolan's secret life as a homosexual and noted that his gay friends had held a separate memorial service for him. While Dolan's family was upset at the invasion of privacy, the revelation seemed justified to many media people because he had allied himself with people who bashed gays in their fund-raising letters.

But the press seemed to employ a more charitable standard when the homosexual in question was a champion of the liberal establishment. Barney Frank was friendly with dozens of editors and reporters. Journalists admired the Massachusetts congressman for his wit and tenacity and valued him as a news source. There was no question of hypocrisy, for Frank had supported gay rights long before he disclosed his homosexuality. Still, the gentler treatment Frank received when he was enveloped by scandal suggests that the press is more sympathetic to a public figure who has been certified one of the good guys.

Frank edged out of the closet on his own terms. In the mid-1980s, he says, "I was out among other gay people. I would go to bars, to parties. Some people knew, some people didn't know.

"The press began to ask me if they could write about it, and I would say no. I was teasing the press. I would drop hints. A variety of reporters approached me and said, 'If you're interested in talking about being gay, we would like to write the story.' People are ambivalent about it, basically out of good motives. The press wanted to write about it, but they didn't want to invade my privacy. They wanted me to volunteer it. They would call up to say we want to ask you, but they wanted my permission."

John Robinson, the *Boston Globe* reporter who covered Frank in Washington, had heard as early as 1979 that he might come out of the closet. Robinson knew Frank socially; they had discussed the matter over dinner.

"Barney for years had been unraveling this to a wider circle of people," Robinson says. "The only issue was when he was going to do this publicly. The *Globe*'s position was, Barney has to decide for himself when he's going to come out; we're not going to push him. I communicated this to him many times."

In the spring of 1987, soon after the Gary Hart episode, the congressman gave John Robinson a signal: "If you ask me the right question, you'll get the right answer."

"It was clear Barney wanted to dictate the terms of the story," Robinson says. "He wanted a long piece about his life and, oh by the way, in line fifty, Barney Frank is homosexual. He said to me outright, 'I do not want a headline that says "Barney Frank Is Gay." ' "

But Frank felt more comfortable speaking to a gay journalist. He canceled a scheduled interview with Robinson, saying they would talk when Robinson returned from vacation. While Robinson was away, Kay Longcope, a *Globe* feature writer who is openly lesbian, called Frank and said she wanted to ask him The Question. He said he would answer it, and Longcope flew to Washington.

"I've known Barney for years and years," she says. "My third question to Barney was, are you gay? He said yes, and we went on from there. He knew in advance what I wanted to talk about. He sounded extremely relieved just to get it out . . . to finally be able to be honest about that part of himself."

Robinson was livid when he learned that Longcope had scooped him. When he started calling Massachusetts politicians for reaction, Frank accused him of unethical behavior and tried to convince the *Globe* to hold up the story. "Barney had a long-standing view of how the story should be written and did everything in his power to get that kind of story," Robinson says.

Frank says Robinson is suffering from "paranoia" and that he merely wanted to delay the story so he could warn friends it was coming. But Frank admits he didn't want the story on the front page, and Longcope's feature was for the Living/Arts section.

John Robinson's story ran at the top of page one the next morning. "People say, why did you do it? I didn't want to keep lying," Frank says. "It would just make my life easier. The only lies I have ever told in my public career were to cover up my homosexuality."

Ironically, this man who did not disclose his homosexuality until he was forty-seven later threatened to out other gay lawmakers. In the spring of 1989, some Republican staffers on Capitol Hill were spreading rumors that Tom Foley, the House majority leader, was gay. These veiled suggestions became a full-fledged story when Mark Goodin, communications director of the Republican National Committee, circulated a memo headlined "Tom Foley: Out of the Liberal Closet." The memo slyly compared Foley's voting record with that of Barney Frank.

Frank quickly announced that unless the other party's operatives stopped spreading such garbage, he would start naming closeted gay Republicans in Congress. "Would I have? No one will ever know, including me," Frank says. "The morality of threatening people to get them to back off, that ain't even close. That's the nuclear deterrent."

Frank's bare-knuckles maneuver infuriated the right wing and particularly *The Washington Times,* the capital's fiercely conservative newspaper. Wesley Pruden, the paper's managing editor, used his column to toss a few homosexual slurs at Frank.

"The humiliation of the Republicans," he wrote, "was total—done in by a Democrat in lavender drawers."

Most newspapers, whatever their political leanings, attempt to deliver the news straight, part of the mantle of objectivity the press has worn since World War II. But *The Washington Times* is a throwback to the days of unbridled partisanship. The *Times'* handling of the Barney Frank story is instructive because it mirrors the way most papers chase a hot story, only in exaggerated form. With a liberal homosexual as its target, the *Times* became a caricature of a newspaper on the warpath.

By any measure, *The Washington Times* is a strange entity. The Reverend Sun Myung Moon, a self-proclaimed messiah from South Korea and leader of the Unification Church, founded the *Times* in 1982 and kept it afloat with $1 billion in church funds over the next decade. The church's global network of businesses, from auto parts to soft drinks, subsidized losses that reached $35 million a year.

Moon was an ardent opponent of homosexuality. His ministry included matching men and women as "blessed couples" and performing mass weddings, such as a 1982 event at Madison Square Garden involving 2,075 couples. Moon says he founded the *Times* "because I believed it was the will of God" and saw the newspaper as "an instrument to save America and the world" from "the collapse of traditional values."

The *Times* had some fine journalists, most of whom were not church members, but it seemed to lurch from one ideological controversy to the next. In 1984, James Whelan resigned as the paper's publisher, charging that it had become a "Moonie newspaper" that is "firmly in the hands" of the Unification Church. In 1987, editorial page editor William Cheshire and several assistants resigned, saying they had been ordered to defend political repression in South Korea. In 1988, reporters Gene Grabowski and Amy Bayer quit after the editors hyped their story about the false rumors of Michael Dukakis having seen a psychiatrist. Grabowski called the episode "trumped-up" and "shameful."

Gays were always a subject of special sensitivity. The paper ran upbeat pieces on right-wingers who crusade against homosexuality, but in 1992 Pruden would kill a profile of a gay conservative author, Marvin Liebman, saying he was "not interested in stories that elevate the lifestyle."

A few weeks after the Foley incident, the *Times* started pumping up stories about a supposed "call boy ring" within the federal government. Soon the paper was citing concerns that "a nest of homosexuals" in the government "may have been penetrated by Soviet-backed espionage agents posing as male prostitutes." The editor, Arnaud de Borchgrave, a conspiracy-minded former *Newsweek* correspondent, insisted the story would prove to be "much like Watergate," but it quickly fizzled.

On August 25, 1989, the *Times* fired a new salvo on its front page: "Sex Sold from Congressman's Apartment." The banner story, by Paul Rodriguez and George Archibald, described how Barney Frank had lived with a male prostitute for nearly two years. Frank admitted he had met the man, Stephen Gobie, by answering a personal ad in the local gay paper that said: "Hot bottom plus large endowment equals a great time."

Gobie said he was running an escort service from Frank's Capitol Hill apartment. Frank, who had hired his lover as a housekeeper and chauffeur, said he knew Gobie was working as a prostitute but had no idea he was using the apartment for sex. When he learned this from his landlady, Frank said, "I kicked him out."

There were other wrinkles that cast grave doubt on Frank's judgment. Gobie, thirty-two, was on probation for cocaine possession, oral sodomy and sex offenses involving a juvenile, and Frank had written at least four letters for him on congressional stationery that wound up in the hands of Virginia probation officials. He hadn't paid Social Security and unemployment taxes on Gobie's $20,000 salary. And the *Times* would later report that Frank used his office to fix thirty-three parking tickets for Gobie.

All newspapers play up their own scoops, but *The Washington Times* flogged the Frank story with almost religious zeal. From August 25 to September 22, the paper ran forty-five stories on the Barney Frank case, twenty-two of them on the front page, plus an editorial calling for Frank to resign. Most of these articles involved less than breathtaking revelations. They were little more than horse-race stories, stressing Frank's precarious position over and over:

"Frank Losing Ground as Hill Recess Ends." "GOP's Strategy in Frank Case: Sit Back, Enjoy." "Embarrassed Leaders Want Frank to Go." "Outrage Grows in Mass." "Tide Is Rolling Against Frank." "Democratic Leaders Desert Frank." "Deserted by Press, Frank Stands Firm Against Resigning." A low point came on September 22, with a front-page story that knit together highlights of anti-Frank editorials from other newspapers.

George Archibald defends the paper's coverage as anticorruption, not anti-gay. "We were going to force the hand of the ethics committee," he says. "Some of the strategy on the part of the editors was to push this thing as hard as they could so that Barney would cooperate. We felt if we could keep the pressure on him, he would help us to break a larger story about this underworld operation" involving "a whole network of congressional gays." It was a strategy more suitable for prosecutors than journalists. Nor was it particularly fruitful, since Frank had stopped speaking to the paper.

"I would have played the story the same way whether it was a Republican conservative or a liberal Democrat," de Borchgrave insists. "If we'd gotten the same story on Jesse Helms, he'd have been run out of town in twenty-four hours."

If Frank's ordeal was made to order for *The Washington Times*, it clearly put more liberal newspapers on the spot. They had an instinctive reluctance to make a public issue of private homosexual conduct, based on little more than the claims of a male prostitute. But they also felt that Frank had stumbled badly and should not be given a free ride.

Nowhere was the dilemma more acute than at *The Boston Globe*, the dignified voice of New England liberalism, whose staff had been close to Frank for two decades. The *Globe* initially painted the episode in rosy colors. "Little Long-term Damage to Career Seen," its front-page headline said, coupled with a profile titled "Frank Has History of Overcoming Obstacles." Many *Globe* staffers were uncomfortable with the Gobie tale.

"I probably dragged my feet a little," John Robinson says. "I didn't think that was the kind of story the *Globe* should pay very much attention to. It just smelled to me. To cover the objections of some boyfriend —who the hell cares? It's a disgusting focus on irrelevant things."

But the *Globe* soon recognized it had blown the initial story. A day later, the new line was "Frank's Career Jeopardized, Analysts Say."

Journalism often turns on personal relationships, and for the Boston pundits who had joked and sparred with Frank over the years, the scandal was no abstract public-policy issue. They felt Barney Frank's agony.

"It made a tremendous difference to me that I had known him since 1967, when I was in college and he was a graduate assistant," says Thomas Oliphant, a *Globe* columnist. "It was really a matter of trust. I was aware of what it felt like to go through the trauma of coming out. I felt sympathy for Barney's loneliness during that period."

Oliphant wrote that Frank was threatened by "a modern version of mob rule: a newspaper publishes a story; politicians react; pressure builds; incestuous pols and writers conclude that so-and-so is 'finished'; the poor slob in question validates the conventional wisdom by quitting." It seemed a bit much, though, when Oliphant defended Frank on television as "a man of surpassing integrity" and "impeccable judgment."

Some of Frank's other journalist friends reached the opposite conclusion, determined not to let personal feelings, or the element of homosexuality, cloud their judgment. To go easy on Frank would be to confirm the conservative lament that there really was a double standard for lefties whose politics matched those of all the closet-liberal reporters.

Ellen Goodman, the syndicated *Globe* columnist, says that "I liked, admired and enjoyed Barney's humor and pointed style over many years." Nevertheless, Goodman called for his resignation, saying: "Barney, it won't wash. Give it up."

David Nyhan, an acerbic *Globe* columnist who had known Frank since the early '70s, wrote of Frank's "mindless pursuit of a gutter-dwelling lowlife. . . . He's got to be ashamed of himself, of his stupidity, of the way his private life went to hell as his public life prospered."

After three weeks of silence, the *Globe* finally urged Frank to resign. Martin Nolan, then the editorial page editor, says he wanted to spare Frank an ugly ordeal. "We were trying to do a favor for him. . . . Geez, we go way back," Nolan says.

The editorial page was swamped with calls and letters accusing the paper of homophobia. Some of the complainants got personal. "I was at a natural food store in Cambridge, shopping for bionic bean sprouts or hydroponic lettuce or whatever the hell it was. This woman comes up to me and says, 'Are you Marty Nolan? I think what you've done to

Barney is despicable.' I said, 'Sorry, ma'am.' Then she spits at me. I'm backing out, and she has a good roundhouse right and whacks me on the side of the head."

Frank's moment of crisis was viewed quite differently at the *Boston Herald,* a working-class tabloid that had little use for liberal do-gooders. It was yet another example of how a newspaper's ideological filter can color its view of the news. Howie Carr, the *Herald*'s bad-boy columnist, wrote a scathing piece describing Frank as "a sicko who happens to be a pol."

"I think we enjoyed the story," Carr says. "Barney has always been one of the *Globe*'s darlings. If you're Irish, it's assumed you're corrupt. Barney is from Harvard, Barney is Jewish, Barney is liberal, no he's got to be a good guy. It was nice to see one of their guys suddenly in deep doo-doo. I was just ecstatic and gleeful that he couldn't hide behind their skirts anymore."

The House ethics committee later rejected the most serious charges against Frank, saying there was no evidence the congressman knew that Gobie was using his apartment for prostitution. The panel's report said two key witnesses had denied what *The Washington Times* quoted them as saying. But the committee also found that Frank had violated House rules, and the House voted 408 to 18 to reprimand him.

"The fact that the committee whitewashed this thing is no surprise," Archibald says. Frank, however, believes he triumphed over an attempted smear by an anti-gay newspaper. "It was a contest between their version and my version, and my version won," he says. "It also had the advantage of being true."

A week before the 1990 elections, *The Boston Globe* endorsed Frank for another term. "It's always hard to say you were wrong," says Marty Nolan. "Hey, we were wrong."

In the end, most of the press—with one obvious exception—struggled to strike the right balance in covering the Frank scandal. But the sordid element of male prostitution somehow made it irresistible. Three other congressmen were battling allegations of sexual misconduct during this period, yet each received a fraction of the publicity devoted to Frank. The very novelty of an openly gay congressman who acknowledged hiring prostitutes made it impossible for the press to treat Barney Frank as just another lawmaker under investigation.

· · ·

In January 1992, Kim Foltz, a business reporter for *The New York Times*, wrote a moving article for the Sunday magazine about his struggle with AIDS:

"The virus seemed to tighten its psychological grip on me. If I coughed too much in a crowd, I felt guilty, even though I knew I hadn't put anyone at risk. I shied away from kissing friends." Foltz even complained about the *Times'* health benefits, saying that once he was unable to work he would be eligible for only a few months' disability pay. Foltz died a year later.

It was, quite simply, an article no *Times*man would have dared write in the climate of fear that prevailed seven or eight years earlier. "Your career was in jeopardy if people found out you were gay," said Jeffrey Schmalz, a reporter who later died from AIDS.

Times have obviously changed. When the National Association of Lesbian and Gay Journalists held its second convention in New York in 1993, a dozen major news organizations sent recruiters; being gay had actually become a plus. The *Detroit News* now has a lesbian journalist, Deb Price, writing a column about gay life. But such writing remains anathema to some readers: 475 people canceled their subscriptions to the Minneapolis *Star Tribune* after it began carrying Price's column in 1993.

As gay journalists have become an increasingly outspoken force, they have had an unmistakable impact on the profession. Just as the growing number of black reporters demanded more sensitive coverage of minority communities, a generation of openly gay reporters has changed the way newspapers write about AIDS and other issues of importance to gays. They have insisted that the press do more than cover the occasional discrimination case or the latest celebrity—Rock Hudson, Liberace, Magic Johnson, Arthur Ashe—to contract AIDS. They want gays and lesbians to be woven into the fabric of everyday coverage, rather than thrust into the headlines when big names or scandals are involved.

Still, some newsrooms remain uncomfortable with the subject. In 1991, top editors at *The Houston Post* barred columnist Juan Palomo from disclosing his homosexuality in a column about a gay-bashing murder case, then fired him for talking about it to reporters from other publications. Palomo was reinstated after an outcry from his colleagues and the gay community.

Perhaps no newspaper has undergone a more dramatic turnabout than *The New York Times*. Once considered a hostile workplace for gays, the *Times* in recent years has undergone what the *Advocate* dubbed the "Lavender Enlightenment." Arthur Sulzberger, Jr., the new publisher, makes the point explicitly, saying the paper's coverage "has to be influenced by my people who are gay. . . . We've taken the handcuffs off. . . . We are covering the totality of gay life, that gays are more than just victims of AIDS."

Richard Meislin, the graphics editor, says that "the level of sensitivity has changed dramatically. The *Times* really does a far, far better job of covering the gay community than it did five years ago. It was easier for the *Times* to start covering AIDS because it was a public health crisis than to start covering the gay community as a community. Now there is a more human and sensitive coverage of how people live. People here feel they're part of the process."

Many staffers blame the years of intolerance on former executive editor Abe Rosenthal, whom Schmalz, Meislin and other gays have described as homophobic. They have said that Rosenthal abruptly recalled Meislin as Mexico City correspondent in the early '80s in part because he had learned that Meislin was gay.

Rosenthal strongly denies transfering Meislin for that reason and dismisses the broader charge of homophobia. He says he tried to hire an arts critic who was gay as early as 1966, a time when "people were still being refused for employment because they were gay. He had to take a medical test. He was refused because he was homosexual. I got into a big fight. The doctor said, 'Don't you know these people go into homosexual rages?' "

On one point, however, there is little dispute: In the news pages, Rosenthal was clearly out of step with his era. He refused during his tenure as executive editor to allow the *Times* to refer to homosexuals as "gays," dismissing the term as part of an effort by activists to use the paper "for political purposes." Things have obviously changed on West 43rd Street. In 1991, five years after Rosenthal stepped down, the *Times* ran a page-one story about militant gays demanding to be called "queer."

Once Rosenthal's tenure ended, Jeff Schmalz said, "People who were gay started coming out, and then began saying we should be covering things differently." Schmalz, a twenty-year *Times* veteran, became a dramatic symbol at the paper in 1990 when he suffered a seizure in the middle of the newsroom and was diagnosed as having AIDS. He also became a leader in changing the culture of the *Times*. Schmalz profiled the two HIV-positive speakers,

Bob Hattoy and Elizabeth Glaser, who addressed the 1992 Democratic convention, and an HIV-positive woman, Mary Fisher, who spoke to the Republican convention. (When Hattoy insisted he had come to terms with AIDS, Schmalz told him, "Bullshit. I know what it's like. I know what it's like to wake up in the middle of the night and to think you're dying"—and Hattoy broke down and cried.) When some Republicans tried to make homosexual rights into a major campaign issue—and President Bush continued to insist that being gay was "not normal"—it was Schmalz who examined the controversy on the front page. He later wrote a cover story for *The New York Times Magazine* on how gays were coming "out of the shadows of American politics."

The changing attitudes have affected virtually every section. After years of lobbying by gay staffers, the *Times* agreed in 1992 that its obituaries would identify gay lovers as "survivors" of the deceased. The op-ed page prominently displayed a piece by former *Times* reporter Dudley Clendinen, saying how pleased he was that some presidential candidates were openly courting the gay vote. Even the much-criticized Abe Rosenthal began assailing anti-gay discrimination in his *Times* column.

The new climate was also apparent during the outing of the Pentagon official, when editors solicited the views of gay staffers. Schmalz said he told Max Frankel that the *Times* should write about the official on grounds of hypocrisy, but that management was too shell-shocked by the fallout over the naming of Patricia Bowman a few months earlier. The editorial page, however, ran a lengthy piece urging Dick Cheney to drop the ban on gays in the military.

The change was long overdue. It is hard to imagine the press devoting so little attention over the years to a policy that barred some other group—blacks, women or Jews—from serving in the armed forces. Most editors, knowing no one who was personally affected, accepted the rationale that gays were "bad for morale" without a second thought. It took a series of "self-outings" by highly successful military men and women—such as Navy aviator Tracy Thorne, who announced his homosexuality on "Nightline"—to give the story page-one prominence. *The Washington Post* later ran a front-page piece questioning whether the military was engaging in a "witch hunt" by tracking down gay servicemen with "homophobic zeal." Once the policy had a human face, it became impossible for the press to ignore, even before President Clinton relaxed the ban.

Press coverage of gays became so sympathetic, in fact, that it often took on an air of political correctness. Most journalists sanitized their reports on the 1993 gay rights march in Washington, making little or no mention of the topless lesbians, drag queens and leather-clad exhibitionists who made up a minority of the crowd, or the obscene performers seen by anyone watching C-SPAN. The approved script for the demonstration was one of well-dressed and well-mannered gays marching for civil rights, and mainstream newspapers, which once described homosexuals as deviants, largely refused to recognize the presence of extremists who might mar that picture.

The wave of involuntary outings continued, and it was no longer limited to Republicans who were deemed hostile to gays. Queer Nation charged that Donna Shalala, the chancellor of the University of Wisconsin and Bill Clinton's choice to run the Department of Health and Human Services, was a lesbian. Using Shalala's denial as an excuse, *The Capital Times* in Madison published the charge, which was promptly picked up by *Newsday, USA Today, Newsweek,* the Associated Press and, of course, *The Washington Times.* "Some editors no doubt feel intimidated by the gay and feminist lobby, but I don't," Wes Pruden said.

Most newspapers ignored the incident, but the echoes continued to reverberate. At the gay march on the capital, *The Washington Post,* which had refused to print the gossip about Shalala, chose to report that gay activist Larry Kramer had told the crowd that "thousands" of people knew that Shalala was a lesbian, "so why is she denying it?" The *Post* included a denial from Shalala's spokeswoman, but the damage had been done.

I again had to confront the issue of homosexuality in early 1994, and this time the person in question was a journalist. David Brock, a reporter for the ultraconservative *American Spectator* magazine, was under attack by several liberal columnists for disclosing some Arkansas state troopers' seamy tales about President Clinton's alleged extramarital exploits. In the most scathingly personal column, Frank Rich of *The New York Times* accused Brock of being a misogynist and seemed to suggest that Brock was gay. Rich insists he knew nothing of Brock's personal life and that the column was not, as Brock put it, a "thinly veiled outing."

My dilemma arose in writing about whether the journalistic assaults on Brock were unfair. I happened to know that the thirty-one-year-old reporter was gay but not openly so, which made it difficult to write about the issue. In a series of sometimes awkward interviews, Brock and I discussed whether he would talk publicly about his homosexuality. I assured him I would not write about it unless he chose to address it. He was torn between wanting to keep his private life off-limits and a concern that some publication might out him. He eventually decided to make a statement, and we negotiated over the wording of the article. "My sexual orientation has never been a factor in my journalism and never will be," Brock said. I deliberately played down that aspect of the story. I am not a defender of David Brock's journalism, but no reporter of any ideological stripe should have his sexual preference disclosed against his will.

Still, for a profession that was once openly hostile to gays, the signs of greater sensitivity were encouraging. In a few short years, gay journalists had helped place homosexual rights high on the media agenda. While newspapers, like the gay community itself, continued to be badly divided over attempts to out people against their will, or even whether to disclose that someone has AIDS, these issues somehow seemed less abstract when they affected newsroom friends and colleagues. It was a pattern that would repeat itself time and again as newspapers, once the preserve of white male heterosexuals, dragged themselves into the era of diversity. Two months after the Pentagon outing, women reporters would help force a particularly nasty issue from the journalistic closet. The subject was sexual harassment.

9

A Question of Harassment

The woman on the phone spoke in a hushed voice as she asked if we could meet for a private talk. She didn't want her name used. Reporters get such secretive calls all the time.

What made this one unusual was that the woman worked in my office. And she wanted to talk about one of our most prominent colleagues, Juan Williams, who was very much in the news.

The day before, *The Washington Post* had run a stinging op-ed piece in which Williams championed the cause of Clarence Thomas, the embattled Supreme Court nominee. He said there was "no credible evidence" for the allegations by Anita Hill, Thomas's former aide, that Thomas had sexually harassed her a decade earlier. Hill, said Williams, seemed to have become the tool of liberal activists, whom he assailed as "abusive monsters."

Williams had been all over television that morning, talking to Peter Jennings on ABC and stopping by C-SPAN. He kept defending Thomas and challenging the charges of sexual harassment. Women in the *Post* newsroom were absolutely livid, my informant said. The reason was that Williams himself was the subject of an inquiry by the paper into complaints that he had harassed several female colleagues.

It was a classic collision of rights. Juan Williams was the subject of complaints by anonymous accusers and had been found guilty of nothing; his reputation was on the line. On the other hand, the *Post*'s credibility could be tarnished by the disclosure that it had allowed an employee accused of sexual harassment to hold forth on that very subject on the newspaper's opinion page. And that, uncomfortable as it made me feel, was news.

By the time the episode ended, I would learn how difficult it is to report on your own paper

—and what it is like to be on the other end of a barrage of media inquiries. Three other reporters would be singed by the white-hot controversy surrounding the Thomas nomination. And some journalists would demonstrate that they were not above using the power of the press to score ideological points or settle personal scores.

Politicians weren't the only ones who looked awful in the Clarence Thomas affair. The news business was also splattered with mud as it wrestled with an issue that stirred intensely passionate feelings.

One reporter who clearly believed the Thomas nomination was more important than his journalistic responsibility was Arch Parsons, a veteran black newspaperman at the Baltimore *Sun*. Shortly before the nomination was announced, Parsons, who had known Thomas for years, tried to reassure the administration that the civil rights community would not automatically oppose him. Parsons quietly passed such information from Benjamin Hooks, executive director of the NAACP, to the White House through a conservative lawyer named Clint Bolick. Parsons later wrote about the NAACP and the Thomas nomination, despite the fact that he had played a backstage role in promoting his old friend. The reporter, who later admitted this was a conflict of interest, probably would have been fired had he not retired by the time the incident came to light a year later.

While the overriding issue for Arch Parsons was maintaining a black presence on the Supreme Court, for others it was abortion, or gender politics. The old notions of objectivity were thrown to the winds. Over and over, women journalists would write that men "just don't get it" when it comes to sexual harassment. It was a deafening feminist roar that stunned many middle-aged male editors who, like the senators on the Judiciary Committee, were slow to grasp the depth of resentment over leering remarks and obscene jokes.

Part of it was the power of television, as millions of Americans were transfixed by the drama of Anita Hill's anguished accusations and Clarence Thomas's angry denials. Part of it was the racial overlay, as Thomas declared himself the victim of a modern-day lynching. There was also the tawdry spectacle of United States senators discussing oral sex and the porn movie star Long Dong Silver, and the vicious negative campaign that Thomas supporters used to discredit Hill.

Journalists, as we have seen, are uncomfortable with stories about sex and have difficulties writing honestly about race. They love to reduce complex subjects to simple morality plays, with the protagonists—

Tawana Brawley or Marion Barry, Barney Frank or William Kennedy Smith—fighting for the highest possible stakes. These forces would intersect in the most racially charged confrontation of the Bush administration.

Against that backdrop, it was hardly surprising that reporters served as lightning rods in the Thomas case. The press was assailed by the right for disclosing Hill's secret Senate affidavit—a neat bit of hypocrisy in a city where Republicans and Democrats leak information every day to advance their partisan agendas.

The media have been pilloried over leaks for decades. After Daniel Ellsberg slipped copies of the Pentagon Papers to *The New York Times* and *The Washington Post* in 1971, the Nixon administration grew so obsessed with leaks that it created a "plumbers" unit to plug them. The administration tried to prosecute Ellsberg, but the case was thrown out of court after the disclosure that White House operatives had burglarized the office of Ellsberg's psychiatrist.

Journalists have been made scapegoats in several other cases. In 1976, the House subpoenaed CBS reporter Daniel Schorr after he leaked a secret House report on CIA and FBI activities to *The Village Voice,* and CBS suspended Schorr. Jan Schaffer, a *Philadelphia Inquirer* reporter, was ordered jailed in 1981 for refusing to disclose her source for a story about the Abscam investigation. In 1989, Attorney General Richard Thornburgh threatened to subpoena the phone records of CBS reporter Rita Braver over her report on an inquiry involving Representative William Gray of Pennsylvania.

The battle over Clarence Thomas resembled several other hotly disputed nominations of the Reagan-Bush years—Edwin Meese, William Bradford Reynolds, Daniel Manion, William Rehnquist, Robert Bork, John Tower—in that leading Democratic senators and liberal lobbying groups were arrayed against the administration's choice. Judicial nominations had become more and more like political campaigns, and there was a tendency on the right to see reporters as handmaidens of such liberals as Ted Kennedy, Howard Metzenbaum and Paul Simon, and such groups as People for the American Way, Alliance for Justice and the Leadership Conference on Civil Rights, whose charges against the nominees invariably got big play in the media.

The reality is that those on the political attack always get plenty of ink, if only because "Nominee Under Fire" is a better story than "Nominee Sails Through." The press had jumped on scandals with equal vigor in Democratic administrations, as Bert Lance can attest. But after almost eleven years of Democratic congressmen battling Republican presidents, the press seemed to many conservative activists to be part of the permanent opposition.

In Clarence Thomas, the White House appeared to have a formidable candidate, a black conservative who had risen from an impoverished home with no indoor plumbing in Pin Point, Georgia. Thomas had emerged from his confirmation hearings without a scratch, so overcoached by his handlers that he even insisted he had never discussed *Roe* v. *Wade* with anyone. To the dismay of liberal activists, who feared that Thomas's confirmation would enable the court to overturn its 1973 decision legalizing abortion, the Senate vote, scheduled for October 8, 1991, seemed a mere formality.

The weekend before the vote, Nina Totenberg of National Public Radio and Timothy Phelps of *Newsday* told the world of Anita Hill's allegations. The leak was unquestionably sleazy, since Hill had asked the Senate Judiciary Committee to keep her name confidential, and the Republicans were furious. But all the handwringing about this dastardly breach of "the process" ignored the fact that someone, as is usually the case with leaks, had a strong reason for making the information public. The disclosure was embarrassing because it revealed how casually the all-male committee had brushed off Hill's charges. It was easier for red-faced senators to holler about leaks than to explain how they had bungled the job.

Earlier in the process, Bush administration officials had themselves selectively leaked information from the FBI background check on Thomas. Soon after the nomination, an administration official told Ann Devroy, a White House reporter for *The Washington Post,* that Thomas had once used marijuana. The official told Devroy, who hadn't even raised the subject, that Thomas had tried marijuana in college and "perhaps once" in law school, and that the White House saw this as no problem. The idea was to defuse a damaging story by putting it out with a positive spin, and it worked. The spate of stories that followed Devroy's adopted the same no-big-deal tone, and the revelation of prior pot-smoking—which had sunk Supreme Court nominee Douglas Ginsburg four years earlier—quickly faded.

The charge that reporters had joined an unscrupulous conspiracy in publicizing the Anita Hill leak was just the beginning of an increasingly angry indictment of the press. The Thomas hearings would become one of those rare national moments that everyone watched on television, like a political Super Bowl, and then argued about for weeks. Reporters took sides at their peril. There was no neutral ground.

From the moment she went on the air with the Anita Hill affidavit, Nina Totenberg found herself under attack from the right.

Totenberg, forty-seven, had always shown a flair for self-promotion. She had a way of sweeping into rooms as if she were the star of the event. A Boston University dropout who had started on the women's page of the old *Boston Record-American,* Totenberg had taken a workmanlike assignment—covering the courts for radio—and turned herself into a celebrity. *People* magazine put her on a list of the most underpaid people, along with Mother Teresa (Totenberg was making $65,000 at the time). She was almost a cult figure in legal circles, on a first-name basis with dozens of federal judges.

Nina Totenberg also had a knack for personal controversy. She was a prodigiously hard worker, but her scoops produced much innuendo about whether she had an intimate link with certain powerful Washington men. In the late '70s Totenberg started dating Senator Floyd Haskell, who was twenty-eight years her senior; they were later married.

When Totenberg broke the 1987 story about Douglas Ginsburg's having smoked marijuana as a Harvard law professor, it led to questions about her own past. "People tried to bait me into saying whether I ever smoked pot," she says. "I said I hadn't, and then I remembered I'd had two drags in my life and I got called a liar."

Although *Newsday*'s Tim Phelps had broken the Anita Hill story the night before Totenberg, it was the NPR reporter who basked in the media spotlight. Print reporters, after all, are anonymous, while Totenberg's voice was heard by millions. Her growing fame was certified with an invitation to appear on "Nightline." The other guests were Paul Simon and Alan Simpson. The Wyoming senator quickly lit into Totenberg: "What politicians get tired of is bias in reporters. You've been beating the drums on this one almost every day since it started in the most extraordinary way. Let's not pretend that you're objective here. That just would be absurd."

"Senator, you've attacked me," Totenberg said. "May I respond?" After several interruptions, she said: "I do not appreciate being blamed just because I do my job and report the news."

"I didn't ask you to appreciate it," Simpson shot back.

After the program, Totenberg was walking toward the car ABC had provided to take her home when she heard a loud voice. It was Simpson, waving a copy of a journalistic ethics code and railing about how she had violated it.

"Nina, I just wanted to tell you those things I said were not said lightly. I meant everything I said," he declared.

Totenberg whirled and shouted, "Fuck you! You big asshole. You are so full of shit."

She got into the car, but the senator held her car door and continued his tirade. "Nina, you love to dish it out, but you sure don't like to take it," he said.

"Fuck you! I don't have to listen to this shit! You're a bitter, evil man." With that, Simpson released the door and Totenberg's driver sped off.

Totenberg would later be sorry that she had lost her temper. She knew she had become part of the story, a dangerous thing for a journalist to do. Totenberg was scheduled to anchor the Judiciary Committee hearings on Anita Hill's allegations, and the world knew she had cursed out one of its most prominent members. I had gotten a tip and, after confirming it with Totenberg and Simpson, recounted the exchange (with several expletives deleted) in *The Washington Post*.

Totenberg immediately became a favorite target of *The Washington Times*, which was denouncing Clarence Thomas's critics with the same intensity it had displayed in going after Barney Frank. Managing editor Wesley Pruden, who had snickered about Frank's "lavender drawers," was now assailing "the hysterical feminists and their thoroughly emasculated male toadies."

Pruden said the Judiciary Committee had paid no attention to Hill's allegations "until Nina Totenberg and the government radio network, who have been leading the campaign to discredit Judge Thomas, got a dump of the confidential Senate files—from Howard Metzenbaum, by all accounts—to create her 'October Surprise.' " Without an iota of evidence, Pruden accused Senator Metzenbaum of "thievery" for supposedly leaking the Anita Hill affidavit.

Soon afterward, I began work on a quick profile of Totenberg. She said she was uncomfortable with all the attention but invited me to her office. As we spoke in her cluttered corner cubicle, I waited to pop a sensitive question. Totenberg had told a number of women around town that she had been sexually harassed by an editor at a newspaper job many years earlier. The newsworthy angle was obvious: the reporter who helped make Anita Hill a household name had herself been a victim of sexual harassment. After twenty minutes of innocuous chat, I asked her about the episode.

"I had a boss who made passes at me repeatedly," Totenberg said, looking down. "It wasn't just talk. I was embarrassed. I didn't want to tell anybody. I was very young. It was a long time ago, when the term sexual harassment wasn't even used. It was awful. There's no other word to describe it."

I pressed for details, but she cut me off. She wouldn't say who the man was, which newspaper they worked at or whether she had quit. "It happened and I left. . . . I'm not going to say any more about it," Totenberg said. "I don't want to be the issue."

I tried a different tack. Perhaps the experience had made her more sensitive in dealing with Anita Hill? Totenberg acknowledged that she could not completely divorce her personal history from her reporting. "Most people, men and women, find it hard to believe this goes on," she said. "If you've had it happen to you, it becomes slightly more believable."

Totenberg said she warned Hill that "she would be the subject of great trauma and controversy. I wanted her not to be misled. This was an incredibly important charge she was making, and the decision had to be hers." After all, she said, "I'm a woman, too."

Later in the day, as I was making calls for the profile, several people said they had heard that the *National Observer* had fired Totenberg for plagiarism in the mid-'70s. I called Totenberg back and asked her about the allegation.

"I told you I'm not going to talk about that!" she snapped.

I was puzzled, since that was what she had said about the sexual harassment and now I was asking her about plagiarism. It suddenly dawned on me that both events must have occurred at the *National Observer* and that they were somehow linked. She acknowledged the plagiarism incident but wouldn't discuss it for the record.

Totenberg went on the offensive, saying I was dredging up twenty-year-old matters and that she didn't see how they were relevant. The irony was stunning: Nina Totenberg had just tossed Anita Hill into a national maelstrom by exhuming an account of sexual harassment that was itself nearly a decade old. As a seasoned reporter, she knew she could not simply declare certain parts of her life off-limits, but journalists often make the worst interview subjects because they know all the tricks of the trade.

It was close to deadline, and checking out the plagiarism story wasn't easy; the *Observer* had been defunct for fourteen years. But I reached a former employee who confirmed that Totenberg had been fired for plagiarism. After two more go-rounds on the phone, Totenberg acknowledged that the *Observer* had fired her for lifting part of a story. She said she had made a mistake. She obviously believed that the real reason for her dismissal was that she wouldn't have sex with the boss, but she wouldn't say that for the record.

What I didn't know at the time was how extensive Totenberg's plagiarism had been. Her offense was far worse than the conduct that had prompted *The Washington Post* to fire Laura Parker three months earlier. In a 1972 profile of Tip O'Neill, Totenberg led with a five-sentence quote from O'Neill that was lifted, word for word, from the last paragraph of a *Post* story by Myra MacPherson. Totenberg also stole another long anecdote recounted by O'Neill, a quote from his son, and quotes from two other congressmen, one of whom she disguised as "one liberal." It was a pretty blatant heist.

My story the next morning led with Totenberg's account of how she had been sexually harassed at the *Observer*. It also said the paper had fired her for plagiarism, and noted that she would not discuss whether the two events were connected. The matter remained as murky as the conflicting accounts of Anita Hill and Clarence Thomas.

I felt bad. I had not set out to rattle an old skeleton in Nina Totenberg's closet, but when I opened the door, it came tumbling out. Still, scrutiny is a two-way street. The episode was a sign that even the best reporters cannot fully separate their personal experiences from the way they perceive and shape the news. And it was a reminder that selective candor, always dangerous for public officials, is also risky business for journalists.

On the day after Anita Hill's televised press conference, the voices of angry women practically jumped off the front page of *The New York Times*.

For decades, the leading lights in the *Times*' Washington bureau had been accomplished men writing about affairs of state. Arthur Krock. James Reston. Tom Wicker. Max Frankel. R. W. Apple. Thomas Friedman. But now, for the first time, the bureau's premier writer was a woman.

Maureen Dowd covered the White House, but she did it with a feminist twist. While others wrote engagingly about George Bush's fondness for golf, tennis and horseshoes, Dowd saw a male locker-room atmosphere that almost totally excluded women. "The capital has always been a man's town, a monochromatic landscape of button-down and gray flannel, and this White House is no different," she had written five months earlier. Dowd sometimes missed the mark, as she had in writing about Kitty Kelley, but she had an uncanny ability to interpret events in a way no one else had thought of.

While the pillars of the Washington establishment were harrumphing that there was no need to delay the vote on Clarence Thomas, Dowd weighed in with an article called "The Senate and Sexism." It was a startling piece, all the more so because the *Times* rarely afforded its reporters such stylistic and analytical freedom.

Dowd described Washington as "a city where men have always made the rules and the Senate remains an overwhelmingly male club." She said that "the story of how members of the all-male Judiciary Committee handled the accusations had touched off an angry explosion among women in legal and political circles." Democratic activist Ann Lewis, Barney Frank's sister, was quoted as saying that Hill's allegations had sent "an electric current of anger through women." Dowd noted that "even some female journalists seemed to have a flash of gender-based anger."

Ironically, in light of the conservative criticism that followed, the story was not Maureen Dowd's idea. Her bureau chief, Howell Raines, had suggested a piece on gender politics, and she had resisted it. "I started making calls," Dowd says, "and there were all these women law professors and women's groups, admittedly activist women, swarming around the Hill. I said, 'Okay, I was wrong and you were right.' "

The Senate agreed to delay the vote for a week, and the floodgates were opened for a torrent of sexual harassment stories, most of them by women. I found the indictment a bit sweeping—no newspaper, after all, would publish a story saying that Jews didn't get it, or blacks didn't get it, or gays didn't get it—and thought readers should be reminded that not all men were Neanderthal pigs. But there was no denying the intensity of the feelings that poured forth as if some kind of emotional dam had burst.

Day after day, the *Times* saved space on the front page for Dowd's

Clarence Thomas stories, sight unseen. In *The Washington Post,* Marjorie Williams had this to say about Anita Hill's failure to file a complaint against Thomas or find another job: "Women make these calculations everywhere, every day. We just didn't talk about it anymore until this week, when we suddenly found ourselves angry, all of us, at the same insult. We are so afraid of whining, sounding like victims, or earning the bad labels. . . . Strident. Humorless."

Donna Britt, a *Post* reporter who is black, had been in the news a few months earlier. She was at the White House Correspondents' Dinner when a stranger grabbed her around the thighs and yanked her across his lap and onto a dinner table. The man turned out to be Dr. Burton Lee, President Bush's personal physician. "There's a world of men out there who just don't get it," Britt wrote after the incident. "Who don't get that almost no woman wants to be manhandled, nuzzled or sexually remarked upon. . . . Who can't fathom why, for a black woman in particular, the slightest presumption of ownership is anathema."

Now Donna Britt took up Hill's cause, saying: "It's a hell of a thing, being female, black and credible all at once, a feat sort of on a par with running a marathon while singing an aria."

While the story was exploding with nuclear force in most of the American media, it barely caused a ripple at one newspaper—*The Wall Street Journal.*

On Monday, October 7, the day after *Newsday* and NPR broke the story, Hill's allegation was front-page news in the *New York Times, Washington Post, Washington Times, Los Angeles Times* and many other papers. The *Journal* gave it one paragraph in its front-page roundup column, saying Hill's charge "appeared unlikely to delay or affect the outcome."

The following day, the Thomas story led the three major networks. The *New York Times* and *Washington Post* each carried six stories, two apiece on the front page, plus excerpts from Hill's news conference, which was broadcast live on CNN. *USA Today* had four stories on the Thomas case, two of them on the front page.

The *Journal* ran two paragraphs in the roundup column.

I wrote a short piece about the *Journal*'s seeming indifference to a story that was not only on everyone's lips but threatening to sink a Supreme Court nomination. "They just didn't get it," said one female staffer in the Washington bureau, invoking the now-familiar mantra. "We have no women editors here, except one on the desk. They made a collective decision that it wasn't that big a deal."

Al Hunt, the bureau chief, told me he regretted not having moved sooner: "I was really taken aback by the reaction of women on the staff. The women made it clear to me that this story was much bigger."

The *Journal* tried to recoup the following day by running four stories on the Thomas case and sexual harassment. The lead story described how "an unanticipated outpouring of rage" had prompted "an embarrassing and painful about-face on Capitol Hill." And at some newspapers.

Juan Williams and Clarence Thomas had known each other for more than a decade.

They had met in 1980, when Williams, a young editorial writer for the *Post*, went to a conference of black conservatives in San Francisco, hoping to spend some time with Thomas Sowell, a prominent economist. Sowell brushed him off, but Thomas, then an aide to Missouri Senator John Danforth, was more than willing to engage him intellectually. Williams mentioned Thomas in a column, which drew the attention of the Reagan transition team and led to Thomas's first presidential appointment, as assistant secretary of education for civil rights.

When Williams started covering the White House in the early '80s, Thomas, by then promoted to chairman of the Equal Employment Opportunity Commission, became a regular source. There were, after all, few important blacks working for Ronald Reagan. "He was always willing to entertain ideas and notions that if you talked to people in the civil rights community would have been heretical," Williams says. "As a journalist I found him fascinating. This guy was not an ideologue. He would go to a different level with me as a journalist."

By 1991, the two had much in common. Williams, thirty-seven, had grown up in subsidized housing in a poor Brooklyn neighborhood. Thomas, forty-three, had been raised by his grandfather in Georgia and forced to study in a blacks-only library. Both had doggedly climbed the ladder of success during the 1980s. Williams was the most visible black reporter in the capital and a fixture on such television shows as "Crossfire" and "Inside Washington"; Thomas, a federal judge, had been the second-ranking black in the Reagan administration, after Sam Pierce. Both had become estranged from the civil rights establishment.

Williams decided to write a lengthy magazine piece on Thomas, and they began to meet regularly. In his 1987 article for *The Atlantic*, Williams described Thomas as "sad, lonely, troubled" and said he "accurately captures the frustration of many middle-class blacks; people who are educated, employed in challenging and high-paying positions, and yet somehow still angry." In some ways, Williams might have been describing himself.

Juan Williams knew all about racial discrimination. At his elementary school, he says, the smartest classes were reserved for whites, the slowest classes all black. Williams also got plenty of hate mail from whites—one called him an "apologist for niggers"—and once struggled to explain to his seven-year-old son why a Washington nursing home didn't admit black people.

Williams, like Thomas, did not embrace the racial remedies advocated by such groups as the NAACP. He caught hell from the black community when he criticized Marion Barry long before it was fashionable. Some of Williams's colleagues believed he deliberately took a contrarian stance, opposing whatever the black establishment supported at the moment, because it made him more marketable as a television personality. But there was no question he felt strongly about his positions.

"Even as I struggle as a black writer in the smug white world of Washington journalism," he once wrote, "I find myself in a trap set by some blacks: they want me to limit my writing rather than addressing problems among blacks, including black politicians who hide their failures behind their skin color."

The nomination of Clarence Thomas propelled Juan Williams toward center stage. Senate staffers and liberal lobbyists started calling him for information that could be used against Thomas in the confirmation hearings. As the questions became more personal, Williams grew angry at the desperate effort to block Thomas. "I wasn't close to the guy by any means," he says. "I was friendly with him like I was friendly with any source." But he says Thomas was being unfairly "caricatured as this all-consuming conservative."

After the initial hearings, Williams wrote: "The entire Clarence Thomas episode illustrates the degree to which representatives of organized labor, of black interest groups, of women's organizations—much of the American Left, in fact—have lost their influence over mainstream thinking."

The following week, a seemingly minor incident triggered a series of events that would soon snowball out of control. On a Saturday in late

September 1991, Jo Ellen Murphy, an art director at the *Post,* says
Williams made some offensive remarks, such as that he had been thinking about holding her in his arms. Murphy says she had had problems
with Williams asking about her sex life a year earlier, and had moved
her desk to avoid him. This time, however, a male coworker heard of
the incident and reported it to an editor. The paper's personnel department began an inquiry, and some other women came forward with
complaints.

Two weeks later, when the Anita Hill charges surfaced, Meg
Greenfield, the *Post*'s editorial page editor, asked Williams for an opinion
piece on the situation. Williams wrote what he knew would be a highly
provocative column, and Greenfield accepted it for publication.

By now Len Downie, who had succeeded Ben Bradlee as executive
editor a month earlier, had been briefed on the harassment allegations
against Williams. Under the "church-state" separation in place at most
newspapers, Downie did not usually read submissions for the op-ed
page. Despite the obvious potential for controversy, he did not feel it
necessary to read the Williams column. And, in what Downie would
later acknowledge was a mistake, he did not tell Greenfield about the
confidential inquiry. So the editor who approved the piece didn't know
about the inquiry, and the editor who knew about the inquiry didn't read
the piece.

On Wednesday, October 9, personnel officials told Williams about
the harassment investigation. He was given an opportunity to withdraw
the op-ed piece, but decided not to. Williams felt strongly that the article
was based on his reporting and his ten-year knowledge of Thomas, and
had nothing to do with his personal situation.

The column was stripped across the top of the *Post*'s op-ed page
the next morning. Williams assailed the "smear tactics" against Thomas
as "indiscriminate, mean-spirited mudslinging supported by the so-called
champions of fairness. . . .

"Hill and the Senate staffers who called her were specifically interested in talking about rumors involving sexual harassment. She had no
credible evidence of Thomas's involvement in sexual harassment, but
she was prompted to say he had asked her out and mentioned pornographic movies to her. She rejected him as a jerk, but said she never
felt her job was threatened by him, he never touched her, and she
followed him to subsequent jobs and even had him write references
for her."

Williams sprayed other targets with rhetorical fire. He assailed

Maureen Dowd's "The Senate and Sexism" piece as illogical. He claimed, with no demonstrable proof, that the Hill affidavit had been leaked to the press through the Leadership Conference on Civil Rights. The group's director, Ralph Neas, would later call the charge "malicious, ugly and untrue."

The campaign against Thomas was a "slimy exercise," Williams concluded, that had produced a "blood-in-the-water response from reputable news operations, notably National Public Radio. They have magnified every question about Thomas into an indictment and sacrificed journalistic integrity for a place in the mob."

Williams was accosted as soon as he arrived at the *Post* that morning. "What happened in the newsroom was incredible," Williams says. "I never saw anything like it in my fucking life. The morning I got here, I had three shouting matches before I got to my desk. People were calling from all over the country. It was unbelievable."

Williams was accustomed to taking heat, but usually from the outside world. "I had always taken this as my sanctuary, like in the business with Barry, when people were attacking me from the left and the right," he says.

From Williams's vantage point, it seemed that much of the rage over Thomas had to do with abortion. Abortion was the one issue that touched women journalists in a personal way, the one issue that could make a reporter like Linda Greenhouse join a political march. Women's groups were fired up about the nomination, and Williams, by embracing Thomas, seemed to side with the enemy.

"The issue crystallized around abortion. . . . The politics washed into the newsroom and exploded in a way I had never seen before," Williams says. But he also underestimated the degree to which women were angry at him over the allegations of sexual harassment.

The next morning, Anita Hill told the Senate Judiciary Committee and a nationwide audience that Thomas had talked to her about pornographic films, women having sex with animals, the size of his penis and so on. Thomas denounced the charges as lies.

That was also the day I learned of the harassment inquiry involving Williams. I didn't know the extent of it and made a couple of calls to try to find out. Len Downie quickly got wind of this and called me into his office. He told me I could not write about the inquiry because it was an internal personnel matter and the *Post* would not allow the confidentiality of the process to be violated.

My position was that while we had to be careful about unproven allegations, the controversy swirling around Juan's column had made it a public matter. If a reporter at another paper was in such a jam, we would consider it news. Besides, it was inevitable that other news organizations would hear about it, and then we would be in the embarrassing position of playing catch-up on a story about our newsroom. It would be better to get out front now with an accurate account. But Downie had made up his mind: There would be no story, at least until the process had run its course.

Many women in the newsroom were particularly angry to see Williams popping off about sexual harassment on television. Downie ordered him not to discuss the subject on TV—all *Post* staffers need approval for outside appearances—until the inquiry was completed. He said Williams's column had become part of the story.

The next day, a Saturday, Senator Orrin Hatch quoted from Juan's column at the committee hearings, praising Williams as "a great journalist." Word of the *Post* inquiry, meanwhile, was spreading around town. A couple of reporters from other papers called me at home to ask about the inquiry. I ducked as best I could. *The Wall Street Journal* came close to writing a story, but decided against it because none of the women would speak on the record.

By Monday, things had reached fever pitch in the newsroom. Several women marched into Downie's office. They were upset with how the paper was handling the situation and felt it should be made public.

That afternoon, I was called by the *Journal*, the Baltimore *Sun*, *Time*, *Newsday*, *The Village Voice*, *The Washington Times*, WUSA-TV and WRC-TV. It got to the point where I couldn't answer the phone. Was it true, they asked, that the paper had killed my story about the Williams inquiry? I told them all the same thing—I couldn't help them, they had to call Downie—and I felt lousy about it, since I often asked reporters for help in just such difficult circumstances. Everyone tried to get me to confirm the story off the record, but I refused. I wanted to be able to say honestly that I had not cooperated with anyone.

Shortly after 6:00 P.M., WRC, the NBC station in Washington, put the story on the air. That pried open the door for us. Just before seven, Downie and Robert Kaiser, the managing editor, gave me the green light to write a story. They were preparing an editor's note to explain the situation. Less than two hours remained before deadline.

I felt a jumble of emotions as I started typing. I felt sorry for Juan, whose work I admired, but I was relieved the story was finally coming out. I empathized with the women who felt they had been mistreated, yet I also wondered how much of their accounts could fairly be published. None of the women would be quoted by name, and it didn't seem fair to push them.

I quoted one unnamed woman as saying that Williams, who is married, had made a number of sexual or insulting remarks to her and that she was "really upset." Another unidentified employee said Williams often commented on her clothes, made sexual comments and asked her out, making her "very uncomfortable." But the sordid details were left out.

I reached Juan Williams shortly before deadline. He was clearly unhappy, but relatively subdued. He said he had written the column "before I had any knowledge of any investigation. My journalistic ethics and the ethics of the newspaper were never compromised."

Williams called me at home at eleven to add some comments for later editions. He called the harassment allegations "absolutely false" and said they "amount to nothing more than women taking a passing word in the wrong way." He said that "the *Post* seems to have labored mightily to produce some charges against me and they have come up with a big zero. It seems to me to be terribly unfair."

The story and the editor's note appeared on Tuesday, October 15. That evening, the Senate voted 52–48 to confirm Clarence Thomas as an associate justice of the Supreme Court. But the Williams story had not played itself out, and the rest of the press caught up the next day.

"Newspaper Discloses Op-Ed Conflict," *The New York Times* said.

"Thomas Supporter in the Hot Seat," said *USA Today*.

The *New York Post* delivered a reliably tabloid headline: "Anti-Anita Scribe in Sex Harass Probe."

Williams told the *Times* he was "socially awkward" and that perhaps the women had misunderstood his jokes. "I love *The Washington Post*, and I'm so disappointed that they would treat me this way," he said. "It's heartbreaking to me."

The Clarence Thomas nomination had energized the troops at *The Washington Times*, where Wes Pruden, Barney Frank's chief tormentor, was now running the show.

Pruden had taken the helm four months earlier, and there was talk that the paper's conservative tilt might become even more pronounced. Pruden insisted the news coverage would be straightforward, but reporters sometimes complained that their stories had been "Prudenized," or rewritten with a blatant political slant.

Pruden assigned his Supreme Court reporter, Dawn Weyrich Ceol, to the Thomas hearings. Ceol, twenty-seven, had spent three years at the paper trying to erase the right-wing image conjured up by her maiden name. She was the daughter of Paul Weyrich, a prominent conservative fund-raiser. Although a conservative herself, Ceol prided herself on her journalistic balance. She did not want to be known as Daughter Of.

The *Times* was now defending Thomas, its new hero, against the liberal onslaught. "Thomas Sexism Charges Refuted," the paper declared in a front-page story the day after the Anita Hill allegations broke, as if the dispute had been conclusively settled. Another front-page "news" story was titled "Women Speak Out for Judge." Pruden attacked the coverage of Hill's charges as "distorted," "delirious" and "media harassment."

On the first day of the Judiciary Committee hearings, Dawn Ceol led her story with Thomas's charge of "a high-tech lynching for uppity blacks." But Pruden had added the words "as lethal as hanging him from the limb of a tree." Worse, Pruden had taken Anita Hill's graphic allegations of sexual harassment, which Ceol had described in the third paragraph, and pushed them down to the ninth paragraph, where the story jumped to an inside page. Ceol complained to the national editor, Francis Coombs, who explained that Pruden always used colorful language.

On Sunday, the third day of the hearings, Ceol filed her story about 10:00 P.M. It had been a grueling day, with a parade of pro-Thomas and pro-Hill witnesses, and she was tired. Ceol wrote her lead paragraph straight down the middle, quoting some witnesses as attacking Hill and others as supporting her charges. The banner headline in the first edition was equally balanced: "THOMAS ACCUSER LAUDED, ASSAILED."

A few minutes later, Ceol's editor, Alan Bradford, called her in the Senate press gallery. She had been listening with one ear as John Doggett III, a Texas lawyer, told the committee that Anita Hill had pursued him for dates and once lectured him about leading her on. Bradford said that Pruden had been struck by Doggett's testimony and wanted her to rewrite the story.

Ceol didn't think Doggett deserved much; most papers would dismiss him as a minor witness with a couple of paragraphs. She typed a few sentences about Doggett and inserted them as the third and fourth paragraphs of the story.

Twenty minutes later, Ceol checked her story by computer and was surprised to see something called "New Thomas Top—Pruden." The new lead on her story said: "An extraordinary Senate Judiciary Committee hearing stretched into the early-morning hours today as the senators wrestled with witnesses who painted Anita Hill as a woman who fantasized relationships with men with whom she worked."

The new banner headline: "Miss Hill Painted as 'Fantasizer.' "

The story now led off with eight paragraphs about Doggett's negative assessments of Anita Hill. The first reference to Hill's defenders was buried in the thirteenth paragraph. Pruden had also added several mistakes to the story. He said "witnesses" had charged that Hill had fantasized about "men," when it was actually just one witness, Doggett.

Ceol was furious. The piece was totally slanted; her reputation would be ruined. She grabbed the phone and called Bradford.

"I just lost my shit," she says. "I just started screaming. I said, 'This is my work. It looks like I've been smoking crack cocaine. I want my byline off of it, and if my byline doesn't come off, I'm resigning.' But it was too late; the presses were rolling. The next morning, Dawn Ceol quit *The Washington Times.*

"It's an editors' newspaper," Pruden explained, "and we edit stories the way newspapers used to, and sometimes a reporter is unhappy about it." He said the story was "absolutely not" tilted for political reasons, but that he was trying to capture "the early-morning drama. . . . Certainly the accusers of Anita Hill painted her as a fantasizer." But other *Times* reporters were also upset.

"He told people the reason I quit was that I was having some sort of adolescent rebellion against my father," Ceol said. "I really think the man has lost his sense of journalistic integrity." She began looking for a job, but it was the middle of the worst newspaper recession in decades and nobody was hiring. She took a job as a waitress.

There was a brief postscript. Clarence Thomas called Paul Weyrich, an old friend from the Reagan administration, to ask about his daughter's welfare. Thomas later spoke to Ceol for about fifteen minutes. "He was very supportive," Ceol recalled. "He said, 'Your name is the only thing you've got.' "

. . .

The Juan Williams affair had the right wing's attack dogs salivating with excitement. They were not about to let a few inconvenient facts spoil the fun.

The Wall Street Journal pounced on the red-meat issue with a lead editorial titled "Politically Correct Newsrooms." It began: "Juan Williams, a black journalist, has been taken hostage by *The Washington Post.*" The paper said Downie had "ordered Mr. Williams to stop saying nice things about Clarence Thomas." It ended with a plea to "Free Juan Williams."

The *Journal's* diatribe artists also chastised *The New York Times* for having "turned its front page over to editorials by Maureen Dowd." And they took a slap at me: "Policing the troops, *The Washington Post's* media reporter/critic, Howard Kurtz, ripped *The Wall Street Journal's* decision to limit its coverage of the Hill accusations Monday and Tuesday to its page-one World Wide summary of major news events. . . . No keeping your cool when the pack is running."

Unfortunately, this PC business bore little relation to reality. For one thing, the *Post's* editorial page had *supported* Thomas's nomination against what it called Hill's "unproven" allegations. Indeed, the *Post* had given Juan Williams a forum for backing Thomas in the first place. To be sure, women at the paper would not have been so angry had Williams not defended Thomas against the sexual harassment charges. But the newspaper's credibility problem centered on the allegations against Williams, not his political stance.

The *Journal* editorial was the first artillery blast in a conservative counteroffensive. Media analyst Robert Lichter, in a later *Wall Street Journal* piece, would decry "the growing influence of feminists at major media outlets, and their tendency to assume all women would react as they did."

"It was like the primal scream of the male locker room," Maureen Dowd says. "If you thought the hearings should be taken seriously and that Hill should have an airing, you were (a) wrong, (b) feminist and (c) liberal."

Dowd readily concedes that everyone involved in the Thomas hearings had a political agenda. "The women's groups had to believe Hill before she even told her story, since they thought the issue of sexual harassment was important and should be taken seriously." But, she says, "the right wing's premise from the very beginning was that Anita Hill was lying and Clarence Thomas was telling the truth, and if you didn't go along with their premise, you were skewed. To me the central issue was not who was telling the truth, but that the Senate set up the rules in such a way that you could never find out the truth."

The *Journal* had one other target on the day it excoriated "politically correct newsrooms." Alongside the editorial was a column by Al Hunt, dredging up the gory details about Nina Totenberg's nineteen-year-old plagiarism incident.

Hunt complained that Totenberg, in her interview with me, had "left the impression that the harassment was behind her firing over charges of plagiarism." He then detailed how Totenberg, while at the *National Observer*—owned by Dow Jones, like the *Journal*—had lifted five quotes from a *Washington Post* story. "Purposeful plagiarism is one of the cardinal sins of journalism from which reporters can never recover their credibility," Hunt declared. "There is no statute of limitations on that judgment." It looked to many people like a corporate hit job. Totenberg says Hunt had been prosecutorial on the phone and simply ignored her contention that her boss had made sexual demands of her, although Hunt says he knew the editor in question had a reputation as a harasser.

Hunt calls the idea that he had a hidden agenda "utter, complete nonsense" and says he wrote about Totenberg only because she insisted she had not been fired for plagiarism. "She did exactly what people were accusing Anita Hill of doing: she used sexual harassment as a camouflage for something else," he says. "If she had told me 'I got fired for plagiarism, and separately there was a case of sexual harassment,' I wouldn't have written one word. I sure as hell wouldn't gratuitously bring up something that happened nineteen years ago. But when someone uses sexual harassment falsely, it becomes terribly relevant."

But even Al Hunt considered the *Journal*'s PC editorial an embarrassment. Its contention that Juan Williams had been silenced contradicted the *Journal*'s own conflict-of-interest policy. The day it was published, Hunt posted an internal memo in the Washington bureau saying: "If any reporter in this bureau were a party to sexual harassment charges he or she clearly would have a vested interest in that subject matter." If such reporters had been writing about the Thomas-Hill controversy, "they would have been taken off the moment this conflict became known. In short, we would have done what Len Downie of *The Washington Post* did last Friday."

But the clarion call had been sounded. The *Richmond Times-Dispatch* assailed what it called Downie's "gag order," saying it "has the flavor of harassment of a professional journalist for expressing opinions that are politically incorrect in liberal newsrooms." *The Washington Times,* delighted to see its rival struggling with the Williams matter, said the *Post* "chose to shut him up" and described the incident as "the latest lynching."

A more serious line of criticism came from the *Post*'s ombudsman, Richard Harwood. He wrote that *Post* officials who violated the confidentiality promised Williams "are guilty of a tawdry act that stains the reputation of the newspaper and of journalists in general."

But Harwood failed to address the other side of the dilemma: The *Post*'s reputation for fairness was also on the line. And the fact that other news organizations were about to trumpet the story made it impossible to sweep under the corporate rug.

Most critics concluded the *Post* had bungled the affair. The *Columbia Journalism Review* awarded the paper one of its "darts" for "self-serving ineptitude." Mark Jurkowitz of the *Boston Phoenix* said Downie had made "a serious screw-up" by not warning the editorial page about the allegations. Jonathan Alter spread the blame around in a *Newsweek* piece. He took a swipe at " 'Don Juan' Williams" and another at "several angry women reporters known informally as the Fem Police." Alter also said that Al Hunt, "bashed by the *Post* for his slowness . . . shook off any embarrassment and took off after Totenberg. . . . Even some of Hunt's friends saw his tone as gratuitous."

The *Washington Times* offered a particularly nasty item about Nina Totenberg and her account of sexual harassment at the *Observer*, where Wes Pruden once worked. " 'She used to fantasize that . . . the editor of the *Observer* . . . a man with a rake's eye for the young women in the newsroom, was hot for her,' recalls one former colleague. 'But if she felt abused it was probably because she was the only woman not being hit on.' " It was a bad joke: Nina Totenberg, like Anita Hill, was being dismissed as a fantasizer.

Totenberg believed that sexism was fueling some of the attacks. After all, not a word had been written about Tim Phelps of *Newsday,* while her personal life was being scrutinized by *People* and *Vanity Fair.* Of course, no one had forced Totenberg to appear on "Nightline" and "PrimeTime Live," and slings and arrows are part of the price of fame.

Still, I belatedly understood why Totenberg had been so reluctant to talk about her experience with sexual harassment. Although she clearly should have been more forthcoming about her plagiarism mistake, she also knew her detractors were waiting for the chance to shred her reputation. "I felt like hamburger meat," Totenberg says. (A special counsel named by the Senate to investigate the Anita Hill leak later threatened to subpoena Totenberg and Phelps after they refused to reveal their sources, but embarrassed Senate leaders ordered the subpoena dropped and the probe ended inconclusively.)

Soon *The Washington Times* was off on a new crusade to find the leaker. A front-page box trumpeted a "$5,000 Reward" for information leading to the culprit. "Bounty for Leaker Climbs," a page-one story announced the next day, listing the new reward as $32,995. The paper's earlier certainty that Senator Metzenbaum was the leaker was dropped without explanation. The *Times* soon offered up a new suspect: Paul Simon. In a remarkable front-page story, Paul Rodriguez and George Archibald, the same team that did the Barney Frank stories, fingered the Illinois senator: "Senate Judiciary Committee members of both parties said yesterday that Senator Paul Simon, Illinois Democrat, is the man who leaked to the media the confidential FBI report that led to the spectacular conclusion of the Thomas hearings."

Then, this amazing second paragraph: "The accusers asked not to be identified and produced no evidence. Mr. Simon told *The Washington Times* he was not the culprit."

That was it. Not a scintilla of supporting information. Just the obvious irony of unidentified senators leaking a story about who they believed the leaker was. Archibald said that three senators had provided the reporters with "very credible information" about the leak, but that they could not disclose the information without jeopardizing their sources.

"I don't necessarily believe that Paul Simon was the one," he said. "I don't know what to believe. . . . It was inconclusive, as the Clarence Thomas–Anita Hill situation was."

It seemed likely that once *The Washington Post* announced to the world that it was conducting a sexual harassment inquiry, it would have to disclose the outcome.

But when Juan Williams returned to the newsroom after two weeks away from the office, the paper refused to say how the complaints had been resolved. Len Downie twice turned down my request to write about the inquiry, even to say that Williams was back at work and management had no comment on whether disciplinary action had been taken. I started getting press calls again. It seemed inevitable that the rest of the story would come out.

The controversy died down for a couple of days. Then Williams minimized the allegations in an interview with James Cox of *USA Today*: "What happened was that [the *Post*] said basically, 'Come back to work. We're sorry this happened.' The resolution is basically, 'You've got to watch what you say.' "

Williams told the paper that the complaints arose from "my attempts at being friendly and trying not to be aloof, [saying,] 'Hi. How are you?'

I thought saying, 'Hey, did you have a date? How was your weekend?' was part of being a good coworker and friend."

These comments ignited a revolt in the newsroom. More delegations marched into Downie's office. About fifty women met with Downie in the second-floor cafeteria, complaining that the *Post* was remaining silent while Williams trivialized the whole affair.

More than one hundred staffers signed a letter to Downie that said: "We feel Juan's unrefuted false statements to the national media continue to cause anguish and professional harm to the women involved. They also have left many people inside and outside the *Post* with the impression that either the complaints were not serious or were not taken seriously."

For the second time in three weeks, Downie reversed himself and said I could write a story about the controversy. Seven women agreed to go on the record. They said Williams had been making sexually explicit or hostile remarks for months or years, and that he had persisted despite a complaint to his editor three years earlier.

The women described such comments as "I want to be your gynecologist" and "Did your feet hit the ceiling last night?" One staffer, Karen Tanaka, said Williams called her "an old hag" who "can't get a man." Jo Ellen Murphy said that "he was obsessed with my sex life." Molly Roberts, a former staffer, said that "it wasn't really that he wanted to have a date with me. . . . It was that his comments were bothering me, were hurting me, and he just liked that game." But Williams believed he was engaging in good-natured bantering, and later maintained that some of the accounts were exaggerated.

Management clearly wanted my story to be the final chapter of the mess. Just after 7:00 P.M., Downie posted an apology from Williams on the newsroom bulletin board. Williams's letter said he had "repeatedly acknowledged that certain verbal conduct of mine in the past was inappropriate. It pained me to learn during the investigation that I had offended some of you. I have said so repeatedly in the last few weeks, and repeat here: some of my verbal conduct was wrong, I now know that, and I extend my sincerest apology to those whom I offended." Downie also posted his own letter, saying the complaints were found to be "serious" and that Juan would "apologize to women he offended."

Williams, for his part, now believes he was caught up in a larger battle. "If the man on the moon came down," Williams says, "he would say what happened to me was in the context of a highly charged political situation having to do with the Clarence Thomas nomination, and did not have much to do with me."

In another time and place, the whole controversy would have been handled quietly and everyone's privacy respected. But the supercharged atmosphere of the Clarence Thomas hearings had turned the media's blinding spotlight back on itself, and we didn't like what we saw.

Nearly everyone involved seemed to have a political agenda: The women who wrote angry pieces about sexual harassment. Nina Totenberg, who had had her own brush with sexual harassment. Juan Williams, who accused the liberals of smearing Thomas while facing allegations of harassment himself. The *Washington Post* staffers who tried to turn Williams's case into a cause célèbre. The *Wall Street Journal* editorialists who charged the *Post* with muzzling Williams. *The Washington Times,* which rewrote Dawn Ceol's stories with a pro-Thomas slant. It was as though the worst conspiracy theories about the press—that it is filled with passionate ideologues who cover their raging bias with a thin veneer of objectivity—had suddenly come true.

Every so often we stumble across an emotional issue that makes true objectivity all but impossible. When *The Philadelphia Inquirer* linked poverty and birth control, virtually everyone on the paper had to take sides on whether the editorial was racist. When the New York press investigated Tawana Brawley, there was no middle ground on whether she was lying. When *The Washington Post* tried to prove that Marion Barry was using cocaine, the newsroom grew as polarized as the city.

The Thomas hearings were particularly baffling because they defied the usual stereotypes about black criminals, black welfare mothers and black basketball stars. This was the tale of two bright, successful, well-educated black lawyers who were telling diametrically opposite stories. It was impossible to write, as some reporters had a few months earlier in the William Kennedy Smith case, that Thomas had been wounded by some low-class bimbo. Anita Hill had a quiet dignity that shielded her from the sort of she-asked-for-it portrait *The New York Times* had painted of Patricia Bowman. This time there was no room for the usual journalistic straddling. Either Hill was spinning wild exaggerations as the tool of liberal interest groups, as Juan Williams suggested, or the man who would be the second black justice in the history of the United States Supreme Court was a bald-faced liar. Once the hearings receded from memory, the media would help build Anita Hill into a feminist hero, and within a year the polls would shift, showing that more people believed her than the reclusive Justice Thomas. But the core of the story remained an ideologically charged mystery, with conservative writers defending Thomas and liberal columnists championing Hill's cause, endlessly debating the arcane details like some latter-day Alger Hiss case.

The stark racial overtones of the Thomas hearings were matched by the vast perception gap separating men and women. If the kind of sexual harassment that Hill was charging was indeed commonplace in America, as an avalanche of stories and women's confessions seemed to suggest, where the hell had the press been all along? Were male editors really so out of touch? Had they been blind to the anger in their own newsrooms, where, according to a later survey, more than a third of the women said they had been harassed? The media's dramatic discovery of sexual harassment was all too typical of a business that is frequently late in recognizing important social trends, then overcompensates through overcoverage till everyone is sick of the subject.

The Thomas-Hill clash was a classic opportunity for newspapers to marshal their investigative resources and, while everyone watched the gripping drama on television, uncover what had really happened. Perhaps, as *The Boston Globe*'s Greg Moore said after the Charles Stuart saga, some cases simply can't be cracked. Or perhaps the press, mesmerized by the racial and sexual maelstrom that enveloped so many of its own members, didn't try hard enough.

10

Outflanked

Long before the first bomber hit Baghdad, the press and the Pentagon had radically different ideas about how America's first full-scale war in two decades should be covered. The press was armed with First Amendment platitudes, while military officials (whose livelihood depends on analyzing and outsmarting the enemy) controlled the airspace, the rules of engagement and the reporters' copy.

The press got its butt kicked.

In fact, it was worse than that. The press became an object of ridicule. Day after day, as reporters clamored for the smallest crumbs at televised briefings, they appeared churlish, ill-informed, even unpatriotic. Journalists badger uncooperative officials with provocative questions every day, but suddenly the whole country was watching. The Pentagon briefers stonewalled on the most basic questions about casualties and bomb damage, but it was the reporters, many of them young and inexperienced, who sounded cocky and unreasonable.

The very fact that they were covering the Persian Gulf war from a hotel in Dhahran, rather than being out with the troops, as they had been in Vietnam, showed how desperate their situation had become. You don't find out how the war is going from a five-star hotel, and they knew it. But the generals, who felt badly burned in Saigon, weren't letting anyone onto the battlefield without a "minder," as the military escorts were called, and those who ventured out on their own were promptly detained and sent back to Dhahran, like schoolboys caught without a hall pass.

There was much editorial tut-tutting about this state of affairs, but the public was overwhelmingly in the military's corner. Eight in ten Americans thought the level of censorship was just fine, and a majority said even stiffer restrictions would be welcome. The country was at war, wasn't it? Didn't reporters have a responsibility to fall into line? What was the idea of giving Saddam Hussein a megaphone to spread his propaganda? The media's explanations fell flat, particularly when things seemed to be going so well. The United States of America was finally standing up to a little tinhorn dictator, the military was getting the job done in superb fashion, and these arrogant reporters were bitching and moaning about not getting enough information! The press was fighting the last war, and it showed.

As *The Washington Post*'s Henry Allen put it: "The Persian Gulf press briefings are making reporters look like fools, nitpickers and egomaniacs; like dilettantes who have spent exactly none of their lives on the end of a gun or even a shovel; dinner party commandos, slouching inquisitors, collegiate spitball artists; people who have never been in a fistfight much less combat; a whining, self-righteous, upper-middle-class mob jostling for whatever tiny flakes of fame may settle on their shoulders like some sort of Pulitzer Prize dandruff."

The war would stand as the most embarrassing moment in media-military relations—that is, until the infamous night in December 1992 when Navy SEALs hitting the beach in Somalia were surrounded by a small army of reporters and photographers who blinded them with television lights, clamored for interviews and generally acted like obnoxious adolescents. That sorry performance, turning a humanitarian mission to aid starving Africans into a Fellini-esque photo op, underscored what the Pentagon had been saying for years: that the press simply could not discipline itself, that reporters would blithely endanger the safety of American troops for the sake of journalistic drama.

The six-week gulf war was perhaps the ultimate metaphor for the daily struggle between the press and those at the highest levels of power. The techniques of secrecy, spin control and obfuscation had been well honed at the White House, where successive administrations had tried to control the timing and flow of information. The very notion of limiting coverage to a small pool of reporters, who must share their dispatches with their colleagues, had evolved from the restrictions slapped on the press whenever the president travels. The Bush administration ran the public relations aspect of the war like a modern political campaign, putting out a line of the day, making the right pictures available for television and responding to criticism in the same news cycle. In politics, however, reporters can always gravitate to competing power centers: disgruntled officials, members of Congress, rival candidates. In time of war, the Pentagon holds all the cards, and even partisan critics tend to hold their fire.

Journalists justified their inquisitions by brandishing the usual clichés about the "public's right to know." Indeed, Americans were hungry for news about the war, and newspapers were perfectly positioned to furnish the detail, the analysis, the perspective that television couldn't provide. But the public had a different agenda. Most readers and viewers believed that bad news might undermine the war effort and should be suppressed. They were perfectly comfortable with the idea of military officials' deciding what could be published, despite the long-standing tendency of these same officials to cover up embarrassments and weapons failures even in peacetime. Any effort to tell the Iraqi side of the story, as CNN's Peter Arnett learned in reporting from Baghdad, brought angry charges that reporters were helping the enemy.

The problem for the press is that its core values, such as objectivity and skepticism, do not mesh well with the rally-round-the-flag passions that swept the country in wartime. Had the gulf war gone badly, our adversarial role would have looked very different. With the swift American success, we were reduced to cannon fodder for our harshest detractors. It was not until months had passed, with a defiant Saddam still firmly in power and the emir of Kuwait still an autocratic ruler, that the media's questions about the war achieved much resonance.

Long after the war, we learned from *Newsday*'s Patrick Sloyan and the *Army Times* that some Iraqi soldiers had been buried alive in trenches by U.S. plows and earth movers. And, in *The Washington Post,* Barton Gellman reported that the military had waited months to tell the families of thirty-three dead servicemen that their loved ones had been killed by friendly fire. These were the kinds of grisly details that Pentagon officials were able to keep from the press, though they had nothing to do with military security.

It was not until a year after the war that we learned that key weapons like the stealth fighter and the cruise missile had struck only about half their military targets, compared to the 85 to 90 percent rate claimed by the Pentagon. Or that the Patriot missile had not worked as well as initially advertised. Or, after months of official denials, that American-led bombers had inflicted serious damage on Iraqi generators, contributing to thousands of postwar civilian deaths. Or that at least twenty-four female soldiers had been raped or sexually assaulted by American servicemen. Or, as Henry Gonzalez, the much-ridiculed whistle-blower of the S&L affair, helped discover, that the Bush administration had given Saddam billions of dollars in agriculture credits and advanced technology until shortly before the invasion. The buildup of Saddam would even be given a scandalous name: Iraqgate.

Perhaps the greatest indignity for the press—the one that convinced the strategists in the Bush White House that they were capturing the hearts and minds of the American people—took place when the media mob in Saudi Arabia was lampooned on "Saturday Night Live." Here, after all, was the hipper-than-thou show that had defined the youth culture in the mid-'70s, when Chevy Chase was ridiculing Gerald Ford and many of today's middle-aged reporters were smoking dope and listening to the Eagles. In 1991, the reporters themselves were cast in the role of buffoons.

"I am happy to take any questions you might have," the handsome Pentagon briefer in khaki fatigues began, "with the understanding that there are certain sensitive areas that I'm just not going to get into, particularly information that may be useful to the enemy."

A scruffy reporter piped up: "What date are we going to start the ground attack?"

Another shouted: "Where would you say our forces are most vulnerable to attack and how could the Iraqis best exploit those weaknesses?"

And a haughty woman: "I understand there are passwords our troops on the front lines use. Could you give us some examples of these?"

For all the snickers, there was a darker side to the way the press got snookered in the gulf. For the first time in fifty years, Americans were reading stories marked "Censored by the U.S. Military." Reporters had been shut out and blacked out, disrespected, detained and fed disinformation. The government set a new standard for manipulation of the media that may well have lingering effects for years to come.

Sydney Schanberg, who won a Pulitzer Prize as the last remaining American reporter in war-torn Cambodia in 1975, says the press felt "embarrassed and humiliated and mortified" over its Persian Gulf performance—and with good reason. "The worst thing you can do is lock yourself in a briefing room, which is what we did," he says. "You're in a room with people who know more about military affairs than you do. You're in a room where you're going to look foolish. We looked like a bunch of little babies."

. . .

When Saddam Hussein sent his troops into Kuwait on August 2, 1990, the American press was as unprepared as the Bush administration for the prospect of war.

Almost overnight, editors and reporters had to grapple with the daunting logistics of a desert battlefield. There were frantic meetings about gas masks, Saudi visas, satellite phones. When the Defense Department got approval from the Saudi Arabian government to bring in the first press pools, the major news organizations—*The New York Times, The Washington Post,* the *Los Angeles Times, The Wall Street Journal,* AP and the networks—gobbled up the spots and refused to relinquish them. Editors insisted that their reporters stay in the gulf for weeks, even months. No one wanted to be caught napping if war broke out, or find their pool slot usurped by some upstart from Kansas City or Des Moines.

Yet once the initial excitement faded, the first wave of reporters didn't have much to report. By September there were 425 media people in the desert, but real news was as scarce as water. The press was granted occasional outings with the dusty troops, but did little more than watch them eat breakfast or change the oil. Tank formations were staged for the networks, reversing field when a better camera angle was needed. Newspapers carried stories about the overpowering heat, the shortage of soap and razors, the daily rations of sodas and Q-tips. Nearly everyone wrote home about MREs, or Meals Ready to Eat, such as franks with bean component. Some of the stories read like travelogues. One *New York Times* reporter described how he regaled soldiers with the latest sports scores and dropped oatmeal cookies into the turret of an M-1 tank. Soon the headlines took on a numbing sameness.

The Pentagon was stingy with details of the buildup, refusing even to talk about troop levels. Consider the stories that graced the nation's front pages on November 9:

"Bush Orders 200,000 More Troops to Gulf," *The Washington Post* said.

"120,000 More Troops Ordered to Gulf," said *USA Today.*

"U.S. Will Double Force in Gulf," said the *Los Angeles Times,* pegging the increase at 240,000 troops. *The New York Times* put the number at "more than 150,000."

The problem was that administration officials would not say precisely how many troops were being added to the 230,000 already in the gulf. They merely listed the Army, Marine and Air Force divisions being dispatched, forcing reporters to make their own calculations. Even families couldn't agree on the numbers. Ann Devroy, *The Washington Post*'s White House correspondent, went with the 200,000 figure, while her husband, Mark Matthews of the Baltimore *Sun*, was more conservative, saying the number "could reach" 170,000.

There were other early-warning signs that the Pentagon was prepared to exploit the media's voracious appetite for news, or at least the appearance of news. While the major news organizations clamored for more access to the troops, the military brought in 960 journalists from smaller papers and television stations under the "Hometown News Program." The locals were flown to the gulf on Air Force jets at government expense and squired around by military escorts for three- and four-day visits. The result was "Hi, Mom" journalism, soft-focus picture postcards from the desert with reporters asking softball questions.

"There was just a safer feeling," Michael Cox, an Air Force lieutenant colonel, told *The New York Times*. "If they know that they're getting a free ride and they can't afford the $2,000 ticket, there's probably going to be a tendency to say, 'We'll do good stuff here.' " Good stuff, naturally, from the Pentagon's point of view.

Even more disturbing, newspapers and TV stations started lobbying members of Congress to help them get their reporters into the gulf. A Miami station, WTVJ-TV, turned to Representative Dante Fascell, chairman of the House Foreign Affairs Committee, who pressed its case with Defense Secretary Dick Cheney and General Colin Powell, chairman of the Joint Chiefs of Staff. A Norfolk station, WAVY-TV, contacted every member of Virginia's congressional delegation, all of whom sent letters of support to the Saudi ambassador and faxed copies back to the station. Several news organizations, including KCBS-TV in Los Angeles, sought help from Senator Dennis DeConcini—conveniently forgetting that they had castigated the Arizona Democrat for pressing federal bank regulators on Charles Keating's behalf.

Every news organization, it seemed, had to have its own man or woman in the gulf. Even *Mirabella* magazine sent a correspondent. Sixteen hundred journalists, more than three times the number that covered World War II, would pass through Saudi Arabia by the war's end, and this stampede only buttressed the Pentagon's argument for the pool system. Hundreds of reporters obviously could not be allowed to roam the battlefield at will. Some of them would probably be killed, and military commanders could not accommodate large numbers of ill-equipped civilians during a lightning-fast ground war. No journalist wanted the Pentagon running a pool system, but the press corps was simply too large and competitive to police itself.

It was hard to argue that there was a compelling First Amendment case for having *Mirabella* tag along with the troops. Yet under the rules of the pool system, the big newspapers could not get a second reporter into a combat pool until all other print organizations had been accommodated. This became known as "the *Mirabella* problem." Jane De-Lynn, the *Mirabella* reporter, spent much of her time writing about the sex lives of female soldiers.

But even the best newspaper reporters were not allowed to do much. Walter Robinson of *The Boston Globe,* frustrated at his lack of access to the troops, tried to interview a few soldiers at a Hardee's restaurant in Dhahran, but a military officer ordered him to cease and desist.

The Pentagon devised ways to entertain reporters. In November, the Navy staged an amphibious landing exercise, code-named Imminent Thunder, for the press. While much of the exercise was washed out by bad weather, the military got what it wanted: a spate of stories about allied plans to attack Kuwait from the sea. This, we would learn later, was a deliberate attempt to float false information through the media, part of a ruse to distract Saddam Hussein from the actual plan to encircle his forces from the west.

By December, the press, with its relentless focus on predicting what happens next, had become obsessed with the question of when the war would begin. Here again, the administration, still hoping to bluff Saddam out of Kuwait, engaged in some masterful spin control—or what Stephen Hess of the Brookings Institution calls "honest lying."

General Calvin Waller, the deputy gulf commander, told reporters that his troops would not be ready for war by the January 15 deadline set by the United Nations. The next day, a senior Pentagon official, speaking "authoritatively" for Secretary Cheney, said that air strikes against Iraq *could* begin on that date. Every day the official line seemed to change. To add to the thickening fog, reporters recruited dozens of sound-bite experts whose conflicting predictions would become so annoyingly familiar during the war.

It is clear in retrospect that the administration was using the press to scare and confuse Saddam Hussein. And that we, having no independent way of gauging where the truth lay, took the bait.

In October 1983, reporters asked Larry Speakes, Ronald Reagan's White House spokesman, about rumors that the United States was about to invade Grenada. "Preposterous!" Speakes declared. U.S. troops hit the island a day later.

It was the first military operation in modern American history intentionally designed to exclude the press. There were no pictures of the eighteen Americans killed in the invasion, no live reports of gunfire, only interviews with the medical students who had been rescued. And that suited the Reagan administration just fine.

A senior administration official told reporters there had been no civilian casualties in Grenada. Four days later, U.S. officials admitted that a Navy plane had accidentally bombed a mental hospital on the island, killing at least twenty patients and orderlies. The Pentagon had insisted the day before that it had no knowledge of such an incident.

After news organizations complained about being frozen out of Grenada, a Pentagon commission recommended that a press pool be mobilized in strict secrecy for future military operations. During the 1989 invasion of Panama, the pool of fourteen journalists arrived hours after the invasion began and was whisked to a hotel, where an American diplomat held forth on the history of Panama. The press was less than thrilled with this arrangement. "Here we were sitting in the middle of an invasion, watching CNN and listening to some guy tell us when the Panama Canal was built," said UPI photographer Matt Mendelsohn.

A Pentagon study blamed the fiasco on poor planning by Pete Williams, the chief Pentagon spokesman, but there were political overtones as well. The report noted that President Bush and Vice President Quayle had been worried that secrecy might be compromised if the press pool were activated before the invasion.

All this was a far cry from World War II. While there was formal censorship after Pearl Harbor, accredited reporters went where the action was, assisted by military drivers, and their dispatches did not hide the ugly face of war. On June 6, 1944, within hours of the D-Day invasion of Normandy, a UPI correspondent reported that "some of the first American assault troops storming the French beaches went down under a withering German crossfire. . . . They swarmed ashore over the bodies of their dead until they established a foothold. . . . At one point Nazi machine guns wiped out some of the first troops as soon as their landing craft swung open." Such vivid accounts would not be permitted to mar Operation Desert Storm.

In Vietnam, the military opted for voluntary security guidelines, with reporters promising not to disclose information that could jeopardize U.S. forces. From 1964 through 1968, while two thousand journalists were involved in covering the war, only a half-dozen had their credentials revoked for violating the guidelines. Reporters roamed the jungles at will, often hitching rides on choppers with friendly units. But as the futility of that tragic, televised war became increasingly clear, many military officials blamed the press for turning public opinion against them. Never again, they vowed, would they allow themselves to be humiliated by the media. When Iraq invaded Kuwait fifteen years after the fall of Saigon, many of the field-grade officers in Vietnam had become senior commanders in the Persian Gulf.

Twelve days after the invasion, a top aide to General Norman Schwarzkopf, the gulf commander, began drawing up plans to require full-time military escorts for all pool reporters. By the fall of 1990, news executives were meeting repeatedly with Pete Williams in an attempt to soften the proposed restrictions. After each round, the newspapers and networks would fire off another joint letter, pronouncing the conditions unacceptable. But this was mere saber-rattling; the basic restrictions never really changed.

Reporters had no problem with the standard wartime precautions, barring them from disclosing troop movements, downed aircraft and the like. But the idea of military authorities approving all pool reports— what the Pentagon called "security review"—smacked of censorship. And the use of tightly controlled pools, which the press had always seen as a temporary measure, somehow evolved into the sole means of coverage for the coming war.

In the first days of 1991, Williams offered some changes in the rules. But the proposals would still bar pool reporters from conducting "ambush" interviews with military officials that had not been cleared in advance. Television could not show "personnel in agony or severe shock" or "images of patients suffering from severe disfigurement." Coverage of religious services in Saudi Arabia would be banned. And any journalist deemed physically unfit would be subject to expulsion.

A few days later, Williams unveiled a boiled-down set of rules that turned out to be final. All copy would still be subject to security review. Battlefield reporting would still be limited to pools. The pool reporters would be required to "remain with your military escort at all times, until released, and follow their instructions regarding your activities." The guidelines promised, however, that military censors would not delete material "just because it is embarrassing or contains criticism." It turned out to be a hollow promise.

Journalists had to decide whether to trade control for access, and access, at the moment, seemed more important. News organizations found the rules offensive, but they had no way of forcing the issue, and most grew absorbed with the preparations for war.

As the January 15 deadline approached, a jingoistic tone crept into some of the news coverage. "Time's Up—Saddam's Deadline for Doom," the *New York Post* roared.

"The whole country, including the press corps, is kind of with the president. . . . We're Americans," CBS's Lesley Stahl told viewers.

But some conservatives found the press, which occasionally made room for antiwar voices, too skeptical for their taste. Representative Mel Hancock, a Missouri Republican, accused the media of trying "to undermine support for the president" and "give aid and comfort to our enemies." Hancock posed a question that would reverberate over the next few weeks: "Whose side are they on?"

Twenty years ago, there were no television sets in the vast, football field–sized newsroom of *The Washington Post*. A couple of executives had sets in their glass-enclosed offices, but that was it. News moved at a slower pace in those precomputer days, with wire machines occasionally clanking out a bulletin and television carrying no national news until the three networks weighed in at 7:00 P.M.

Nowadays, a half-dozen TVs are mounted along the newsroom ceiling, and hardly a day goes by without a knot of reporters huddling around to watch live coverage of a presidential news conference or congressional hearing or some other event. The bigger the story, the bigger the crowd.

At 6:35 P.M. on January 16, 1991, hundreds of reporters stood transfixed around these sets, heads tilted upward, as they listened to the first sounds of war on CNN. There were no pictures, but that seemed to make the radio-style narratives of Peter Arnett, John Holli-man and Bernard Shaw all the more gripping. Within minutes I was sitting at a Rayedit computer terminal, tapping out a story about the extraordinary drama unfolding on a network that did not exist a decade earlier.

Many staffers stayed up through the night putting out several extra editions. But since most print reporters had abandoned Baghdad earlier in the week, nearly all our information was coming from television, and our readers had seen nearly all of it on the tube hours before their morning paper arrived.

Never had newspaper people felt so utterly obsolete as during the first days of the Persian Gulf war. It was a CNN war and we all knew it. The story was changing by the hour and we came out only once a day. We were constantly overtaken by events. With the gulf seven hours ahead of Washington, even the time difference conspired against us. We would work all day gathering information for the next day's paper, only to toss it out by midnight after fresh allied assaults on Iraq.

On January 17, dozens of print reporters filed stories on the wide-spread relief that Saddam Hussein had not attacked Israel, as he had threatened. Those stories had to be hastily rewritten when the first of seven Scud missiles hit Israel at 7:15 P.M. Eastern time. Had the Scuds landed a few hours later, the morning papers would have carried no word of the attacks, a modern-day replay of "Dewey Defeats Truman." We were like bike riders trying to keep up with a bullet train.

Yet newspaper circulation soared, with some papers selling 200,000 to 300,000 extra copies a day. In those first days of the war, people were buying papers from the back of delivery trucks. Television had whetted viewers' appetite for news and they rushed to read about what they had watched the night before, like Redskin fans devouring the Monday-morning analysis after the big game.

Other factors were also at work. The television coverage had im-mediacy and visual impact—you could hear the air-raid sirens, see the sky light up, watch the correspondents fumbling with their gas masks. But it was as if the reporters were reading us their raw notes, repeating unconfirmed rumors and conflicting accounts. They got plenty of facts wrong. One TV reporter announced that Iraq's elite Republican Guard had been wiped out. Another said that chemical weapons had been used against Israel. Casualties were overstated. Viewers were drowning in disconnected facts as the networks hopscotched from one country to the next. They wanted some guidance, some context, someone to help them sort it all out.

Not that newspapers didn't also make mistakes. "Iraqi Troop Loss Is Put at 150,000," the *San Jose Mercury-News* said in a wildly erroneous front-page headline after twenty-four hours of allied bombing. But by and large the print press gave some coherence to the fast-moving events, delivering what Steve Hess calls "processed news." And there were the endless sidebar stories—the war's effect on gas prices, airline travel, the Democratic Party. Newspapers' greatest strength is detail, and readers were being showered with it. I watched with amusement one day as CNN's Wolf Blitzer read from a *Washington Post* story describing how a two-thousand-pound U.S. bomb leaves a crater thirty-six feet deep and fifty feet wide—the kind of perspective usually lacking in broadcast reports.

Still, too many papers—including the *Post*—insisted on running long, tedious "lead-all" stories recounting each battle and official statement from the previous day. They couldn't quite abandon their long-standing practice of writing for the historical record. *The New York Times*, in a single day, carried more than fifty stories and columns on the war. No one I know, including all the news junkies in the business, tried to read more than a fraction of the coverage, and many people barely skimmed it. Bombarding readers with that kind of payload was probably more a matter of journalistic pride than informing the public.

At one point I watched NBC and read the *Los Angeles Times*, a behemoth of a newspaper, in an effort to compare print and broadcast coverage of the war. It was a fascinating exercise. The *Los Angeles Times*, while slower and heavier, achieved a form of air superiority, delivering page after page of war news. There were reports on Baghdad radio propaganda; the love life of women soldiers; possible defects in the Army's Bradley Fighting Vehicles; the Navy trying to weed out lesbians; the war's impact on the city of Norfolk, Virginia; the military's problems with the media; the impact of CNN on the Arab world; the massive oil slick reaching the Saudi coast; and on and on. There were half-page graphics crammed with little factoids, columns by a retired colonel and, appropriately, a daily feature called "TV and the Gulf War." If you had nothing else to do, you could spend all day reading about the war.

Reuters scored a coup with a dispatch about how allied bombers had destroyed an Iraqi hotel, full of families, that was located near a communications tower. Television would not catch up until pictures became available that evening.

NBC's reports, while largely limited to the "Nightly News" and updates on the "Today" show, were quite vivid. There was drama—correspondent Brad Willis, in helmet and goggles, with pictures of charred Iraqi tanks in the desert. There was poignancy—a report on a Palestinian family on the West Bank that opened with a shot of a toddler putting a gas mask on his Mickey Mouse doll. There was pathos—reporter Bill Lagattuta interviewing the crying widow of a slain American serviceman. "Her grief was almost unwatchable," Lagattuta said. Television showed it anyway.

But the TV coverage took on a certain sameness after a while, as when Willis appeared with his sand-swept footage for the third consecutive night, although he had nothing new to report.

Flushed with success from their news management on the battlefield, Pentagon officials decided to try their luck at home. They barred reporters from covering the arrival of casualties at Dover Air Force Base in Delaware. There was no conceivable national security rationale, just a flimsy argument about the privacy of families that had never manifested itself in previous conflicts. It was clear the government wanted no pictures that would shatter the illusion of a bloodless war.

Both newspapers and television were captivated by the Pentagon's selective release of gun-camera videos, which showed "smart bombs" destroying their targets with pinpoint accuracy. The military had proven once again that in the electronic age, controlling the pictures meant controlling the story. Few reporters questioned why we weren't seeing pictures of the more prevalent "dumb bombs," which were more likely to cause what the Pentagon obliquely called collateral damage. Nor were pictures of B-52 carpet bombing, which would have shown the devastation being visited upon Iraq, made public. When news organizations demanded videotape of unsuccessful bombing runs, Pete Williams promised to look into it. No such pictures were ever released. It remained a Nintendo war, all flashing lights and no dead bodies.

"I think that colored the press and the public's perception of how swimmingly things were going," said Mark Thompson, a defense reporter for Knight-Ridder Newspapers. "Reporters went, 'Wow! She-bang! This is great!' I'd like to see some bombs not destroying buildings with a single bound." Terry Eastland, a media columnist for the *Ameri-*

can Spectator, said some of the early hype was fueled by a "patriotic fervor" among reporters.

"You experience the adrenaline," Thompson conceded. "There seemed to be a silent chant of 'Okay! Let's go!' We are sort of rooting for the home team."

If the press had kept up that sort of cheerleading, it would have been perfectly in tune with the public mood and a hell of a lot more popular. But within a few days our skeptical instincts returned, and we began to demand more than the sketchy victory statements the military was churning out. It seemed to the outside world that reporters were determined to make our fighting men and women look bad, rather than just pressing for an honest accounting, and the public quickly turned against us.

On January 22, I went to the Pentagon to see how the press was faring in the daily briefings. The first-floor briefing room is located at the end of Correspondents Corridor, dedicated in 1972 by Defense Secretary Melvin Laird "in honor of a free and strong American press." It seemed somewhat less than free and strong at the moment, especially when I saw a group of TV technicians who had hooked up a Nintendo game in the briefing room.

Lieutenant General Thomas Kelly, a ruddy-faced man with a chest full of medals, took to the podium, facing seventeen minicams and nearly sixty reporters. We would learn later that Kelly had rehearsed extensively for each three-thirty briefing, with Pentagon officials peppering him with the questions they had picked up from reporters wandering the halls.

Most of the inquiries were reasonably intelligent, as might be expected from the regular beat reporters. Here are some of Kelly's answers: "We're not discussing the number of Patriot missiles expended. . . . We have air superiority. I'm not going to give you actual numbers. . . . I'd be reticent to hang a percentage on it right now. . . . The Israelis are working hard on that. You'll have to go ask them what the specifics are. . . . I'll have to check on that and get back to you."

A total stonewall. When John Tirpak of *Aerospace Daily* asked Kelly which one of three standard missiles American pilots had used to shoot down Iraqi planes, the general bristled. "You're buttin' into a policy there," he said, as if that were somehow against the law.

The tension level increased when Pete Williams took over the briefing. Shouts of "Pete! Pete!" filled the air, and the questioning turned from jargon-laden subjects to the Pentagon's attempts to manage the news.

Reporters were upset about the military's initial claim that 80 percent of its bombing raids had been successful. Officials later admitted that the number of "sorties" had included reconnaissance, refueling and other support missions, and that "success" had been defined as the pilot releasing his payload and returning to base, regardless of whether the target was destroyed. We had been snookered again. But Williams turned aside the hostile questions with polished ease.

When the televised briefing ended, a Senior Defense Official—you can probably guess who—retreated to the hallway for a fifteen-minute "background" briefing with twenty or so reporters. He could not be identified under the ground rules, an arrangement designed to allow for more candor. But the backgrounder yielded little more than promises of more information. One reporter, uttering that dreaded phrase from the Vietnam era, asked whether the Pentagon was facing a "credibility gap."

"If that were true, I would be concerned," said the senior defense official, who did not look concerned.

I asked some of the Pentagon regulars what they thought of the briefing.

"I wouldn't say it was wildly informative," said David Lynch of *The Orange County Register*.

"They've sharpened their ability to tell you why they can't tell you something," said Melissa Healy of the *Los Angeles Times*.

My color story on the briefing ran in *The Washington Post*'s Style section, along with two other reports on military-media relations. The next day, Secretary Cheney and General Powell took over the daily briefing, apparently to counter criticism that the military wasn't being forthcoming. To my surprise—after all, he had a war to run—Cheney began by taking note of the three Style stories and wondering whether the press didn't have something more important to do. It was clear that the Pentagon was certainly taking this matter of managing the news very, very seriously.

Carol Morello of *The Philadelphia Inquirer* was aboard the aircraft carrier USS *Kennedy* when the war broke out. As pilots started shouting and giving each other high-fives, a military escort hustled Morello and other reporters to a small room below decks.

"He rounded us up for that first crucial hour," she said. "I tried begging, I tried arguing, I tried banging my head against the wall. I said, 'History is being made.' By the time we got out, that initial euphoria had died down."

Military officials were suddenly functioning like editors, and some wielded a heavy blue pencil. When pilots on the USS *Kennedy* told an AP reporter that they had been watching porno movies before their bombing missions, a public affairs officer deleted the information as "too embarrassing," according to Morello.

There were other incidents of outright censorship. When Frank Bruni of the *Detroit Free Press* filed a story describing pilots returning from bombing missions as "giddy," a military escort changed the word to "proud."

"You're trying to portray military people as human beings; not everybody's a hero," Bruni said. "When you have a situation where access is everything, and people in the same channels are looking at your stories, it's impossible not to be a little afraid that how much access you get will be affected by what you write."

Malcolm Browne of *The New York Times* lost what would have been a major scoop. Officers had told Browne that U.S. air strikes had destroyed many of Iraq's nuclear facilities, but a unit commander blocked his pool report on the grounds that it could aid Iraqi intelligence. Schwarzkopf later disclosed the same information at a briefing. "We were essentially unpaid employees of the Department of Defense," Browne said.

In theory, the Pentagon could not force reporters to change their stories, and disputes were to be appealed to Pete Williams, who would take up the matter with the reporter's editor back home. But the journalists were well aware that the military had the power to revoke their credentials, and no one wanted to hold up a hot story for a lengthy bureaucratic wrangle over a few sentences.

Blatant attempts at censoring copy faded after the first couple of weeks. The larger problem, the pool reporters soon realized, was that the escorts controlled their every movement. John King of the AP says his escort frequently interrupted his interviews when he asked servicemen what the escort deemed to be "political" questions. "I think we have every right to ask these kids if they think this is worth dying for," King said.

When Stephanie Glass of the *San Antonio Light* complained that her escorts were stopping her from asking questions, she was told she would be "put back on the bus" for "being a smart ass."

Then there were the seemingly endless permutations of security review. Doug Jehl of the *Los Angeles Times* says that after each of his stories was reviewed by his Army escort, "it moved to the 1st Armored Division public affairs officer, who not only reviewed the copy himself but was under orders to show it to the division chief of staff. It then moved to the Army VII Corps, where public affairs officers conducted a similar review. It next headed to a field officer of the Army Central Command, where another review was conducted. At every step, a new set of eyes and interpretations were applied to the copy."

Whether by accident or design, the military had come up with a brutally efficient method of controlling the press: censorship by delay. Pentagon officials had constructed a Rube Goldberg system in which pool reports were placed on Humvee jeeps and had to be handed off three times before they reached the headquarters at Dhahran. Missing a rendezvous point by five minutes could mean a twenty-four-hour delay. Yet the authorities refused to allow reporters to use their own satellite phones to file their stories. Reporters were also refused access to fax machines. Many journalists risked their lives against Iraqi artillery fire and land mines, only to learn that most of their stories never made it back home.

"You turn over control of your copy to them and they don't care whether it gets there or not," says Edward Cody, a veteran foreign correspondent for *The Washington Post*. "It's not part of their culture. We, the newspapers, did it by buying into this stupid system of take-me-along."

Marine commanders were more receptive to accommodating reporters during combat than the Army, with the result that Marine units, which played a much smaller role in the war, got far more favorable publicity. But even the Marine pools were sometimes kept away from the action.

No single event more graphically underscored the Pentagon's attempt to stage-manage the news than the brief but intense battle for the Saudi town of Khafji. At first, U.S. officials insisted that only Arab forces were battling the Iraqis. But John King and another AP reporter made it to Khafji on their own and found a Marine unit on the scene.

"We hooked up with a Marine colonel in his thirties who was getting ready to go to battle in five minutes, and he assigned a couple of guys to protect our asses," King says. "He let us tag along and see things no one else could see." The wire reporters soon discovered that a group of Marines was trapped in an abandoned building in Khafji. They withheld this information because they did not want to endanger the Marines' safety.

The press pool didn't reach the outskirts of Khafji until the fighting was eighteen hours old, and by then several other reporters had arrived in their four-wheel-drives. Tensions immediately flared between the officially sanctioned press and the outsiders. Robert Fisk, a British reporter for the *Independent*, says that when he approached the Marine unit, NBC's Brad Willis, a pool member, shouted at him: "You asshole! Go back to Dhahran!" Willis called over a Marine public affairs officer and pointed out Fisk.

"I don't like some American network guy telling me to leave an area on behalf of the U.S. Marines," Fisk says. He says the pool members had "lost some of their critical faculties and become part of the military machine."

Military officials detained several other newspaper reporters at Khafji, temporarily lifted their credentials and sent them back to Dhahran. Their offense? Reporting outside the pool system. Wesley Bocxe, a *Time* photographer, was blindfolded and held for more than twenty-four hours by a National Guard unit.

Other attempts at manipulation were more subtle. James LeMoyne, a *New York Times* reporter, says he tried for nearly two months to obtain an interview with General Schwarzkopf. A Pentagon press officer would call with periodic updates on the request: " 'The general liked your last story,' the officer would say. Or, more ominously, 'The general did not like your last story.' " LeMoyne's interview was canceled after he wrote a piece in which Army enlisted men questioned why they had been sent to Saudi Arabia.

"For the next six weeks," LeMoyne wrote, "almost all print news reporters were denied visits to Army units. . . . They were told there was no transport available or that units were changing position." LeMoyne says Schwarzkopf later denied that the story had scuttled the interview. (By contrast, after Schwarzkopf was interviewed by Joseph Galloway of *U.S. News & World Report*, the general circumvented the pool system to order up an extra combat slot for Galloway. As related by author John Fialka, Galloway later wrote a glowing profile of Schwarzkopf as "a general who knows soldiers and loves them, who knows war and hates it.")

Sometimes the press did little to enhance its image. R. W. (Johnny) Apple, who was running *The New York Times* bureau in Dhahran, got involved in a shouting match that caused a few titters back home. Incensed by the fact that the *Times'* only pool reporter was not seeing any action, Apple chewed out Colonel Bill Mulvey, the man in charge of the Pentagon's Joint Information Bureau.

"He said he'd be sure my career would be ruined and I would be fired," Mulvey recalled. According to Mulvey, Apple made a point of telling him that he would be sitting next to Dick Cheney at the upcoming Gridiron Dinner, an annual bash for Washington's top movers and shakers. "He was very abusive. . . . He said I had used everything in my power to favor his competition and keep *The New York Times* from covering the war," Mulvey said.

A few days later, Apple wrote in the *Times* that Mulvey had "lost the confidence of the press corps."

Apple denied threatening the colonel's career. "I did say I was going to take this up with General Schwarzkopf," he said. "I was extremely angry. I told him Cheney was an old friend of mine, and a sufficiently good friend that he's my guest at the Gridiron. I did not say he'd be sitting next to me."

Apple, who later regretted losing his temper, had good reason to be mad, for the *Times'* pool reporter had been cooling his heels in a hotel. The pool system was like a lottery—some units might spend weeks in combat with a front-line unit, while others were kept waiting for weeks without explanation. "The Defense Department is determined to have this war covered on its own terms, through military briefings that are less informative than they were in Saigon," Apple said.

The daily briefings often deteriorated into low comedy. Pentagon officials referred to them privately as "nitwitness news." One reporter asked if we had put a limit on the number of Iraqis we would kill. Another asked if Schwarzkopf had known before the war began of the damage an oil spill could do, and whether he had considered the moral implications of such damage before deciding to start the war.

"A lot of people went over there to make a name, get a byline, and the pool system homogenized everything," a senior military official said. "It was hard to stand out and be a star war correspondent. . . . Some generals are more savvy and understand the press better. Other reporters got treated like dirt."

It remained a sanitized war, with few stories on casualties and almost no pictures of injured soldiers. One notable exception was provided by John Balzar of the *Los Angeles Times*, who was assigned to an Army helicopter brigade. Pilots allowed Balzar to look at footage of a nighttime raid. Here is what he wrote:

"They looked like ghostly sheep, flushed from a pen—Iraqi infantry soldiers bewildered and terrified, jarred from sleep and fleeing their bunkers under a hellstorm of fire.

"One by one they were cut down by attackers they couldn't see or understand. Some were literally blown to bits by bursts of 30mm exploding cannon shells. One man dropped, writhed on the ground, and struggled to his feet. Another burst tore him apart."

The Army was not pleased. Balzar and his pool saw no further combat for the rest of the war.

On February 7, I got word that Senator Alan Simpson had made a harsh personal attack on CNN's Peter Arnett, the only correspondent for an American news organization still reporting from Baghdad. At a luncheon with Capitol Hill reporters, the Senate Republican whip said that Arnett was "what we used to call a sympathizer. . . . He was active in the Vietnam War and he won a Pulitzer Prize largely because of his antigovernment material. And he was married to a Vietnamese whose brother was active in the Viet Cong."

I called Arnett's daughter, Elsa, a reporter at *The Boston Globe*, who told me the allegation about the brother-in-law was simply not true. She said her mother, Nina, had two brothers—a heart doctor who was forced into early retirement by the Viet Cong and died in the 1960s, and a math professor in Hanoi who was not politically active during the war. But even if Simpson's charge were true, so what? Hadn't many Vietnamese families found themselves torn apart by what was essentially a civil war?

The slashing attack was typical of the senator from Wyoming. Al Simpson is smart, funny and generally liked by reporters because of his facility with razor-sharp quips. He's good copy. Simpson had a tendency to shoot first—he once referred to civil rights activists as "bug-eyed zealots"—and apologize later. Later in the year he would get into his celebrated shouting match with Nina Totenberg. But Simpson had risen to become the second-ranking Republican in the Senate, and his verbal assaults were beginning to strike some people as mean-spirited.

I got Simpson on the phone, fully expecting him to soften his words with some version of what-I-really-meant-to-say. Instead, he repeated the charge and threw in some new ones, such as that the Communist regime in Vietnam had allowed Arnett to roam the country after the fall of Saigon.

Simpson said he had been told about Arnett's brother-in-law "by an AP man who was involved in reporting during the Vietnam War . . . a friend I've known for thirty years." He did not know the brother-in-law's name or the nature of his supposed Viet Cong connection. He would not identify his source, he said with obvious relish, any more than reporters would reveal their anonymous sources.

"I find a lot of those used in your line of work. . . . They slap guys like me around day and night," Simpson said. He loved to bait the press. Simpson was convinced that reporters were out to get him because of his embarrassing visit to Baghdad before the invasion. Simpson not only toed the Bush administration line by playing down the Iraqi threat, he told Saddam that his problems were being caused by the "haughty and pampered press" in the West.

Here again was the classic newspaper dilemma, one that has plagued reporters since the days of Joe McCarthy. Do you print scurrilous charges by a public figure even if you have no reason to believe the charges are true and the person offers no concrete evidence? Or do you refuse to publish them, even if their very sensationalism reveals something about the character of the person making the allegation?

We decided to run the story, balanced by strong statements from Arnett's friends and colleagues. The *Post* was the only major newspaper to play up Simpson's charges, which soon became a cause célèbre in the media. (*The New York Times* didn't carry a word for days.) Even conservatives who found Arnett's reporting from Baghdad downright scandalous would not defend Simpson on the brother-in-law charge. The Wyoming senator came under considerable pressure to retract the allegation.

Six weeks later, Simpson finally admitted he had no evidence for his charge and apologized to Arnett. But rather than call Arnett, who had returned from Iraq, Simpson's apology took the form of a letter to *The New York Times,* which had run a poignant op-ed piece on the subject by Arnett's son, Andrew.

"While I still strongly criticize him for his reporting from Baghdad during the Persian Gulf War," Simpson wrote, "I do feel the deep personal need to apologize for repeating the rumors about Mr. Arnett's family connection to the Viet Cong. I said from the outset that if it couldn't be proven, I would apologize. . . . I greatly regret any hurt, pain or anguish that I have caused his family." Still, the senator couldn't resist a few more swipes at Arnett. Instead of calling him an Iraqi sympathizer, Simpson said, he should have used the word "dupe" or "tool."

I asked Simpson whether it had been irresponsible of him to make such charges in the first place. "You just take your lumps in this game," he snapped. "I'm not going to go into a shrink session about it."

Arnett told me he was struck by the "audacity" of a man of Simpson's stature spreading such unsubstantiated "rubbish." He attributed it to the long-festering wounds of Vietnam.

"The specter of Vietnam will just not go away for my generation," he said. "We were tarred and feathered because of our coverage. The right will not let it die. . . . That war was not lost by the press. It was a wrong war, wrongly conducted in the wrong place."

On the night of February 23, Dick Cheney went on television to announce that the ground war had begun and that all news of the assault would be blacked out until further notice.

Many editors were stunned by the move. No one had thought the Pentagon would go this far. But most tempered their remarks on that tense Saturday night, perhaps aware that the press was already being routed in the court of public opinion.

Still, there were a few voices of dissent. Jack Nelson, Washington bureau chief of the *Los Angeles Times,* called the move "total censorship. . . . They don't want anybody to see the ugly face of war because they're afraid of how the public could turn against them."

The following morning, less than twelve hours after the blackout was declared, Schwarzkopf called a news conference to announce that the allies were having "dramatic success." Cheney appeared on "Face the Nation" and declared himself "pleasantly surprised" by the light casualties. Pool reports started flowing again from Saudi Arabia. The blackout was history.

It seemed clear that the blackout was a political security blanket designed to smother any reports of heavy casualties, only to be whisked away when Iraqi resistance turned out to be weak. "What they've put in place is a mechanism to block out bad news and to keep good news in the forefront," said Howell Raines of *The New York Times.*

The pool system virtually collapsed during the four-day ground war. When allied troops marched into Kuwait City, only those who had broken away from the pools—a few print reporters, CBS's Bob McKeown, ABC's Forrest Sawyer—were on hand to record the event. Those who stayed with their military escorts faced seemingly interminable delays in getting their copy back home. Only the war's sudden end prevented a full-scale revolt against the cumbersome pools.

For all the snide attacks on the press's patriotism, it should be noted that key news organizations—including CBS, NBC and *The Washington Post*—knew of the secret "Hail Mary" plan to attack Saddam from the west, but never reported it. The notion that reporters would knowingly jeopardize American forces was always a fat red herring.

As the country celebrated its victory—and reporters declared George Bush a shoo-in for reelection—military officials expressed no regrets at having misled the press. Schwarzkopf said he was "delighted" that news accounts the previous August had exaggerated the U.S. buildup at a time when he felt vulnerable to Iraqi attack. And he said he was glad the press had played up the phony amphibious-assault plan that had fooled Saddam. Reporters were somewhat less enthused about having been used.

There was one last footnote to the media debacle. In early March, when thirty Western journalists—including reporters from *The New York Times,* CNN and National Public Radio—were captured by Iraqi forces, several news organizations demanded that the United States government do something about getting them released. All that lofty rhetoric about freeing the press to do its job was somehow forgotten; when reporters got into trouble, it was the government's responsibility to bail them out, as Pentagon officials had said all along that it would be. Fortunately, the thirty journalists were freed a few days later.

In the months that followed—once it was too late to do anything but whine—the press engaged in considerable hand-wringing about military censorship and the pool system. But the press began to sing a different tune during the U.S. intervention in Somalia in the fall of 1993. Conditions had become so dangerous there—four journalists had been shot and stoned to death by a mob—that all American reporters had fled the country. Although they had free access to a dangerous battle zone, some editors complained that the Pentagon wasn't inviting reporters out with the troops or granting them military protection, and a press pool was quickly formed and flown to Mogadishu. The editors were understandably concerned about the safety of their reporters, but it looked to many observers that the press was determined to have it both ways.

If news organizations had fumbled and bumbled their way through the Gulf war, they were determined to recoup when it came to hyping the seemingly endless Desert Storm victory parades. *The New York Times* donated $50,000 from a special "advertorial" section to a fund for military families. *Newsday,* the *Daily News* and the *New York Post* each contributed $25,000 to the big New York homecoming parade. "Celebrate America's Persian Gulf Victory!" *Newsday* declared in an ad inviting readers to buy a *Newsday* "Victory!" T-shirt. Seven *Newsday* reporters refused to fall in line, protesting the corporate sponsorship by pulling their bylines from two special sections on the parade.

"Having given up their birthright with barely a whimper," Sydney Schanberg wrote, "the newspapers compound their disgrace by blithely becoming sponsors of a parade to celebrate a war that they were in effect not allowed to cover as professionals. Bravo!"

11

The Media Primary

In the first days of 1992, the press worked its conspiratorial magic in anointing Bill Clinton as the Democratic presidential front-runner.

Much of the country had never heard of the Arkansas governor. Not a single vote had been cast in any primary. Yet a relative handful of newspaper reporters, acting like some metaphysical screening committee, divined that Clinton was the man who would face George Bush in the fall.

The magazines quickly followed suit. "Is Bill Clinton for Real?" *Time*'s cover asked six weeks before the New Hampshire primary. "Who Is This Guy?" Joe Klein demanded in *New York* magazine. The networks fell into line, giving Clinton more bursts of airtime than the other anonymous members of what was derisively called the Democratic six-pack.

This was the infatuation stage, the period in which reporters paid homage to Clinton's awesome political skills, his keen grasp of government, his unique ability to inspire. Many rising political stars get this sort of initial gush, when the courtship is still young and their faces seem so fresh. It is inevitably followed by a period of reappraisal, when their warts are soberly examined, and then by a round of attack-dog journalism, when snarling reporters savage the candidate's record and character.

Clinton's rise, fall and subsequent resurrection became a morality play in which the press was on trial along with the candidate. He had gotten such an easy ride early on, and yet the battering that followed was suffused with an aroma of sleaze that sent the news business into seizures of self-doubt. Clinton was crucified on the trinity of baby-boomer sins—sex, drugs and the draft—by a press corps that had vowed not to trivialize another presidential campaign and yet again found itself obsessed with the dirty laundry of personal conduct.

In a year of economic pain and deep voter anger, newspapers felt a special responsibility to focus on the problems facing the country. This had become our principal franchise in an era when the signature events of presidential campaigns—the photo ops, the commercials, the conventions, the debates—are staged for television. If newspapers are no longer the primary means through which voters get to know candidates, they still help define the agenda on which these politicians will be judged. They still carry on the substantive conversation of an election year, since the networks often have neither the time nor the inclination to explore the fine print of what the candidates are saying. And, with much greater forcefulness since 1990, they referee the political advertising, blowing the whistle on misleading claims amid the blizzard of thirty-second spots. Still, if our professed goal during the primaries was to keep the public spotlight on important issues, the verdict is clear: We failed miserably.

In the fall of 1991, print reporters were in the unusual position of having the presidential arena to themselves. The networks, badly squeezed by the recession, had not yet begun to focus on the fledgling campaign. Bush looked strong and the Democratic field strikingly weak. And so newspapers tried to impose order on a shapeless contest, to cook up a story line that could be developed day after day.

We began with the script for which every political reporter was privately praying, the Mario Scenario. We had been through it all in '88, conjuring up a hundred plots that would see the governor of New York triumph at a brokered convention. Now Cuomo was again running semantic circles around reporters, insisting he had "no plans to make plans" to run for president.

Why was the press so fixated on Mario Cuomo? The simple answer is that reporters find the man endlessly fascinating. Where most pols repeat their hackneyed applause lines with robotic precision, Cuomo engages you in intellectual swordsmanship, quoting Sir Thomas More one minute and his mother the next. "The dirty little secret of political reporting is that most of these guys aren't very interesting," Joe Klein says. "Most of these guys were the student body leaders in high school that the reporters, who were the nerdy little iconoclasts in the back of the room, made fun of. Cuomo is a hell of an interesting human being."

On a more pragmatic level, the press believed that Cuomo had the best chance of giving George Bush a stiff challenge, and we all have a deep-seated bias toward close elections. And so reporters churned out hundreds of upbeat stories about the noncandidate who had deigned to consider running. "If Cuomo doesn't run, he's a jerk!" Richard Reeves complained in *The Philadelphia Inquirer. The Washington Post* started a daily Cuomo Watch. It was a bit much.

When Cuomo ended his flirtation ninety minutes before the New Hampshire filing deadline, the press was left high and dry. Within days, however, the new betting line was Bill Clinton, front-runner, with a dark-horse challenge from Bob Kerrey, war hero.

The favorable assessment of Clinton was not entirely conjured out of thin air. Clinton had the most polished message of the Democratic contenders. He had impressed the political professionals with a series of substantive speeches. He had raised more money than his rivals. And he had courted reporters for years, David Broder had picked him as a future president back in 1980. Now he was winning the invisible Media Primary.

Still, all those front-runner headlines reflected nothing more than the buzz among a few hundred activists and reporters, reverberating through the Washington–New York echo chamber. Clinton had been certified by the same people who decided that Ed Muskie was unstoppable in 1972, that Gary Hart was going nowhere in 1984, and that George Bush couldn't shake the "wimp" label in 1988.

But we all knew about one problem that could derail Bill Clinton's bandwagon. Rumors of womanizing had dogged Clinton throughout his eleven years as governor. Most national reporters believed Clinton had passed up the '88 race in part because he had a zipper problem. The Arkansas rumor mill cranked up again during Clinton's 1990 reelection, fed by two gentlemen of dubious credibility. One was Larry Nichols, who had been fired from his state job for making more than $1,300 in phone calls on behalf of the Nicaraguan contras. Nichols sued Clinton, charging the governor with using state money to finance affairs with five women (one was Gennifer Flowers). The other accuser was Robert "Say" McIntosh, a longtime gadfly who was handing out fliers that said, "Governor Clinton . . . will be remembered as the governor whose dick just couldn't say no! . . . Clinton just knocked off 2 darkies and is disappointed because 2 white gals did not show up."

Suggestions of Clinton's womanizing kept seeping into the press. In the summer of 1991, John Brummett, a columnist for the *Arkansas Democrat,* wrote a piece saying the local press should stop acting like "rumor-mongers and wimps." A week later *The Washington Times,* always quick on the trigger when Democrats and sex are involved, weighed in with a front-page story that slyly repeated the allegations. "The five-term governor insists he won't answer tough personal questions—like those about extramarital affairs, illegitimate children and having used drugs," the second paragraph said.

Wes Pruden, an Arkansas native, made no apologies for the piece. "Everyone in Arkansas is talking about it," he said. "We owe the reader the courtesy of telling the reader what it is we're talking about."

I wanted to write a story about the media's dilemma in dealing with these rumors, making clear that they were unsubstantiated. The buzz had grown so loud that it was creating a problem for Clinton, and several news organizations had sent reporters to Little Rock to investigate.

But the *Post*'s editors were unanimous in deciding that even a media story would unfairly give credence to the rumors. I argued that the story was going to pop somewhere; it was only a matter of time before we were forced to deal with it. Why not address it now, on our terms? But the editors wanted more information. They sent a reporter to Arkansas, but he couldn't nail anything down.

The *Washington Times* piece roiled the political waters for a few weeks. *The New Republic* quoted it in an editorial criticizing the press. George Will wrote a similar column, quoting the allegations about "extramarital affairs, illegitimate children and having used drugs." The column ran on the *Post*'s op-ed page, thus slipping into the back of my newspaper, in far more explicit detail, what I had failed to get into the front. It was a reminder of the hydra-headed beast the media had become: Kill a story in one place and it came slithering back in three others.

Although Clinton tried to defuse the issue by appearing with his wife, Hillary, at a breakfast with Washington reporters—admitting that their marriage "has not been perfect"—newspapers continued to run just enough tantalizing hints to mystify readers. *The Boston Globe* said Clinton was having trouble filling campaign jobs "in part because of nervousness over potentially embarrassing questions about his personal life." *The New York Times* said Clinton had "been forced to deal with a rumor campaign pressed by political opponents here in Arkansas." There was no elaboration.

Such stories added to the sense that newspapers were conducting a dialogue with the political insiders, that mere readers couldn't be trusted with the sensitive details. It is, ultimately, an elitist view: We in the press can sort through this uncorroborated garbage and make the proper judgments, but those who buy our product are too dumb to make such distinctions. When we decide something ought to be a character issue, we'll let you know.

On the Republican side, the line between the press and politics grew increasingly blurry. Pat Buchanan abandoned his newspaper column and CNN perch to launch a conservative challenge to President Bush (CNN promptly hired John Sununu as his replacement). Buchanan's candidacy —leaked in advance to *The Washington Times* and the Manchester *Union Leader*—tapped into a rich vein of discontent with Bush's handling of the recession. But it also got a nice boost from Buchanan's former talk-show colleagues—John McLaughlin, Bob Novak, Fred Barnes and others—who pretended to take seriously the notion that someone who yakked away on television was qualified to be president. Some of Buchanan's former partners tried to gloss over his history of anti-Semitic, anti-gay and racially insensitive statements, comments that would have sunk any candidate with lesser ties to the media establishment.

The Union Leader, which had urged Buchanan to run, began crusading on his behalf. Publisher Nackey Loeb assailed Bush in a series of front-page editorials ("We Need a Fighter, Not a Wimp"). Editor Joseph McQuaid, whose wife and daughter were Buchanan volunteers, chipped in with a glowing front-page commentary. While less vitriolic than in years past, *The Union Leader* still acted more like a right-wing pamphlet than a newspaper.

Faced with a surprisingly stiff challenge, the Bush White House started leaking like a sieve. Putting aside their recent indignation over the Anita Hill leak, administration officials whispered to reporters about the goodies in the president's forthcoming budget. Once again we were blinded by the "scoop" mentality, publishing locally tailored non-stories under big headlines: "Bush Sends Maryland $45 Million to Aid Bay Cleanup," said the Baltimore *Sun*; "Bush's Budget to Seek Money for Old Redwoods," said the *San Francisco Chronicle*; "Bush Plans to Unveil a 90-Day Moratorium on New Regulations," said *The Wall Street Journal*; "Bush to Drop Resistance to New Jobless Benefits," said *The Washington Post. The Boston Globe* discovered there would be another $100 million to clean up Boston Harbor—a particulary cynical leak, since Bush had used the polluted harbor as a cudgel against Michael Dukakis four years earlier.

When Justice Department officials passed the word one weekend that they were beefing up immigration patrols along the Mexican border, the "news" led that Sunday's *New York Times* and *Washington Post*. And both papers bit when "administration officials" leaked yet another story about secret maneuverings to topple Saddam Hussein.

One morning the *Times* devoted its lead story to the president's sudden budgetary concern for feeding and vaccinating poor children. At least reporter Robert Pear added a dash of salt, citing Bush's "economic recovery plan to save millions of jobs, including his own."

After each election, journalists swear off the bottle. No more silly scandals or mindless horse-race stories. No more photo ops and thirty-second smears. Never again will we allow ourselves to be manipulated by campaign consultants. This time we will stick to substantive issues, whether the candidates want to talk about them or not.

And then, like struggling alcoholics, we take one drink and fall off the wagon.

On a cold January afternoon in Nashua, New Hampshire, the candidates were talking substance and the press corps was bored. Bob Kerrey and Tom Harkin were touting their health care plans to an audience of senior citizens. The reporters had heard it all before. Candidates say the same things over and over on the campaign trail, and once you've written a health care story or two, it no longer fits the definition of "news." Besides, the subject was terribly complex. Who really knew whether Paul Tsongas's "managed care" plan was better than Bob Kerrey's "Health USA"? How many readers would peruse the fine print? We all yearned for something new and exciting.

Moments later, we got it. Bill Clinton arrived at the Nashua hotel and was surrounded by a gaggle of fifty reporters with microphones and tape recorders, shouting questions as he emerged from his car. *The Star,* a trashy supermarket tabloid usually concerned with such fare as "Cher's Botched Breast Job" and "John Denver Divorce Turns Ugly," had just dredged up the two-year-old Larry Nichols lawsuit. The seamy tale had moved up the media food chain, just like the naming of Patricia Bowman nine months earlier. "WILD BILL," said that morning's *New York Post.* "I'M NO GARY HART," wailed the New York *Daily News.* The *Boston Herald* and Fox television had also trumpeted the charges.

"It is old news at home," Clinton calmly told the media mob. "It was thoroughly investigated, and it's not true." In a weird sort of way, Clinton had legitimized the story; now we could all lead with his denial.

Adam Pertman, a *Boston Globe* reporter, pronounced the spectacle "nauseating."

I called the *New York Post* and asked Jerry Nachman how he could justify a banner headline for an old lawsuit by a fired state worker who had produced no evidence for his charges. "This is absolutely public information," Nachman said. "It's become part of what we do, going over the character thing." In other words, who cares whether it's true? Some clown files a lawsuit, and that's good enough for the press to leap into action.

Most newspapers played the story modestly. The following week, however, *The Star* made Gennifer Flowers a household name. This time the story was a bit harder to ignore: an on-the-record interview with a former TV reporter and nightclub singer who claimed to have had a twelve-year affair with Clinton, and excerpts from what she said were taped phone conversations between her and the governor.

Of course, the fact that *The Star* had paid Flowers a reported $100,000 made her something less than a model witness. But when someone with a real name and real face says publicly that she slept with a presidential candidate, the press has little choice but to deal with it, however gingerly.

What followed was one of the most schizophrenic episodes in the history of journalism. There was no way to overlook the Flowers extravaganza because it froze the Clinton campaign in its tracks. The media's designated front-runner was under siege, peppered with questions by local reporters at every stop. Of course, this was circular reasoning: Clinton couldn't talk about anything else because we in the press were making the bleached-blonde's tale Topic A, and the fact that he couldn't talk about anything else was news. But that is how the process works.

The networks didn't broadcast the Flowers allegations at first (except for a couple of sentences on NBC), but they soon followed the newspapers' lead. Clinton, meanwhile, boosted the story into the media stratosphere by denying the charges with his wife on "60 Minutes." If the candidate wanted to talk about Gennifer Flowers to forty million viewers on Super Bowl Sunday, it was hard for editors to say the story had to be suppressed.

Still, the pundits and editorialists plunged into an orgy of breast-beating and self-flagellation. It was a curious spectacle: Newspapers published the salacious details on the news pages, then denounced themselves for doing so on the editorial pages.

Jim Gannon of the *Detroit News* called it "sickening . . . a new low for the media, if that's imaginable." David Broder of *The Washington Post* spoke of "the degradation of democracy." *The Philadelphia Inquirer* called it "the Geraldo-ization of presidential politics." The *Globe*'s David Nyhan complained of "grab-your-crotch journalism." Tom Oliphant called on voters to fight back against "Big Media."

When Flowers held a news conference at the Waldorf-Astoria, the press pack's despicable behavior was broadcast for all to see on CNN, just as the pathetic Persian Gulf war briefings had been. After one shouted question—"Did Governor Clinton wear a condom?"—many viewers had no trouble believing it had come from a typical reporter. In fact, it was "Stuttering John" Melendez, whose job is to insult celebrities for Howard Stern's radio show. The Clinton campaign had become a soap opera, more grist for the talk show mills.

Even as Flowers went on "A Current Affair" to embellish her story, some legitimate questions emerged. Clinton's staff had helped Flowers get a $17,000 state job, raising the prospect of a mistress on the public payroll. And no one who heard Flowers tell Clinton on the tapes that he ate "good pussy" could doubt that she was more than a casual acquaintance. Even if their affair was not as extensive as Flowers claimed, there was the very real possibility that Bill Clinton was lying. The New York tabloids were already calling Clinton the "Luv Guv."

One newspaper, however, virtually pretended that Gennifer Flowers didn't exist. *The New York Times,* still reeling from the backlash over its Patricia Bowman profile, insisted on allocating only a few paragraphs to the story, usually on the bottom of an inside page. The *Times* reduced Flowers's press conference, which was front-page news around the country, to one paragraph in a story headlined "Clinton Attempts to Ignore Rumors." Several reporters and editors argued strenuously that the *Times* had to do more, but Max Frankel wouldn't budge. "I am ashamed for my profession," Frankel told me. "We don't want to report on the candidates' sex lives." He was bending over so far backward that his paper was missing the biggest event thus far in the '92 campaign.

"There was literally daily hand-wringing over this," says one *Times* reporter. "There were closed-door meetings every day. It was very frustrating. At some point you had to recognize that this had the potential to derail a legitimate candidate. We were worried Clinton was going down in flames and we wouldn't have written about it."

The paper was in a particularly awkward position when Clinton apologized to Mario Cuomo for having said, in a taped conversation, that

Cuomo "acts like" a member of the Mafia. The *Times,* which had ignored the Flowers tapes, buried the apology in the thirteenth paragraph of a Clinton story. The next day the paper had to throw together a catch-up piece acknowledging that the Cuomo-Clinton dustup "became front-page news today in many New York newspapers and was picked up elsewhere across the country"—everywhere except the *Times.*

"We didn't want to be on the cutting edge of that particular story. . . . It's not the *Times'* kind of story," says Howell Raines, who was running the Washington bureau. But, he admits, "if I was doing it over, I'd like to see us pick up the pace and the volume a little bit earlier than we did." The *Times* didn't apply the same standard to all rumors; during this period it ran a front-page piece titled "Yeltsin, Out of Sight, Prompts Anxiety and Rumor."

Many journalists wondered what purpose was served by the media's obsessive focus on the candidates' private foibles. In the past, says the Baltimore *Sun*'s Jules Witcover, who has covered every presidential race since 1956, "You didn't intrude on their personal lives. By giving them a longer leash, they were willing to relax in your presence. They would come into a bar at night and have a few drinks and you would shoot the bull. Now, with tape recorders and boom mikes, no candidate feels at ease anymore. Older reporters are criticized by the younger reporters who say, 'You guys paid a price for cozying up to these people,' and I wouldn't deny that. But there was a payoff as well."

As polls showed that most people didn't care whether Clinton had had an affair, a backlash began to build against the press. Some of this sanctimony was a trifle overstated—someone, after all, was buying those 3.5 million copies of *The Star* each week. But with Flowers's picture staring out from every checkout counter, the nation's elite newspapers no longer had exclusive control of the campaign dialogue.

Some journalists grew overly protective of Clinton, and perhaps some were seduced by him as well. At forty-five, Clinton was a member of their generation, and he clearly loved the game of politics, just as the reporters did. He spoke their language. He would stroll to the back of the plane and chat about solutions to government problems, joining a debate that neoliberal journalists had been conducting for years. Many thought Clinton was a superb politician and astute policy wonk who would be far preferable to George Bush.

For the daily reporters on the bus, Clinton's success meant a steady diet of page-one stories, and if he made it to the White House many would follow him there. Some of the liberal pundits may have dreamed of a new Camelot, of advising a Democratic president after twelve years in the Republican wilderness.

But if some journalists crossed the line, it doesn't follow that the press went into the tank for Bill Clinton. There is a unfortunate zeitgeist in the press that saying nice things about a politician is tantamount to swooning over him, and that only those who trash the candidate have proven their mettle. Many savvy reporters, such as Joe Klein, simply made the judgment that Clinton was the class of the Democratic field, and they turned out to be right, although they underestimated the degree to which voters would find him slippery.

Even the most skeptical correspondents were impressed by Clinton's stamina as he battled back from the Flowers debacle, shaking hands from dawn till midnight. Nearly all hoped the *Star*'s cash-for-trash story would die; nobody wanted blood on their hands for killing off another Gary Hart. They were rooting for Clinton to win what Klein called "the Bimbo Primary."

When the Flowers headlines began to fade, it was much to the consternation of *The Washington Times,* which insisted there had to be a partisan conspiracy. Wes Pruden wrote that the liberal media were "trying to expatiate the sins of the past, when they pilloried the likes of Dan Quayle, John Tower and Clarence Thomas as brutal and insatiable beasts of the boudoir. . . . The Clintons easily intimidated *The New York Times,* the *Post* and the other mighty organs of the media into a cowed and respectful disobedience." Well, not exactly. In fact, a new feeding frenzy was about to begin.

On February 6, *The Wall Street Journal* ran a story by Jeffrey Birnbaum which raised new questions about Clinton's draft record, and the issue quickly achieved critical mass. The story had three things going for it. First, it appeared in a respectable publication. Second, it involved the military, presumably a more relevant subject than sex for a potential commander-in-chief. And third, it seemed to build on the Flowers mess by casting fresh doubt on Clinton's character.

The press had already reported the basic outlines of the story: Clinton had strongly opposed the Vietnam War, had secured a deferment while he was a twenty-three-year-old Rhodes scholar, and then drew a high lottery number and was never drafted. The *Journal* now quoted a former ROTC official in Arkansas as saying that Clinton had gotten his deferment by promising to join the ROTC program, but never enrolled.

The decibel level rose still higher when ABC obtained a copy of a 1969 letter in which Clinton thanked an ROTC official for "saving me from the draft." Clinton launched a preemptive strike, calling a press conference to release the letter before Ted Koppel could broadcast the story. Clinton's letter was quite eloquent, filled with a young man's anguish about Vietnam. But in the sound-bite culture of politics, it was clearly damaging. Headlines and television anchors reduced the moral ambiguities of 1969 to one damning phrase: draft dodger. "New Letter Reveals Clinton Shunned Draft," said the *Boston Herald.*

The irony was that many of the reporters on the campaign trail were part of the Vietnam generation. They, too, had despised the war as unjust and immoral. Just as some of the reporters who wrote about Donna Rice and Gennifer Flowers had had extramarital affairs, just as some of the reporters who wrote about Douglas Ginsburg's drug use had smoked plenty of dope in the '60s and '70s, so too had many of Clinton's chroniclers done what they could to avoid the draft. They knew it was unfair to take the most painful ethical dilemma of that era and condemn it by the flag-waving standards of the '90s. Yet they were also trained professionals, and their journalistic judgment was that Clinton was badly wounded. Many pundits wrote him off. "I think Clinton is dead," said columnist Charles Krauthammer. "He's a goner," agreed Carl Rowan. "Dead meat," said Al Hunt.

As Clinton plummeted in the polls, he started running against the press. In one television ad he lashed out at the "pundits" and "tabloids" for trying to destroy his candidacy. This phony populism was laughable from someone whose lead in the polls had essentially been created by rave reviews from the folks he was now attacking. Clinton had gone from *Time* cover boy to press-basher in just one month.

One frigid February evening in Manchester, dozens of reporters filed into the Palace Theater for a Paul Tsongas rally. Nobody in the press had taken Tsongas seriously—he was too dour, too uncharismatic, another Greek liberal from Massachusetts—but now, in the wake of Clinton's troubles, Tsongas, with his eighty-six-page economic plan, was on the verge of winning New Hampshire. Perhaps there was a lesson here, the guy we had dismissed as a joke overtaking the telegenic candidate we had seen as invincible. Tsongas gave a moving speech about his battle against cancer and began taking questions from the audience.

As Tsongas droned on, Tom Oliphant began leafing through the latest issue of the *Globe,* the trashy Florida tabloid that had published

Patty Bowman's name and picture the previous spring. It had a screaming headline: "Bill Clinton's 4-in-a-Bed Sex Orgies with Street Hookers —He's the Father of My Child, Claims Ghetto Gal He Had Sex with 13 Times." Inside was a reproduction of the disgusting "Say" McIntosh flier I had laughed off the previous summer. Just when it seemed the press had sunk as low as humanly possible, there was always another surprise. This time, however, no mainstream newspaper touched the story.

During a televised debate in early March, Bill Clinton held up a front-page headline from *The New York Times*: "Even Among the Well-Off, the Richest Get Richer."

"You see this *New York Times* story today . . . that in the '80s, the top 1 percent of the people had 60 percent of the net economic growth," Clinton said, launching into a pitch for "people-based economics."

A few minutes later, ABC's Peter Jennings asked Paul Tsongas how his economic proposals differed from the president's. "Well, I was endorsed last Sunday by the Atlanta *Constitution*," Tsongas began.

This is the "read my clips" approach to campaigning. Politicians love to use newspapers to drive home a point or demonstrate that they have been certified kosher for Election Day. A favorable editorial makes a great prop to wave before the cameras.

Newspapers lend a certain stamp of authenticity in these matters. In the era of the 7.3-second sound bite, they still devote considerable space to issues, however fleeting their attention span. It's almost as if the real election debate takes place in print, and each day the participants stage a briefer, punchier version for television, with print reporters standing around as extras.

No presidential aspirant cited the judgment of newspapers more often than Paul Tsongas, largely because his upscale supporters were the kinds of folks who underlined *New York Times* editorials. Tsongas announced at one debate that his opposition to a middle-class tax cut "is the same as *The New York Times*," as if that settled the matter. When seven Florida papers backed him, Tsongas stumped the state with blown-up copies of the editorials. At a Chicago debate he quoted from the *Chicago Tribune* editorial endorsing him.

Newspaper stories are even more useful for skewering the other guy, especially when they're quoted out of context. At one debate, Tom Harkin held up an *Arkansas Gazette* article with the ominous headline,

"Clinton's Plan Sticks It to the Little Guy." In fact, it was an opinion piece by a columnist who had never liked Clinton.

Candidates and their handlers were constantly pitching their ideas to newspaper reporters, hoping for articles that would play into their strategy. When a *Wall Street Journal* story declared Bob Kerrey "the candidate with the best developed proposal" on health care—and said Clinton didn't really have a plan—Kerrey aides quickly used the piece to attack Clinton.

Candidates who fared poorly were quick to blame their troubles on a media conspiracy to deny them their rightful place in the polls. Jerry Brown grumbled about the "corrupt media game" and the "media college of cardinals," complaining that "a few media executives" determine who are "the approved candidates." Tom Harkin warned one audience: "The national news media are trying to tell you people in New Hampshire how to vote." The White House, meanwhile, grew so frustrated at coverage of the president's faltering campaign that spokesman Marlin Fitzwater called the beat reporters "lazy bastards."

It is no exaggeration to say that the most important events of the primaries revolved around newspaper stories. Two days before Super Tuesday, Jeff Gerth of *The New York Times* reported on a questionable Ozarks land deal between the Clintons and James McDougal, an old Arkansas friend. McDougal later bought a savings and loan that was regulated by the state, and represented by Hillary Clinton, before federal regulators shut it down. But the densely written Gerth story, rushed into the paper under pressure from editors, was too complicated for television; like the early S&L stories, it quickly faded. (Although reporters soon lost interest in the Whitewater land deal, it would come back to haunt Bill Clinton nearly two years later in a media frenzy that led to the appointment of a special prosecutor.)

A week later *The Washington Post* raised questions about Hillary Clinton's role as a partner in one of Little Rock's largest law firms. The *Post*'s David Maraniss and Michael Weisskopf found that the firm had received $175,000 for state bond work and another $115,000 from the Arkansas public service commission.

The piece triggered some televised fireworks that night at a debate in Chicago as Jerry Brown ripped into Clinton: "It's right on the front of *The Washington Post* today. He is funneling money to his wife's law firm for state business."

Clinton shot back: "You ought to be ashamed of yourself for jumping on my wife. You're not worth being on the same platform as my wife."

They jabbed their fingers and glowered at each other. Brown tried again: "It was in *The Washington Post.*"

"That doesn't make it true."

"Are you saying that they lie?"

"I'm saying that I never funneled any money to my wife's law firm, never, never."

Clinton was right. Brown had misquoted the *Post* article, which in no way suggested that the governor had played a role in steering work to his wife's firm. But such distinctions were lost on viewers as Brown invoked the *Post* to cover his exaggerated charges.

Most news accounts noted that Brown had misrepresented the article, but almost as an aside to the verbal jousting. Tom Oliphant wrote that Brown's "slander" and "intentional falsehoods" were "magnified by unforgivably stenographic treatment by the press. . . . Brown's lies were designed to trap the press in its own childish preference for drama in political coverage, to become the story of the debate, and they succeeded."

Perhaps no part of a presidential campaign touches more voters than thirty-second ads. Repeated again and again between pitches for dog food, Diet Coke and deodorant, these propaganda assaults reach millions of viewers who have tuned out of politics but are tuned into sitcoms and docudramas.

For twenty-five years, beginning with LBJ's famous "daisy" ad against Barry Goldwater, newspapers had been little more than spectators to this televised warfare, reporting on the action as if it were a baseball game. But now we have cast ourselves in the role of umpire, calling each attempt fair or foul. The transformation began in 1990, when the *Post*'s David Broder wrote a column challenging his colleagues to do more than passively parrot the false and misleading charges contained in so many ads.

Calling a candidate a liar, in effect, required the press to break the shackles of objectivity that had long restricted campaign coverage. But once editors decided they would no longer allow political consultants to get away with falsehoods, the "ad watch" became a permanent feature of the newspaper landscape. Sophisticated admen began using newspaper criticism in counterattack ads. The press was finally making political consultants pay a price for stretching the truth.

The '92 primaries had more than their share of nasty commercials. Pat Buchanan used slow-motion footage of half-naked homosexual men in leather harnesses to accuse Bush of supporting pornographic art. As news stories quickly pointed out, the footage was from a film about black homosexuals, which had received a $5,000 grant from the National Endowment for the Arts in 1988, before Bush took office. Moreover, only a tiny fraction of the NEA's funding went to controversial artists who peed onstage or covered their bodies with chocolate. Buchanan, as the press duly noted, was making a blatant anti-gay appeal.

A Bush ad, which aired during the Georgia primary, said that Buchanan's protectionist policies would threaten 164,000 Georgia jobs. When asked for documentation, campaign officials said the figure assumed that Buchanan would wipe out every last dollar of Georgia's $7.2 billion in annual exports, a totally ludicrous charge.

Clinton and Tsongas began to use increasingly subtle distortions in their advertising, some of which slipped through the "ad watch" net because it was hard to prove them literally false. One Clinton ad quoted *Time* magazine as saying, "Much of what Tsongas proposes smacks of trickle-down economics." True enough—except that the same article said that on many economic issues, "Tsongas is clearly the more courageous" of the two. A Tsongas spot accused Clinton of borrowing "from our children" to finance his proposed middle-class tax cut. This neatly ignored Clinton's pledge to pay for his plan by raising taxes on the wealthy. The *Washington Post, New York Times, Boston Globe, Los Angeles Times,* NBC, CNN and other news organizations tried, with mixed success, to illuminate such half-truths and misrepresentations.

In those first few weeks in New Hampshire, the press coverage was unusually substantive. Reporters filed lots of serious stories about people who had lost their jobs, their homes and their health insurance, and what the candidates intended to do about it. *The New York Times* ran several pieces on how the candidates were espousing a kind of pain-free economics that had little to do with the massive budget deficit. Newspaper reporters, who rode the campaign planes with their laptop computers and cellular phones, had to be more probing and interpretive, for the events they wrote about were now instantly available on CNN and C-SPAN.

But the daily drumbeat of tracking polls soon began to drown out the lofty debate. The old adrenaline started flowing: Could Kerrey edge out Harkin for third? Would Buchanan crack 30 percent? Before we knew it, the horses were out of the gate, around the bend and headed for the home stretch, and we slipped into our handicapping mode.

One week in mid-February, *USA Today,* which was conducting daily polls with CNN, could no longer restrain itself. "Clinton Slips, Bush Strong," said Monday's front page. "Poll Shows Tsongas in N.H. Lead," said Tuesday's front page. "Tsongas Holds Lead in Final Weekend in N.H.," said Friday's front page.

Polls have become a journalistic addiction. Reporters who gathered for dinner at the Sheraton Wayfarer each night would rush to the phones when the latest numbers came in, although the surveys involved just two hundred voters in each party. We were again using polls to manufacture news.

Ask political reporters about their horse-race fixation and you get a pretty standard response. "I think the horse race is what people really care about," says Paul West, Washington bureau chief of the Baltimore *Sun.* "They want to know who is going to win." But the polls we trumpet so loudly have inherent weaknesses. Among other things, they can't predict which respondents will actually turn out to vote, a crucial factor in a low-turnout primary.

Exit polls are more valuable, since they give us demographic data on people's motivations, but they can also lead us astray. On the night of the New Hampshire primary, reporters wrote their stories and television based its broadcasts on exit polls projecting that Buchanan would capture a whopping 44 percent of the vote. It wasn't until the next day that we learned that Buchanan's actual total was 37 percent. Never mind.

The first results of the season also gave us the chance to engage in our favorite game: spin. Forget what the voters say, it's the media interpretation that counts. Bush may have won the primary by sixteen points, but his showing was a "jarring political rebuke," *The New York Times* said. A "stunning setback," *The Wall Street Journal* announced. A "potentially disastrous pounding," *The Boston Globe* declared. "Read *Our* Lips," the Manchester *Union Leader* crowed.

The issues were quickly overshadowed by a headlong rush to follow the action in a dozen states at once. Would Kerrey drop out after Colorado? Would Tsongas go negative in Illinois? Almost no one reported on such matters as who would be affected by Clinton's middle-class tax cut and how much money they would receive. It was old news to us, but not to millions of voters who were tuning in for the first time. Instead the press went into the crystal-ball business. On the Sunday before the Illinois and Michigan primaries, *The Washington Post*'s lead story was "2 Big Wins Predicted for Clinton."

The political commandos of the press sprinkled their copy with war metaphors. Candidates would "rally the troops," roll out their "fire-power," conduct a "blitz," mount an "offensive," move into "crucial battlegrounds," "ambush" rivals, "torpedo" opponents, fight the "air war." But a Times Mirror poll in early March provided a sobering reminder that much of this stuff is consumed by junkies and insiders: Only 19 percent of those surveyed said they were closely following the campaign.

When Tsongas dropped out after his drubbing in Illinois and Michigan, many reporters were depressed at the prospect that the Democratic race was over. One group of journalists drank a dinner toast to the political health of Jerry Brown, the only person standing between them and months of boredom.

We had all dismissed Brown as a space cadet and a charlatan. No national reporters followed him around the country. But when Brown narrowly upset Clinton in Connecticut, the media conveniently brought him back to life. Although a front-page *New York Times* headline the next day declared that "Brown Surges," he didn't have a prayer of winning the nomination. Still, Jerry Brown put the press in touch with its most deep-seated fantasy: a brokered convention.

Brown provided us with reams of colorful copy: his Moonbeam persona, his 800 number, his inexhaustible ability to reinvent himself. But few reporters bothered to examine the details of what Brown was saying, such as his proposal to scrap the income tax system and replace it with a 13 percent flat tax and 13 percent value-added tax.

There was a glaring double standard at work here. The press simply doesn't give the same scrutiny to so-called marginal candidates as to those it deems potential presidents. Pat Buchanan is the classic example. Anyone with his history of incendiary remarks—calling Congress "Israeli-occupied territory," saying AIDS is nature's "awful retribution" against gays, defending accused Nazi war criminals, saying "Englishmen" would be easier to assimilate than "Zulus"—would have been pounded mercilessly by reporters if they thought he might one day sit in the Oval Office. But since Buchanan's chief function was to embarrass

Bush, his intolerance was treated as an interesting quirk, although he received somewhat tougher scrutiny after New Hampshire.

The problem with this approach is that we are frequently wrong about those we so cavalierly write off. Few in the press took Tsongas seriously, and only after he won New Hampshire did *The Wall Street Journal*—followed by the *New York Times, Los Angeles Times* and *Washington Post*—bother to examine his record as a lobbyist for polluters and other corporate interests.

After Connecticut, as Brown emerged from what he called "the black hole of media nonexistence," the press finally started holding him accountable. *The Boston Globe* called Brown's tax plan "startlingly regressive." Jodie Allen of *The Washington Post* wrote that Brown's plan was "snake oil" that would boost the deficit by $200 billion a year. Lars-Erik Nelson of the New York *Daily News* called it "the single greatest rip-off of American working people in this nation's history." Clinton quoted these stories endlessly and used them in a TV ad in New York. (When the same ad ran in Wisconsin, he substituted a quote from the *Milwaukee Sentinel*.) With Tsongas out of the race, Clinton became the new "read my clips" candidate. He constantly invoked a *Philadelphia Inquirer* series on how the middle class got screwed in the '80s.

The press corps, however, was more interested in the constant rumors that some publication was about to run an article on a new Clinton affair, or even a Hillary affair. Soon the grapevine had it that the May issue of *Playboy* would feature Elizabeth Ward, a former Miss America from Arkansas, saying she had had an affair with Clinton. *The New York Times* published a flimsy piece about the gossip, saying that Clinton aides had "shown reporters a statement from a former Miss America denying that she had an affair with the Governor." In other words, the paper that had all but refused to report on a woman who said publicly she had an affair with Bill Clinton was now writing about a woman who denied having such an affair. "We're using what even *Playboy* says is a non-story as a way of rehashing all the stuff we wouldn't write about the first time," one *Times* staffer sniffed.

For a few brief, hysterical moments, the steamy world of the tabloids fused with the organized chaos of presidential politics. Bill Clinton came riding into the New York primary as the presumptive Democratic nominee, and the local press corps was determined to rip him to shreds. Lars-Erik Nelson of the *News* called Clinton "an alien in our Yankee midst." *Post* columnist Mike McAlary denounced him as a "fraud" and "Liar Bill." Another *Post* columnist, Ray Kerrison, assailed Hillary Clinton as a "buffoon" and "radical feminist." The papers resurrected the whispers about marijuana use, and Clinton finally confessed to Marcia Kramer of WCBS-TV, adding his famous "didn't inhale" caveat. The tabloids were so determined to live up to their reputation as character assassins that their coverage quickly degenerated into self-parody. It was less an election than a Manhattan mugging.

The national media continued hounding Clinton as he closed in on the nomination. The behemoths of the business—the *New York Times, Los Angeles Times* and *Washington Post*—each sent a half-dozen reporters to Little Rock, putting Clinton's record under the journalistic microscope. What followed was a steady drumbeat of pseudo-scandals, pieces that appeared to raise ethical questions about Clinton but, in truth, fell short of the mark.

Editors justified such articles with high-minded statements about the need to examine the record of a Man Who Might Be President. But we all knew what was really going on. Each paper was trying to come up with the prizewinning story that would blow Bill Clinton out of the water. Dig into any governor's record and you'll find a long trail of political deals and favors for fat-cat donors. That's how business is done in state capitals, and it's a legitimate part of the story. But the press lost all perspective for a time, hyping each small episode into a new "character" issue.

Later on, the big papers would take a stab at illuminating the larger questions about Clinton—how he governs, what he stands for, what he had accomplished on education or civil rights. At the start, though, most of the stories amounted to a prosecutorial game of "gotcha"—whether it was Clinton's real estate deals, his relationship with prominent Arkansas businessmen, his half-brother's drug addiction or his wife's law practice.

Typical of the genre was a *New York Times* front-page story on the 1988 passage of an Arkansas ethics law, which Clinton viewed as a major achievement. The legislature had balked at a stronger version, so Clinton had compromised by removing a conflict-of-interest provision that would have required greater disclosure from all state and local officials, down to library board members. The *Times* twisted this into an attempt by Clinton to shield himself from the law, implying that he was trying to hide some awful conflict of interest.

No one in the press was holding George Bush to a similar standard.

The lingering questions about Bush, from his role in Iran-contra to his secret dealings with China to his son Neil's involvement in the S&L scandal, were dismissed as old news. Bush was a familiar figure, a known quantity. The media's investigative guns were trained elsewhere.

The negative headlines about Clinton invariably produced a barrage of questions on the campaign trail, which in turn were reflected on the network news. Newspapers were clearly setting the tone for television coverage in these matters. The focus of press coverage also turned inward, not only from media reporters like me, but from the networks as well. "How much scrutiny can or should any candidate be subjected to?" asked NBC anchorman Garrick Utley during a newscast in late March. As pictures of newspaper articles flashed on the screen, Andrea Mitchell told viewers that Clinton had been hit by "a series of front-page allegations, some of which have not fully checked out."

What saved Clinton in the New York primary was that the media pendulum finally swung against Jerry Brown. After months of failing to scrutinize Brown's record, the press belatedly discovered that the self-styled outsider had been a canny insider. The *San Francisco Chronicle* reported that the man who denounced big money in politics had lobbied against campaign-donation limits in California two years earlier, and his law firm had billed the taxpayers $178,000. *The Washington Post* reported that Brown had been a director of a biomedical firm whose parent company paid a $400,000 fine to settle federal charges that it falsely promoted an anti-AIDS drug. ABC would later broadcast an awful story, based on anonymous sources, charging that drug parties had been held at Brown's home while he was governor of California.

Clinton was again running against the press, singling out the New York tabloids in a television ad. "We live in a world where if anybody says anything about you that's bad, you folks will publish it and worry about whether it's true later," he told Phil Donahue after the talk show host had grilled him about Gennifer Flowers.

Even after a bloodied Clinton had virtually clinched the nomination in New York, the character cops of the press were still chasing bimbo rumors. This led to some wild-goose chases. At the *Post,* Bob Woodward got a tip that the former secretary of a Washington lawyer claimed to have had an affair with Clinton. The paper sent Sharon LaFraniere to Little Rock to find the woman; while she was in the air, reporter Michael Isikoff learned that the woman had moved to Tulsa. LaFraniere got on another plane. Then Isikoff discovered that the law firm had fired the woman for forging checks. And her former roommate said the woman was a chronic liar who sometimes claimed to be vacationing with the Kennedys. "She's a convicted embezzler whose roommate said she was a pathological liar," Isikoff says. "What are you going to do—put it in the paper?" When LaFraniere finally found the woman, she denied having an affair with Clinton.

The two reporters visited another woman rumored to have slept with Clinton. She denied it. Even if it was true, Isikoff says, "Why the hell would anybody tell us? Why would you want to step into that media maelstrom and have ten thousand tabloid reporters descend on you?"

It was probably inevitable, with so much mud being dumped on Clinton, that some of it would splatter the White House. The first hint that the adultery issue might not be limited to the governor of Arkansas appeared in the *Los Angeles Times*. Jack Nelson wrote a story quoting Ron Brown, the Democratic chairman, as suggesting that if reporters kept badgering Clinton about his private life then Bush should have to answer the same questions.

Nelson recounted how Bush's son, George W., had told *Newsweek* in 1987, "The answer to the Big A question is N.O." And how the *L.A. Weekly* had in 1988 regurgitated the rumors that Bush had had an affair. Was this now fair game for the press? The decade-old gossip that Bush was sleeping with a staffer who went on to hold a prestigious post in his administration was one of the great open secrets of our time. Across the country, reporters were constantly asked: When are you going to print the story of the Bush affair?

"One area which I find most curious is the press reluctance to report on the very well-known rumors about George Bush and his mistress of long standing, whose name is certainly no secret in Washington," an Alexandria, Virginia, man wrote me. *The Philadelphia Inquirer* published a similar letter with the none-too-subtle headline, "Bush's Girlfriend."

Even Hillary Clinton joined the chorus, telling *Vanity Fair* that Bush's "carrying on" was being shielded by the media's double standard. "HILLARY GOES TABLOID," chided the *New York Post*.

The problem is that we had absolutely no proof, no Gennifer Flowers telling the world of an adulterous relationship. In the early '80s, Ann Devroy, then working for Gannett, had spent two months on the story, even interviewing the alleged mistress herself, and found no evidence of an affair.

By the spring of 1992, few newspaper readers could have been unaware that Bush's supposed girlfriend had the same first name as Clinton's alleged paramour. The *New York Post*'s Deborah Orin, with a wink and a nod, noted that a Democratic consultant had dubbed the issue "the Jennifer question." The paper went into its Marla Maples mode, reducing the controversy to a celebrity catfight. "BABS BITES BACK," Orin's cover story said, hyping a single anonymous source who said that Barbara Bush was "spitting mad" over Hillary Clinton's "hypocritical" remarks about her husband.

But the seamier side of the campaign was no longer limited to the tabloids. Everyone wanted a piece of the action. In a front-page *New York Times* piece, Andrew Rosenthal noted that "long-denied rumors that Mr. Bush had an extramarital affair are already back in play." Indeed they were.

Newspapers, which had started the campaign season with such high-minded promise, had once again lost touch with their readers. We had been sidetracked into sleaze. We had played along as the candidates danced around the issues, offering painless solutions to intractable problems. As we raced from one "crucial" state to the next, turnout in the primaries fell below 20 percent, an all-time low. It was a game that was fascinating mainly to journalists and their friends in the political subculture. Again and again we wrote that the voters were angry at incumbents. What we didn't realize was that they were also angry at *us*.

Just as reporters were catching their breath from four months of scandal-mongering, poll-watching and bimbo-hunting, two events unfolded that made the frenetic primary season seem irrelevant. The fury of the Los Angeles riots underscored that what was on the front pages bore little relation to the anger and racial hostility on the streets of urban America. And the press belatedly discovered that millions of voters, disgusted with the two-party system and our role in it, had found an alternative.

12

The Talk Show Campaign

By the late spring of 1992 it was clear that the presidential campaign had broken free of the establishment press.

Frustrated by the narrow, cramped agenda of daily journalism, the candidates began to sidestep the national press corps and take their message to a broader audience. If fewer people were reading newspapers and watching the network news, then perhaps they could be reached through Arsenio Hall and Larry King and MTV. If voters were disgusted with the antagonistic queries of Washington reporters, they could ask their own questions on call-in shows and at televised town meetings. The candidates, tired of having their words sliced and diced into a few sentences in the paper, or challenged by the Sunday-morning pontificators, would simply cut out the middleman. All this threatened to make the newspaper reporter obsolete, his narrative function usurped by television, his mediating role awarded to millions of ordinary citizens plugged into 800 numbers.

It became fashionable to speak of the Old Media (newspaper hacks and starched-shirt talking heads) being eclipsed by the New Media (movies, rap, talk radio, infotainment shows). The New Media had all the elements that newspapers lacked: passion, excitement, attitude. The new forms spoke to young people who had little interest in bloodless press accounts. They were on the cutting edge with racially and sexually charged messages that only gradually percolated into the headlines. Facts were less important than point of view; Oliver Stone's conspiratorial *JFK*, widely debunked in the mainstream press, was more vivid to many people than the Warren Commission report. The Old Media flacked for a tired establishment; the new version was in touch with "the people." The newspapers that were once the main conveyor belt for news, and the broadcast networks that once commanded mass audiences, now had to compete with hundreds of impudent upstarts.

The idea of using alternative formats to circumvent the national press was not as newfangled as it seemed. FDR gave fireside chats when radio was the hot new medium. Bobby Kennedy appeared with Jack Paar on "The Tonight Show." Richard Nixon tried to soften his image by popping up on "Laugh-In." Jimmy Carter sought regular-guy status by telling *Playboy* he lusted in his heart; Ronald Reagan preached conservatism on Mutual radio; Gary Hart did "Saturday Night Live." That politicians would now rush to appear on the new breed of confessional programs, which catered to movie stars and sex therapists and women who love transvestites, simply underscored how tabloid culture and political culture had merged into one great ooze of celebrification. And the candidates' forays into Oprah-style campaigning were invariably recounted the next day in the newspapers, which were at once mesmerized by their new competitors and resentful at being shoved to the sidelines.

The New Media were particularly important for Bill Clinton as he struggled to reintroduce himself to an electorate that knew him largely as a media caricature. Clinton's negatives were so high after his mugging by the press that many pundits pronounced him unelectable. (Fred Barnes wrote a cover story in *The New Republic* titled "Why Clinton Can't Win.") He needed a looser, more relaxed format—broad enough so he could talk about his modest upbringing in rural Arkansas, present his basic message of economic change (which was old news to the campaign reporters) and, yes, even play the saxophone. None of that was possible under the conventions of traditional journalism, which had dismissed the likely Democratic nominee as old news.

Meanwhile, the spotlight shifted to a man who had seized the possibilities of live television more aggressively than anyone before him. Ross Perot refused to play by the standard rules: He would not subject himself to press conferences or hit the hustings with a planeload of reporters in tow. Instead, he communed with the country from TV studios, reducing political reporters to armchair critics who had to watch him on the tube like everyone else. He was the talk show candidate for president, making his electronic pitch at the elbows of Larry King and Barbara Walters and Katie Couric. He had little use for print journalists, dismissing the Beltway press corps as a relic of old-style politics.

Newspapers "don't matter," Perot insisted, because "what happens on TV is what really impacts on people. I think you could print any story you want on the front page of *The New York Times* and there's no reaction. It just blows away."

Perot seemed far more in touch with the pulse of America than the pack of reporters rushing from one airport to the next. Newspapers religiously chronicled the guests on "Meet the Press," "Face the Nation" and "This Week with David Brinkley," but entertainment shows like "Larry King Live" were off their radar screen. The *consiglieres* of organized journalism paid no attention when Perot told Larry King on February 20 that he would run for president if supporters could get him on all fifty state ballots. It would take a full month before the *Los Angeles Times* and *The Washington Post* gave page-one recognition to the hundreds of thousands of phone calls that were flooding Perot's office. We were not yet tuned into the New Media.

It gradually dawned on reporters that the armies of disaffected Perot volunteers reflected something broader than just a rich gadfly who could bankroll his own challenge. Once the mainstream media had certified Perot as a genuine phenomenon, he was buoyed by a gusher of fawning coverage. The infatuation stage had begun. Perot was Mr. None of the Above, thumbing his nose at a bankrupt political system and an arrogant press corps that seemed to embody its values.

"The elfin, crewcut Texas billionaire is poised to cast himself as a kind of Lone Ranger from the Lone Star State ready to ride into Washington to clean up the mess," *The New York Times* observed.

"Computer tycoon, business reformer and unabashed patriot . . . a billionaire entrepreneur who has spawned a folklore of almost mythic proportions . . . perhaps the greatest threat to the political establishment in a generation," proclaimed *The Wall Street Journal.*

The effusive prose masked a growing indignation among reporters that this Dallas maverick could soar in the polls without getting down in the trenches with them. He was, *The Boston Globe* sniffed, "a crewcut billionaire who sounds more like a cow town sheriff than a world leader." Perot was running on platitudes, promising to wipe out the budget deficit "without breaking a sweat," an absurd claim he had no intention of clarifying. Yet voters loved the way he brushed off reporters like nettlesome gnats. It was like the White House press corps trying to nail Ronald Reagan for stretching the truth; Perot seemed to stand for something, and many people simply didn't care whether he met some journalistic threshold for specificity.

The press turned on Perot in a few short weeks, telescoping the normal process as if to compensate for his avoidance of the primary gauntlet. Soon the *New York Times, Wall Street Journal, Washington Post, Los Angeles Times,* Associated Press and *Dallas Morning News,* his hometown paper, were giving Perot the flyspeck treatment: He had won a special tax break by donating $55,000 to members of the House Ways and Means Committee. He had convinced the government to invest in a Fort Worth airport near land his family owned. He had received special favors from the Nixon White House and had discussed spending $50 million—perhaps to buy *The Washington Star* or ABC— on a PR campaign to burnish Nixon's image. His computer firm, Electronic Data Systems, had fired people for wearing beards or committing adultery. He had discussed business opportunities with Vietnamese officials during his much-ballyhooed mission to find missing American servicemen. He had hired private detectives to investigate employees and rivals. Despite his stance against raising taxes, he had written in *The Washington Post* in 1987: "We must cut spending and raise taxes to pay our bills. We all know it."

Some columnists—the *Times'* William Safire, the *Post's* Richard Cohen—began crusading against Perot. The press dug up almost daily examples of his weird behavior. In 1955 Perot had sought an early release from the Navy, calling it "a fairly Godless organization" where he had to endure the spectacle of sailors drinking and cursing like, well, sailors. Richard Connor, publisher of the *Fort Worth Star-Telegram,* recalled how Perot, upset about coverage of his son's business dealings, had warned that he had photographs to prove that one of Connor's employees was having an affair with a city official.

David Remnick, then a *Washington Post* reporter, offered a similarly strange tale. During a routine interview, Perot had opened his office safe and produced a photograph of a top Pentagon official, Richard Armitage, and a young Asian woman that he said "completely compromised" Armitage.

Yet Ross Perot was soaring above the reach of the Old Media. He often denounced his press critics in personal terms. When asked about a 1988 column by Laura Miller of the *Dallas Times Herald,* reporting that he had called for house-to-house searches in the war on drugs, Perot accused her of "flights of fantasy." When Linda Wertheimer of National Public Radio pressed him on the air about his failed effort to rescue a New York brokerage firm in the 1970s, Perot accused her of a "classic setup . . . and I'm sure you had a smirk on your mouth as you got me into this." Perot insisted that hostile interviews worked to his advantage by making voters angry, and perhaps he was right: By mid-May he had passed both Bush and Clinton in the polls.

"This country does have a weird fixation on the businessman/savior," columnist Jack Newfield wrote. "Remember, four years ago people were talking about Donald Trump running for president."

As spring turned into summer, the prospect that Perot might actually become president was unnerving to many reporters, who interviewed his volunteers as if they were strange fanatics. What they found were ordinary, middle-class folks disgusted with the kind of slash-and-burn politics the press specialized in covering.

"Are Perot's supporters on a dangerous flight from reality?" Don Kimelman asked in *The Philadelphia Inquirer.* "Or, worse yet, are they crypto-fascists looking for a führer who will end the political deadlock that our messy democracy has produced? Hardly. . . . They are, for the most part . . . decent, levelheaded people." *Boston Globe* columnist Derrick Jackson, however, was more dismissive: "Millions of blind mice are running into Ross Perot's cage. Stupid little creatures they are."

Perot's rivals quickly followed him onto the talk show circuit, hoping for a whiff of his magic formula. Clinton jammed for Arsenio, did breakfast on "Good Morning America" and rapped with young folks on MTV. Bush fielded questions on "20/20" and "CBS This Morning." The candidates got hours and hours of free airtime and relished the chance to make their case, unedited and unfiltered. They got plenty of softballs they could knock out of the park, and without the adversarial follow-up that had become a journalistic trademark. As a bonus, they could reach younger, more alienated viewers who had little use for newspapers.

On a deeper level, the talk show campaign was a rejection of the prosecutorial culture of the national press that had reached its apogee with Watergate. It was, at bottom, a healthy development. Millions of people had become disconnected from the kind of poll-driven, battering-ram politics chronicled by the Old Media. If professional reporters were more persistent than Aunt Millie from Omaha calling in from her kitchen, they were frequently less substantive and more concerned with strategy and inside baseball. When Bush held a prime-time news conference on June 4 (which the Big Three networks pointedly refused to broadcast), nearly half the questions were about Perot, the polls and other horse-race matters. Some were downright inane; a *USA Today* reporter asked what Bush would say to Perot if he ran into him on the street. It was yet another reminder of why people were tuning us out.

In his disdain for details, however, Perot had underestimated the ability of newspapers to set the campaign agenda, even in the television age. His dealings with one rather famous reporter were about to come back to haunt him. During the 1988 campaign, Perot had gathered a wealth of documents and allegations about George Bush and passed them to Bob Woodward. The *Washington Post* sleuth was investigating the then vice president, and Perot, who detested Bush, was only too eager to help.

Perot told Woodward he had looked into a controversial Texas land deal that might bear Bush's fingerprints. Woodward and a colleague, Walter Pincus, say they spoke to the billionaire on "background," meaning they could use the information but could not attribute it to him (Perot recalls the discussions as being totally off the record). Perot described the situation as a "mini–Teapot Dome" and gave the reporters two vinyl binders full of documents.

Perot offered to obtain the records on two of Bush's Texas investments and later sent them to the reporters. He dropped other tantalizing leads, recalling how he had once warned Bush that two of his sons were associating with unsavory characters.

The leads went nowhere, and the *Post* never published Perot's material. Four years later, however, Perot's Watergate-style penchant for investigating his enemies had become big news. Woodward faced a thorny dilemma: Perot had been a confidential source, yet the very transaction for which Woodward had promised him anonymity was now part of the hottest story in town.

Woodward called Perot. "I've got to write about you as an investigator," he said.

"I don't want any of that out," Perot replied, saying it would distract from the real issues of the campaign.

"The situation's changed," Woodward said. "I've got an obligation. I'm going to write about it in some form. You're running for president and it describes who you are."

Perot refused to put their conversations on the record. Woodward told James Squires, the former *Chicago Tribune* editor acting as Perot's spokesman, that he was going with the story. Squires left a message confirming that Perot had passed information on the Texas land deal to the *Post,* but he disputes Woodward's contention that this amounted to putting it on the record. As for the other "background" material, Woodward and his coauthor, John Mintz, artfully worded their article so that they never said exactly where the stuff was coming from, although readers could infer that Perot was the source.

The *Post*'s banner story on June 21 caused a sensation. The image of Inspector Perot, private eye, took hold in the popular culture. The electronic town hall candidate reacted like an old-style pol: He summoned David Broder, dean of the political press corps, for an interview. Perot told the *Post* columnist that the recent spate of negative stories were the product of "Republican dirty tricks." (This was demonstrably false in the case of the *Post* story, which had obviously come from Perot's own lips.) After weeks of ignoring reporters at his rallies, Perot called his first news conference to defend himself.

The talk around Washington was whether Woodward, who was still protecting Deep Throat twenty years after Watergate, had burned his source. Bill Safire charged that the *Post* had been a "patsy" for Perot and that Woodward had "confessed" to the secret dealings for fear of being exposed. Once again, I had no choice but to do a story about my own paper.

Woodward told me he had been "very aggressive" with Perot, but said he had "other sources" for much of the information and that "the ground rules were strictly observed. . . . I feel absolutely comfortable." But Squires suggested that Woodward had violated his confidentiality pledge. "One of the most famous reporters in the country, doer of good deeds, pursuer of sin and corruption in high places, is calling Perot, working on a Bush investigation," he said. "It's Woodward who was investigating Bush. Perot gives Woodward what he asked for. That act, right there, turns into Perot 'investigating' Bush and Bush's children."

The *Post* compounded the problem by not being straightforward about the origins of the story. We were pointing the finger at Perot for investigating Bush when the paper had been a willing accomplice. And while there is a difference between a newspaper and a private businessman conducting such inquiries, we failed to make that argument by fudging the facts.

Unfortunately, a *Post* editor killed my explanatory piece after the first edition, ostensibly to make room for late-breaking news but creating the perception that the paper had something to hide. I complained to Len Downie that we still had not adequately explained how the Woodward story got into print, and he agreed to let me write a longer piece about the controversy, which ran two days later.

Other newspapers, meanwhile, were pummeling Perot regularly, with television following suit. The attack-dog stage had arrived. Perot started sinking in the polls. He tried to explain away his comment that he wouldn't have homosexuals in his Cabinet. He addressed an NAACP audience as "you people." Days later, on July 16, Perot pulled the plug on his candidacy.

The newspaper reporters that Perot so casually scorned had helped blow him out of the race. It was done like "a Mafia hit, with smooth professionalism," Richard Cohen said admiringly. Perot had a fine time running against the press, but when the press started hitting back, he quickly folded his cards. He couldn't take the heat, couldn't abide having snotty reporters challenge the mythologized version of his life story and point an accusatory finger each time he lied. It was journalism at its best, for the searing spotlight of press scrutiny essentially exposed this billionaire populist as a paper tiger.

Some publications clearly enjoyed kicking the Texan while he was down. "The Quitter," said *Newsweek*'s cover. "WHAT A WIMP!" declared the *New York Post*. The *Kansas City Star* called him a "fraud," *The Miami Herald* a "chicken." The man who declared every problem "pretty simple," who said he could easily eliminate the deficit, belatedly embraced a plan to raise taxes and cut Social Security and other entitlement programs. It was a tacit acknowledgment that his no-sweat assurances had been wrong all along.

It turned out that those annoying Old Media reporters had been right to press Perot about the issues he so calmly finessed at Larry King's elbow. Ross Perot had bowed out in large measure because he could not stomach the daily combat with the press, and that spoke volumes about his unsuitability for the Oval Office.

When Dan Quayle misspelled "potato" at a Trenton school, it was hardly front-page news. The press had been polishing Quayle's tarnished image for months, most notably in a seven-part *Washington Post* series by Woodward and David Broder that portrayed the vice president as a canny and underestimated politician. "Quayle's Moment," proclaimed the cover of *The New York Times Magazine*. After four years of ridicule, Quayle was finally being taken seriously, at least by the elite press. The "potatoe" gaffe was a minor embarrassment, surely not worth much ink. The *Los Angeles Times* ran an eighty-seven-word wire story on page 21. *USA Today* kissed it off with a one-paragraph item. *The Washington Post* relegated the matter to its gossip column. *The New York Times* ran a story inside the paper two days after the fact. And yet the gaffe, silly and inconsequential as it was, instantly became part of the New Media culture, providing nightly fodder for Jay Leno and David Letterman and spawning a thousand T-shirts and buttons. It was the ultimate metaphor for Quayle as a guy who just didn't measure up, and yet the newspapers managed to miss it.

Editors at the most prestigious papers sometimes have a tin ear for the news that everyone is talking about. When Quayle attacked Murphy Brown for having a baby out of wedlock—using a sitcom character to hammer home his "family values" message—much of the press had a field day. "Quayle to Murphy Brown: YOU TRAMP!" blared the New York *Daily News*. But *The New York Times* and *The Washington Post* missed the point. The *Times'* Andrew Rosenthal and the *Post's* John Yang each mentioned Murphy Brown at the top of their front-page stories on Quayle's speech, but editors at both papers buried the comments on an inside page. A mere TV sitcom was simply too frivolous to warrant page-one treatment. After blowing the initial story, both papers followed up with days of saturation coverage on the absurd spectacle of the vice president assailing a fictional journalist and the tenuous link to the millions of struggling single mothers. Better late than never.

Days later I got a call from a source who disclosed that Dan Quayle, protector of family values, was renting his McLean, Virginia, home to an unwed couple with two kids from the woman's previous marriage. But the *Post's* national desk brushed off this delicious bit of hypocrisy and suggested I give it to our gossip columnist, Lois Romano. Her item produced headlines around the country. "DAN, HOW COULD YOU?" the *New York Post* demanded. "DO AS DAN SAYS, NOT AS HE DOES," the *Daily News* tittered. For all their excesses, the New York tabloids sometimes have a better feel for the average reader than their high-rent cousins.

Rap music is another avenue through which information ignored by the Old Media seeps into pop culture. Rap seethed with images of black violence long before the white press caught on. After the L.A. riots, Sister Souljah, a black rap singer, told *Washington Post* reporter David Mills: "I mean, if black people kill black people every day, why not have a week and kill white people?" This remarkable statement went largely unremarked upon, except by Richard Cohen, who denounced it as "raw race hatred." When Clinton later assailed the Souljah remarks before Jesse Jackson and his Rainbow Coalition, he did what few white politicians (or journalists) have dared to do: criticize a prominent black for reverse racism.

When the establishment press refuses to deal with rumors that everyone is whispering about, other outlets invariably fill the vacuum. It was only a matter of time, therefore, until the Bush infidelity story made its way into print. "He Cheats on His Wife," *Spy* magazine's cover blared in June. *Spy* named as Bush's mistress his longtime aide Jennifer Fitzgerald, the subject of years of low-level gossip. Bush had named her the State Department's deputy protocol chief in 1989 (prompting *The Washington Post*'s wry observation that Fitzgerald had served Bush "in a variety of positions"). Although *Spy* had no proof, its story was picked up by *Newsweek,* the *Chicago Tribune,* the *New York Post* and *USA Today* (which described *Spy* as descending "right into the sewer of sleaze and unnamed sources"—while still naming Fitzgerald).

The story took center stage on August 11 when the *New York Post,* in a replay of the Kitty Kelley episode, ran a banner headline ("THE BUSH AFFAIR") based on a new book called *The Power House.* The "evidence" consisted of a single footnote. Author Susan Trento said her husband, a former CNN reporter, had been told by the late U.S. ambassador Louis Fields that he had arranged for Bush and Fitzgerald to share a guest house in Geneva during arms-control talks there in 1984. Fields claimed no firsthand knowledge of an affair; he simply said the living arrangements made him uncomfortable. It was pretty thin gruel, but that didn't stop the tabloid from sneering about Bush's "lakeside love nest" with "the alleged First Mistress."

Various Democrats had been trying to peddle the tale to reporters for weeks. Jack Nelson of the *Los Angeles Times* had interviewed Trento but decided that the word of a dead ambassador hardly justified accusing the president of adultery. Still, as with the Gennifer story, tabloid headlines put the Jennifer charge in play. CNN's Mary Tillotson asked Bush about the *Post* report at a Kennebunkport news conference carried live by her network; he called it a "lie" and scolded her for asking "sleazy questions." Stone Phillips, cohost of "Dateline NBC," asked the president later that day if he'd ever had an affair. All the major newspapers (except *The New York Times,* which reverted to its Gennifer mode by burying a small article on an inside page) dealt prominently with the controversy the next morning. My piece in *The Washington Post* led with Bush's angry denial, just as I had led with Clinton's denial seven months earlier. Once again, even though the press had absolutely no proof that the allegations were true, we could not take a head-in-the-sand approach to a seamy story that had been all over television. But this time the editorial hand-wringing lasted only a day or so; by the abysmal standards of 1992, even sleaze was becoming old hat.

By early July, Bill Clinton was undergoing a remarkable political resurrection. Battered mercilessly by the press, he began to recover only when journalists started ignoring him. All the investigative reporters had abandoned Little Rock for Dallas, digging for dirt on Perot. The attack-dog phase was finally over for Clinton, and his message of moderation finally broke through the static. Clinton's image-makers settled on an MTV media strategy, one focused more on *People* magazine (which obligingly put Bill, Hillary and Chelsea on the cover in July) than *The New York Times*.

As the Democratic convention approached, reporters grew consumed by feverish and monumentally useless speculation over Clinton's vice presidential choice. It was the press at its worst, day after day of inside-baseball gossip on a matter that would be announced soon anyway. Jack Germond said it would be Bob Kerrey; David Broder put his money on Al Gore; NBC's Tim Russert picked Lee Hamilton; *Time*'s Margaret Carlson bet on Jay Rockefeller. *The Boston Globe* said Clinton was "seriously considering" Florida Senator Bob Graham. *Newsday* revived the faint hope that Mario Cuomo might say yes. "Clinton 'Close to Decision' on Ticket," *The Washington Post* said in its second straight front-page story on the matter. "WHO'S IT GONNA BE?" the *Daily News* demanded.

"There is, quite simply, no way to write about this process and retain any sense of journalistic self-respect," Joe Klein said. "No source ever knows anything useful; all rumors are inevitably false."

When Clinton picked Gore, a senator who had begun his career as a reporter for the Nashville *Tennessean,* it reminded me of the time Gore had called me at home to leak a story. The Tennessee congressman was running for the Senate in 1984, and his staff slipped me some documents about mismanagement at the Federal Emergency Management Agency. There is a tacit understanding with such Hill leaks that the story will include a paragraph saying Congressman So-and-So is investigating the matter, but Gore wasn't taking any chances. "I know these things are usually unspoken, but I'm in a tough race for the Senate," Gore told me. "I want to make sure I get some credit on this." I assured Gore that I would make note of his role.

When the Democrats convened in New York in mid-July, fifteen thousand journalists descended on Madison Square Garden in search of news. The endless parties, schmoozing and free booze were a reminder that these political gatherings are really a quadrennial excuse for a journalists' convention. To justify our expense accounts, we all churned out stories that pretended something of cosmic significance was going on. *The New York Times,* covering the hometown event, inflicted as many as nine pages a day on its readers.

The convention and the telegenic bus trip that followed gave Clinton and Gore a huge bounce in the polls. A *Washington Post* survey showing Clinton with a twenty-nine-point lead over Bush seemed so ludicrous that the paper's political reporters argued against putting it on the front page (they lost). Such polls produced a bandwagon effect that gave the Arkansas governor a period of glowing, even giddy, coverage. "Clinton and Gore, New Heartthrobs of the Heartland," declared *The Washington Post*'s Style section, praising their "gloriously triumphant" bus trip. *Newsweek*'s Eleanor Clift described the nominees as "the all-beefcake ticket." *The New Republic*'s Hendrik Hertzberg called Clinton's choice of Gore "magical." The *Post*'s David Maraniss filed a dispatch from one bus trip that began: "Bill and Al are back together again after two long and lonely weeks apart."

The local coverage was even more fawning. On a Clinton-Gore trip to Nashville, I was struck by the boosterish tone of the local news outlets, as if the candidates had honored their community just by showing up. Local anchors gushed, and the newspapers weren't much better. "It's a Grand Ol' Evening," *The Tennessean* proclaimed after the duo took the stage at the Grand Ole Opry. Clinton also appeared on the Nashville Network, where the Democratic presidential nominee demonstrated his hog-calling skills. It was the same story in town after town. "Waco Hails Clinton-Gore Team," said the lead story in the *Waco* (Texas), *Tribune-Herald.* "Wow, What a Crowd!" roared the Madison (Wisconsin), *Capital Times.* "Gore Voices Hope for Future," said *The Burlington* (Vermont), *Free Press.*

As in the Reagan years, we were once again falling for photo-op politics: Bill and Al jogging, Bill and Al tossing a football, Bill and Al on a haystack talking to farmers, the events all choreographed by a Hollywood producer. *The New Republic* started a "Clinton Suck-Up Watch." To be sure, the Democratic ticket was drawing big crowds, but it was Clinton's big lead in the almighty polls that was making him look like a genius. Had Clinton been trailing, there would have been a spate of stories questioning why he was wasting his time on a stupid bus.

Many black journalists, however, were less enamored of Clinton than were their white colleagues. Some black reporters openly criticized the governor's relentless focus on white, middle-class voters. Sam Fulwood III of the *Los Angeles Times,* joining a Clinton-Gore bus trip through the Midwest, wrote of "what is likely to be conspicuously absent in the next two days: Black people." Several blacks on the campaign trail wrote pieces criticizing Clinton for doing little to court minority voters or address urban poverty, but Fulwood says such stories "largely disappeared into a black hole of obscurity." Still, not all black reporters covering Clinton hewed to this line. Gwen Ifill of *The New York Times* said black journalists should not behave like activists pursuing a narrow agenda. "When you talk about a tax cut, you're talking to black people too," Ifill says. "I resist the notion that you only talk to black people when you talk about poverty." Once again, the prism of race was producing sharply divergent views of the world within the press corps itself.

The Bush campaign, meanwhile, was being widely ridiculed as the gang that couldn't shoot straight. The Bush-Quayle team was so disorganized that it made little news, and the press had to make do with a steady stream of rumors. There were rumors that Bush was ill, that Quayle was ill, that Quayle was close to being dumped from the ticket. "Bush's Doctor Denies Rumors of Poor Health," a front-page *New York Times* headline said, demonstrating anew that at least some rumors were fit to print.

The flood of Quayle-must-go stories, like the earlier dump-Sununu drumbeat, reflected an orchestrated attempt by senior campaign officials to oust the vice president. Even after Bush insisted he was keeping Quayle, the damaging leaks continued. "Once the rumor game puts a person 'in play,' few things are more difficult than stopping the cycle," the *Los Angeles Times* observed. Next the press latched onto the unlikely notion that Bush himself might withdraw from the race. Even the most conservative columnists—George Will, Robert Novak, William Safire—had deserted the president. Will, who had detested Bush for years, said he should not run because he "almost certainly will lose, perhaps in a landslide." With most liberal pundits openly rooting for Clinton, these defections added to the sense that the media were ganging up on Bush.

The growing Republican anger toward the press was palpable at the GOP convention in Houston, where "Blame It on the Media" T-shirts were a hot-selling item. As Nina Totenberg tried to conduct interviews on the floor, a group of young Republicans shouted "Nina, Nina, have you had an affair?" (They had confused her with CNN's Mary Tillotson.) There was a cultural clash between the wisecracking reporters and members of the religious right. Most of the press thought the convention—particularly the anti-gay, religious-war rhetoric of Pat Buchanan —was "dominated by hate-mongering and fear-mongering," as Molly Ivins put it. For once the media elite had it right: Many Americans also found the Astrodome antics distasteful.

Like Bill Clinton, Jerry Brown and Ross Perot before them, George Bush and his surrogates began carping about a media conspiracy to discredit their man. Dan Quayle said the press wanted "to hurt the president and help Bill Clinton." Barbara Bush said reporters were "liberals." Her husband, who had taken to blaming the media for public pessimism about the economy, called the coverage "one-sided." The old GOP tactic of assailing the press, which dated to Spiro Agnew and his "nattering nabobs of negativism," was designed to make reporters feel guilty about beating up on Bush.

There was, in fact, more than a grain of truth to these charges, although not in the partisan sense the Bush folks had in mind. The contrast in coverage of the two campaigns was so stark that I felt compelled to write a piece about the pro-Clinton tilt in the press. While Bush was a weak incumbent running an awful campaign, the pack mentality was such that reporters assailed almost everything he did as stupid, cynical or politically motivated. We simply didn't judge Clinton's pronouncements and fence-straddling in the same harsh light.

Many reporters privately believed that Bush had been a mediocre, do-nothing president who did not deserve to be reelected. They felt more of a cultural affinity with the forty-six-year-old Elvis fan than the sixty-eight-year-old patrician from Greenwich and Kennebunkport. Some had close friends working for the Clinton camp. What's more, a second Bush term would be a snooze for the press—some reporters openly mused about leaving Washington if he was reelected—while a Clinton administration would usher in an exciting era of activism. Journalists may have savaged Clinton during the primaries, when he looked unelectable, but now he had, in their eyes, the aura of a winner. Many of the reporters on Clinton's plane would become White House correspondents, perhaps enjoying special access to the new president. As *Time*'s Walter Shapiro put it: "It's wanting to be Ben Bradlee to Bill Clinton's Jack Kennedy."

The Republicans, naturally, enjoyed quoting my article on the talk shows, and not one of my colleagues called to say it wasn't true. But there was a larger dynamic at work here as well. Reporters felt they had been badly burned by Bush's Willie Horton tactics four years earlier, and they were determined not to let him get away with a repeat performance. All politicians stretch the truth, but Bush and his operatives indulged in far more blatant distortions than Clinton. And that, not the president's conservative philosophy, was what roused the media truth squads into action.

The press turned an important corner as the 1992 campaign wore on. Journalists began examining the daily sound-bite warfare with a far more critical eye. Thematic, interpretive stories—about Bush showering key states with federal largesse, or Clinton repeatedly hedging on trade and other issues, or both men preaching pain-free economics— became more important than what-happened-yesterday pieces. And the press finally shed its reluctance to make an issue of false or distorted charges.

When the Republicans claimed that Hillary Clinton supported the right of children to sue their parents, *The New York Times* and *The Washington Post*, among others, pointed out that this was a distortion of her writings from the 1970s, which dealt with extreme cases of abuse. Reporters also blew the whistle when, despite Bush's vow to avoid personal attacks, political director Mary Matalin spoke of "bimbo eruptions" plaguing Clinton, and U.S. Treasurer Catalina Villalpando called him a "skirt-chaser." The *Times* observed that "the Republicans have perfected a rhetorical two-step: say something nasty about the opposition, then apologize."

The new media approach was evident when the Bush camp began assailing Clinton for raising taxes in Arkansas 128 times. Michael Kinsley exposed this charge as blatantly false in his syndicated newspaper column. The Bush camp was counting some taxes more than once, subdividing taxes that applied to different types of alcoholic beverages, counting as a tax a measure that lengthened the dog-racing season, and so on, while ignoring Clinton's offsetting tax cuts. In fact, Arkansas ranked forty-sixth in the nation in per capita tax burden. By this sort of accounting, Bush himself had raised taxes 133 times. Yet even after this fraud had been thoroughly aired in the press, the president repeated the 128 figure in his acceptance speech. *The Boston Globe* gave Clinton fresh ammunition by quoting an unnamed Bush aide as saying the campaign knew the 128 charge was untrue but kept using it because "it works."

I found myself in the middle of one such brawl as a member of the "ad police," as the reporters who critiqued campaign commercials had been dubbed. The Bush campaign launched a television ad charging that middle-class folks could expect a hefty tax increase from a Clinton administration. The thirty-second spot showed pictures of ordinary people and flashed their supposed tax hikes with chilling specificity—steamfitter John Canes ($1,088), scientist Lori Huntoon ($2,072), and so on.

It was voodoo arithmetic, for Clinton had proposed to raise taxes only on people earning more than $150,000 a year. The Bush ad rested on a series of assumptions as shaky as a house of cards. One had to assume (1) that Clinton's revenue projections were wildly exaggerated; (2) that $58 billion of Clinton's proposed spending cuts were phony; (3) that Clinton's health plan would cost $117 billion more than he claimed; and (4) that Clinton would abandon his plan for a middle-class tax cut. Even if all those predictions turned out to be true, one had to further assume that Clinton would ignore other options—such as scaling back his spending plans—and sock it to the middle class.

To be sure, Clinton's budget, like Bush's, was filled with ambiguities and exaggerations that avoided the painful choices the next president would face. I had myself criticized a Democratic Party radio ad for making a similar leap of logic in charging that Bush would slash Medicare and veterans' benefits (he had merely listed that as an option). The Bush deception, however, was far worse. Charles Black, Bush's senior strategist, insisted to reporters that the ad was fair because—and this was truly sad—it used the word "could." The campaign figured that no newspaper article could catch up with the power of a televised accusation. "If there are stories accusing us of distortion, so what?" a top Bush adviser told me. "Just repeat the charge by the third paragraph."

I described the ad's flaws in a front-page story and, in an accompanying graphic, called it "misleading." Unbeknownst to me, Clinton's media adviser, Frank Greer, dispatched an aide to buy the *Post*'s first edition at 10:30 that evening, and his team worked until 4:00 A.M. to produce a counterattack ad, using my piece as ammunition. The Clinton rebuttal hit the airwaves the next evening: "George Bush is running attack ads. He says all these people would have their taxes raised by Bill Clinton. Scary, huh? 'Misleading,' says *The Washington Post*. And *The Wall Street Journal* says, 'Clinton has proposed to cut taxes for the sort of people featured in Bush's ad.' " (Clinton's tax increase the next year nicked the middle class for only a small fraction of the numbers featured in the commercial.)

Clinton's counterattacks—his aides sometimes obtained Bush's ads twenty-four hours early and faxed rebuttals to reporters even before they had aired—helped neutralize the president's phony charge. But Clinton's strategy depended on an energized press corps. Journalists had decided not to mindlessly repeat campaign charges as we had done in 1988. If one side wanted to use our words to neutralize the other's false claims, well, that was the free market at work.

When Bush started using the Old Media—in this case, radio—he peddled even more egregious distortions. Radio was a way of flying under the political radar because it was hard to track ads that varied from one market to the next. One spot charged that "Bill Clinton's policies have been called 'fiercely protectionist' by papers like *The Washington Post*." When I asked about the quote, the Bush campaign cited a 1985 *Post* editorial about a long-forgotten textile bill in Congress which had made no mention of Clinton. Campaign spokeswoman Alixe Glen said that since Clinton had supported the textile bill, and the *Post* had called the bill protectionist, the paper was, ipso facto, calling Clinton a protectionist. It was, in other words, a lie. I felt a bit uneasy about criticizing the Bush ads more harshly than Clinton's ads, but the fact is that the Democrats, while occasionally shading the truth, were far more careful about documenting their charges. I was not going to equate jaywalking with bank robbery just to create an artificial "balance."

While the networks followed up with similar reports, some news organizations remained cautious about pointing out lies in the Bush radio ads. Even as a new wave of false spots hit the airwaves—accusing Clinton of backing a "carbon tax" and "farm taxes" that he had never proposed—*The New York Times* said that "aides to Governor Clinton say the radio ads have no basis in fact," as if it were just another exchange of political jabs. Still, the barrage of negative ads ultimately had little impact on the race—polls showed that many people simply didn't believe them—and the press clearly had a hand in that. For all their bad habits, reporters were finally giving voters a reality check on the wild exaggerations of a presidential campaign.

Inevitably, the media pendulum swung back against Bill Clinton. His period of press coddling ended on September 2 with a *Los Angeles Times* report that raised new questions about whether his uncle had helped him duck the draft. A defensive Clinton accused the press (with considerable overstatement) of a new "feeding frenzy." Reporters stuck with the draft story, in part because Clinton kept fumbling it and in part because it was the only juicy "character" issue around. Again, however, the public responded to the media's latest obsession with a resounding yawn: 79 percent of those questioned in a *New York Times* survey said the draft issue wouldn't affect their vote. Some journalists, however, had an ideological interest in flogging the story. Wes Pruden wrote in *The Washington Times* that "many of the people who defend Slick Willie's draft dodging, and his later lies," and his organizing "hate-America rallies in London," were journalists—"many of whom were slackers themselves." The right was still intent on fighting the Vietnam War.

But even the draft issue was soon overshadowed by the endless waves of polls. "Bush Pulls Close in Poll," a front-page *New York Times* story announced after the GOP convention. Four days later, the *Times* ran a page-one "correction": "Bush's Gains from Convention Nearly Evaporate in Latest Poll." Nine days later it was *USA Today*'s turn for a banner headline on Bush losing his "bounce" (it's only news when your own pollster makes the discovery). *The Washington Post*'s polls were equally unpredictable. When a *Post* poll showed Clinton up twenty-one points in late September—which we all knew was out of line with other surveys—the paper broke with its usual practice and touted the figure in a front-page headline and story. But when Clinton's lead dropped to nine points in the following week's poll, the paper ran an analysis on an inside page: "Clinton Slide in Survey Shows Perils of Polling."

Managing editor Robert Kaiser says the paper's principal sin was allowing the twenty-one-point lead into the headline, despite constant lobbying by David Broder and other reporters who believed that polls were not front-page news. ("It was a slow news day," Kaiser says.) By the following week, Kaiser notes, "We had lost some confidence in our poll. There was a discussion: Did we owe it to the Bush campaign to put the story on the front page because of what we did the last time, or were we compounding an error? I took the latter position." Having sinned once, however, the *Post* convinced many skeptics that it was deliberately tilting the news by suddenly turning agnostic about polls when Clinton's lead seemed to plummet.

Despite such distractions, by mid-September the press was filled with substantive stories about the economy, health care, North American free trade and other campaign issues. Reporters were making a concerted attempt to listen to the voters, and not just to the political handlers. *USA Today* ran a weekly "people's press conference" in which the campaigns responded to readers' questions. *The Boston Globe* ran a regular box called "One Voter Speaks." *The New York Times* took the electorate's pulse in an "Off the Trail" feature. The television networks began blowing off staged events and scripted sound bites in favor of analysis, voter interviews and focus groups. Suddenly, substance was in.

Recalling our silent complicity on the S&L mess, the press seemed determined to spotlight the issues the candidates were ducking. *The Wall Street Journal* detailed how Bush and Clinton, in an "eerie replay" of 1988, were ignoring the increasingly troubled condition of commercial banks. Another *Journal* piece accused the candidates of flunking basic math, saying both men were "promising hundreds of billions of dollars more in tax cuts, spending increases and deficit reduction than their specific proposals will pay for." *The Washington Post* ran a three-part series on the budget deficit. The *Los Angeles Times* carried a skeptical report on the job-training programs that both candidates were touting as an all-purpose remedy. There were richly detailed portraits, particularly by the *Post*'s David Maraniss, of Clinton's approach to governing. Several newspapers reexamined Bush's role in Iran-contra, reviving the complicated scandal as a television story. The talk shows may have taken over the campaign, but time and again the interviewers' questions were drawn from the morning papers.

The issues were finally eclipsing boys-on-the-bus journalism, in part because the electorate seemed to demand more serious coverage. Besides, the horse race was becoming a study in creeping incrementalism. Day after day Bush and Clinton made the same charges and we found new ways to slice the salami. Most reporters grew bored watching Clinton sit on his double-digit lead. How many times could we say that the economy was the dominant issue, that the public had soured on George Bush and that Reagan Democrats were returning home in droves? The press began to talk up the possibility of a landslide. Jack Germond spoke of a Clinton "blowout." "The Bush-man is toast," crowed *The Boston Globe*'s David Nyhan. *The Washington Post*'s Richard Harwood said Clinton was headed for "a landslide on the order of the Johnson victory in 1964." Editors started planning for a Clinton transition. With five weeks to go, we were about to declare the thing over.

Just as the press was desperate for a new story line, Ross Perot came riding to the rescue. The billionaire started making the talk show rounds, pushing his new book and dropping hints that he just might run again. The networks showered Perot with free airtime; in one two-week stretch he appeared on the "Today" show four times, on "Larry King Live" and "Nightline," "The MacNeil/Lehrer NewsHour" and C-SPAN, "Good Morning America" and "CBS This Morning." Perot had become America's guest, his presence a guaranteed ratings-booster.

When Perot jumped back into the race on October 1, the press welcomed him with a second honeymoon. Having initially missed the Perot phenomenon, we were now determined to overcover a guy who had plummeted to single digits in the polls. Perot had absolutely no rationale for resuming his campaign, other than salvaging his reputation and living down that "WHAT A WIMP" headline. The transparent fiction that he was obeying the will of "the volunteers" was belied by reports that he had spent $7 million on his campaign after supposedly dropping out.

To be sure, some pundits were openly hostile toward Perot II. *The Philadelphia Inquirer*'s Steve Lopez called Perot a "liar," a "bozo" and "obscenely self-important." The *Los Angeles Times* called his reentry a "charade." The *New York Post*'s Pete Hamill dismissed him as a "head case." Perot, in turn, seemed more determined than ever to run against the press, grousing about "gotcha journalism" and accusing reporters of making up "fairy tales." It seemed like old times.

But this sort of jousting masked a fundamental failure by the media. Perot was using his personal fortune to mount the most expensive television blitz in presidential campaign history, churning out sixty-second ads and half-hour "infomercials" that depicted him as an American hero, and we were still treating him like an amusing vaudeville act. It was the Jerry Brown syndrome all over again. We spent little time examining Perot's controversial plan to raise gasoline taxes and income taxes and cut Social Security and Medicare. We forgot about his strange penchant for investigating people. All that we had learned about his behavior the previous spring—the paranoia, the conspiracy theories, the secret photographs—had suddenly become irrelevant. Perot was determined to circumvent the Old Media by running a Wizard of Oz campaign that existed almost entirely behind the curtain of television. He wagered that reporters would be too focused on the final leg of the horse race to resurrect all those Inspector Perot stories. And, for most of October, he was right.

With Ross Perot leading the way, the New Media were once again in the ascendancy. Bush, who earlier in the year had assailed "weird talk shows," booked himself twice on Larry King King, a great schmoozer who made no pretense of being a newsman, slapped the president's thigh and served up friendly questions ("You like campaigning?" "Is Millie writing another book?"). In the new media universe, Larry King was now more important to the race than David Broder or Johnny Apple or Jack Germond.

But campaign controversies still seemed to move along a conveyor belt from newspapers to chat shows. The trick for political operatives was to slip their filthiest wares onto that conveyor belt. Republican strategists had been whispering to reporters that there was something ominous about Clinton's 1969 sightseeing visit to Moscow as an Oxford student. Robert Dornan, a far-right GOP congressman, spent day after day railing about the trip to an empty House chamber (and a C-SPAN audience). But no one would bite—that is, until *The Washington Times* obligingly bannered the story on October 5. The piece dripped with innuendo: Clinton had "quietly" turned up in the Soviet Union "during the dead of winter." He refused to comment on the "unusual" trip, but Dornan had suggested that "the former antiwar activist and draft evader may have been duped by Soviet intelligence officials." An unnamed British intelligence expert "said Mr. Clinton 'fit the profile perfectly' of someone the Soviets might cultivate and recruit as an 'agent of influence.' " It was almost a parody of attack-dog journalism. Wes Pruden even speculated that someone from the Soviet Peace Council might have put Clinton up in a fancy hotel "with an Anna to stroke his youthful beard and a Natasha eager to draw a nice hot bath."

Other newspapers ignored the *Times* story, but the New Media were happy to pick up the mudball and run with it. Phil Donahue, who had badgered Clinton about Gennifer Flowers the previous spring, pressed him about the Moscow trip, forcing reporters to cover the governor's denials. When Bush himself discussed the Moscow trip issue on Larry King, it became an automatic front-page story and led all the network newscasts. Four years earlier, this sort of charge might have degenerated into yet another media circus. This time, however, the press slammed on the brakes, putting more emphasis on Bush's descent into McCarthyism than on the sleazy allegation itself. "The red-baiting tactics that President Bush rolled out this week reflect a train of desperation that is running through his campaign," Curtis Wilkie wrote in *The Boston Globe*. "A new low . . . un-American," said Lars-Erik Nelson in the New York *Daily News*. "Slime," sniffed Anthony Lewis in *The New York Times*. "A GOP dirt-bomb," snapped the Baltimore *Sun*.

One columnist unwittingly provided the ammunition that Clinton needed to even the score. Tom Oliphant recounted in the *Globe* how Senator Prescott Bush had denounced Joe McCarthy in 1954, contrasting his bravery with his son's latest smear tactic. A Clinton campaign aide noticed the piece, and in their first televised debate Clinton turned to the president, recalled Prescott Bush's role and said: "Your father was right to stand up to Joe McCarthy; you were wrong to question my patriotism." It was the defining moment of the debate.

When Bush attacked Clinton's character in the second debate, the Democrat again turned to a newspaper for defense. This time it was the *Post*, which had endorsed him days earlier. *"The Washington Post* ran a long editorial today saying they couldn't believe Mr. Bush was making character an issue, and they said he was the greatest, quote, 'political chameleon' for changing his positions, of all time," Clinton said. It was in that town-meeting debate in Richmond that Clinton demonstrated his mastery of the New Media, connecting with the audience as he roamed the stage, Donahue-style, with a hand-held mike. Bush, checking his watch, seemed detached and awkward, and even Perot's one-liners fell flat. But it was the audience that gave the journalists a lesson in conducting a debate. It was as if the campaign had come down to a single talk show, with ordinary people taking the place of reporters and, in their utter seriousness, taking control of the election. No reporter would have dreamed of telling the candidates, as the third and fourth questioners did, that they were tired of negative attacks. And no reporter would have asked the president, as Marissa Hall of Richmond did, how the recession had personally affected him, the question that provided Clinton with his best moment.

Newspapers insisted on scoring the debates like a boxing match. "Some Fury, No Knockout," the *Chicago Tribune* said after the first encounter. "Jabs, No Knockouts," agreed *USA Today.* "Round 2: They Keep the Gloves On," the *Tribune* said. "President Comes Out Slugging in Final Debate," *The Washington Post* said. The debates dominated the campaign in mid-October, but it was hard for television to sort out the swirl of charges and countercharges. After the raucous Quayle-Gore debate, ABC's Peter Jennings told viewers there had been so many misstatements and distortions that they should read a newspaper the next day to get the full story.

Clinton, the first Democratic nominee since 1964 to win a majority of the nation's newspaper endorsements, became the ultimate read-my-clips candidate. On talk shows, in his ads and on the stump, he would recite anti-Bush editorials from the *New York Times, Washington Post, Sacramento Bee* and Portland *Oregonian.* The candidate who had denounced reporters back in January was now using the press for protective cover. Suddenly all the news, from the unraveling "Iraqgate" scandal to an investigation of the FBI director, seemed to be breaking Clinton's way. The *Post*'s Mike Isikoff disclosed that a senior State Department official had personally ordered the U.S. Embassy in London to search for files on Clinton's years in England, including documents related to his draft status and citizenship. It turned out that political appointees had led a bizarre nighttime search for the papers, even dredging up the file of Clinton's mother. A smiling Clinton held up the *Post* article for the television cameras.

Two and a half weeks before Election Day, Gennifer Flowers surfaced one last time. Flowers had sold new details of her alleged affair to *Penthouse* (and posed for the inevitable nude layout), including the unsubstantiated allegation that she had had an abortion while dating Clinton in 1977. The Republicans obtained advance copies of the piece and faxed it around town. Most news organizations decided they had had enough of Flowers's cash-for-trash charges, which rated only a few paragraphs in the *New York Post* and *USA Today.* But *The Washington Times,* which had been quick to publish the Clinton adultery rumors in the summer of 1991, gave front-page play to the *Penthouse* story. "Most of the article," the *Times* said in upholding the people's right to know, "is devoted to her vivid descriptions of their sexual relationship, including frequency, positions, techniques and pet names they had for parts of their bodies."

But even Gennifer in the raw could not slow our headlong rush to declare the election over. "President Clinton?" asked *Newsweek*'s cover two weeks before the election. "The Democrats: Measuring the Drapes," said *Time.* "Running Away with It," the *New York Post*'s headline agreed. One newspaper after another ran speculative pieces about the Clinton Cabinet and plans for his first 100 days. The polls quickly tightened; the press was turning Bill Clinton into the incumbent in an anti-incumbent year. "It feels like Clinton has been president for so long that I'm already tired of him," Russell Baker observed.

Bush fought back by bashing the press, relentlessly attacking "biased" reporters and "nutty talking heads" and "crackpots" who analyze the news. "Some in the media are trying to tell you the election's over," he told one crowd. "Don't let these newscasters tell you what's happening," he said the next day. He drew cheers by reciting his favorite bumper sticker: "Annoy the Media, Reelect Bush." Later Bush would snap that he had run a tough campaign, "and if *The Washington Post* doesn't like it, too damn bad."

It was quite a spectacle: Two of the three candidates for president running flat out against the press, denouncing us daily as arrogant insiders. Perot, still smarting over his media beating the previous summer, would launch into anti-press tirades at unexpected moments. He told reporters they were "jerks" and "teenage boys" who would do "anything that'll get you a headline, get you a bonus; anything that among your peers will get you a high five. . . . You guys hate that I'm in the race."

In fact, we loved that he was in the race, for Perot added spice to what otherwise would have been a Clinton runaway. And he deserved credit for focusing attention on the massive budget deficit, which his two opponents were doing their best to ignore. Still, as Perot inched up in the polls, most journalists continued to treat him with kid gloves. The computer magnate had turned his candidacy into a prime-time miniseries, reducing reporters to little more than drama critics.

And then, without warning, he crashed and burned. In the most spectacular act of self-destruction in modern political history, Perot told "60 Minutes" and the *Boston Herald* that the real reason he had quit the race in July was a bizarre plot by the Bush campaign to disrupt his daughter's wedding. He had no proof, only irrational theories. Shadowy Republican operatives would somehow doctor a photograph to show his daughter Carolyn in a lesbian embrace. The "dirty tricks" supposedly included plans to wiretap his office. The only source Perot would identify was Scott Barnes, a con man with a long history of making outlandish allegations. Perot repeated the charges at an angry news conference carried live on CNN, telling reporters he was "sick and tired of you all questioning my integrity."

Suddenly the newspapers and network shows were filled with dark tales of "Perot-noia" (such as the Texan's insistence that a Black Panther hit squad dispatched by the North Vietnamese had stalked his property in 1970, but that an alert guard dog had taken a bite out of one assassin's rear end). These stories made it clear that Perot was a fervent conspiracy theorist, the perpetual victim of strange and elaborate plots. But where had the press been? After all our digging the previous spring, why did we see fit to warn the American electorate only after Perot had his public meltdown? For all its bleating about the "character" issue, the press clearly fell short when it came to illuminating the most important question about Ross Perot's fitness to be president.

As the candidates raced through a final, frenzied round of talk shows —Bush, after disdaining the "teenybopper" network, even did his thing on MTV—reporters were confronted with one last burst of sleaze. Newsrooms across the country were swept by false rumors that *The New York Times* or ABC was about to release a picture of Clinton burning an American flag in his student days. Senior Bush campaign officials started urging reporters to investigate a groundless rumor that Clinton was having an affair with a reporter on his campaign plane. Representative Guy Vander Jagt, head of the National Republican Congressional Committee, even made the charge at a news conference. The press wisely resisted this eleventh-hour slime. Of course, no journalist could ignore the filing of a revised indictment of Caspar Weinberger by Iran-contra prosecutor Lawrence Walsh, which contradicted Bush's repeated denials that he knew in 1986 the United States had been trading arms for hostages. If the timing, four days before the election, seemed politically motivated, the subject—whether Bush was lying about the biggest scandal of the Reagan administration—was certainly fair game.

The endgame plunged us into a spasm of polling mania. Reporters gorged on three or four polls a day in the final week, some showing Clinton leading by ten points and several *USA Today*/CNN polls putting the margin at as little as one point. (The *USA Today*/CNN polls, however, were widely criticized because their pollster, the Gallup Organization, abruptly shifted its sample from registered voters to its own estimate of likely voters, thereby making comparisons misleading.) A collective shudder could be heard in many newsrooms at the thought that President Bush might win after all. A Bush comeback would show that all our stories had been wrong, that we had misread the electorate once again, and—worst of all—that we were consigned to four more years of excruciating boredom. It would ruin all those "end of an era" pieces that reporters had already written for the day after the election. The press was once again banking on Clinton, as it had in anointing him the front-runner back in the snows of New Hampshire.

Just before 10:30 P.M. on Election Night, as I sat typing in *The Washington Post* newsroom, a copy aide handed me the first edition of the next day's paper, with the headline "Clinton Elected 42nd President in Sweeping Victory over Bush." Even though the western states were still voting, we had called the election because exit polls were showing a decisive Clinton victory. On television, however, Dan Rather, Tom Brokaw, Peter Jennings and Bernard Shaw were still pretending that the race was not yet over—although they had known since mid-afternoon, from the same exit polls, that Clinton would easily surpass the required 270 electoral votes. The networks were constrained by their commitment to withhold state-by-state projections until the local polls had closed, and so did not declare Clinton the winner until 10:50. For once, newspapers had beaten television on a breaking story.

Clinton's electoral landslide shattered the media myth that the Democrats were permanently locked out of the White House, humbling all those journalistic geniuses who had insisted that a small-state governor with Clinton's personal baggage was unelectable. The American people had been telling us all year that they were ready to hand George Bush his walking papers, and for all his desperate attempts to blacken Clinton's character, Bush never got above 38 percent in the polls. The desire for change was so strong that Ross Perot pulled an impressive 19 percent of the vote, confounding the pundits once again. The year-long drama was over, and now there was a new president to swoon over. But there was an extended news vacuum as an exhausted Clinton rested after the campaign, and newspapers quickly reverted to creeping incrementalism: "Clinton May Quickly Announce Transition Chief." "Clinton Sleeps Through Foreign Leaders' Calls." "Clinton Passive in Role as President-Elect." There were stories on Clinton jogging to McDonald's, Hillary's fashion role, Chelsea returning to junior high and

Socks, the First Cat–elect. There was an attack-dog phase as Clinton began backing away from some of his campaign promises. The press had come full circle.

In the end, a campaign that frequently managed to bring out the worst in the news business ended on a hopeful note. Despite the distractions, both newspapers and television had managed for two solid months to elevate the level of discourse, listen to the voters and avoid the quicksand of sleaze and scandal. Having gotten a good kick in the pants from the New Media, newspapers finally plugged into the anger of an aroused electorate that could now take its case directly to Larry King. The talk show campaign had stolen our thunder, forcing us to jettison some of our traditional ways of doing business, to focus less on the insiders and more on the great, angry mass of readers and viewers and the issues they insisted were important.

Before the self-congratulations get out of hand, however, it's worth noting that we didn't have much choice. The 1992 election was decided by larger forces—the ailing economy and the deep-rooted fear that the country was headed down the wrong track—and that made the horse-race stuff that reporters like to write about almost irrelevant. All our fancy graphics, our forays into key battleground states, our pulse-taking among southern evangelicals, urban Catholics and left-handed Hispanics seemed beside the point. Strategy, polling and attack ads didn't matter much; nor did family values and the draft and pot-smoking and crime and homosexuality and all the other wedge issues that Republicans had so successfully exploited for two decades. The whole campaign came down to the famous inscription on the wall at Clinton headquarters: "The economy, stupid." For months we waited for the corrosive Bush attacks to destroy Clinton and not much happened, leaving us little to analyze. It was like sitting in the anchor booth during a 42–10 football game.

In another campaign season, a tighter horse race, a year in which divisive social issues or personal foibles have more resonance, the Old Media may well revert to its old habits. Our immunity to the temptations of a new Donna Rice or Gennifer Flowers story may melt away in the heat of the moment. Newspapers could easily miss the next Perot phenomenon, the next tax revolt, the next urban explosion in our frenetic effort to cover the thrust and parry of political battle. But for one brief moment, we seemed to rise to the magnitude of the task. The country had finally forced the press to get serious.

13

White House Warfare

Ruth Marcus was downright livid. Here she was, a White House correspondent for *The Washington Post*, stuck inside a van on a rainy Saturday in April in Scranton, Pennsylvania, being ordered around by a bunch of impudent twenty-two-year-olds determined to ensure that she did not lay eyes on the man she was covering, the president of the United States.

It had been like this for days. Marcus was the pool reporter, which meant she was supposed to be whisked along at President Clinton's side and file reports that could be used by her colleagues in the White House press corps. But she had barely gotten a decent glimpse of the president. When Clinton was speaking at the Little Rock funeral of his father-in-law, Hugh Rodham, the White House had decreed it a private function from which all journalists were barred. But the funeral was open to members of the public, and

Richard Berke of *The New York Times* had simply walked in like a fellow mourner and quietly covered it. Marcus, who was playing by the administration's rules, had been stuck out on the street like some hapless Pentagon reporter who never made it to the battlefield.

Now she was stranded again outside the Court Street United Methodist Church in Scranton, where a second funeral service was being held. "I went into the church basement to file the pool report," Marcus says. "As I was heading for the ladies' room—looking dangerous, I'm sure—a woman wearing a Secret Service badge comes up and says, 'You can't be out here.' " Informed that Marcus was simply making a pit stop, the agent announced: "I have to go in there with you."

"I was tired and beaten down after three days of the most useless and degrading professional experience of my life," Marcus says. "I thought about throwing a fit but I just didn't have it in me. I was sitting in the stall peeing and this woman is standing outside. I yelled to her, 'I hope you find this as humiliating as I do!' "

The White House beat, for all its supposed glamor, is the gilded cage of American journalism. There is, to be sure, the heady sense of being close to the seat of power, of posing momentous questions at televised press conferences, of traveling around the globe with the world's most important newsmaker. There is no more automatic ticket to the front page.

Yet it is also one of the most frustrating assignments any reporter can draw. You have limited access to the president's inner circle. You must tag along for dozens of meaningless trips and hundreds of empty speeches, herded behind ropes like cattle. You are a stenographer for functionaries determined to put their spin on the day's events.

Despite these obstacles, some of the two thousand correspondents accredited to the White House manage to do some fine reporting. But much of the daily coverage is exceedingly mediocre. Dozens of reporters write the same superficial story about what the president said yesterday or what he plans to do next week. It is almost a parody of pack journalism. While scandals go undetected at HUD or the Energy Department or the Federal Home Loan Bank Board, news organizations spend vast sums covering routine events that are quite competently handled by the Associated Press. It is the peacetime version of the Gulf war, the prestigious assignment where government officials control your movements and everyone is spoon-fed the same pabulum.

"I always thought of the White House as being the jewel, the thing you spent your career trying to get to," says Susan Milligan, who has covered Clinton for the New York *Daily News*. Instead, she says, "It's just grueling. You spend so much time chasing the story of the day. I look back on some of what I've written and wonder why I wrote it. We get caught up in bullshit."

The media mob, led by the major newspapers, turned in a spectacularly sorry performance in the first few months of the Clinton presidency. The press canceled Clinton's honeymoon, pronounced him dead time and again, hyped each minor setback into a national crisis and generally lost all sense of perspective. To be sure, Clinton made plenty of mistakes and compounded his difficulties by treating the establishment media with open disdain. But journalism's headlong rush to judgment on a man who had barely unpacked his bags spoke volumes about the prosecutorial nature of the Washington press. To say anything positive—indeed, even to withhold judgment until the president had more time to push his program—was to be dismissed as a cheerleader. Biting criticism had become a badge of journalistic manhood.

This slashing approach was yet another sign of the talk show culture that had turned news into entertainment and helped make the White House the most overcovered beat in American history. With an explosion of media outlets from *USA Today* to the *National Enquirer,* from "Capital Gang" to "Crossfire," from Rush Limbaugh to Larry King to Tom Snyder, we seemed to take a rectal thermometer to the Clinton presidency every few hours. Hero or bum? Genius or goat? In a profession that increasingly valued sweeping judgments, there was no middle ground. Each twist and turn became a seismic event requiring endless analysis and perpetual punditry.

"You listen to these hot-air boys, these naysayers, and we're idiots," says James Carville, Clinton's colorful Cajun consultant. "Then we're the smartest people in the world. The stimulus package fails and Clinton is the most unpopular president in the history of mankind. Then he gives a health care speech and we're geniuses again. Hell, even a broken clock's right twice a day."

The tunnel vision of daily newspapers—Is the president up or down today? What's he gonna do tomorrow?—gave Clinton little credit for tackling the intractable problems of a huge budget deficit and a wasteful health care system and a bloated federal bureaucracy. He made more blunders than George Bush in part because he took more risks. Yet even modest achievements, like the family-leave law or national service program, were dismissed as one-day stories. In the fickle political subculture of which journalists are a part, Clinton's inevitable compromises were routinely portrayed as a sign of weakness. Our preferred story line—the young outsider struggling to prove himself—mattered far more than exploring the complexities of governance. That powerful forces were arrayed against an inexperienced president—special interests, obstructionist Republicans, ambivalent voters who demanded leaner government so long as their sacrosanct benefits were protected—was played down by the press. We made it our job to keep reminding the public where Clinton had fallen short of his campaign promises, rather than grant him credit for gaining yardage on treacherous political turf.

The talk show campaign helped accelerate this polarization between the president and the press. The gnawing fear among White House reporters—that they had become mere props in the daily staging of presidential drama—came to a head after Bill Clinton's election. Here, after all, was a politician who knew how to work the call-in shows. His aides openly boasted about their technological acumen and their plans to circumvent the traditional media through satellite interviews and televised town meetings and computer bulletin boards. Print reporters were dinosaurs, in their view, and an MTV-savvy president planned to race right by them on the information highway.

Arrogance was in vogue after the election, with Clinton carefully keeping his distance from the press. To be a newspaper reporter in such an environment was to live at the bottom of the media food chain, always hungry for news and constantly scrounging for tidbits. Print reporters quickly grew restless in this news vacuum, and that meant trouble for the administration-in-waiting, for journalists with nothing to write about will create their own stories based on spin and speculation. They wound up making Clinton the first modern president whose honeymoon ended before he took office. "Bill Clinton is preparing to walk away from some of his campaign promises," *The Wall Street Journal* complained in early January 1993, while *The Boston Globe* groused that he was replacing his election-year pledges "with more amorphous 'goals.' "

It was almost as if the White House reporters had made a secret pact to prove they could be just as tough on a Democratic president as they had been on Ronald Reagan and George Bush. Many of them had grown to like Clinton and his squadron of young aides, and as the adrenaline of the campaign faded, some began to wonder whether they had let down their guard, whether this new team really measured up. It was time for that post-election ritual, the cataloguing of all the world's ills and the stunning discovery that the president-elect might not be able to solve every problem in his first hundred days. The pace of the transition seemed alarmingly slow. The novelty of the nation's new celebrity-in-chief was beginning to wear thin.

For weeks there had been a great media gush about the vigorous new leader and his wide-ranging intellect and his politically shrewd wife and his morning jog to McDonald's. Clinton took the capital by storm simply by hitting the Georgetown party circuit. Pamela Harriman threw a big Democratic bash for Clinton and the media elite—Katharine Graham, Donald Graham, David Brinkley, Tim Russert, Bob Schieffer—

turned out to greet him. Johnny Apple went as a guest and turned the soiree into a front-page *New York Times* story about "the privileged ninety or so"—including him, of course—"as giddy as debutantes."

Next Clinton paid his respects at the court of Kay Graham. It was another A-list affair where working-stiff reporters were reduced to rounding up quotes on the cold sidewalk outside. As Clinton worked the room, even William Safire was impressed. "Kay introduced us," he recounted in his *New York Times* column, "and the president-elect promptly said what goes over well with Republicans who reluctantly voted for him: I hope you won't be disappointed. . . . I hope to get good advice in the papers. You write it, I'll read it." Here was a president who knew how to play to the pundits, and they were all too happy to cozy up to the new leader of the free world. Bill Moyers flew to Little Rock to take in a movie with the Clintons and stay over at the governor's mansion. Rick Kaplan, executive producer of "PrimeTime Live," played a round of golf with Clinton, as did Michael Kramer, *Time*'s political columnist. *Time,* which seven months earlier had wondered on its cover "Why Voters Don't Trust Clinton," now anointed him Man of the Year. "For the first time in more than thirty years the nation has elected a president with sex appeal," the magazine burbled.

But the magic soon wore off. Once again it was the newspapers, with their insatiable need for a new story each day, that grew testy. Not only were White House reporters stranded for weeks at Little Rock's Capitol Hotel, but the president-elect had the temerity to refrain from making news. To fill the gap, reporters rushed into print with the latest rumors about who was in line for which Cabinet post. They openly joked about this descent into gossip-mongering, but many fervently wanted to prove to their bosses that they were plugged into the new administration. Their editors were salivating to know who would be the next HUD secretary, even though most would again ignore HUD for the next four years.

The papers were full of misinformation and leaky trial balloons. Jack Nelson wrote in the *Los Angeles Times* that Colin Powell was "under increasingly serious consideration" for secretary of state, a notion seconded by *The Boston Globe.* Evans and Novak reported "confidential word" that Lloyd Bentsen did not want the job of treasury secretary. Stories would evolve from secondhand rumor to informed speculation to done deal—Tim Wirth would be energy secretary, and William Daley transportation secretary—but the deals kept coming undone.

When Thomas Friedman of *The New York Times* was dispatched to Little Rock, he was struck by the pointlessness of the exercise. One evening he was asked to confirm a wire report that Clinton planned to name the Arkansas health director, Joycelyn Elders, as surgeon general. Friedman tracked down Elders, who chatted freely about her appointment even though the current surgeon general had not even been told of her dismissal. Friedman decided not to use any of her comments. "I told her, 'I shouldn't be doing this, but I'm going to give you some advice: Don't talk to any other journalists,' " Friedman recalls. "I felt this was a woman who had no idea what the game was. I didn't care whether I was first or not on Joycelyn Elders. It just didn't matter enough to me to get someone in trouble."

The speculation sweepstakes soon shifted to the various women said to be in the running for attorney general—all except Clinton's eventual choice, Zoe Baird. Baird's brief moment in the spotlight would expose a far greater shortcoming in the Washington press corps than merely betting on the wrong horse. The talk show campaign had rudely reminded us how out of touch we were with the public pulse, and we soon got another humiliating lesson.

On January 14, *The New York Times* reported that Zoe Baird had acknowledged to the Clinton transition team that she had hired illegal aliens as her nanny and her driver and hadn't paid Social Security taxes for the Peruvian couple. The collective judgment of the media establishment was that this was a minor infraction. Some senior editors at *The Washington Post*, who were not unacquainted with the illegal babysitting market, insisted it was no big deal. Lots of professional couples around town did it. Reporters called the usual suspects—senators and political analysts—who calmly predicted that the nomination was not in jeopardy. "Baird's Hiring Disclosure Not Seen as Major Block," said the *Post*'s follow-up story, buried on page 14. *The Hartford Courant* called Baird's confirmation "an almost sure thing." Anna Quindlen acknowledged that she was among the mothers who "have sometimes hired the person they thought best for the job although that person was undocumented."

But the folks out there—our readers—had different ideas. To them, the idea of a $500,000-a-year corporate lawyer saying she just couldn't find a legal baby-sitter smacked of arrogance. How could someone who had knowingly violated the immigration laws function as the nation's chief law-enforcement officer? Talk radio shows were flooded with angry callers. Rush Limbaugh had a field day. The Capitol switchboard lit up. Slowly, the press realized that perhaps this would be an issue after all. Newspapers belatedly assigned a spate of stories on the day care crisis and the underground nanny network. Journalists with no-green-card baby-sitters looked vaguely embarrassed when the subject came up in casual conversation.

Len Downie admitted that the *Post* had blown the story, in part because the paper was less than enthusiastic about chasing a rival's scoop. The fact that "many journalists, among others, were in this situation in Washington" may have contributed to "a more sympathetic initial reaction," he said. Zoe Baird was forced to withdraw her nomination on January 22 in a debacle that made the establishment press seem more remote than ever.

The plain fact is that most big-city journalists earn more money and enjoy more privileges than the great majority of people who buy their newspapers and watch their newscasts. Most of us have little in common with struggling parents who must feed three kids on $25,000 a year. We had a great deal more affinity with the whiz kids of the incoming administration, people like George Stephanopoulos, Dee Dee Myers, Mark Gearan, Mandy Grunwald and Paul Begala, many of whom had become our friends during the Democrats' twelve-year exile from the White House. Newspaper reporters, once the champions of the little guy, now shared the same upper-middle-class values as the officials we covered.

This was never more obvious than when Clinton announced that he was sending his daughter, Chelsea, to Sidwell Friends, a private school in northwest Washington where the tuition was $10,000 a year. The media reaction to this decision by a president who had campaigned as a supporter of public schools was noticeably muted, and for good reason.

Donald Graham, Bob Woodward and Bob Kaiser of *The Washington Post* all sent their kids to Sidwell. Kathy Sulzberger, the daughter of *New York Times* chairman Arthur Ochs Sulzberger, not only sent her children to Sidwell but served on the school's board. When columnist Mark Shields praised Sidwell on "The MacNeil/Lehrer NewsHour," he had to note that his children went there, as did Jim Lehrer's kids and Judy Woodruff's kids. Woodruff's husband, Al Hunt, made a similar disclosure while defending Clinton on CNN's "Capital Gang." Carl Rowan touted Sidwell on "Inside Washington," pointing out that his grandchildren attended the school. Howard Fineman, a *Newsweek* political reporter whose daughter was in kindergarten at Sidwell, told me he "shamelessly" lobbied Bill and Hillary Clinton to pick the school at a social event. It was little wonder that many people viewed the press as elitist.

The cultural bias was showing in other ways as well. Few reporters made an issue of Clinton's insistence that his attorney general be a woman, undoubtedly because they saw such a quota as politically correct. One exception was Lars-Erik Nelson, who assailed Clinton in a *Daily News* column called "Men Need Not Apply."

Similarly, many reporters were surprised when Clinton's stance on allowing gays to serve in the military sparked a national furor. After all, Clinton had pledged to do so many times during the campaign. But now he had the power to make it a reality, and the press, viewing Clinton's position as quite reasonable, misjudged the emotional divisiveness of homosexuality.

The new president's stumbling start in office—Zoe Baird, gays in the military, abandoning campaign promises on Haiti and a middle-class tax cut—immediately transformed him from Man of the Year to punching bag of the week. The press dismissed almost everything Clinton did as wrong or politically dumb. A front-page *Washington Post* story even complained that Clinton's early-morning jogs through the capital were tying up traffic—and when he responded by raising funds for a White House jogging track, the press made fun of that as well.

Once again, reporters were out of step with the country. Most people were willing to give Bill Clinton a chance, while the press was all but calling him a one-term president. The talking heads were unanimous: "Incredibly inept," said Mark Shields. "The president is stumbling," said Tim Russert. Newspaper coverage was equally downbeat. "Hope is rapidly turning to chilly uneasiness, even dismay," said the *Los Angeles Times,* making the dreaded comparison to Jimmy Carter. "The new president now desperately needs a victory," *The New York Times* announced just two weeks into his administration. It was as though we had all been infected by the blowhard nature of the talk shows, rushing to render a thumbs-up or thumbs-down verdict on a president who had just arrived in Washington. We could no longer see beyond the next twenty-four hour news cycle.

For some journalists, the subtle seductions of covering the White House have a way of blurring the adversarial lines.

"A lot of guys over there are so self-important," says John Yang, a *Washington Post* editor who spent time covering the Bush presidency. "Their entire existence is based on the fact that they're White House reporters. They've got T-shirts and luggage tags that say 'White House' and have the presidential seal. It makes you look like you're on the team, and a lot of people feel that way."

For much of this century, the press and the president really were on the same team. In 1908, a *New York Times* reporter obtained a stunning interview with Kaiser Wilhelm II in which the German leader said he expected to go to war with Britain. So shaken were the *Times* editors that they had the reporter, William Bayard Hale, show his notes to President Theodore Roosevelt. The president said the interview should never be published, and *Times* publisher Adolph Ochs agreed to suppress it.

During the twelve years that Franklin D. Roosevelt served in the Oval Office, the press never saw fit to tell the American public he was barely able to walk. Not much had changed by the time John F. Kennedy was charming and cajoling reporters, especially close friends such as *Newsweek*'s Ben Bradlee. The press in those days could still be wielded as an instrument of diplomacy. In a private chat at Hyannis Port in 1961, Kennedy told James Reston that it would be "helpful" if Reston would write in *The New York Times*, on his own authority, that any Soviet move to restrict U.S. access to Berlin would prompt a military response.

"Any assumption that the United States would acquiesce to the defeat of its command on the ground without resorting to the ultimate weapons of nuclear power would be highly reckless. . . . Mr. Khrushchev . . . would be well advised to take this into account," Reston wrote—after the language had been approved by Kennedy.

In a few short years, Lyndon Johnson's prosecution of the Vietnam War and Richard Nixon's covert war against his domestic enemies would permanently alter the cozy relationship between presidents and their chroniclers. But another, less momentous event of that era also changed the way White House reporters perceived their job. It was the publication of Theodore White's book, *The Making of the President, 1960.*

"Before Teddy White, political journalism was hacks writing about hacks," says David Hoffman, who spent a decade covering Reagan and Bush for the *Post*. "It wasn't very gripping. White made it more interesting by telling a long, beautiful mosaic of a story. We all started practicing that kind of journalism: What were they eating? Did they have

304 / Media Circus

eggs Benedict? And which guy didn't finish his coffee? He created a whole generation of reporters who thought that adding some style to the coverage was sufficient."

Editors grew enamored of the behind-the-scenes story, not so much to expose the hidden machinery of policy-making but to re-create the atmospherics of great men making decisions. Such pieces became known as "tick-tocks," a reconstruction of past events. The genre goes something like this: "Richard Darman slammed his fist on the cherry-wood desk after his top aide delivered the news. Dammit, he thought, I must tell the president. Darman reached for the phone, the one with the secure line to the Oval Office. He checked his Rolex watch: it was 7:21 P.M. His half-eaten turkey sandwich would have to wait. Thus began one of the most important turning points of the Bush presidency. . . ."

Such stories, of course, are difficult to write without help from one of a handful of top officials. But most White House correspondents are reduced to shouting questions at Dee Dee Myers at the daily briefing, a ritual that has passed for aggressive reporting since the days of Watergate.

In such a news-starved environment, small details about upcoming events can be transformed into major revelations. Editors love to be able to report, before the official announcement is made, that the president will take a trip, make a speech, unveil an initiative or appoint a task force.

Tom Friedman, a former Middle East correspondent more interested in analysis than ephemeral scoops, was baffled by this culture when he was assigned to the Clinton White House. He found that reporters would write about minor blips "protectively," just to spare themselves a late-night call from editors who would see the incremental development in a rival newspaper.

"As a foreign reporter you're out on the streets," he says. "There's no structure, no afternoon briefing, no official to confirm everything. Reporting from the White House means being the first to report about a decision that has been made and not announced, or a decision that's about to be made and not been announced. . . . My mother is probably the only person who reads past the jump on half these stories."

To be sure, White House reporters must be generalists, able to slide from banking to Bosnia without missing a beat. It's hardly realistic to expect them to break complicated stories of bureaucratic malfeasance. But they also do a poor job of evaluating the administration's performance or following up on past promises. If Bill Clinton vows to revamp the welfare system by forcing recipients to get jobs or lose their benefits, few reporters bother to ask him about it a year later. The beat reporters are wedded to the blow-by-blow, the uproar du jour.

"The White House press corps is attuned to politics rather than substance," says David Lauter, who covers Clinton for the *Los Angeles Times.* "A lot of them are political reporters and they get energized every two years. Some administration policies didn't get nearly the scrutiny they should have until they became political stories. The coverage tended to be oversimplified."

Newspapers in particular are obsessed with anticipating events. "All the time, I could get on the front page by saying Reagan was about to do something," David Hoffman says. "I confess: It was wrong to constantly be making news out of impending events without knowing what the exact words were. We tend to slack off when the deed is done or the analysis is required afterward."

Hoffman once got a twenty-four hour break on the news that George Bush and Mikhail Gorbachev would hold a shipboard summit off Malta. "I thought that was a huge scoop," he says. "But was the world any better off? There's a lot of ego involved in covering the president, a lot of 'we got it first.' No wonder the historians look down on some of our work, because it's so damn superficial."

In the summer of 1993, Tom Friedman was invited to play golf with the president of the United States.

Friedman, an avid golfer, was hesitant. He did not want to be thought of, or to think of himself, as Bill Clinton's golfing buddy. He had often been accused—unfairly, he said—of being a conduit for leaks from George Bush's secretary of state, James Baker; he did not want to get too close to the man he was now covering. But how could he pass up such a coveted invitation?

"I thought about it long and hard," Friedman says. "My editor said if you can spend six hours with the president, do it. We all know this isn't about socializing. Everyone understands the game."

Friedman accepted, but with one condition. He told White House aides the outing could not be off the record. Otherwise it would be useless to him as a reporter. "They thought about it and agreed, as long as there were no quotes," he says. "You could say Clinton believed, thought, indicated, but no direct quotes. He didn't want to be sitting there in the golf cart with a guy with a notepad."

The morning at the Army-Navy Country Club was pleasant. Clinton mostly wanted to talk golf, but Friedman occasionally steered the conversation toward policy. "For me it was a six-hour interview," he says. "I went home and wrote myself six pages of notes."

And what did Clinton get out of it? "The illusion and hope," Friedman says, that the *Times* might go a bit easier on him. But the outing may have helped Friedman as well: Clinton later granted him an exclusive interview aboard *Air Force One* on the weekend before Israel and the Palestine Liberation Organization signed their historic peace treaty in Washington.

White House reporters concede that a president who socializes with them reaps some journalistic benefit. Maureen Dowd says she found Clinton warm and likable after dropping by for dinner and a movie. "The reaction of most reporters who've gone to these events is 'Hell no, you're not going to buy me with a dinner at the White House,' " says Ann Devroy, a veteran White House correspondent for *The Washington Post.* "But any time you see a person acting like a human being, you give them the benefit of the doubt."

One reporter who found White House parties "thrilling" is Jessica Lee, who covered the Bush presidency for *USA Today.* After attending a state dinner for the president of Brazil in 1991, she shared the experience in a computer memo to her colleagues.

"Going to a state dinner at the White House is unbelievably seductive," Lee began. "It was like being Cinderella at the prince's ball. . . .

"Driving through those big iron White House gates and up to the circular drive was awesome. A military aide opened the car door and said, 'Welcome to the White House, Miss Lee.' Waiting to escort me was a handsome hunk of U.S. Marine—captain class—with biceps as big as footballs. He gave me his arm. He strolled slowly. . . . He chatted pleasantly. He made sure I had a glass of designer water. He knew when it was time for me to go through the receiving line. . . . His performance was flawless."

When Lee reached the front of the receiving line, "I chatted with the president and first lady." The awestruck reporter marveled at Barbara Bush's Scaasi gown and the exquisite menu, from tomatoes stuffed with crabmeat to mocha bombe with Tia Maria sauce, all served on the Johnson china.

As an Army band began to play, and the captain escorted Lee to the Blue Room for "mix and mingles," Gloria Estefan, resplendent in a sequined minidress, belted out some entertainment.

After dancing in the grand foyer, "my captain escorted me out with compliments on my looks and charisma. . . . He opened the car door. I got in and turned into a pumpkin just outside the White House gates."

Lee later insisted that such glittering evenings had no effect on her coverage of the president. "I'm not really sure that he gets anything out of it," she said.

George Bush, a master of personal diplomacy, favored selected journalists with personal attention in a way that Ronald Reagan and Jimmy Carter never bothered to do. By jogging and fishing with reporters, writing them thank-you notes and inviting them to private White House lunches, Bush bought himself some goodwill even during the lowest periods of his presidency.

On one of Bush's first weekends at Camp David, he studied photographs of the 150 White House regulars so he could remember their names at press conferences. He invited certain reporters to the White House for off-the-record chats. He threw an annual summer picnic for the press at Kennebunkport. So many reporters started bringing their friends—some of whom swiped the towels from Barbara Bush's bathroom—that the White House barred all outside guests except spouses. Shouting matches erupted as reporters' friends and dates were turned away.

Howell Raines of *The New York Times* spent a day at sea with Bush for a book on fishing. Tim McNulty of the *Chicago Tribune* went boating and played horseshoes with Bush and went to the White House for an off-the-record lunch. While such social occasions are "no big fucking deal," McNulty says, "Of course it's a kick to sit down to lunch with the president of the United States. You get a sense of what he's thinking and what really interests him and what makes his eyes glaze." Yet all this socializing did Bush little good when he plummeted in the polls and wound up running against the press in 1992.

Bill Clinton, having been roughed up by the media mob during the campaign, decided after the election that courting reporters was a waste of time. He would take his case directly to the people rather than playing the Beltway game with reporters who were fixated on inside baseball. Like Ross Perot, he failed to grasp how badly the establishment press could wound him.

And so George Stephanopoulos and Dee Dee Myers barred reporters from the area outside their offices in the upper White House press room. This restricted area, dubbed the "no-fly zone," prompted weeks of journalistic whining. The president held televised town meetings, had satellite chats with local anchors, spoke to children with Peter Jennings and fielded questions on MTV. He granted no interviews to national print reporters and held no formal press conferences for his first two months in office. "You know why I can stiff you on the press conference?" Clinton asked reporters at the Radio and Television Correspondents Dinner, one of those black-tie affairs where journalists rub shoulders with the government elite. "Because Larry King liberated me by giving me to the American people directly."

This was a frontal attack on the White House press corps, which considers televised news conferences an important perquisite. Here is the chance for reporters to strut their stuff for the folks back home, to influence the national dialogue, to go toe-to-toe with the president. That, at least, is the illusion. The reality is that the president gives mostly prepackaged responses and deflects any question he doesn't want to answer. Meaningful follow-up is all but impossible because once Clinton stakes out a position on health care, the next query may be about New Zealand or interest rates or welfare reform. The reporters are little more than extras in a White House production.

Still, when Clinton at first refused to hold a formal news conference, the heavyweights of the press corps felt personally affronted. How dare he refuse to meet them in the East Room, to engage them on their terms in those big prime-time extravaganzas that had turned the reporters into TV stars? Sure, Clinton had answered three hundred questions from the White House press at various gatherings in his first few weeks —more than Bush, Reagan or Carter at that stage—but the press monopoly had been broken.

When Clinton finally held a news conference on March 23, some of the questions served to underscore the media's obsession with Beltway politics. "How do you plan to handle [Perot's] criticism?" "Are you losing your political grip?" "Did you underestimate the power of Dole?" The only real news Clinton made was in not ruling out the notion that gays in the military might have to be segregated. This touched off the kind of one-day flap that reporters love, reinforcing the president's view that such sessions allowed the press to control the agenda.

News conferences are greatly overrated as a vehicle for eliciting information. In 1991, *The Washington Monthly* analyzed the 1,865 questions asked at news conferences during the first two and a half years of the Bush presidency. Two-thirds were about foreign policy—and this from a press corps that was constantly sniping that Bush had no domestic agenda. Only four dealt with AIDS, four with public schools, two with the collapse of commercial banks and none with homelessness. Many queries involved the political flap of the day, from John Tower to Clarence Thomas. As the magazine noted: "Reporters asked twice as many questions about the president's health—'Have you been gaining weight up here, sir?'—as about health care for the rest of America."

Bill Clinton, policy wonk, could reel off detailed answers with ease. He simply chose to keep the press at arm's length. Many big-league reporters were miffed at this smug approach from a member of their own generation. Others grew resigned to their reduced status. "During the campaign, I really felt I knew what was going on," says Adam Nagourney, then with *USA Today,* who often kidded Clinton about gaining weight during the primaries but rarely saw the president after the election. "Now I feel that I'm in the audience. It ends up being boring. You wind up doing stories that are a silly waste of time for talented people, like who's on the short list for attorney general. It's monotonous, stenographic work. There are a million reporters all trying to do the same story, the conventional wisdom."

Still, says Nagourney, "They won the election and there's nothing anywhere that says they have to give me an interview. I don't feel like I have a right to whine about it. I'm not going to grovel at his feet."

Ruth Marcus was more frustrated by the isolation from Clinton. "I have almost no contact with the man," she says. "I see him speak; I've been at his press conferences. I doubt he knows who I am. It's like covering the Wizard of Oz." Like many of the new White House reporters in their thirties, Marcus, a brash woman with a Harvard law degree, had never covered a Democratic administration. Most of her friends were Democrats, some of whom had landed jobs in the new administration. She was engaged to a Democratic Senate staffer. One of her closest friends was Ricki Seidman, a former Ted Kennedy aide who now worked in the White House. A fellow *Washington Post* reporter, Alison Muscatine, had signed on as a White House speechwriter. Marcus had first met George Stephanopoulos at a dinner party years earlier, when he was "just some guy named George." In the older and grayer Bush administration, she had expected to feel like an outsider. Now, in a

White House peopled with young liberals she had known for years, Ruth Marcus ought to have been perfectly wired.

And yet it didn't seem to matter much. To be sure, senior aides were quick to call her back and talk off the record—"there's definitely a trust factor," she says—but she got few exclusive leaks. Marcus had no more access to Bill Clinton than any other print reporter. Her friends on the White House staff often fed her the same propaganda they dished out to everyone else, even when it was obviously bogus. Liberal or not, they were now on opposite sides of the fence. "They're not used to having adversarial press relations," Marcus says. "They understood how to use the press as a tool of opposition, but there's a general lack of understanding about how to use the press as an affirmative message-delivery system."

Tom Friedman isn't sure why reporters were so tough on the new administration, especially since officials from chief of staff Thomas "Mack" McLarty on down were usually quick to return phone calls. "Is it because the press are mostly liberal Democrats and you judge one of your own more harshly?" he asks. "I may subconsciously be holding them to a tougher standard, and I'd be the first to admit that. This was also an issue as a Jew covering Israel, wither I was holding Israel to a higher standard."

A newspaper reporter who was repeatedly spun by White House officials put it this way: "You expect this sort of disingenuous bullshit from Republicans, but you don't expect it from people you're philosophically in tune with. It's sort of fun to watch them fuck up, but it's horrifying. We want Clinton to succeed not only as Americans, but because we basically agree with him. And when he fucks it up he gets worse coverage because you think about having to cover another Republican administration after '96. There's a little bit of a backlash."

The web of incestuous relationships between the Clintonites and the journalism community occasionally backfired on the press. *The New York Times* was left with egg on its face in early February after the president dropped Kimba Wood as his second choice for attorney general over her hiring of an illegal immigrant as a baby-sitter (although, unlike Zoe Baird, she did so before the current law had gone into effect). In the finger-pointing that followed, the *Times* quoted "one person familiar with her version of events" as saying that Wood had fully disclosed her nanny problem to the White House more than a week earlier. This unnamed source also took a poke at Clinton, saying, "If you can't make the distinction between somebody who did something wrong and somebody who didn't, what good is the moral authority of a president?"

It wasn't hard for me to discover that the source was none other than Kimba Wood's husband, Michael Kramer, the *Time* political columnist, and I wrote an article identifying him as the unnamed critic. It's not likely that *The New York Times* would have accepted such anonymous, self-serving spin from another nominee's spouse had he not been in the news business. Kramer told me he was merely "helping to clarify the facts" because his wife, as a sitting judge, felt she could not defend herself publicly.

A day later, in what amounted to a front-page correction, the *Times* quoted a letter from Wood in which she disavowed the source's account and supported the White House version of events. The paper blamed the foul-up on a "misunderstanding" between reporter Robert McFadden and the mysterious source. Bound by its pledge of confidentiality, the *Times* was unable to tell its readers what everyone in Washington now knew, that its secret informant was a prominent journalist who within days would again be passing judgment in print on President Clinton.

The tone of the White House coverage began to veer wildly according to Clinton's standing in the polls. When the president unveiled his $500-billion package of tax hikes and spending cuts in February, most journalists were convinced that he was committing political suicide, that voters would never forgive him for jettisoning his campaign pledge to cut taxes for the middle class. "BILL'S FLIP FLOPS," sneered the *Daily News*. But when the public revolt failed to materialize—polls showed that two-thirds of the electorate actually like the Clinton package—newspapers beat a quick retreat. "Clinton's Early Moves Find Support Across N.E.," *The Boston Globe* said. "Clinton Plan Enjoys Strong Public Support," echoed *The Washington Post*. "Congress Hears the Public and Moves Behind Clinton," noted *The New York Times*. The same might have been said of the press.

Soon the newspapers were paying tribute to a president who had thrown away the rule book. "Mr. Clinton is proving to be a far better chief executive than might have been expected on the basis of his sometimes haphazard campaign," *The Wall Street Journal* said in March. *The Boston Globe* saw "a president who is tireless, who is resilient, who is politically gifted and who is committed to change, both substantive and stylistic." A front-page *Washington Post* headline said Clinton had "dazzled" the capital.

Yet this brief period of admiration was followed by six weeks in which the media relentlessly savaged the president. A series of stumbles beginning in late April pushed Clinton's approval rating down to 37 percent, the lowest of any modern president in his first months in office, and that sent his roller-coaster press coverage plummeting again.

On one level, of course, the media were merely reflecting reality. There was the botched raid in Waco, Texas, that resulted in the deaths of David Koresh and his cult followers. (*The Wall Street Journal,* in a leap of logic, likened Clinton's handling of the mass suicide to Kennedy's Bay of Pigs.) There was the Republican filibuster in the Senate that killed Clinton's economic stimulus package. There was the embarrassing retreat on intervention in war-torn Bosnia. There was the humiliating withdrawal of the nomination of Lani Guinier, the law professor and old friend whom Clinton had picked to head the Justice Department's civil rights division. No one in the White House had bothered to read Guinier's extreme-sounding legal writings on racial quotas and voting rights, which proved her undoing. Conservative activist Clint Bolick had branded Guinier a "quota queen" on the *Journal*'s op-ed page, launching a campaign of vilification that forced the president to abandon one of his most visible black nominees.

As if to underscore that gossip was big news, there was also the most politically expensive haircut since Samson's, the $200 shearing by celebrity stylist Cristophe aboard *Air Force One,* disclosed by *Washington Post* gossip columnist Lois Romano. The president's tarmac trim was widely reported to have held up planes at the Los Angeles airport, but when *Newsday* later revealed that there had been no such delays, few news organizations bothered to report the belated finding. The symbolism was too good to mess up with mere facts. The man who had dazzled the capital was now, as *Time*'s cover put it, "The Incredible Shrinking President." Even the liberal columnists abandoned Clinton, likening him to visionless old George Bush.

But there was more at work here than just Clinton's political incompetence. The press was clearly piling on, magnifying each misstep with laserlike intensity. "Almost everyone in town is wondering the same thing: Will this be just another failed presidency?" *The Washington Post* asked in late May. "It doesn't get much worse than this. To the people who cover them every day, the White House staff has become a joke," the *Los Angeles Times* observed. The *Daily News* simply branded the president "BUMBLIN' BILL."

Clinton was badly stung by this criticism, which exacerbated an already tense relationship with the press. "He was boiling over with resentment," a senior White House official said. "He was lashing out at the press coverage. To this day he feels he was given a bum rap on the haircut. He would say, 'Why am I getting killed like this?' There was still some lingering resentment from the campaign. The frenzy [over the Gennifer Flowers allegations] left him scarred. Those wounds are not very far beneath the surface."

The coverage of George Bush's first months in office had been nowhere near as hostile, and Bush had not even attempted to tackle the budget deficit or health care or the other thorny problems that Clinton was taking on. *The New Republic* accused reporters of acting like "spurned lovers." The attack-dog journalism was widely seen as the revenge of the White House press corps.

What some of the esteemed correspondents failed to realize is how petty and unprofessional all this made them look. Who really cared whether they liked the president, or got to schmooze with him, or had regular access to his top aides? They were paid to report fairly on the nation's leader and to keep their personal feelings out of it. By giving in to an us-versus-them mentality, they fed the perception that journalists were a bunch of pampered potentates determined to trample anyone who failed to treat them with the proper deference. And the public clearly recognized this: A Times Mirror poll found that 43 percent of those surveyed believed the press was treating the new president unfairly.

"We should not have declared him dead; that was silly," says Gwen Ifill of *The New York Times*. "In fact, the guy was dropping precipitously in public opinion. We didn't cause that, even though we did our best to keep it going. When you keep saying the guy's dead, he's dying, after a while that has an impact on the American psyche."

Ifill says a few of her fellow beat reporters don't bother to hide their view that Clinton and his top aides are hopeless amateurs. "There are people who have an ingrained disdain for this administration. They are mean and nasty about it," she says.

In hindsight, says Adam Nagourney, "I might have written three or four stories that were jumping on the Washington bandwagon by bashing Clinton: 'He's down, he's not gonna get up.' I wonder if any president can succeed because we all tend to be so negative. We were all too quick to judge him as being inept."

Nor was Clinton's staff immune from the boom-and-bust syndrome. Three weeks after the election, *The Washington Post* described George Stephanopoulos as a "young Capitol Hill wizard" with an "unflappable demeanor . . . a fellow who looks so young and dresses so hip yet behaves with such maturity." Six months later, when Stephanopoulos lost his job as communications director, the paper said he had become "a symbol of everything that's wrong with Bill Clinton's presidency . . . callow, arrogant and obsessed with image over substance."

Reeling from the awful publicity, Clinton stunned official Washington by asking David Gergen, a former aide to Republican presidents Richard Nixon, Gerald Ford and Ronald Reagan, to help rescue his presidency. Gergen's hiring was a declaration that one moment you could be a columnist for *U.S. News & World Report* and commentator for "The MacNeil/Lehrer NewsHour," and the next you could be spinning reporters as a top White House official. As Gergen slipped easily through the revolving door, it was not hard to fathom why many people no longer saw a difference between the political establishment and the establishment press.

Gergen wisely called a truce with White House reporters, and the press was soon filled with anecdotes about how Gergen was brilliantly pulling the strings offstage. The "no-fly zone" was reopened. The president and his wife hosted a big barbecue for the press on the White House lawn. Clinton began inviting newspaper folks—Johnny Apple, David Broder, Jack Nelson, Katharine Graham, Len Downie, Jack Germond, Abe Rosenthal, Mary McGrory—to small luncheons, dinners and movie screenings at the White House. He held four news conferences in a single week. He gave interviews to *The Boston Globe* and *Los Angeles Times* and *USA Today* and the newsmagazines. Suddenly, print reporters mattered again. The White House correspondents, too, seemed to pull back, sensing that they had gone too far, perhaps not wanting to take the blame for crippling a president so early in his term.

It was no accident that the dismissal of seven obscure staff members from the White House travel office in May 1993 became a huge front-page story, for here was a move that hit reporters where they live.

To be sure, White House officials had bungled the matter from beginning to end. They axed the employees suddenly, without a shred of due process, and hired a distant cousin of the president as a replacement. They responded in part to a memo from Bill Clinton's Hollywood pal, Harry Thomason, who was seeking White House travel business for his consulting firm. They improperly called in the FBI in an attempt to use a criminal investigation to justify what was little more than old-fashioned cronyism.

Yet even before these facts came to light, White House reporters were treating the affair as a scandal of Watergate proportions, asking spokesmen 161 questions about the firings in a single day. The firings melded perfectly into the media's theme of the moment, that Clinton and his crowd were pitiful bumblers. On one level, the travel scandal was fueled by a basic human reaction—reporters had known the employees for years and did not believe their buddies would do anything wrong. But there was also a self-protective element, for the travel office's primary mission is the care and feeding of White House correspondents. (Even the Clintonites belatedly recognized this by contracting with a luxury plane service called MGM Grand.)

Traveling with the president is always a first-class affair, with the press well pampered aboard a chartered jet. News organizations pick up the tab, but most reporters are not particularly concerned if the bills get a bit steep. The travel office folks help cushion the journalists from the smallest discomforts on the road, making all hotel reservations and worrying about the luggage. They hold up the plane if a straggler is running late. They also help spouses and children, who accompany reporters to Santa Barbara or Kennebunkport at bargain-basement rates. They make sure there is a fully equipped pressroom, with phones and fax machines and instant transcripts, at every stop. It is a seductive lifestyle.

"They feed you a lot," John Yang says. "They sort of sedate you, so you can't move very fast. The bar on the plane is always open. It's the same crew over and over, so the stewardesses learn what you like."

On trips abroad, some reporters would bring back cases of Russian caviar or room-sized Chinese rugs, and while they are supposed to declare such purchases, no Customs agents inspected their luggage. Local regimes would shower them with goodies. When the Turkish government provided a cruise and lavish dinner for George Bush, it also rolled out a second boat with identical food for the press.

"You get all these freebies," Yang says. "In London, we got a tote bag filled with tour books, maps, cuff links, a tie and a scarf. In Greece we got these incredibly tacky Alexander the Great ashtrays, a big bottle of Greek champagne, a big bag of pistachio nuts and a big bag of raisins. In Ankara we got these very nice briefcases. You get on the press plane and everyone's carrying these briefcases. I left mine; it was very expensive and I didn't feel right."

I once filled in for a White House correspondent when President Carter took a vacation trip to Jekyll Island, Georgia, in 1979. The plane left Andrews Air Force base at 7:00 A.M., and I was startled when several of my colleagues started downing Bloody Marys. Spouses and kids were along for the ride and no one had the slightest intention of doing any work. The days consisted of swimming, suntanning, reading, and checking in twice a day at the makeshift press room, where utterly routine announcements were posted: The president caught several fish. The president and Amy took a walk. The president made some minor appointment. (This turned out to be the trip where Carter was attacked by the "killer rabbit," probably the creation of an overheated media imagination, but that didn't come out until later.)

Traveling "with" the president really means arriving in places hours before he does. Only a handful of pool reporters actually fly on *Air Force One*. The rest can go for days with only fleeting glimpses of the man they are supposedly covering. "They grind you down," Yang says. "When you travel, the logistics are so difficult and convoluted. You have incredible delays. They have a 5:00 A.M. baggage call for a 10:00 A.M. speech. They drain all the curiosity and initiative out of you, so when they come out and tell you ridiculous things in the press room, you say, 'Oh, OK,' and just write them down."

The Travelgate scandal reinforced the notion that how the White House press corps handles a story is more important than the magnitude of the offense. The petty corruption of the travel office firings resonated with the veteran correspondents in a way that a distant procurement fraud at HUD never would. Indeed, the media's take on any story tends to be colored by reporters' feelings about how they are being treated. This was especially evident after Clinton ordered a bombing raid on Iraq in retaliation for an alleged plot to assassinate George Bush.

Press secretary Dee Dee Myers told reporters the day before the June 26 attack that Clinton had not yet received an FBI report on the plot against Bush. Myers had been misinformed, for the president had already reviewed the report that he used to justify the bombing. On the

Saturday afternoon of the attack, White House officials—understandably determined to protect the operation's secrecy—announced a "lid" on further news, meaning that reporters were free to leave for the day. Half the *New York Times'* Washington bureau went off to an Orioles-Yankees game in Baltimore. They and other reporters had to scramble back to work when Clinton announced the air strikes on television.

The Monday press briefing was consumed by angry questions and accusations about why Myers had misled reporters. Tom Friedman, for one, was appalled by the questioning. "I don't think there was a single person outside that room who either cared or didn't understand there was a national security issue there," he says. Had news of the raid leaked out, Friedman says, journalists would have said, "Look at these amateurs: They told the press before they attacked Baghdad!"

While the president remained constantly at odds with the press, Hillary Rodham Clinton was getting far better coverage than her husband, in part because she tightly controlled reporters' access with a discipline he would never have dared impose. She had set the tone by granting her first newspaper interview to *New York Times* food writer Marian Burros—on condition that Burros ask only about the First Lady's hostess duties. The result was a frothy page-one piece about Mrs. Clinton choosing place settings and banning smoking at White House dinners, unmarred by inconvenient questions about her policy-making role.

Despite some early carping about Hillary Clinton as "co-president," most of the press was in a full swoon. *Time* hailed her as "the icon of American womanhood." A *Washington Post* profile, praising her "charm" and "depth" and "gravitas," said she was "replacing Madonna as our leading cult figure." A *New York Times Magazine* cover story dubbed her "Saint Hillary."

The First Lady repeatedly turned down requests for interviews about her work as head of the administration's health care task force, in one case insisting that *USA Today* submit written questions in advance. But she spoke freely to magazines she knew would treat her like royalty: *Good Housekeeping, Family Circle, Redbook, Mirabella, Parade.* Like Princess Di, she had become a bankable cover girl.

As spring turned into summer and the president continued to struggle in the polls, the White House coverage remained predictably downbeat. Clinton's budget plan, which had seemed so bold back in February, was now under assault from all sides. Hypocritical congressmen who had done nothing to curb spending for a decade now loudly proclaimed that the package didn't go far enough, and we obliged them with the media spotlight. Ross Perot, once again getting a stunningly free ride from the press, assailed the budget plan on one talk show after another. To be sure, no reporter could ignore that the Democrats were in disarray, and the president made so many compromises that the package seemed an awful muddle. But the journalistic fixation on legislative process—day after day of newspaper stories on whether Congress would raise the gas tax by 4 cents or 6 cents or 8 cents—was obscuring the larger picture. The press gave Clinton little credit when Congress finally passed his budget by a one-vote margin in both houses.

Clinton would later complain to *Rolling Stone* that it was "the press's fault" that he wasn't getting "one damn bit of credit" for taking on tough battles. He snapped that he was "sick and tired" of being given such short shrift by the "knee-jerk liberal press." This was a strange lament for a Democrat, but the president had a point. He had succeeded in the first serious attempt in a dozen years at slicing the massive deficit. Yet the media did such a poor job of explaining the program that 78 percent of respondents in a *Wall Street Journal* poll mistakenly believed that middle-income people, who were barely nicked, would pay a bigger share of new taxes than the wealthiest taxpayers. Clinton had kept his campaign pledge to raise taxes on the rich, but that went largely unheralded in the press. The president was again being pilloried by the pundits. Bill Clinton couldn't even take his family to Martha's Vineyard without being subjected to media ridicule. His difficulty in choosing a vacation site, the newspapers declared, was a metaphor for his unfocused presidency.

The Vineyard trip did, however, provide a summer excursion for Ruth Marcus, who spent hours stranded in a yellow-and-white tent in a field far outside the Clinton vacation compound. As she reported to her colleagues: "Picking up the existential theme of the last . . . report—the pointlessness of it all—your pool can dutifully report this: Nothing happened by 3:00 P.M. No jog. No golf. No sighting."

Every so often there is an event that turns the media's unblinking spotlight back on itself. Such a moment came on July 20, 1993, when Vincent Foster shot himself in a deserted Virginia park. The ghoulish tendencies of the press were quickly placed on public display.

No one would deny that the suicide of the deputy White House counsel was an important news story. Here was Bill Clinton's boyhood friend, a loving father of three, a lawyer at the peak of his profession, suddenly ending his life for no apparent reason. It didn't add up. There had to be an explanation.

But even as the pieces began falling into place—Foster had been depressed, felt tarred by his role in Travelgate, despaired over Washington's cynical combat, believed he had failed the president—reporters remained dissatisfied. The press hounds smelled blood, certain that some dark scandal had yet to be unearthed. White House officials fed these suspicions through repeated foul-ups, such as their thirty-hour delay in turning over to investigators a note found in Foster's briefcase.

In one newspaper story after another, the underlying tone suggested the possibility of skulduggery. Typical of the genre was a *New York Times* report headlined "Palm Print Raises Questions on Inquiry in Aide's Death":

"Contradicting the assertions of federal law enforcement officials who said this week that only a smudged, unreadable palm print had been found on an anguished note left by Vincent W. Foster Jr., Government officials said today that a partial but identifiable palm print had been found but had never been investigated."

But what was there to investigate? The man was depressed and had killed himself. The press seemed unable to accept that suicide is an irrational act, that some people are haunted by demons that have no public policy implications. Washington journalists were so bent on navel gazing, so determined to analyze whether the media environment had contributed to Foster's death, that they kept on flogging what was essentially a private tragedy.

Once the Beltway rumor mill began spinning at full speed, it was only a matter of time until unsubstantiated gossip found its way into print. *The New York Times,* noting that the capital was "rife with rumors," proceeded to publish one: that *The Washington Times* had been preparing a damaging story about Foster before the suicide. But Wes Pruden and his staff insisted there had been no such story.

The first newspaper to truly descend into the gutter was Rupert Murdoch's *Sunday Times* of London. The paper reported a "salacious rumor" which "suggested Foster had been having a passionate affair with Hillary Clinton, who used to work in the same Arkansas law firm. This had been discovered, according to the gossip, and unable to bear the exposure of his betrayal of the president, Foster had killed himself. But there is no evidence of an affair."

That, of course, didn't stop the *Sunday Times* from putting the Hillary rumor in play. It quickly resurfaced in the *New York Post*, which provided a roundup of unproven Foster theories, ranging from "suicide over a sizzling affair with Hillary, to a tawdry gay murder, to a hit by a drug gang." Before long this gossip was fodder for the talk-show circuit.

Foster's final lament—"Here ruining people is considered sport," the note in his briefcase said—sent a shiver through Washington and its attack-dog press corps. In truth, the press had barely taken note of Foster, except for a string of cheap-shot editorials in *The Wall Street Journal*, which made no secret of its disdain for the entire administration. But even these pieces, accusing Foster of cronyism and legal manipulations, were pretty tame stuff. Still, every reporter in town knew that Foster's critique of the press climate was chillingly accurate.

In September 1993, Bill Clinton finally figured out how to manipulate the print press. Two days before his televised address on health care reform, the president and his wife invited David Broder, Johnny Apple, Jack Germond, Al Hunt, Jack Nelson, Michael Kinsley and other columnists and reporters to a White House luncheon to pitch the plan.

Clinton reaped substantial benefits from this meal, just for providing journalists with some food and inside tidbits. One guest, Gerald Seib of *The Wall Street Journal*, led off his piece the next day: "Near the end of a White House luncheon yesterday, President Clinton wound around to a powerful argument for his health care proposal: In the long run, it's about creating jobs."

Apple, in a page-one *New York Times* story, marveled at the White House effort to sell the plan: "Government activism was back in vogue, and this was a great chance to watch the show." Jack Nelson wrote a front-page *Los Angeles Times* story and talked about attending the lunch on "Washington Week in Review." Amazing what a little schmoozing over rolled veal and baked apples can accomplish.

Gwen Ifill says such access is crucial to the pundits. "They can go on TV and say, 'When I was with the president this week . . .' These guys trade on it. It's their cocktail-party chatter. It's their reason for being. It's their way of elevating themselves."

Hillary Clinton drew a new round of media genuflection as she dazzled five congressional panels with her testimony. The *Times* hailed the First Lady as "feminism's first mainstream icon." Broder, in his *Washington Post* column, observed that she "may be the stronger part of the team. . . . It was not until I saw the president and his spouse together, at a luncheon briefing for Washington columnists . . . that it became clear how completely they share proprietorship of this plan."

It was hardly coincidental that the tone of the coverage began to improve just as President Clinton's approval ratings were on the rise. And when two-thirds of those who saw Clinton's health care speech said in a *Washington Post* poll that they approved of his plan, the media fell into line with similarly upbeat reviews.

"Health Plan Gets Thumbs-Up" said *USA Today*'s banner headline, touting (naturally) a *USA Today* poll showing that Clinton's approval rating had jumped to 56 percent. The Baltimore *Sun* had the White House "riding a wave of post-speech euphoria." Johnny Apple wrote admiringly that the president was sporting "not only a new, slimmer haircut, but a sense of unflinching purpose and renewed self-confidence." Even the much-hyped Cristophe trim had been forgotten.

The new story line was clear: The president had picked himself off the mat. "I've been getting a lot of calls about the 'Clinton comeback,' " James Carville said a week after the health care speech. Carville's own analysis was more matter-of-fact: "If you're a smart guy and you take on a tough job, you're better at it after nine months. But that's not a dramatic story."

What was temporarily lost in the praise for Clinton's speech was the sheer complexity, daunting cost and breathtaking bureaucracy of the program. It was only a matter of time before the coverage turned sharply negative as lawmakers, physicians, hospitals, insurance companies and other interest groups began picking apart the plan. Newspaper headlines shifted from a single, impassioned speech to the messy legislative process. Reporters eyed the polls like doctors monitoring an electrocardiogram. "Skepticism Increases As Support Shrinks for Health Care Plan," said a *Washington Post* report on a poll taken three weeks after the speech. "Health Plan Support Slips," said another banner headline in *USA Today*. The press was again following the well-worn path that always seemed to take Clinton from inspirational peaks into the valley of disaster. In October, when eighteen Americans were killed in Somalia and turmoil erupted in Haiti, health care quickly dropped off the front page.

The Clinton comeback was over—at least for a few weeks. In November, the media again hailed Clinton as a masterful leader after he convinced Congress to pass the North American Free Trade Agreement. The president had achieved what the pundits had declared nearly impossible, and he had done it on behalf of a cause that the media establishment, from Anthony Lewis on the left to George Will on the right, had deemed vital to America's future. *USA Today* announced that Clinton "may have come into his own." *The New York Times* likened his deal-making prowess to that of Lyndon Johnson, calling Clinton "relentless and resourceful." All those harsh obituaries the previous spring now seemed silly and shortsighted.

The president might have celebrated Christmas on an upbeat note, but yet another spasm of sleaze journalism intervened. This time, however, it wasn't the supermarket rag *Star* or the *New York Post* that put Clinton's sex life back in play. The *American Spectator,* the right-wing monthly that despised Clinton and had previously attacked the First Lady as "Boy Clinton's Big Mama," published charges from two Arkansas state troopers who said they had facilitated a marathon of extramarital affairs for Clinton when he was governor. The author was David Brock, the conservative young journalist who had previously attacked Anita Hill in the *Spectator* as "a bit nutty and a bit slutty" and had turned his indictment into a best-selling book. The new *Spectator* piece, assailing Clinton as a "sexual predator," freely mixed graphically explicit allegations and secondhand gossip, even recycling the rumor of a Hillary Clinton affair with Vince Foster, although Brock admitted the evidence for this was merely "circumstantial."

It was as if someone had tossed a stink bomb onto the front porch of the establishment media, and few could ignore the stench. The *Los Angeles Times,* which had been investigating the troopers' allegations for four months but had agonized about publishing them, now ran a lengthy piece on the charges, much as *The Washington Post* had been prodded by NBC's "Exposé" into publishing its story on Chuck Robb. CNN rushed the charges on the air after doing quick interviews with the troopers. The *New York Post* ("BILL'S NEW SEXGATE") and *Daily News* ("BILL'S CUPID TROOPERS") gleefully joined the fray. *The Washington Post* ran the allegations on the front page (along with two of my stories examining the media's behavior), and ABC and NBC aired reports near the top of their newscasts. Even the high-toned "MacNeil/Lehrer NewsHour" got into the act, inviting me to a panel discussion on the latest media circus.

A handful of news organizations tried to resist the stampede. *The New York Times,* which had doggedly refused to cover the Gennifer Flowers episode, ran nothing on the troopers' charges the first day and buried a seven-paragraph wire story the second day. "I am not interested in Bill Clinton's sex life as governor of Arkansas," Johnny Apple told me. Still, when Hillary Clinton denounced the allegations as "outrageous" and "terrible," the *Times* played her comments at the top of its front page. This, of course, was inevitable: the media may ignore salacious charges for a time, but when a public official heatedly denies them (as President Bush had done in condemning CNN's "sleazy questions" about his supposed mistress), it suddenly fits the conventional definition of news. One of the last holdouts was *The Wall Street Journal,* which printed almost nothing about the allegations even after the president and Hillary Clinton denied them.

News executives who jumped on the story solemnly insisted it wasn't about sex at all. It was about "character," "judgment," "veracity" and "abuse of power," Peter Jennings said. This was the old abuse-of-government-gasoline argument that the press often uses as a fig leaf when covering steamy stories. It was still, at bottom, about illicit sex. Had the troopers been doing Clinton's laundry instead of supposedly driving him to late-night assignations, no one would have cared about state employees being misused. There was, however, one clearly newsworthy aspect to the story. In an inexplicably dumb move, the president had called some of the troopers, sparking charges (which Clinton denied) that he was trying to silence them and had offered one trooper a federal job.

Some of the troopers' tales sounded implausible. But most journalists believed that Clinton probably did his share of fooling around as governor, and believed just as strongly that it really didn't matter—he had tacitly admitted as much in his 1992 appearance on "60 Minutes"—unless he continued this behavior after the election. The public, for its part, greeted the latest media flap with a big yawn. Reporters soon learned that the troopers were not only angling for a book contract but had lied in an insurance company lawsuit over their drunken smashup of a state police car. The seamy story quickly faded, to the relief of most journalists, who were more interested in reviving another campaign issue: the murky Whitewater case involving the Clintons and the owner of a failed Arkansas savings and loan. While the complicated transactions were barely comprehensible, they carried an aura of journalistic high-mindedness in a way that tales of furtive sex most definitely did not.

Perhaps it was inevitable that an increasingly tendentious White House press corps would continually clash with a young president who had learned the dangers of letting the media define him. But the manic-depressive coverage of Bill Clinton's first year in office laid bare the media's growing tendency toward snap judgments and knee-jerk negativity. The cycle repeated itself after the Democrats' electoral debacle in 1994, when the press all but wrote Clinton's political obituary, declaring him irrelevant, only to chronicle his subsequent recovery.

Beyond the constant carping lay an even more disturbing truth: We exaggerate what any president can do because that inflates our own sense of self-importance, of covering history in the making. By buying into the central lie of American politics—that one man can change the course of a trillion-dollar economy, create millions of jobs, whip the bureaucracy into shape and fix a massive medical system—the press builds up expectations that no politician can meet, neatly positioning us to chronicle the failures that follow.

The White House correspondents rightly held Clinton accountable for his overpromising and his mistakes but stubbornly refused to give him the slightest break, lest they be seen as too soft on a Democratic president. Too many reporters allowed their coverage to be colored by personal pique, as if the president's relations with them were somehow more important than how he was running the country. The self-absorbed organs of daily journalism had turned Bill Clinton into just another celebrity, an entertainer-in-chief whose job was to feed the great maw of publications and programs whose reporters were already growing bored waiting for the '96 election.

14

The Smell of Death

In the spring of 1975, even the trash at *The Washington Post* was considered valuable.

All the world knew how two young, shoe-leather reporters had helped topple a president, and now their story was being processed and merchandised and burnished for the glitzier precincts of the entertainment world. The moviemakers descended on the newsroom; Dustin Hoffman sat on the floor during an editors' conference, while Robert Redford eavesdropped on a reporter working the phones. The film people were building a $200,000 replica of the newsroom in Burbank Studios, and no detail was deemed too small, not least the awesome clutter piled high on reporters' desks. At one point thirty-seven boxes of authentic junk was collected and shipped to Hollywood.

It was a heady time for the newspaper business, not just for Bob Woodward and Carl Bernstein but for anyone who shared the same line of work. There was much self-conscious prattling about the media and the movies, about the chroniclers of news finding themselves at the other end of the camera, about the dawning of a new mythology built around the workaday reporter and his once-lowly craft.

It was a heady time, too, for an industry that had lived through the trauma of Vietnam and Watergate, the years of pitched struggle with an administration that treated the press as an enemy. Reporters for *The New York Times* found their phones tapped by federal officials trying to unmask their sources. The Washington Post Company had to fight off a government attempt to revoke its Florida television licenses. Columnist Jack Anderson was the target of a bizarre murder plot cooked up by G. Gordon Liddy. An adversarial culture had flourished in the press, rooted in the media's role in exposing the futility of the distant war in Southeast Asia and the unconstitutional attempts to crush dissent at home. A decade and a half earlier, Jack Kennedy could with a single phone call persuade the publisher of *The New York Times* to tone down a story about the impending Bay of Pigs invasion. Now Richard Nixon, who railed against the press inside the Oval Office, had been driven from Washington, and reporters were getting most of the credit.

All this was a bit unsettling for those who made their living chasing after people with pen and pad, scribbling down the words of the powerful. The younger practitioners tended to be creative types who had strayed from the conventional path of success, for even during the 1960s becoming a journalist was an offbeat thing to do. They were liberal, to be sure, but not so radical as to reject the whole system. They were committed to change, but not so passionate as to feel uncomfortable in the observer's role. They were willing to work erratic hours for mediocre pay, even as the best and the brightest of their generation became lawyers and doctors and academics.

Most news organizations were run by establishment-minded editors who tended to hire white, middle-class men like themselves. The older reporters, not unlike firemen, liked to drink and play poker while waiting for the next bell to ring. The popular stereotype that newspapers were peopled by hacks and ambulance-chasers and frustrated authors had not changed all that much since the *Front Page* days of the 1930s.

And now, without warning, it all seemed so chic. Timothy Crouse had romanticized the likes of David Broder and Johnny Apple and Jack Germond in *The Boys on the Bus*. The Redford-Hoffman film, *All the President's Men*, would become a box-office smash the following year. David Halberstam was writing a book that would portray media moguls as the true power brokers of American society. Ed Asner would soon star in a hit television series that served up realistic slices of newsroom life. Lou Grant was America's city editor.

The investigative reporter, that lonely nerd who spent his days in dusty file rooms, was becoming the new antihero. Seymour Hersh, who once had trouble peddling his exposé of the My Lai massacre, was now telling tales of CIA malfeasance on the front page of *The New York Times*. Journalism schools were flooded with applications from idealistic young men and women who dreamed of meeting shadowy sources in parking garages. Salaries improved. More papers opened foreign bureaus. More reporters got book contracts. Cable television was still a blip on the media horizon. It was the beginning of an era in which newspapers would become fabulously lucrative properties and many print reporters, harnessing the power of television, would achieve celebrity status.

The money men on Wall Street had always regarded newspapers as a troublesome business hobbled by constant labor strife, featherbedding and outdated equipment. By the early '80s, however, that perception began to change. Most of the big newspaper companies had gone public, and that meant they now had to worry about shareholders and dividends and quarterly profits. Aggressive managers were brought in, and they started buying up other papers, magazines, paper mills and cable franchises.

Allen Neuharth, the charismatic chairman of Gannett, had mounted a propaganda campaign to change the industry's image on Wall Street. And Gannett delivered the goods: The company would report increasing profits each quarter for twenty-two years, a streak that would not be broken until the 1990 recession.

But many journalists were troubled by the new emphasis on stock prices. "There was a time when *The New York Times* made the money in order to strengthen the news operation," says Bill Kovach, the former *Times*man who now runs the Nieman Foundation at Harvard University. "The profit margin was 5, 6, 7 percent, and the Sulzberger family was perfectly content with that. The minute *The New York Times* had to go out to the market to raise capital, they had to play the Al Neuharth game. The market recognizes only one thing, and that's quarterly profits. That's the thing Al Neuharth brought to the newspaper business."

As newspaper executives became more focused on the bottom line, the power of organized labor began to fade. A year after its Watergate triumph, *The Washington Post* achieved a different sort of notoriety by breaking its pressmen's union after a violent strike. As more newsrooms switched to computers, automation ended the unions' stranglehold on production. The technological revolution promised greater profits through the elimination of thousands of jobs, and the unions were painfully slow to accept this.

The media business was soon swept up by the takeover frenzy of the '80s. *The Des Moines Register* and three smaller papers were sold for $200 million, the *Louisville Courier-Journal* for $306 million, the *Chicago Sun-Times* for $145 million, the Baltimore *Sun* and a television station for $600 million. Some papers even started using junk bonds.

The industry's bottom line never looked better than in the Roaring '80s. Some newspaper stocks tripled in value. The New York Times Company, which in 1975 posted earnings of less than $13 million, turned a profit of $266 million in 1989. The Washington Post Company saw its annual profits rise from $12 million to $197 million over the same period. Other highly profitable newspaper companies that year included Gannett ($397 million), Knight-Ridder ($247 million), Dow Jones ($317 million) and Times Mirror ($298 million). "They just sat back and raked in the money," says industry analyst John Morton.

They weren't the only ones getting rich. The '80s were the decade when print journalists hired agents and became television stars. Rowland Evans and Robert Novak published three newsletters and hosted a weekly show on CNN. Columnist George Will, better known for his Sunday-morning appearances on David Brinkley's show, took in $15,000 a speech. Jack Germond, little known to the public as a Baltimore *Sun* columnist, became a food-fight panelist on the "McLaughlin Group" and started taking in an extra $100,000 a year or so from speeches and TV appearances. *Wall Street Journal* reporter Bryan Burrough, coauthor of *Barbarians at the Gate,* the story of the RJR Nabisco takeover, won a million-dollar contract for his next book. He was twenty-nine years old.

There's nothing wrong with talented journalists cashing in on their prominence. But some of my colleagues began spending so much time chasing the bucks—rushing from studio to studio to sound off on talk shows, flying from city to city to give the same speech again and again—that they had little time for the kind of reporting and writing that made them successful in the first place. The media world rewarded simplistic sound bites over hard digging, insults over insights.

The zeitgeist had clearly shifted since the days of Woodward and Bernstein. Success soon brought a new sense of caution and restraint. The corporate mind-set grew so dominant by the late '80s that *Columbia Journalism Review* ran a piece called "When MBAs Rule the Newsroom." Many newspapers took on an insurance-company atmosphere, with serious young people churning out serious stories as if they were legal briefs on product liability. The oddballs, louts and curmudgeons of yesteryear became a dwindling presence.

"Newspapers have gotten more homogeneous, filled with yuppies and vipers," says Phil Gailey, editorial page editor of the *St. Petersburg Times.* "There's no tolerance for people who get a little older or drink a little too much at lunch. These days most journalists are interested in getting on TV or writing books or both. The soul has gone out of the business."

Soon the spectacular profits vanished as well. The bottom fell out in 1990, with newspaper earnings plunging by 30, 40, or even 60 percent. Classified advertising stalled with the collapse of the real estate and employment markets. Department stores such as Macy's and Blooming-dale's, the traditional linchpin of retail advertising, were bankrupted by debt-laden corporate takeovers. Less advertising invariably meant less news. Most newspapers froze hiring and offered buyouts to induce older employees to quit. Others cut their news pages, closed bureaus and slashed travel budgets. The *New York Times, Miami Herald, San Francisco Examiner* and *Atlanta Constitution* were among those laying off dozens of employees. *The Wall Street Journal* shut its Philadelphia bureau and dropped some foreign correspondents. The *Chicago Sun-Times* put its staff on a four-day work week. Many papers doubled their prices. Circulation took a nosedive. "The Party's Over," a *Forbes* cover story announced.

The smell of death permeates the newspaper business these days. Every few months there is a repetition of the now-familiar ritual: the desperate search for a buyer, the anguished countdown, the farewell edition, the grieving in the community, the latest batch of reporters and editors tossed out on the street. More than 150 daily newspapers have folded since 1970. Big, deep-pocket corporations—Time, Gannett, Hearst, Cox—have proved as helpless at bucking this tide as small-town owners.

Some newspapers, in their rush to transform themselves into hip, video-age products, have badly misjudged their audience, alienating long-time readers without attracting many new ones. Others, hampered by union strife, have been unable to gain control over inflated labor costs —a condition epitomized by the seven-month Teamsters' strike that killed *The Pittsburgh Press* (with help from a bullheaded management at Scripps Howard) at the end of 1992. Still others have hemorrhaged until they were abandoned by corporate owners, as the *San Antonio Light* was in January 1993 when Hearst folded the paper and bought its more profitable rival, the *San Antonio Express-News*. And in 1995, corporate executives shuttered *The Houston Post,* the Baltimore *Evening Sun,* and *New York Newsday.*

In a larger sense, however, all defunct newspapers share a common failing: They could not carve out a niche in a rapidly changing marketplace. Somehow they allowed themselves to become redundant, like trolley cars in the subway era.

To understand how newspapers in the '90s can survive, it is necessary to examine how once-great papers have died, or are slowly committing suicide. While there is no miracle vaccine that can inoculate the press against demographic decay, there are obvious danger signs to be heeded.

Afternoon papers in Richmond, San Diego, Louisville, Baton Rouge, Shreveport, Spokane, Tulsa, Durham, Charleston and Knoxville have folded or been swallowed by morning editions. The circulation of P.M. papers, most of which were aimed at blue-collar workers, has dropped 42 percent since 1970. They have become relics of an earlier era.

Ninety-eight percent of American cities are now monopoly markets. Los Angeles, Philadelphia, Baltimore, Cleveland, Pittsburgh, St. Louis, Newark, Atlanta, Miami and Dallas are served by one newspaper (or two papers owned by the same corporation). Newspaper chains, which in 1960 accounted for less than half of all daily newspaper circulation, now control 80 percent of the nation's 1,580 daily papers.

It is far easier for a distant owner who doesn't rub shoulders with readers and advertisers to pull the plug on a newspaper. To some owners a newspaper is less a journalistic venture than a bottom-line proposition, no different from a plastics factory. When Houston publisher William Dean Singleton closed the *Elizabeth* (New Jersey) *Daily Journal* in 1992, he said the city's ailing retail core would never recover and that he planned to invest his money in suburban papers. It is hard to imagine a local owner so casually writing off a 212-year-old paper and its community. The biggest acquisition in newspaper history, The New York Times Company's billion-dollar purchase of *The Boston Globe* in 1993, was also part of the trend toward consolidation. While the Taylor family was fortunate to find a buyer committed to quality journalism, it is nonetheless sad that New England's proud Yankee newspaper is now just another branch office of a big out-of-state landlord.

Sometimes newspapers are bought and resold like used cars. The Times Mirror Company bought the *Dallas Times Herald* in 1969, then sold it in 1986 to Singleton, who flipped it two years later to John Buzzetta, a longtime associate. Buzzetta closed the paper in 1991. As has been the case with other failed papers, most of the abandoned readers simply disappeared from the newspaper market.

Some twenty cities, among them Detroit, San Francisco, Nashville, Cincinnati and Seattle, have preserved the veneer of competition through joint operating agreements (JOAs). These government-blessed arrangements prop up failing papers by allowing them to share printing and business operations with a stronger rival. But even this well-intentioned attempt to maintain competing editorial voices became perverted during the '80s.

When Cox Enterprises shut down the *Miami News* in 1988, it did so under the terms of a twenty-two-year-old JOA with Knight-Ridder's *Miami Herald*. The result is that Cox continues to draw a share of the *Herald*'s profits until 2021. Virtually all the money has flowed to two Atlanta sisters, Anne Cox Chambers and Barbara Cox Anthony, whose fortune is worth more than $4 billion. In other words, under an antitrust exemption designed to preserve newspaper competition, two billionaires are being paid not to publish a newspaper. Now that's free enterprise.

But JOAs are not always guaranteed money machines. When Gannett's *Detroit News* and Knight-Ridder's *Detroit Free Press* joined forces in 1989, the venture lost $12 million in its first year of operation. Even worse, the merger devastated the *Detroit News*, which had been winning the circulation war. Over the next four years the *News* lost nearly half its readership as circulation plummeted from almost 700,000 to 367,000. The *Free Press*'s circulation dropped from 626,000 to 556,000. Many readers, fiercely loyal to their old paper, resented the higher prices and combined weekend editions, and in 1995 the papers would be decimated by a bitter strike. Perhaps the sickest papers should be permitted to die with dignity rather than be hooked up to these rickety life-support systems.

The demise of a newspaper is sometimes compared to a death in the family, and the analogy rings true because of the intimate bond that many readers develop with their daily paper. A good newspaper is a living, breathing organism, with a lively personality and a colorful past and a rightful place in the community. Something irretrievable is lost when it fades into history. And yet such failures are now ho-hum news, a one-day story. Even our obituaries have become routine.

The *Arkansas Gazette*, a gray, respectable paper that modeled itself on *The New York Times*, was 167 years old when its longtime owners, the Patterson family, finally threw in the towel in 1986.

The *Gazette* had a rich legacy as the state's social conscience and the oldest newspaper west of the Mississippi. Founded in a malarial swampland in 1819 when Arkansas was still a territory, it had been edited by the legendary J. N. Heiskell from 1902 until his death in 1972. Heiskell, who bequeathed the *Gazette* to his son-in-law Hugh Patterson, believed that news sold newspapers and that it was his responsibility to keep a watchful eye on government.

In some ways Heiskell's ghost still haunted the place. Two Pulitzer Prize trophies in the high-ceilinged lobby testified to the editor's courage in 1957, when the *Gazette* strongly supported President Eisenhower's effort to integrate all-white Central High School. Advertisers boycotted the liberal paper, backed by the segregationist governor, Orval Faubus, yet Heiskell stood firm.

But the *Gazette* developed a major problem in the person of Walter Hussman, Jr., the balding, soft-spoken publisher of the *Arkansas Democrat*. Hussman had bought the afternoon paper in 1974 for just $3.7 million. The scrappy *Democrat* had only half the circulation of the *Gazette*.

Although Hussman cut costs to the bone and got rid of the paper's unions, he was still losing money. In 1987 he asked Hugh Patterson for a JOA, with 90 percent of the profits earmarked for the *Gazette*. Patterson, who owned the more lucrative morning market, turned him down.

Stung by this rejection, Hussman declared war. He switched to morning publication. He started giving away free classified ads. He lured the state's biggest department store, Dillard's, by offering it unlimited ads for $500,000 a year. (It didn't hurt that William Dillard, the store's chairman, was an old friend of his grandfather.) He published fatter papers than the *Gazette*. And he started losing millions of dollars a year, losses that had to be subsidized by his string of TV stations and godawful small-town papers.

"I kind of like Little Rock," Hussman says. "I've got a nice house here. All these advertisers are friends of mine. I didn't want to leave."

The following year Hussman hired the irascible John Robert Starr to run the *Democrat*. The white-haired Starr posed for a magazine cover in a helmet and Army vest with a knife between his teeth, squatting on a *Gazette* newspaper box. The stunt almost got him fired, but it also served notice that a street fighter had taken charge.

Five years later, it was Patterson's turn to sue for peace. He took the *Democrat* to federal court, charging that Hussman was trying to drive him out of business through predatory price-cutting. Starr called his rivals "crybabies." Patterson lost the suit in 1986. Seven months later he sold the paper to Gannett for $51 million.

The future now looked bright. The *Gazette* had more advertising than the *Democrat*. Its thickly carpeted newsroom, filled with rows of personal computers, hummed quietly like a corporate law firm. Its staff was more seasoned and better paid than that of the *Democrat*.

Four blocks away, the *Democrat* was assembled in a dingy former YMCA building, with cramped desks and mismatched chairs arranged around file cabinets stacked so high you needed a ladder to retrieve the yellowed clips they contained. The few ancient computer terminals had to be shared by the staff.

But the *Gazette* was kind of stodgy by '80s standards, and Al Neuharth's media conglomerate decided to give the paper a facelift. Before long the *Gazette* would be peppered with page-one stories about zoo animals, cheerleaders and children in need of organ transplants.

Gannett gave its papers numerical ratings each month, a practice that offended Carrick Patterson, Hugh's son, who had stayed on as editor. "There was pressure to conform," he says. "We'd go to these meetings in Washington and we'd be preached to about *USA Today* and how wonderful it was."

There were other intrusions. Gannett talked Patterson into starting a Business Monday, but the section drew little advertising. Feature sections were added, but early deadlines were imposed so they could be printed in color, and that made them seem flat and lifeless.

"They had utterly no understanding of news," Patterson says. "Good reporting to them was short stories and not covering meetings. You don't cover the city board of directors meetings because that's boring; you cover some kid who needs a new liver."

Soon Gannett asked Michael Gartner, who would later become president of NBC News, to evaluate its new acquisition. A wonderful clash of cultures was captured in the ensuing war of memos:

Gartner said the weather map was full of "useless tables" showing "water levels of seven rivers at thirty-seven different locations."

Patterson replied: "The river bulletin is very important in this agricultural and flood-prone state. . . . Are you just trying to make us mad with outrageous statements like this?"

Gartner: "The paper has no zip, no sparkle, no twinkle. . . . It is full of news you can't use. . . . You just don't get a feel for Little Rock by reading the *Gazette*."

Patterson: "Our readers, since they live here, already have a 'feel' for the place. If the Little Rock Planning Commission is going to rezone the vacant lot across the street from me I damn well want to know about it and expect my newspaper to tell me. I'm a lot more interested in that than in the fact that 37 percent of Arkansans like disco music."

Gartner: "The editorial page is unappealing . . . editorials are incredibly long . . . invariably deal with leaden issues of little interest or importance to most readers."

Patterson: "We don't try to be dull, but neither are we Pollyannas who try to make the editorial page the functional equivalent of television 'happy talk.' . . . It is our duty to deal with issues that may not be obviously important or interesting but that have significant impact on readers' lives."

But the direction was clear. When the new publisher, William Malone, ordered Patterson to write an editorial saying that newspapers should be exempt from the state sales tax, he threatened to resign. The paper was clearly floundering under Gannett's heavy-handed management.

"This is the thing that really gets to me: there did not seem to be a plan," Patterson says. "I certainly couldn't believe that this multibillion-dollar company that had eighty straight quarters with increased revenues wouldn't be smart enough to manage the business. The direction for this month was, 'Let's spend a bunch of money and drive the bastards back.' The direction the next month was, 'Oh my God, we're spending too much money.' "

Patterson was eased out. In 1988 he was replaced by Walker Lundy, a veteran of newspapers in Fort Worth, Tallahassee, Charlotte and Detroit. To much of his staff, Lundy seemed obsessed with human interest stories and color pictures. He ran front-page articles about the circus coming to town, new gorillas at the zoo, a baby born in the backseat of a car. One classic headline said, "Arkansans Encounter Visitor from Outer Space" (for a story about a meteor sighting). Some headlines carried exclamation points. Much national and foreign news was reduced to one- or two-sentence digests.

"The *Gazette* is like an elegant old woman and suddenly she was made to look ridiculous," said Alan Leveritt, publisher of the weekly *Arkansas Times*. "We had cheerleaders wearing spandex suits on the front page. That was just a little radical for us."

But Lundy viewed himself as an innovator trying to rescue a newspaper in decline. When anyone invoked the old chestnut about the *Gazette's* being *The New York Times* of Arkansas, Lundy would remind them that the *Times* was not even the best-selling paper in New York.

"My belief is that up here are the readers," Lundy says, holding his hand at eye level. "Their lives are changing, their interests are changing. You drop about a foot down"—now he's at chest level—"and here come newspapers; we're changing too, but we're behind the people. Then you drop down another foot and there you find a lot of reporters, who believe newspapers are pandering to readers—God forbid you should do that—and trying to suck up to readers. They think you should keep doing what you were always doing, and think the readers, most of them are too stupid anyway to be on a newspaper subscription list."

Still, Lundy was surprised at how local folks resisted his efforts to brighten the paper. He recalls one Little Rock woman who hated the fact that the *Gazette* had switched to color, though she couldn't quite explain why. "It was as if she was saying that God meant newspapers to be in black and white," he says.

In his zeal to lure new readers, Lundy was driving away many of the old ones. The *Gazette's* circulation began to slip while the *Democrat's* climbed, although both papers were losing millions. Gannett suffered another setback when William Dillard, chairman of the department-store chain, got angry about a negative story in the *Gazette* and promptly pulled his daily full-page ads from the paper. This cost Lundy's bottom line $2 million a year, but that wasn't the worst of it. Dillard's was the only full-service department store in town; now readers couldn't find out if Dillard's was having a sale by reading the *Gazette*.

Walker Lundy was dumped in 1990 and replaced by Keith Moyer, a Gannett editor from the Fort Myers, Florida, *News-Press*. A new publisher was imported as well. Folks at the *Democrat* ridiculed the revolving cast of managers as out-of-state "Gannettoids." Hussman appeared in television commercials, stressing his local roots as proprietor of "Arkansas' newspaper." And Starr's vitriolic column gave the *Democrat* a vivid working-class identity.

"The one thing they had going for them is that they were aggressive," Moyer says. "They were kick-you-in-the-nuts feisty. We always felt we were operating with one hand tied behind our back because we were the big corporation. We played by the rules, and they would come from behind and trip us up."

Hussman dismisses the charge of Gannett-bashing. "I don't think Gannett is an evil company," he says, "I just think it's a profit-oriented company. I think they put profits ahead of journalism. For a company that prides itself on research—the new buzzword—I don't think they understood the feeling readers had toward that paper. They really did turn it into a version of *USA Today*.

"The fact is, our editors were more attuned to what people wanted. Bob Starr grew up in Arkansas. I know a lot about Arkansas. Every week I make lots of story suggestions. I clip things out of the paper when we screw something up. You can't beat that kind of personal attention."

Keith Moyer, a low-key man with a fondness for bow ties, toned down the *Gazette*'s emphasis on frothy features. "Clearly, some of the moves that were made were wrong," he says. "We went back to being a serious newspaper."

Well, almost. Moyer still ran such front-page stories as "Porky the Warthog Found Dead at Zoo" and "Miss Arkansas Follows in Mother's Footsteps." And as part of Gannett's "News 2000" program, he ran a survey asking readers what they liked.

It was paint-by-numbers journalism: Readers could check off whether they wanted more news from Europe or the Middle East. News about the governor. News about the legislature. News from your county. News from other Arkansas counties. Or, from Column B: Coping with infants and preschoolers. Advice on teenagers. Advice on dating, sex, relationships. Advice on retirement. Single parenting. Bob Starr lampooned the survey in his column in the *Democrat*.

Starr and Moyer took off the gloves when the *Democrat* printed the name of a woman who said she had been sexually assaulted by four University of Arkansas basketball players. Starr said he did so because the woman was drunk and did not press charges; he wasn't convinced a rape had taken place. The *Democrat* reporter who wrote the piece (and did not want to identify the woman) promptly resigned and joined the *Gazette*.

Moyer assailed Hussman and Starr for printing the woman's name, saying that "the women of this state . . . are less safe today, more vulnerable than ever before, less likely to report a rape because the men who run the *Democrat* decided to play God." Starr struck back in a column titled *"Gazette* Editor Carries Hypocrisy to New Lows." He followed up with an angry fax, saying that Moyer's column seemed "an exercise in downright lying" and warning: "You are in over your head, Buster."

"Dear Bullyboy," Moyer faxed back. "It is hilarious that you would discuss 'intellectual honesty.' In your case it would be an oxymoron."

"You are way, way, way in over your head," Starr replied.

"My daddy can whup your daddy," Moyer shot back.

Such juvenile antics spilled over into the news pages, where there were constant attempts to knock down the other paper's scoops. This continual sniping obscured the fact that the *Democrat* was a mediocre newspaper that was heavily influenced by Starr's feuds and pet peeves. At times Starr was so close to Bill Clinton that the governor frequently consulted him about legislation; after a falling out, however, he would attack Clinton mercilessly. Arkansas officials say Starr sometimes threatened to write a column if he didn't get his way. It was a vendetta that would continue throughout Clinton's presidential campaign.

The *Gazette* had more balanced political coverage, and its investigative reporting had brought down the state attorney general. The *Gazette*'s staff was also 16 percent black, including several black editors, while the *Democrat* newsroom was virtually all-white. The *Democrat* had an embarrassing rule that no columnist could criticize Hussman's advertisers. "The *Democrat* could do lousy reporting and people would say, 'Well, that's just the *Democrat*,' " Moyer says. "But the *Gazette* was the grand old paper. The *Gazette* was held to a higher standard."

Gannett officials, surveying the wreckage from their headquarters in Arlington, Virginia, were baffled. The lighter-and-brighter formula had worked for them at dozens of papers, but they had forgotten that each city has its own tastes and idiosyncrasies. For all its flaws, Walter Hussman's newspaper had its finger on the state's pulse. It passed the *Gazette* in Sunday circulation, 236,000 to 222,000, and trailed only slightly during the week. Hussman was still losing about $10 million a year but Gannett was losing a staggering $25 million a year. That was intolerable for a publicly owned company.

In the spring of 1991, Gannett officials secretly offered to sell Hussman the *Gazette*'s assets. When Hussman saw the books, he was stunned: Gannett had outspent him by $50 million over five years.

Rumors were rampant, but Gannett officials remained silent as they searched for a buyer. Still, the smell of death was unmistakable. Everyone knew the end was near, but Gannett refused to allow the planning of a final edition.

On October 18, 1991, Gannett announced that it was closing the *Arkansas Gazette* that day and selling the assets to Hussman for $69 million. In just five years, it had killed the oldest paper west of the Mississippi.

The company issued a terse statement saying the decision had been "influenced by market research conducted in 1990 that showed marginal prospects for increases in circulation penetration." But no amount of corporate blather could mask Gannett's failure. John Brummett, who had been the *Gazette*'s top columnist, said that Gannett "changed the soul of the paper. An old gray lady, a southern imitation of *The New York Times,* was transformed into pop journalism."

Seven hundred people were out of work, and the *Gazette*'s building was taken over by the Clinton campaign. Walter Hussman changed the name of his paper to the *Arkansas Democrat-Gazette* and picked up a few *Gazette* writers.

"Having a newspaper here in Little Rock meant a lot more to me than it did to the people at Gannett," Hussman says. "We live here. We worked harder. We realized we didn't have as much money and we had to be smarter. If this newspaper was located a thousand miles from here, I'd be less concerned about it. That's the advantage of local ownership. There's pride in the product.

"When you get right down to it, are people going to remember you for how much money you made, or what kind of newspaper you published?"

The *New York Post* had only hours to live. It was September 14, 1990, and a pack of reporters had gathered at a midtown hotel for the ritual death watch. Negotiators were shouting behind closed doors, working against an 8:00 P.M. deadline. The owner, Peter Kalikow, had lost $80 million on the paper in just two years, and now he was threatening to shut it down unless the unions agreed to major layoffs and pay cuts. As the minutes ticked away, the *Post* prepared two stories: one announcing its demise, the other a dramatic rescue.

It was not the first time I had watched the *Post* teeter on the brink of extinction. Two and a half years earlier, I was in the storied newsroom on South Street (which had been home to the old *New York Journal-American*) as a nervous staff waited to see whether Rupert Murdoch would close the paper. The Australian-born press baron had bought the liberal tabloid from Dorothy Schiff in 1976 and turned it into a sensationalist, right-wing rag. Since federal regulators had decreed that Murdoch could no longer own both the *Post* and his New York television station, he was trying to sell the paper to Kalikow, a little-known Manhattan developer. The sale hinged on Murdoch's ultimatum that the unions make sweeping concessions. A sense of sadness filled the air, and reporters collected autographs from colleagues they might not see again. But a late-night deal was struck, and the next day's paper declared "WRITE ON!"

Now the *Post* was headed toward another nail-baiting climax, and once again the tabloid defied the obituary writers. At 11:30 P.M., more than three hours after Kalikow's deadline, weary negotiators emerged with a deal that slashed the staff yet again and put the remaining employees on a four-day week. The *Post* was becoming a journalistic skeleton, but it was, for the moment, still breathing.

The New York newspaper world was littered with ghostly reminders of such battles between labor and management. In 1900, the city had boasted twenty-five daily newspapers; by 1966 it was down to six, and a year later it was three. The *Herald Tribune,* the *World-Telegram,* the *Journal-American,* the *Mirror* and others had all vanished. The unions, with their notorious waste and incessant demands, had a way of pushing newspapers over the edge. A dozen strikes from the 1950s through the '70s had gradually taken their toll.

The conventional wisdom was that the *Post* and the *Daily News* were in a fight to the finish. With the 1983 launch of a city edition of *Newsday,* the Long Island newspaper owned by Times Mirror, the market had simply become too crowded. New York could not support four newspapers in an era when most big cities had just one. At least one of the tabloids, it was widely agreed, would not survive.

Six weeks after the *Post*'s 1990 brush with death, it was the *Daily News'* turn. The paper's violent struggle seemed to epitomize the self-destructive warfare that was slowly strangling newspapers across America.

Launched in 1919 by Joseph Medill Patterson and Robert Mc-Cormick, owners of the *Chicago Tribune,* the *News* spoke the language of the working-class masses. Billing itself as "New York's picture newspaper," the *News* prided itself on its exclusive photos, from the Hindenburg exploding over New Jersey to the only picture ever taken of a Sing Sing electrocution, snapped with a small camera strapped to a reporter's ankle. Sunday circulation peaked at 4.7 million in 1947, more than twice the sales of any other American newspaper.

But the paper had begun to decline in the '50s and '60s, and by the time of its classic 1975 headline, "FORD TO CITY: DROP DEAD," both the *News* and the city were in financial peril. In 1978, when union demands led to a crippling, eighty-eight-day newspaper strike in New York, the *News* tried to keep publishing, but abandoned the idea after strikers clashed with police and two delivery trucks were firebombed.

The *News* lost $115 million during the 1980s, even while taking in $4 billion in revenues. Circulation dropped 700,000 from 1983 to 1990, to just over 1 million. The *News* could not turn a profit because it simply cost too much to produce.

Publisher Jim Hoge was ready to take on the unions, with help from a law firm that had broken the pressmen's union at the *Chicago Tribune* four years earlier. The Tribune Company began training managers at a mock newsroom, dubbed "Fort Jim Hoge" by the unions, in an abandoned Sears warehouse in New Jersey. It was lining up replacements from its nonunion papers in Orlando, Fort Lauderdale and Newport News. The company even advertised 116 mailers' jobs that might become vacant "in the event of a strike," and 4,000 applicants showed up, snaked around the 42nd Street tower like a 1930s soup line.

Union leaders were incensed by management's saber-rattling. Mike Alvino, head of the drivers' union, grew up running a newsstand near city hall, selling the papers his father delivered by truck. William Kennedy, head of the pressmen's union, was the son of a pressman, and he knew how poor conditions were in the *News*'s Brooklyn plant, where you had to shout to be heard and your skin and clothes were covered with an inky mist. They had nothing but disdain for the Yale-educated Hoge, son of a wealthy Park Avenue lawyer, whom they viewed as a hatchet man for the corporate bean-counters in Chicago.

Still, the company's grievances were real. The *News* was paying fourteen or fifteen men on a press while it needed only six or seven. There was a "buddy system" in which pressmen were said to sign in for colleagues who never showed up. Some of Alvino's drivers were making $100,000 a year with overtime. And a web of featherbedding rules resulted in delivery trucks leaving the plant half full and some drivers getting seven days' pay for five days' work. Hoge was also eager to publicize the fact that the craft union members were virtually all white men, many of them the sons and brothers and cousins of older members.

Union leaders had their own gripes, of course. Kennedy saw the *News* as "the most mismanaged paper in America," one that never lived up to its promise to buy new presses. The Tribune Company seemed to have plenty of dough when it came to paying its chairman, Stanton Cook, $1.5 million a year, or loaning Jim Hoge a million dollars to buy his Gramercy Park apartment, which was featured in *Architectural Digest.*

Management clearly wanted a strike. But newspaper strikes had become a rarity as advanced technology made it almost impossible for unions to shut a paper down. Aggrieved unions were more likely to file lawsuits, ask reporters to withhold their bylines or organize an advertiser boycott. Labor officials were determined not to play into management's hands.

On October 25, 1990, a predawn argument broke out when an injured driver refused an order to stand up as he worked on a conveyor belt. Some men walked off the job. Within fifteen minutes, management had a bus full of strikebreakers on the scene. Several delivery trucks were firebombed, and forty others had their radiators punctured. A bus carrying replacement workers was attacked with sticks and stones. The strike was on.

The confrontation was particularly painful for the Newspaper Guild, which represented reporters, editors and clerical workers. Born during the Depression, the Guild had in middle age become encrusted with seniority rules and work restrictions that somehow seemed the antithesis of the freewheeling reporters' ethic. The notion of quitting a story after precisely eight hours, or toiling for the same wage as the lazy hack who never left his desk, seemed ludicrous to young reporters who wanted to climb as high as their writing skills would take them. Middle-class reporters, many of them graduates of the best colleges and journalism schools, felt they had less and less in common with the brawny pressmen and tough-talking drivers.

The Guild voted to join the blue-collar walkout amid much dissension. "A lot of people said fuck this, why should we go on strike?" said political reporter Adam Nagourney, who later moved to *USA Today*. "I don't feel even remote solidarity with those guys. My contract is fine." Even so, Nagourney still regarded management as "scum," and he could not cross the picket line.

Other staffers refused to strike, ignoring the jeers of their colleagues. "I wouldn't spend five minutes out for some fucking truck drivers and pressmen that make a hundred grand a year," said courthouse reporter Alex Michelini. "Why would I walk out? For what? To put a bullet in the head of this newspaper? Whatever happened to loyalty?"

For the first time in New York history, the Tribune Company published a daily newspaper solely with managers and replacement workers. There was just one problem: they couldn't get the paper to the newsstands. A union-backed campaign of violence and intimidation had scared off all but a handful of dealers, many of them struggling immigrants who made little money on the 35-cent paper.

A Bronx bodega was firebombed hours after a man demanded that it stop carrying the *News*. Three men in ski masks went to a Brooklyn store and warned the proprietor not to sell the *News*; hours later some of the store's windows were broken.

"I can't take the paper or they will kill me," said Ali Nejeli, a Brooklyn newsstand dealer. Carlos Chacon, a replacement driver in New Jersey, was dragged from his truck by twelve to fifteen men with baseball bats, beaten and stabbed in the abdomen and buttocks. Two striking union members were later charged with armed robbery and aggravated assault. A *News* supervisor's car was blown up.

With the distribution channels choked off, major advertisers like Macy's and Alexander's quickly deserted the paper. Windows were repeatedly smashed at stores owned by Hillside Bedding, one of the few advertisers to stick with the *News*. The *News* hired homeless men to hawk the tabloid on street corners, but circulation sank to 300,000.

The unions acted as if they were determined to confirm the old stereotypes of union members as heavy-handed thugs. Some reporters were embarrassed to be on strike with people who fought their battles with knives and pipe bombs, and prosecutors would later charge that the drivers' union was controlled by Mafia families. Although there were more than 1,300 reported incidents of vandalism—including 200 vehicles damaged, 80 people hospitalized and 200 arrests—police officials insisted they could find no evidence of an organized conspiracy.

The *News*, of course, gave the story the full crime-wave treatment: "News Under Siege"; "They Live in Fear of Violence"; "News Dealer Firebombed"; "It's Organized Terror: Hoge." Union leaders harrumphed about the violence but never denounced it. Striking columnist Juan Gonzalez said he was "amazed there was so little violence, given how this company treated its employees. They had an army of goons out there." Union leaders were so consumed by their hatred of *News* management that they began to talk about the prospect of killing the paper as a great victory.

Finally, in January 1991, the Tribune Company announced that it would close the *News* if no buyer emerged. Several potential bidders dropped out until just one suitor remained: Robert Maxwell.

The British media mogul was hailed as a savior as he sailed into town to talk to the paper's unions. The *Times* gushed over Maxwell, saying he had reached Trump-like proportions: "His bustling, baroque persona . . . promises to fill the void left by the nearly departed likes of Donald J. Trump, Edward I. Koch and George Steinbrenner." Allegations of financial chicanery by Maxwell were kissed off in a couple of paragraphs.

Maxwell's dark side was no secret. A British government agency in 1971 had pronounced him unfit "to exercise proper stewardship" of a public company, saying he had falsified records and hidden information from investors. His communications empire was heavily weighted with debt. Since buying the *Daily Mirror* and other London tabloids in the early '80s, he had plastered them with his picture and tales of his exploits. Maxwell also had a nasty habit of using libel suits to silence his critics.

But the New York press chose to celebrate Cap'n Bob as a charming rogue. In a week of negotiations, Maxwell won the sweeping union concessions that the Tribune Company had been demanding for fourteen months. The unions agreed to eliminate 800 of their 2,300 jobs, and the Tribune Company paid Maxwell $60 million to assume the paper's liabilities. "ROLL 'EM," the banner headline said on March 22, 1991. Maxwell had saved the *News* from oblivion.

Or so it seemed. The wounds of the five-month walkout were not so easily healed. Most of the big-name stars had quit during the strike. Jack Newfield and Mike McAlary defected to the *Post,* Liz Smith and Gail Collins to *Newsday.*

Still, the *News* began to rebuild. Major advertisers returned. Readers were lured with a "Lucky Bucks" game, and circulation rose to 800,000. And then, suddenly, on November 5, Robert Maxwell was dead. He had disappeared from his yacht off the Canary Islands and was found floating in the Atlantic Ocean. Insurance investigators later concluded that the sixty-eight-year-old tycoon probably committed suicide.

The Maxwell saga quickly turned into an awful parody of a tabloid melodrama. Within weeks the *News* would declare its onetime savior

"CAPTAIN CROOK." Investigators charged that Maxwell had plundered more than $620 million in pension funds from his Mirror Group newspapers. In the final weeks of his life, Maxwell had been grabbing cash from his public companies and using it to prop up the *Daily News* and his other privately held firms. The press had embarrassed itself on the tycoon beat once again, just as it had in glorifying Donald Trump. Only *The Wall Street Journal* and *Business Week* had examined Maxwell's financial woes in the weeks before his death.

The *News*'s days seemed numbered as the paper filed for Chapter 11 bankruptcy protection. But the stubborn tabloid clung to life, and in early 1993 developer Mortimer Zuckerman, the owner of *U.S. News & World Report*, brought it out of bankruptcy. But Zuckerman's rescue came at a price: He broke the Newspaper Guild, refusing to honor its seniority rules and firing a third of its members. He wanted to bring in his own people to replace those he considered deadwood. "There was no consideration for the people who've been holding this paper together with masking tape for a year and a half," said reporter Susan Milligan. The Guild vowed to organize a boycott against the *News*, but the battle was lost. Zuckerman had cut deals with the powerful pressmen and drivers. Mere reporters no longer had the power to shut down the paper.

The *Daily News* and *New York Post* were engaged in a deadly dance, each reviving only when the other seemed to be dying. Two weeks after Mort Zuckerman bought the *News*, the *Post* was plunged into chaos. Peter Kalikow was bankrupt, the paper was losing $350,000 a week and the banks had cut off Kalikow's credit. No reputable newspaperman wanted to buy the struggling tabloid. Kalikow again threatened to close the *Post*, and the unions agreed to yet another emergency pay cut.

The tragicomic soap opera that followed made clear that a newspaper is more than just a collection of computers and printing presses and real estate. It also has a soul. That doesn't generally count for much in the corporate world, where debt must be serviced and profit margins maintained. But the *Post*'s scruffy rebels were determined to prove that they had as much claim to the 192-year-old newspaper as whatever wealthy businessman happened to be in charge at the moment. They staged a workers' revolt whose very audacity would reverberate through the more refined precincts of the media world.

After Kalikow agreed to sell the *Post* to Steven Hoffenberg, a shadowy Manhattan financier and bill collector, it was revealed that federal authorities were investigating Hoffenberg for securities fraud and that several states had accused his firm of improper conduct. Hoffenberg denied any wrongdoing. When pressed by a *New York Times* reporter, he bristled at the questions and said there would be no such "negative" reporting in the *New York Post.*

Many *Post* staffers were convinced that "Repo Man," as they dubbed Hoffenberg, wanted to milk the paper for its assets. The *Post's* three top editors defected to the *Daily News,* along with columnist Mike McAlary ("I cover crooks, I don't work for them," McAlary sniffed, conveniently forgetting that weeks earlier he had called Zuckerman a "cheap dictator" and a "power-mad Stalin wanna be"). Hoffenberg denounced Zuckerman as a "punk," "coward," "chicken," "vampire" and "body snatcher." He didn't stop there; McAlary testified in a lawsuit that Hoffenberg was "fixated with gays" and had ordered up a baseless front-page story charging that Zuckerman was gay. Hoffenberg called the charge "total garbage." The financier did make one smart move, installing longtime *Post* columnist Pete Hamill as editor. But Hoffenberg's assets were soon frozen in a Securities and Exchange Commission lawsuit and his company went bankrupt.

Thus did the paper fall into the hands of Abe Hirschfeld, a parking-garage magnate whose main interest was in acquiring the *Post's* South Street building. The staff was stunned. Hirschfeld was an eccentric millionaire who had repeatedly run for public office in New York and Florida, his only success a two-year term on the Miami Beach city commission. He had vividly expressed his attitude toward journalists in 1990 by spitting on Bonnie Weston, a *Miami Herald* reporter who had been writing about fire-code violations at Hirschfeld's beachfront hotel.

The Polish-born tycoon wasted no time living up to his reputation for lunacy. He asked the editors to publish his wife's poetry and an op-ed piece by his chauffeur. He declared that the *Post* would become an international spokesman for Israel. He put the paper in bankruptcy, fired Pete Hamill and dismissed seventy-two other staffers, including such top reporters as Jack Newfield. He said he would replace Hamill with Wilbert Tatum, publisher of the *Amsterdam News,* a black newspaper frequently accused of running anti-Semitic articles. During a news conference announcing Tatum's appointment, *Post* staffers shouted "You're a dog!" and "You're an animal!" at Hirschfeld.

Steve Cuozzo, the executive editor, and Marc Kalech, the managing editor, realized the *Post* was doomed if the erratic owner completed his purchase. They refused to put out the paper that day as a show of strength. The following day, they made journalistic history.

On March 16, 1993, the front page of the *New York Post* depicted its founder, Alexander Hamilton, shedding a single tear. Inside, story after story assailed Hirschfeld as a "nut," "madman," "loon," "liar" and "idiot." A cartoon showed Hirschfeld in a straitjacket. There was even a photo of Hirschfeld spitting on Bonnie Weston, with the caption: "Her job was to take a gob from angry slob." The inmates had taken over the asylum.

I had snuck into the newsroom that morning when the coup reached its climax. Pete Hamill arrived in a trench coat, work shirt, jeans and boots and triumphantly lit a cigarette. While the troops cheered and exchanged high fives, Hamill, a high school dropout and former sheet-metal worker, reclaimed his old office and hung up a picture of the 1955 Brooklyn Dodgers. He was "Yeltsin standing on a typewriter," as New-field put it, refusing to submit to Hirschfeld's illegitimate rule. It was a surreal moment, an act of defiance that briefly seemed to recapture the old butt-kicking spirit of newspapers before they became part of the political elite.

Hirschfeld continued his bizarre behavior, telling interviewers how much he liked the edition attacking him and how he had actually planned it as a publicity stunt. On CNN's "Reliable Sources," Hirschfeld ranted and rambled, at one point telling Deborah Orin, the *Post*'s Washington bureau chief, to "shut up," saying that if it wasn't for him she'd be on welfare. As Hamill put it, the man was not playing with a full plate of tacos.

The *Post* refuseniks also published plenty of vitriol directed at Tatum, who was denounced as "slime" and "a force for evil." Some of this was pretty mean-spirited, particularly from a virtually all-white newsroom that had long been accused of insensitive coverage of minorities. But the battle lines had been drawn, and the *Post* was determined to appeal to its heavily Jewish readership, which would not countenance an editor whose newspaper had supported Tawana Brawley.

A federal bankruptcy judge briefly restored Hamill to power as the *Post* was running out of cash. But there was an unlikely hero waiting in the wings: Rupert Murdoch, who had been forced to sell the tabloid five years earlier. Key members of Congress agreed to support a waiver of the anti-monopoly rule that had forced Murdoch to give up the *Post*. The paper's staff, and much of the media, hailed him as a savior. This was an exquisite irony, for it was Murdoch who had debased the paper during his tenure with such headlines as "HEADLESS BODY IN TOPLESS BAR" and "TEEN GULPS GAS, EXPLODES." Murdoch had wielded the tabloid like a latter-day William Randolph Hearst, turning it into a virtual house organ for such allies as Ed Koch and Ronald Reagan and bludgeoning adversaries like Ted Kennedy. And he was no friend of labor, having broken the Fleet Street press unions after buying the *Times* of London in the 1980s.

But Rupert Murdoch now had an aura of respectability, for while his London tabloids had given the world bare-breasted women, his global communications empire also included Fox television and Twentieth Century Fox and *TV Guide* and HarperCollins publishing. The press hailed Murdoch, like Robert Maxwell before him, as a giant. Murdoch told friends he missed the excitement of owning a New York newspaper.

Hirschfeld agreed to sell Murdoch the paper after the bankruptcy judge stripped him of operational control. The new owner immediately dismissed Hamill and replaced him with British journalist Ken Chandler, executive producer of "A Current Affair," Murdoch's tabloid TV show. The first banner headline under Chandler was "AMY'S NUDE ROMPS IN JAIL," a breathless update on the saga of Amy Fisher, the Long Island teenager convicted in the shooting of her lover's wife. Chandler inherited a badly depleted staff and a paper whose circulation had dropped from 900,000 in the '70s to just 400,000. (Another Murdoch man from Britain, Martin Dunn, soon became editor of the *Daily News*.)

The *Post*'s battered staff saw a darker side of Murdoch once he got his federal waiver. He demanded the right to fire Newspaper Guild members at will and refused to pay more than a few weeks' severance, even to reporters who had worked for the *Post* for more than forty years. Isolated and powerless, the Guild took the suicidal step of going on strike in September. Many members were appalled at the union's stupidity. "They had to drag me kicking and screaming from the building," said reporter Colin Miner.

Murdoch shut the *Post* and vowed to abandon his purchase. "SMELL OF DEATH," declared *New York Newsday*, which itself was losing $14 million a year and would succumb in the summer of 1995. The craft union members quickly caved in, crossing the Guild's picket line amid angry taunts from their colleagues. "Rupert Murdoch wants to crush us," said Tom Bonfiglio, a city desk assistant. "It ain't money; he wants to crush us." The destruction was soon complete. When Murdoch reopened the *Post* on September 30, the Guild was shattered, just as it had been at the *Daily News* nine months earlier. Its humiliated members were forced to reapply for their jobs, and only 35 of the 270 strikers were rehired, including just a half dozen reporters. Alexander Hamilton's paper was again back from the graveyard, but without most of those who had kept it alive. This time, no one was cheering.

In an era when corporate owners routinely walk away from money-losing properties, the *New York Post* limped sadly on, a symbol of one man's willingness to subsidize a failing newspaper once he had obliterated its staff. Whether such a fate is preferable to death with dignity is not an academic question for those of us who have been through such a wrenching experience.

Let me state my bias up front: I thought *The Washington Star* was a great newspaper. I worked there for the last three years of its distinguished, 128-year life. Only a decade later it seems a throwback to a much earlier era, when afternoon papers were a vital urban presence. You would cover a morning hearing on the Hill and run to a pay phone and dictate your story from scribbled notes, and when the late edition hit the street you had a sense of actually having broken news. You would get a great adrenaline rush by beating the journalistic behemoth across town, *The Washington Post*, while getting scooped gave you a sinking feeling in the pit of your stomach. The daily combat kept both papers on their toes.

For more than a century, the *Star* was the dominant newspaper in the nation's capital. Abraham Lincoln is said to have delivered a copy of his first inaugural address to the *Star*'s editor right after he finished the speech. It covered world wars, presidential campaigns and the Redskins with considerable élan. But in the '60s and '70s the *Star* got caught in the familiar downward spiral of once-great P.M. papers, and in 1981, after a last exclusive interview with Ronald Reagan, it died.

Economic forces killed the *Star*, just as they killed the *Arkansas Gazette*, but part of me believes it could have been saved. It was backed by the resources of one of the world's great publishing conglomerates, Time Incorporated, but Time succeeded only in driving the final nails into the *Star*'s coffin.

Like the *Herald Tribune*'s, the *Star*'s journalistic heyday came when it was nearly broke. In the mid-'70s, Texas financier Joe Allbritton it was nearly broke. In the mid-'70s, Texas financier Joe Allbritton bought the paper from its longtime family owners and started cutting costs to the bone. He put the staff on a four-day work week. The unions accepted a wage freeze. Two hundred jobs were sliced from the payroll.

But Allbritton also brought in Jim Bellows, who had worked his mumbling magic at the *Herald Trib* a decade earlier. And Bellows helped give the struggling *Star* a magazine-style vitality that soon made it the talk of the town.

Bright writing was showcased throughout the paper. Each day there would be a rambling feature story on page one and a Q&A interview with some important personage. Bellows recruited Diana McLellan, a delightful British journalist, to write "The Ear," a gossip column that skewered Washington's pretentious ruling class. Her favorite targets were the big shots at the "Other Paper," as McLellan referred to the *Post.* Everyone read "The Ear" for the latest gibe at the Fun Couple, Ben Bradlee and Sally Quinn.

The *Star* was on everyone's list of the top-ten American papers. Jack Germond and Jules Witcover were one of the premier reporting teams in the political world. Mary McGrory, the elegant voice of liberalism, had been a Washington institution for decades. Jeremiah O'Leary, who started as a copy boy in 1937, was stationed at the White House, along with Fred Barnes, who would later gain notoriety along with Germond as a verbal brawler on the "McLaughlin Group." The *Star* had one of the nation's best Supreme Court reporters (Lyle Denniston), one of the best sports columnists (Morris Siegel), one of the best book reviewers (Jonathan Yardley), one of the best science writers (Cristine Russell), one of the best cartoonists (Pat Oliphant). The newsroom was sprinkled with little-known workhorses who would become prominent network correspondents, from NBC's Lisa Myers to ABC's Sheilah Kast and Steve Aug.

With no national or international pretensions, the *Star* was a hometown paper with a lean and hungry Metro staff. Maureen Dowd, who would become *The New York Times'* most celebrated feature writer, covered Montgomery County, Maryland. Robert Pear, now the *Times'* domestic policy whiz, covered D.C. politics. Jane Mayer, later a page-one star at *The Wall Street Journal,* covered Arlington, Virginia. Mike Isikoff, now a top investigative reporter at *The Washington Post,* covered Annapolis and Richmond.

The setting was hardly glamorous. We worked in a dingy building sandwiched between the Southeast-Southwest Freeway and a public housing project, miles from the trendy downtown eateries. We used a cranky computer system called Logicon that had a vicious habit of crashing on deadline. We were always outmanned by the *Post,* always having a hard time getting calls returned, always worried about the latest rumor of impending doom.

But we fancied ourselves a sort of ragtag M*A*S*H unit, ambushing the enemy with sweat and stealth and then swinging by the local watering hole, Jenkins Hill, for a few after-deadline brews. The third-floor newsroom was filled with old-time characters, from three-martini editors to society matrons to Charlie McAleer, a rotund Irishman who faithfully monitored the police radio. In the late evenings a bottle of wine might emerge from someone's bottom drawer. Young dictationists (whose number once included Carl Bernstein) translated the deadline prose of grizzled veterans and volunteered when extra bodies were needed on a murder story. Office romances, licit and illicit, were always flourishing. One scribe used to send poetry to his beloved on the computer system, unaware that his colleagues were eagerly reading each sonnet.

The *Star* had a knack for sniffing out scoops, from Billy Carter's Libyan dealings to Marion Barry's cut-rate mortgage from a local bank that employed his wife. On slow days a modest tale or two could always be hyped onto the front page. Anything that happened before 1:15 P.M., from new unemployment figures to a minor Iran-Iraq skirmish, was a potential banner for the night final.

In 1978 Joe Allbritton was forced to sell the *Star* in order to hang on to his more lucrative property, the local ABC affiliate. He found the ultimate deep-pockets buyer—Time Inc. Time bought the paper for $20 million, in part to acquire a prestigious perch in the capital to compete with *Newsweek,* owned by the Washington Post Company. The *Star*'s circulation was only 329,000, compared to 562,000 for the *Post.* But Time made a five-year commitment to reviving the paper.

Installed as Bellows's replacement was Murray Gart, an imperious *Time* lieutenant with a military style of command. Gart, who had virtually no newspaper experience, was ferried to work each morning by chauffeured limousine. He traveled around the globe, interviewing world leaders for articles that drew snickers in the newsroom. He also liked to hire attractive young women he met on the party circuit, who were dubbed "Murray's Angels."

Gart quickly drained the paper of color. Long features were out, interpretive writing was discouraged and investigative pieces were toned down or killed. Short, tersely written stories about press conferences and government reports became the order of the day. "Time wanted to make it stodgy, respectable," says Jack Germond. "Their idea was to make it a duller *Post*. They started running texts of speeches. They were very establishment-oriented."

This was a fatal formula, for there was no way the understaffed *Star* could match the *Post*'s formidable newsgathering resources. Jim Bellows's paper had been uneven but idiosyncratic; there was no compelling reason to buy the new, blander *Star*. A graphic artist from *The New York Times* gave the paper a clean, award winning redesign, with a front-page news digest three years before the launch of *USA Today*. But the paper fumbled away its basic franchise of politics and local news.

Gart tried to position the *Star* as an "unbiased" alternative to the more liberal *Post*, but instead gave the paper a conservative tilt that made much of the staff uncomfortable. Stories that reflected badly on Jimmy Carter were relentlessly trumpeted, no matter how incremental. The glowing coverage lavished on Ronald Reagan proved an embarrassing contrast.

"They thought they were going to acquire a status with a Republican administration in Washington that Time had always yearned for," says Eileen Shanahan, a former assistant managing editor. "They thought the Reagan administration would just swoon into their arms. We saw Murray passionately panting after top officials. The whole style of advocacy journalism drove us crazy. I really think there was a social-climbing motive in a lot of that. There was a lot of whoring for advertisers. It made us all feel lousy."

Time used the *Star* for shameless self-promotion. Lavish coverage was given to the launch of Time's *Discover* magazine, the retirement of Time chairman Andrew Heiskell and the appointment of editor-in-chief Hedley Donovan ("a strapping man with piercing blue eyes") as an aide to President Carter.

One embarrassing about-face took place when Carter named Thomas Watson ambassador to the Soviet Union. A *Star* editorial belittled the appointment, noting that Watson had no diplomatic experience and didn't even speak Russian. But after belatedly discovering that Watson served on Time's board of directors, the editorial page suddenly paid homage to the man's many talents.

Perhaps the biggest fiasco was a decision to split the Metro section into five zoned editions. There was no research to support this high-stakes gamble, just a memo written one rainy weekend by Metro editor Dennis Stern. "What did I know?" Stern says. "My thought was that Time Inc. would have consulted some other papers that had done it or brought in an expert or something. It was hard to take good people and get them real excited about covering minutiae in Fairfax County."

The new creations—the *District Star, Montgomery Star, Prince George's Star, Fairfax Star* and *Arlington/Alexandria Star*—were heavily promoted, and reporters were exiled to expensive new suburban offices. But the sections were a consumer fraud. The *Star*'s local staff was so thin that the coverage was just as haphazard as it had been before. The zoned editions wound up being interchangeable, with Maryland news in the Virginia sections and vice versa.

Time also had an aversion to investigative reporting, at least when the target wasn't the Carter administration. Consumer columnist Goody Solomon was assigned to do a five-part series on the pros and cons of supermarket coupons. Her first piece happened to run while the ad department was pushing a promotion called "Star Coupon Saving Days." Gart killed the rest of the series, dropped Solomon's column and banned her from the paper.

I was involved in an incident that brought the *Star* a sizable dose of bad publicity. Dennis Stern had asked me to look into housing discrimination in the Washington area. I began checking out apartments advertised in the classifieds hours after Hazel Robinson, a black reporter, made the same inquiries. We used our real names, said we were writers and listed the same income. In several instances, I was offered apartments in nice, middle-class buildings right after Robinson was flatly told there were no vacancies.

A wealth of other evidence emerged from court records, government agencies and interviews with victims. A black physician said he was told by a realty agent that "we don't show to blacks" in certain areas. A black couple was blocked from bidding on a home in a lily-white Maryland town (they later bought another house and were visited by President Reagan after someone burned a cross on their lawn). HUD officials acknowledged that federal housing laws were so weak there was little they could do for most victims.

Every editor at the *Star* loved the series—except Gart. He asked other top editors to kill the series and when they refused, he killed it himself, allowing only small chunks into the paper. There was talk that some real estate firms had threatened to pull their advertising. It's just as likely that Gart didn't think discrimination was a big deal and didn't see it as a newspaper's role to challenge the real estate establishment on such a sensitive subject. "The effect on newsroom morale was catastrophic," Gregg Easterbrook wrote in *The Washington Monthly*. He added that "if the *Star* dies, the county coroner will rule it a suicide. . . . Time Inc. has taken the *Star*'s fine collection of able writers and editors and essentially switched them off."

The publisher, George Hoyt, had never worked for a big-city paper. The circulation department under Hoyt was a joke. Seventy thousand people were dropping the *Star* each year because their papers came late or not at all. Even senior *Star* editors had trouble getting home delivery. It hardly mattered what was on the front page if you couldn't get the paper to people's doorsteps.

The paper lurched from one strategy to the next. A morning edition was launched at considerable expense but never sold well. Management lost all interest in the zoned editions after the advertising hype faded. The *Star* kept missing its deadlines because of Logicon meltdowns.

The 1980 recession delivered another blow as hard-pressed merchants dropped the *Star*. Costs could not be slashed because the unions had already made major concessions after Time took over. By the spring of 1981, circulation had fallen to six thousand less than when Time bought the paper. Star officials asked *The Washington Post* for a JOA, but Katharine Graham turned them down.

By now the Time executives who arranged the *Star*'s purchase had retired, and their successors did not have the same emotional attachment to a newspaper that had run up $85 million in losses in only three years. The board of directors voted to pull the plug.

Few employees were notified before the news went out on the wire. We learned our paper was dying when we came to work and were met by a bevy of television reporters demanding our reaction. It was like being kicked in the abdomen.

The usual frantic efforts to find a buyer failed. Many of the fourteen hundred employees who lost their jobs blamed Time for mismanaging the paper and abandoning its five-year commitment. As *The Washington Star* published its last edition on August 7, 1981, some staffers were wearing new T-shirts made for the occasion. "TIME has run out on the *Star*," they said.

15

Pink Flamingo Journalism

Once, not so many years ago, editors edited from the gut. They had an instinctive sense of what people might find important or interesting or titillating. Today's editors have become focus-group groupies, assembling ordinary folks behind one-way mirrors to find out what is wrong with the product. The very notion that newspapers must study their readers' habits, as if they were some exotic species, is a stunning sign of desperation, of the missing synapse that once provided the spark for daily journalism.

Newspaper people have finally gotten it through their heads that major parts of their audience, particularly younger folks, are tuning out, and they are determined to cultivate a new generation of customers. The problem is that the cure may be worse than the disease.

Everyone wants to be "reader-friendly," the buzzword of the '90s. Hard news is out; relevance is in. Hundreds of papers have undergone virtually identical redesigns, with colorful indexes and big color pictures and colorful little boxes above the logo touting fun stories inside.

"Let's Go Barefoot!" says the "skybox" atop *The Charlotte Observer* logo. "Jammin' Jamaica—It's Reggae Time," says *The Miami Herald*'s skybox. "A Star Trek Quiz," says *The Hartford Courant*'s box. "Baby Boomers Hit Midlife Crisis," says *The Arizona Republic*'s box. There are car columns, health columns, gossip columns, advice columns, lawyers' columns, computer columns, photography columns, gardening columns, men's columns, women's columns, fishing columns, finance columns. There are parenting tips, survival tips, pet tips, dining tips, shopping tips, travel tips. There are sections called Rumpus, You, Sunday Brunch, Almost the Weekend, High Style, Home, View, Scene, Tempo, KidNews, WomenWise, Living, Life, Yo, and Yo! Info!

There's nothing wrong with most of these features; newspapers are meant to be smorgasbords, and some people will always buy them for the movie reviews or the grocery coupons. Nor is there any harm in loosening our ties and shedding some of our stuffiness. But the cumulative effect of these changes is to deemphasize news and replace it with a feel-good product that is more frivolous, less demanding, more like television. And television already does it better.

No editor will admit this, of course. They all proclaim their undying commitment to informing the public, even as some reduce national news to a half-page and foreign news to a few wire-service briefs. But too many newspapers have gone into the entertainment business, dismissing serious reporting as a luxury they can no longer afford. And a spate of big libel judgments, including a $34 million award against *The Philadelphia Inquirer* in 1990, has further chilled the atmosphere for hard-edged reporting.

As you travel around the country, it's hard to tell where you are by reading the local papers. They all carry the same wire stories, the same syndicated columns. When there were three or four newspapers serving each city, they had distinct personalities—eccentric or irascible, crusading or corny. Now most of them look like they're put out by the same faceless market-research folks. Once you get beyond the dozen or so top markets, there are hundreds of breathtakingly mediocre newspapers out there. The growth of chains has stamped hundreds of one-newspaper towns with a certain ethos—what Jack Germond calls "corporate journalism"—that is not quite awful, but awfully boring.

"So much of what we do in a newspaper just doesn't have any excitement," says Christian Anderson, associate publisher of *The Orange County Register.* "What is there in newspapers today that has the passion that MTV has? Nothing."

"It is cheaper than blue blazes," says Kurt Luedtke, former editor of the *Detroit Free Press,* "to go to the daily events that government stages for us. Send a kid to city hall and he will bring back two or three things that look and feel like news and we will put it in the paper. People have stopped reading the stuff. Look at the lead story on any local page and 92 percent of the time it's whatever the city council did today and it's duller than hell."

The new emphasis is on yuppie features—coping with divorce or bed-wetting, the lowdown on dating services, where to buy the best shiitake mushrooms—aimed at upscale baby boomers with lots of disposable income. Most editors are aging boomers, and many yuppies live in the suburbs, where newspapers have been redoubling their efforts. Left out of the equation are poor people, blue-collar workers, inner-city residents and minorities, but advertisers are less interested in them anyway.

"Look at the front page," Mike Barnicle says. "More often than not it's full of what I call made-up stories, ideas they cook up at these cluster-fuck meetings: 'Go out and do left-handed teenagers who are thinking of becoming gay.' They do trends, they don't do news. There's a burnt fuse, a lack of connection between people in the business and a large number of people who read newspapers."

Our efforts to repair this burnt fuse are rather awkward. We hire teenagers to review movies for other teens and pretend that we've plugged into the youth culture. We assign reporters to cover shopping malls. We ballyhoo the local football team on the front page. We serve up modest portions of News Lite, congratulating ourselves for not overtaxing the poor reader.

My own view is that newspaper salvation lies in the opposite direction, with detailed, compelling reports on controversial subjects that simply can't be found elsewhere. Of course we must learn to be more concise, more graphically appealing, more creative in packaging our writing for busy readers. And yes, we must conquer our addiction to insider news and wrestle more with the hobgoblins of everyday life. But those who insist on shrinking the news into ever-smaller digests will eventually digest themselves out of existence.

The problem with dumbing-down newspapers is that we're talking down to people, and they know it. Instead of capturing their attention the hard way—with well-written stories about schools and taxes and crime and culture and other things that matter in their lives—we take the easier (and cheaper) way out. We move away from our greatest strength—depth and texture—and assume that everyone in the video generation has an attention span of ninety seconds.

The newspaper of the 1970s—page after page of gray type and boring stories about bureaucracy—would seem unreadable today. But we haven't quite figured out what should replace it. We are changing, evolving, but not nearly fast enough.

. . .

Few marketing tricks are available today that were not trotted out 160 years ago by James Gordon Bennett, who launched the *New York Herald* in 1835. While respectable newspapers were selling for six cents, the *Herald* was one of the first penny papers. Newsboys hawked them on the streets. Bennett introduced lively prose and expanded Wall Street coverage. He played up lurid crimes. He opened a Washington bureau. He assembled a network of correspondents in European capitals and sent boats to retrieve their dispatches from incoming ships.

Bennett was no stickler for propriety. He accepted licentious ads for a "personals" column, serialized romances on the front page and sold ads for quack medicines. The penny-paper phenomenon spread to other cities, and technology gave the industry a major boost. By the 1840s the steam-driven press, ten times faster than the best hand press, dominated the American market. The telegraph became a journalistic fixture after the Baltimore *Sun* opened the first telegraph line between Washington and Baltimore.

Most papers (dating to Alexander Hamilton's *New York Post*) were either owned by politicians or openly partisan, a pattern that would change little for the next half-century. Horace Greeley, owner of the *New York Tribune*, was elected as a Whig member of Congress in 1848 and filed daily reports about waste and corruption in that institution.

Newspapers were never more vital than during the Civil War, when correspondents would race back with their bloody tales by train or horseback, sometimes providing firsthand accounts to President Lincoln. After the war, professional qualifications began to rise. Charles Dana, editor of the *New York Sun*, favored college graduates for his staff in the 1880s. Reporters began receiving individual acclaim. Nelly Bly went around the world in eighty days, a publicity coup for Joseph Pulitzer's *New York World*. Henry Morton Stanley found Dr. Livingstone in Africa. Jacob Riis chronicled the ills of New York's other half. Richard Harding Davis, who wrote for William Randolph Hearst's *New York Journal*, became the nation's most famous war correspondent. In 1897, Hearst (who would later run for president) incited passions with a hyped-up Davis dispatch claiming that Spanish police had strip-searched women on an American ship bound for Key West. But when the *World* exposed the story as overblown, Davis resigned.

The yellow streak permeating journalism left a vacuum for a more authoritative publication. When Adolph Ochs bought the failing *New York Times* in 1896, the paper's circulation was a mere 9,000, compared to 600,000 for the *World* and 430,000 for the *Journal*. The *Times* huffed about journalistic standards and promoted itself as a newspaper that "does not soil the breakfast cloth." It offered complete financial coverage, bought better newsprint and started a Saturday book review and illustrated Sunday supplement. But the breakthrough came from a marketing maneuver: Ochs lowered the price from 3 cents to a penny. Circulation quickly rose to 75,000 and by 1920 it had reached 343,000.

Pulitzer's paper crusaded against such corporate giants as Standard Oil and the New York Central Railroad and exposed squalid conditions at Ellis Island. As Lincoln Steffens, Ida Tarbell and others became known as muckrakers, self-promotion became vital, even at the august *Times*. When the first trans-Atlantic press cable was sent to the *Times* in 1907, the paper ran the Western Union message on page one with the accompanying headline: "Marconi Congratulates The New York Times."

In what would seem an outrageous display of checkbook journalism today, the *Times* paid Admiral Robert Peary $4,000 for exclusive rights to the tale of his 1909 expedition to the North Pole. It did the same thing in 1927, signing Charles Lindbergh to a $5,000 contract (he eventually got $60,000) for the story of his pioneering flight to Paris.

The rise of pundits like Walter Lippmann, who consorted with presidents, gave the profession a sheen of respectability, even as the Depression cut staffs to the bone and the advent of radio news eliminated the market for "extras." But the rise of Hitler shook the industry out of its lethargy. Some World War II correspondents, like Ernie Pyle, were more famous than the units they covered. While many newspapers crammed their pages with advertising during the wartime boom, the *Times* eschewed short-term profits and maintained the scope of its coverage. The resulting benefits suggest a lesson that today's struggling publishers would do well to remember.

The press's role as outside critic blossomed during the civil rights strife of the early '60s and achieved its full flowering during the Vietnam War. Editorial support for the war crumbled under the weight of dispatches from correspondents like David Halberstam, Neil Sheehan, and Peter Arnett. Still, Vietnam was the first American conflict in which newspapers were no longer the principal means of communication. Television reporting came of age in the steamy jungles of that senseless war, achieving a dominance that would haunt the print side of the business for the next thirty years.

The '60s were also a time when writers would begin their flirtation with the New Journalism, an impressionistic art form that seemed particularly suited to the drug-soaked cultural upheaval across the land. It was a welcome transformation, for there was a sense that the old ways of defining news had failed to capture the anger and alienation in society, the changes in people's lives.

If Watergate proved the high-water mark of newspaper influence, it was also the event that permanently put the press into the scandal business. Investigative reporting became a fixture of daily journalism in the '70s, and even small papers started kicking over rocks in their municipal backyards. New disclosure laws made millions of public documents available. Glorified by Hollywood, the press embarked on a new era of self-righteous muckraking.

But the product still looked awful—ink-smudged sheets with muddy pictures and dreary layouts. On the eve of a communications revolution, the press remained wedded to backward technology. And it would stay that way until Al Neuharth created a national newspaper in 1982.

USA Today was, by design, a whole different approach to journalism. How the paper looked—its layout, its color photos, its eye-catching graphics, its little boxes filled with factoids—was as important as what it said. Articles would be light and tight and bright, attuned to the lightning pace of the computer age.

But a funny thing happened on the way to the McPapering of America: *USA Today* got more serious. In the early '90s it rediscovered hard news. Stories grew a bit longer as the paper started providing reasonably good coverage of Washington, politics, the economy, health care and other nuts-and-bolts issues.

"In the beginning we weren't sure if we could sell newspapers if we did the same stories everyone else did," says Peter Prichard, the paper's editor from 1989 to 1995. "We tried real hard—probably too hard —to be different. If you look at our front pages the last couple of years, it's almost all hard news. We've discovered what journalists have always known, that hard news sells newspapers. But I don't think we've changed our emphasis on putting the reader first, on not being boring."

Some executives attribute the new tone to Neuharth's 1989 retirement. "Those stories that used to be stripped across the top of the front page—'Women Have More Sex in Elevators'—they were the staples of morning disc jockeys, but they played to the belief that *USA Today* was not a serious newspaper," says Tom McNamara, the managing editor for news.

Staffers welcomed the new emphasis on news. The front page, once filled with such headlines as "Men and Women Are Different" and "We Still Believe in American Dream," now features stories on civil rights, Russian hunger and Middle East peace talks. The post-Neuharth paper has tackled such potentially dull subjects as the health of life insurance companies. And where Neuharth espoused the Journalism of Hope—symbolized by his famous plane-crash headline, "Miracle: 327 Survive, 55 Die"—*USA Today* now explores such sobering topics as toxic dumping in minority communities. Even Neuharth says the paper has "matured."

USA Today blankets major news events, but slices the coverage into digestible chunks—seven pieces on the release of hostage Terry Anderson, eight on the William Kennedy Smith rape verdict. While the Gannett paper has yet to turn a profit—indeed, it lost more than $800 million in its first nine years—circulation has climbed almost to the two-million mark. Once a second paper for people on the run, it is now the primary information source for nearly 40 percent of its readers.

For all its improvements, *USA Today* has not quite sworn off the frothy stuff. On the day that Peter Prichard gave me a tour of his Arlington, Virginia, headquarters, we came upon an artist preparing a computer graph on "Percentage of Adults Who Say They Sleep Nude." The paper's limitations are also obvious. It has no foreign correspondents, and often runs only one or two foreign stories a day. It makes little pretense of investigative reporting.

USA Today remains a paper that runs a banner headline when Julia Roberts calls off her marriage to Kiefer Sutherland. That can offer seven front-page sentences on a coup in Haiti and pretend it is informing its readers. That panders to teenagers with a cover story on "Girls Who Go Gung-Ho After Guys." That gives page-one play to polls announcing that 69 percent of respondents pee in the shower, or that 7 percent believe that Elvis could still be alive. That puts out bonus sections like Wheels that are thinly disguised advertising vehicles. And that resurrects the Journalism of Hope at odd moments. In July 1993, on the morning after the worst flooding in American history left 250,000 people in Des Moines without running water, the banner headline was "HOPE: RAINS EASE, HEAT EBBS." This ran just below a box touting a new, improved weather page.

Still, even the most curmudgeonly critic would concede that *USA*

Today changed the look of an entire industry. Once it appeared on the newsstands, other papers seemed hopelessly gray by comparison. By the late '80s hundreds of newspapers had switched to color presses. Everyone started using more graphics. A wave of spacious redesigns replaced the cluttered layouts of the past. Indexes and news summaries became standard equipment. Sports sections expanded their coverage. A big weather map became de rigueur.

In redesigning the gas-guzzlers of the past, *USA Today* came up with a sleek contraption that was built for speed and little else. To compress reams of copy into bite-size portions requires a top-heavy bureaucracy in which a single story is often rewritten by two or three editors. For reporters this can be an exercise in frustration, with key facts evaporating in the process. "It changes the whole corporate culture of the newsroom because the reporter is no longer the star, it's the editor," says Philip Meyer, who teaches journalism at the University of North Carolina. "Your words have to be pushed and pummeled and pounded to fit the format."

USA Today reporter Dennis Cauchon complains that "your story is never free from assault. If you strip away the color, the graphics, it reads a lot like the AP. What's lost is style, personality, voice and flavor."

One staffer grumbled that "the place is still peopled with a lot of jerks, a lot of castoffs from mediocre newspapers who don't know what the fuck they're doing." At the same time, this person says, "Their goal is to be a newsmagazine each day. They're willing to spend money like crazy to be taken seriously on a story."

Bill Kovach, one of *USA Today*'s earliest critics, says that "it's become a much more substantial newspaper just at the time all the apes are aping the thing that didn't work."

Kovach has some firsthand experience on the subject. After he became editor of the Atlanta *Journal* and *Constitution* in 1986, he clashed repeatedly with the management of Cox Enterprises. "They would hold up *USA Today* and say, 'This is the kind of newspaper we believe is the newspaper of the future. Why can't you produce this kind of newspaper?' " Kovach recalls.

Kovach shook up the place, beefing up suburban coverage and sending a reporter to Africa to write about famine. He angered the local business establishment with a Pulitzer Prize–winning series on how Atlanta banks were refusing to make loans in black neighborhoods. "The publisher was interested in stories about where women could go to get their fingernails fixed if they broke a nail just before a dinner party," Kovach says. "That was not what I thought I should concern myself with. Serious journalism creates problems. If you write about the banks, the bankers get upset. If you help consumers find furniture at a better price, it upsets the retailers who advertise in the paper. If you send a reporter to the Sudan or Ethiopia, it costs a little money."

Publisher Jay Smith sees it differently. Kovach, he says, was "a great newspaperman, but a miserable disappointment and a failure as an editor. Bill was enamored exclusively of the ten-part, two-hundred-inch-per-part investigative series. That's important, but it's one piece of the recipe. . . . The man once said to me, 'I don't want to put out a paper for fucking hillbillies.' Well, this is still the South."

Kovach resigned under pressure after twenty-three months, prompting more than a hundred reporters to protest with a full-page ad in the next day's paper. He was replaced by Ron Martin, the executive editor of *USA Today*.

The one-story building on South 3rd Street looks like a cut-rate motel. Outside is a pink newspaper box with that day's edition of the Boca Raton *News*, Knight-Ridder's answer to *USA Today*. The paper's logo is emblazoned with a pink flamingo.

For years, *The News* was an aging, black-and-white dowager, not terribly different from hundreds of other small-town papers. But in the fall of 1990, it was reborn as a pastel-colored smorgasbord of snippets, with editors slicing and dicing the news into tiny, tasty morsels.

There was a daily "Critter Watch." There was "Today's Hero," an upbeat little blurb meant to "tell a good story about someone each day." There was "Success," exploring "topics of style and manners that help you shine on the job." There was one absolute rule: No story would jump from one page to another.

And there were maps, endless maps, with little numbers keyed to the two- and three-paragraph briefs that passed for national and foreign news. A local map was dotted with "News Near You." A typical front page had three stories, a five-paragraph column by a local resident and a pink-edged guide to other features called "30 Seconds," which is about how long it took to read anything in the paper.

The News is the brainchild of Knight-Ridder's 25/43 Project, a $2-

million effort to appeal to that all-important age group. "A lot of what we do here I would not be proud of if I was still at *The Miami Herald,*" said Lou Heldman, who launched the project. "It's a different level of journalism. It does a good job of explaining the world for people who don't want the world in great depth."

The paper is packed with yuppie features on children's temper tantrums or working women too busy to sleep. A thirty-five-paragraph *New York Times* story on "chronic anger" was sliced to five paragraphs. It was news you could swallow with a single gulp.

"We must sell ourselves like Chevrolet and Ivory Soap," explained Wayne Ezell, *The News'* editor. During my visit, Ezell pointed to a *Miami Herald* story on a housing scandal. Pretty dull, he said. Then he turned to his own paper: " 'Champagne Prices Soon to Explode'—we're the only paper in America to do an eight-inch story on that. For baby boomers who go to a lot of champagne parties, that's more interesting than whatever Jack Kemp had to say today."

Ezell boasted of doing "a lot less government stuff." He spoke of more than thirty focus groups and the strategy sessions that decided on short stories. "Nobody with a reporter's mentality was allowed in these meetings," Ezell said.

Nobody with a reporter's mentality? What was most striking about this journalistic mélange is that Ezell and Heldman never talked about reporting. It was all cute columns and friendly features and Macintosh graphics. Very little of Knight-Ridder's money had been spent beefing up the staff of young reporters.

I asked Ezell if he would stop carrying foreign news if focus groups pronounced it boring. "That would tell me they're not reading it, so why should I have it? If readers said they wanted more comics and less foreign news, in a market-driven economy, I'm going to give them more comics and less foreign news."

Many press critics were not kind to the Boca Raton venture. "When *USA Today* first began publishing," Linda Ellerbee said, "I described it as a newspaper for people who find television too complex. In some ways, the Boca Raton *News* may be described as a newspaper for people who find *USA Today* too complex."

The News did come up with some interesting gimmicks. There was a daily guide to all the ads in the paper, which would certainly appeal to my mother, who's more interested in Macy's sales than the Middle East. There was a guide on how to read the stock tables. The "Your

Money" section, heavy on personal finance, was tailored to female readers.

But the paper's tone was so boosterish it made *USA Today* look dour. The opening of a new mall, Mizner Park, was greeted with a front-page column about the "tempting little designer shops" that ended: "Let's wish Mizner Park well." There were special sections produced by the advertising department, with such swooning cover stories as "Al Hendrickson's Toyota Wraps Up a Record-Setting Year." The real estate section was filled with similar heartwarming tales. "Camino Realty Celebrates Two Decades of Personable and Professional Service," one headline boasted. Stephanie Murphy, then the real estate editor, said: "I prefer to tell the good story, the happy story. I don't go looking for termites—that's not my role."

Each week, the beat reporters on South 3rd Street also had to turn out one profile, one "Today's Hero" and other vignettes. "I get very, very frustrated having to cover a city council meeting in eighteen lines," said reporter Anne Marie Reidy. "You can't give very much context or very many quotes. If I get in one quote from each side, that's really miraculous, even if forty people are standing up and screaming." Sportswriter Cedric Harmon was even harsher: "This sucks from a writer's standpoint. You don't go to school and bust your butt to write a five-inch story. It makes you feel like an idiot."

Wayne Ezell was undeterred. "Newspapers have failed to treat readers as customers and tailor the product to the interests of those customers," he said. "We are producing newspapers the same way we did twenty and thirty years ago, and our readers have run off and left us."

Despite some fine-tuning—silly features such as "Critter Watch" have been killed—Knight-Ridder officials are urging their other papers to learn from the Boca Raton experience. A bit of pink flamingo journalism is creeping into almost all newspapers, tipping the balance from hard news to light-as-a-feather stories, not always with happy results.

For twenty years, Malcolm Borg had always been a benevolent owner, like his father and grandfather before him.

Borg's newspaper, the Bergen *Record,* published in Hackensack, New Jersey, had a reputation as both a good place to work and as one of the best small papers in the country. It was a writer's paper, a place where young reporters could hone their skills before moving on to bigger markets. It was an aggressive paper whose influence was felt across the state. And it was a profitable paper that dominated its home turf, Bergen County, an affluent collection of bedroom communities across the Hudson River from Manhattan.

The Borg family took good care of its employees. Paternalism had replaced unionism ever since the pressmen struck in 1933 and were promptly fired. The paper paid for college courses, helped arrange home mortgage loans, awarded generous profit-sharing checks. *The Record* remained enormously successful until the early '90s, when Mac Borg lost his financial footing and his paper lost its journalistic soul.

Borg's grandfather, John Borg, a Wall Street financier, bought into the Bergen *Evening Record* in 1920. He passed on the paper to his son, Donald Borg, in 1949. Mac Borg, who started work on the obituary desk, took over as chief executive officer in 1971, a day shy of his thirty-third birthday.

Unlike his father, who was nervous about borrowing money, Borg quickly expanded the family company. Within a year he took on substantial debt to buy three CBS affiliate stations, a weekly paper and two shoppers. "I wasn't concerned," says Borg, puffing on a Winston. "For a paper this size, we were really unbeatable."

A blunt, sad-eyed man with thinning blond hair, Borg never held himself aloof from the community. He assumed the seats his father had held on the board of Bergen Pines County Hospital and as president of the Palisades Interstate Park Commission. He even kept *The Record*'s slogan, "Friend of the People It Serves."

But where Donald Borg had treated the agencies like sacred cows —*The Record* could publish nothing about them without his approval— Mac criticized the management at both institutions and encouraged his paper to investigate them. A decade later, when he was arrested for drunk driving, Borg called his editors to make sure they got the story first. The message was clear: There would be no sacred cows under Mac Borg, not even the owner himself.

I worked at *The Record* for a year and a half in the mid-'70s. It was my first job out of graduate school—I was hired for the princely sum of $10,000 a year—and I was quickly struck by the range of talent amassed by a 150,000-circulation paper in run-down Hackensack. *The Record* had a full-time investigative editor, top-notch bureaus in Trenton and Washington, a great sports staff and a daily "patch"—a boxed, front-page feature whose writing often rivaled that in *The Wall Street Journal*.

Like all raw recruits, I worked nights, covering school board meetings and zoning commissions. Bergen County has seventy towns—from the exclusive mansions of Saddle River, where Richard Nixon lived, in the north, to the gritty meadowlands of East Rutherford in the south, where Giants Stadium was built in the '70s—and *The Record* covered the hell out of each municipality. It seemed like hopelessly small potatoes to a twenty-one-year-old kid, but I came to understand that this was the paper's franchise, what made it indispensable to readers in Paramus and Teaneck and Fort Lee. While the Newark *Star-Ledger* was much larger, *The Record* was widely considered the best paper in the state, a niche that carried added influence because New Jersey had no major television station.

Mac Borg took a major gamble in 1979, spending $110 million—a third more than *The Record*'s annual revenues—to buy state-of-the-art color presses. *The Record* began using color in the summer of 1982, two months before the debut of *USA Today*.

The paper was burnishing its journalistic reputation as well. With Borg's approval, *The Record* published fraud allegations involving its biggest automobile advertiser, a local Chrysler dealer, who promptly pulled his $1.6 million a year in ads. *The Record* also took on *Penthouse* publisher Bob Guccione, who sued the paper for $50 million after it raised questions about his qualifications for an Atlantic City casino license. Guccione settled the suit with no payment by *The Record*.

"Over the years, Mac Borg, and his father before him, were willing to spend for quality," says Robert Comstock, who became the editor in 1977. "To take chances. To do hard-nosed investigative work and analytical reporting. We would spend months on a major series to examine some aspect of society or government. We also put a couple of people in jail. I'm not sure we could defend it on a cost-benefit basis, but we were very proud of it."

The Record's staff more than doubled during the boom years of the '80s. In 1985 Borg bought the *Woodbridge News Tribune,* a small daily south of Newark, for about $25 million, and soon doubled its staff. The horizon seemed limitless. *The Record* was putting out 360-page Sunday papers, the absolute limit of its printing capacity. "Newspapers got fat, dumb, lazy and happy in the '80s," Borg says. "I could have fired my whole advertising staff and saved all that money."

Like Donald Trump and other businessmen caught up in the merger mania, Borg got overly ambitious. In late 1988 he borrowed another $110 million and signed a contract to build a mammoth new printing plant in Rockaway Township, thirty-two miles to the west. He was also eyeing *The Central Jersey Home News,* whose purchase would give him control of a broad swath of northern New Jersey.

Borg, who had always served as de facto publisher, hired Byron Campbell as *The Record*'s first publisher and promised to stay out of his way. "Firin' Byron" replaced Borg's father-in-law as chief financial officer and dumped Bob Comstock as editor. Campbell's new editor was David Hall, who had run the *Denver Post* and *St. Paul Pioneer Press Dispatch.*

Hall quickly took *The Record* in a new direction. Stories got shorter. Page 2 was devoted to Liz Smith's column and a "People" column. Both "Dear Abby" and "Ann Landers" were added, along with Jeane Dixon's horoscope. Local coverage was deemphasized. The liberal editorial page was toned down and the editorials shortened. The investigative editor was moved to a desk job.

Hall, who describes himself as one of *USA Today*'s biggest fans, made no apologies for the paper's new philosophy. He had little use for the long series and magazine-style pieces that were once *The Record*'s signature.

"I don't think people are going to read a newspaper that is self-important and ponderous and dull and patronizing to them, however journalistically excellent it might be," he said. "I'm looking to put out a newspaper that's satisfying for readers rather than gratifying to the reporters. . . . If you want a newspaper that wins a lot of plaudits in the journalism community and wins a lot of prizes, that's one thing. That's not what I'm after."

But many reporters and editors saw Hall as an autocrat who had no understanding of *The Record*'s proud culture. "That son of a bitch is the worst newsman in the country," says Mark Howat, who retired as a senior editor in 1991 after more than forty years at the paper. "He stands against everything good journalists have ever stood for. The editorial page has no bite. They do no real investigative work anymore. The Lifestyle page is all wire. The food page is all wire. We use canned stuff from Hershey's and Chiquita Banana. It's just awful."

Hall gave weather stories so much prominence that reporters joked about winning a Pulitzer for weather coverage. One reporter says *The Record* has become "very much an editor-driven paper. Stories go in the blender and come out sounding the same. Color and graphics really drive news decisions. If you don't have a good picture, forget it, your story will get buried."

Hall's next move was to launch *Your Town Record,* a weekly tabloid that was little more than a vehicle for local advertising. The ten zoned editions featured weddings and engagements, a police blotter, school sports, school reunions and a "scholar of the week." The stories included such fare as "Marching Band Is Stepping Higher" and "Teen Is Driven to Succeed."

Perhaps nothing more clearly symbolized the new *Record* than the Saturday paper, which was launched in 1989. It was a curiously breezy publication, with no Metro section and no editorial page. A third of the front page was devoted to a colorful news index. No story could jump inside the paper. The Saturday Life section consisted of such fluffy features as "Out There Today," "At the Malls," "Smart Shopper" and "For Kids Only." Hall calls it "a throwaway newspaper," saying market research shows that readers "liked all the things that the capital-J journalists don't want to hear, all the shortness."

In the summer of 1990, Borg announced that he planned to buy *The Central Jersey Home News,* offering more than $30 million for the paper. But the recession had begun to take its toll on *The Record.* Advertising revenue plummeted more than 20 percent. Profit sharing was canceled for the first time since 1940.

The sagging finances weighed heavily on Borg. The fifty-three-year-old owner had always been a heavy drinker, and now he began going on binges for hours at a time. He would start with wine, then switch to vodka and stingers. He was losing control. In May 1991, Borg's secretary and his lawyer confronted him, saying he had to deal with his alcohol problem. "The pressures were driving me quietly insane," Borg says. "I knew I couldn't hack it anymore." Borg entered a thirty-day alcohol rehabilitation program.

As the financial situation grew worse, employees were furloughed for five days without pay. Salaries were frozen. College tuition aid was suspended. The news hole was cut. But it wasn't enough. Borg's longtime bankers came to his office and announced that they wouldn't lend him the money to buy the *Home News.*

That summer Mac Borg laid off 138 employees, more than 10 percent of *The Record*'s work force. It was the first time the paper had let anyone go since the Depression. As an added indignity, *The Record* published a story on the layoffs that read like a corporate press release. Hall told the reporter assigned to the story, Patrick McGeehan, that the piece could not include comments from anyone who was laid off. McGeehan responded by taking his byline off the story.

The reason for the layoffs was simple: The paper's net profits—which had dwindled to just over $4 million in 1991—were being eaten up by debt service on the new Rockaway plant. Some employees were bitter about losing their jobs to pay for a huge printing plant that, without the *Home News,* was far bigger than *The Record* needed.

"It was a gamble, but shit, when we made the decision in '88, who the hell expected the economy to go into a nosedive?" Borg says. "I'm not trying to be greedy, but I'm trying to push this franchise further and further out for eventual survival."

The Record's circulation, which had been 173,000 a year earlier, slipped to 158,000. Some of the pressmen tried to organize a union, although the campaign failed after a personal appeal from Borg.

The impact of the layoffs was quickly felt. "Everywhere I go, people want to know, what's happened to *The Record?*" Mark Howat says. "There's no news in it anymore. . . . Mac Borg has been drunk for the last eight years and doesn't know what's happened to his newspaper."

But Borg understood all too well. On the last day of 1991, Borg announced that Campbell had resigned as publisher and that he would again be running *The Record.* In a two-and-a-half-hour meeting with his staff, Borg assailed the Liz Smith column as "drivel," said the editorial page had drifted too far to the right and ridiculed *Your Town Record* for its birth announcements.

In April 1992, Borg dismissed David Hall. Hall says it was a mutual decision, and that he had already lined up a job as editor of the Cleveland *Plain Dealer.* It turned out that Borg detested much of what Hall had done to *The Record.* Hall had "no imagination," Borg says, and did "no local coverage at all. All we're doing is reacting to news. We're not planning stories and we're not doing major investigative work. It makes us look like wimps. It really pissed me off."

Borg and his new editor, Glenn Ritt, quickly beefed up local coverage and replaced *Your Town Record.* "We've gotten into the syndrome of soft news. . . . I want to get back into some pretty hefty shit," Borg says.

The Record had become another victim of the '80s, brought low by overexpansion, oversimplification and the old *USA Today* formula. But no newspaper was immune from the market forces that demanded a tighter and brighter product, not even the journalistic giant across the river.

· · ·

For most of this century, *The New York Times* front page has been a dependably dull repository of official pronouncements about matters of state. The front page of January 2, 1970, for example, was cluttered with eleven stories across eight narrow columns, nearly all of them official news: "Nixon Promises an Urgent Fight to End Pollution." "Administration Expects to Seek ABM Expansion." "Agnew Ends Visit to Vietnam." "Transit Strike Is Averted with 18% Wage Increase." "Israel Rejects French Charges." The only color story, by Max Frankel, was "Mood in Capital: Change Will Be Slow."

Change was equally slow in the newspaper business. The two-section *Times* of that era shows how archaic the designs were. Half the front of the D section was devoted to an unsightly news summary. There was no clear beginning or end to the local news or sports sections. The business page was crammed with thirteen stories, most involving corporate statistics. There was no op-ed page and not a single graphic.

Joe Lelyveld, now the executive editor, describes the old paper this way: "We used to cover a lot of legislative process stories—'The House Ways and Means Committee voted yesterday 12 to 5 on the capital gains tax.' It comes out of the Senate Finance Committee: front page. It comes out of the Senate: front page again. It goes to the joint committee: front page again. Signed by the president: front page again. The same thing on major legislation in Albany, Trenton, City Council of New York."

In recent years, however, the paper has undergone a cultural revolution. After a lifetime of waltzing through history, *The New York Times* has learned a little rock 'n' roll.

The first phase of this revolution began in the mid-'70s when Abe Rosenthal, faced with mounting financial problems, decided to create some new sections. A survey showed that more people liked the *Times* than bought it regularly; the challenge was to draw them in without changing the paper's basic character. Rosenthal describes the strategy as "putting more tomatoes in the soup instead of more water. You can cut costs till your eyeballs bubble, or you can improve it, give yourself a better thing to sell."

The new additions—Weekend and Living in 1976, followed by Home in 1977 and SportsMonday and Science Times in 1978—were dismissed by some as too frivolous. "My feeling was, if we were going to have food, it was going to be as good as the foreign report," Rosenthal says. "The asparagus stories would be as good as the stories from

Paris." The new sections proved magnets for advertising and would help carry the *Times* into the boom years of the '80s.

As for the Tuesday paper, "The business department wanted a fashion section and I didn't," Rosenthal says. "They said science would never get any advertising." He took the space he needed for Science Times without telling anyone, and today it is fat with computer ads.

But the *Times* was still ruled by a heavy-handed copy desk. When Molly Ivins, now at the *Fort Worth Star-Telegram,* worked at the *Times* in the late '70s, she wrote a story that described a man as having "a beer gut that belongs in the Smithsonian." The desk changed it to "a man with a protuberant abdomen." On another story, her description of a fellow who "squawked like a two-dollar fiddle" was recast as "an inexpensive musical instrument." Ivins says she felt "like a horse shut up in a very small stall."

The classic Ivins tale involves her story about an all-day community chicken slaughter in a New Mexico town. Ivins couldn't resist describing it as a "gang pluck," knowing full well the phrase would never make it past the copy desk. Ivins was promptly removed as Rocky Mountain bureau chief and ushered into Rosenthal's office.

"He said, 'You used the word gang pluck.' I said, 'I thought it was a good line.' He said, 'Gang pluck.' I said, 'It was a play on words.' He said, 'Gang pluck. Gang pluck sounds like gang fuck. You were trying to make our readers think of the word fuck.'

"I said, 'Damn, Abe, you are a hard man to fool.' "

But sections like Living and Home demanded brighter writing, and that virus, once unleashed, infected the rest of the paper. Rosenthal began hiring other talented writers like William Geist, Joyce Maynard, Leslie Bennetts, Howell Raines and Maureen Dowd, as well as Anna Quindlen, who would launch the popular "Life in the 30s" column.

The tone of the paper gradually began to lighten, but complete perestroika would not arrive until Max Frankel succeeded Rosenthal as executive editor in 1986. Frankel understood that not even the good gray *Times* could ignore the influence of *USA Today.* The paper started using focus groups. Frankel's front page began dealing with such eclectic subjects as urban pigeons, yo-yos, rising hemlines, three-star French chefs, health-conscious dinner parties, rodeos, growing up gay, menopause, interracial marriage, the Mommy track, goose liver, McDonald's low-fat burgers and teenage tennis camps.

One vivid page-one piece began: "There is a single woman in New

York, bright and accomplished, who dreads nightfall, when darkness hugs the city and lights go on in warm kitchens. The woman's problem: She is nearing forty and unmarried, and there are only so many straight, single men out there."

Says editorial page editor Howell Raines: "People say the front page is lighter now and we've lost gravitas. My feeling about the *Times* is we have so much gravitas that it doesn't hurt to lose a little. We've got to engage the reader in a different way. It's possible to be intellectually serious about something other than arms control and the Middle East."

By the same token, women are no longer confined to the journalistic kitchen. For decades, most female reporters were steered toward "softer" stories, while the heavy lifting—the Pentagon, the politics, the Moscow bureau—was seen as man's work. But by the early '90s *Times*-women had infiltrated the front lines. The top political reporters included Robin Toner, Gwen Ifill and Elizabeth Kolbert. There was Maureen Dowd, the star White House correspondent, and Alessandra Stanley, the top New York feature writer, and Soma Golden, the national editor. Felicity Barringer had been a star in Moscow, along with her husband, Philip Taubman. Just as the influx of black reporters on metropolitan dailies helped produce more racially sensitive coverage, the growing influence of women journalists had a leavening effect on the old, cramped definitions of news.

"We took the ghetto with us," says Anna Quindlen, now a columnist on the op-ed page. "We were all ghettoized—the bright writers, the feature writers, the back-of-the-book writers—in what we called the style sections, but what we all really knew, with a wink and a nudge, were the women's sections. As late as 1978, I was assigned to cover all women's issues, from battered wives to day care. Child care wasn't a congressional issue, it was a women's issue. Abortion wasn't a political issue, it was a women's issue. These turned out to be the cutting-edge issues of the '90s."

The paper was badly hurt when the New York economy hit the skids in 1990. By the fall of 1991, the Times Company's quarterly profits had plunged 79 percent, to just $1.9 million. The paper laid off 60 employees and induced another 160 to take early retirement. The short-term future looked bleak.

Arthur Sulzberger, Jr., who within months would succeed his father as publisher, decided to remake the paper once again. In a radical departure from the industry's obsession with cost-cutting, the thirty-nine-year-old Sulzberger chose to spend more money. Sulzberger was worried about shoring up the home base; the *Times* was reaching only 1 in 10 New York–area households, and editors were concerned about competition from suburban papers, and by *Newsday*'s encroachment into Brooklyn and Queens.

The first move was obvious, for even Max Frankel admitted that some *Times* loyalists were buying *USA Today* for the sports coverage. The paper redesigned its lackluster sports section, increasing the space by 50 percent, introducing flashy graphics and hiring a couple of tabloid sportswriters.

Next came a multimillion-dollar overhaul of the Metro section, which had long been a backwater. *The New York Times* was a paper that covered South Africa more closely than the South Bronx, and editors had always been slightly embarrassed about their weak performance at home. Now that would change. No longer would the *Times* have a half-dozen reporters in California and just one on Long Island. While it could never cover every local sewer hearing like the Bergen *Record* or *Hartford Courant,* it would concentrate on broader regional themes that might interest readers from Paterson to New Haven. The number of suburban reporters was doubled. The city staff was beefed up in Brooklyn, Queens and the Bronx. The Metro section got a glitzy new look, with *USA Today*–style graphics and a news index with Boca Raton–type maps.

Bringing local news alive isn't easy, and the Metro section still had plenty of dull stories on trash pickup and town libraries. It was still possible for the *Times* to utterly fumble the story that all of New York was talking about—such as when Woody Allen announced that he was in love with Mia Farrow's twenty-one-year-old adopted daughter, and the paper ran ten paragraphs on page B-3, below "Moving of Courts Planned in Brooklyn." (Despite the tabloid excesses to come, the Woody-and-Mia story was clearly news.) But the Metro staff also produced some dazzling features, and the paper was clearly inching in the right direction. In 1992 the *Times* added a Sunday Styles section, which tried to be trendy with features about nightclubs, fashion, relationships, even gossip (although it proved an embarrassment and was soon folded inside the Metro section). A decade after *USA Today*'s debut, the gray lady is finally printing some Sunday sections in color.

"This is like changing the Soviet Union," Anna Quindlen says. "It doesn't happen overnight."

. . .

In focus groups conducted for *The Washington Post,* here is what some younger readers had to say about newspapers:

"When you see a plane crash, you are glued to that screen. With a newspaper, you can just throw it down." —Male, 18–34.

"When you tell me about the Trident X-sub missile, forget it. . . . I don't know who the heck they're aiming at. I don't know people that talk like that." —Female, 18–22.

"I don't relate to world news." —Female, 18–22.

"I don't want people to see me as stupid. That's really the only reason I read." —Female, 18–22.

"I can't take a newspaper every day. It's just too much of an information blitz coming at me." —Male, 18–22.

The implications for the republic are not encouraging. A 1990 Times Mirror survey concluded that young Americans "know less and care less about news and public affairs than any other generation of Americans in the past fifty years." It is hardly surprising that these young people have little use for newspapers.

In 1967, 73 percent of American adults said they read a newspaper every day. By 1991 that figure had dropped to 51 percent. Daily newspaper circulation has hovered around 62 million for the last twenty-five years, even as the country's adult population has grown by more than a third.

In the past, even occasional newspaper readers often became steady customers in their mid-thirties, when they were more likely to own a home and put down roots in a community. But studies show that those who never bothered with newspapers when they were growing up are least likely to acquire the habit in middle age. In short, if editors don't find a way to hook the younger generation, they can kiss the future good-bye.

"If you treat kids as if they're somehow inferior and should be put off in a corner, they don't like it," says Robert Kaiser, *The Washington Post*'s managing editor. "They have a place in our world. I'd like our pop music coverage to be so good that if you're really into rock 'n' roll, you're going to learn stuff that's going to make you look cool with your friends."

The *Syracuse Herald-Journal* delivers a weekly youth tabloid to thirty-one area high schools each Thursday. The section covers topics from status sneakers and cheerleading to dieting and weightlifting. A

"What's Hot" column (nose earrings, untied shoes, spiked hair, ripped jeans) keeps kids apprised of fashion trends. Brief profiles of students ("Class Acts") have proven popular with readers.

If all this sounds like a throwback to the days when newspapers ran pictures of newborn babies, it may be no accident. Steve Crosby, editor of the *Lafayette* (Indiana) *Courier,* says newspapers have started "taking us back twenty years to the time when we weren't too important to put in their engagement announcements, or when the community group is going to meet. We sort of lost that homey touch. I call it chicken-dinner news. Staffs hate it; readers love it."

A growing number of papers, from the Baltimore *Sun* to the *Chicago Tribune,* are concluding that the future is local, local, local. *The Hartford Courant* has subdivided itself into seven zoned editions that cover eighty-two communities across Connecticut. Unlike *The Washington Star*'s pseudo-zoning, the *Courant* delivers the real thing. Each edition contains different "Our Towns" editorials, different letters to the editor and different photos, along with school-lunch menus and women's club activities. An expanded sports staff covers the action at 118 high schools. "It's extremely expensive, but we believe it's our franchise," says managing editor David Barrett.

The problem is that reporters assigned to such sections often feel like second-class citizens stranded in the boonies. The *Courant*'s local sections are filled with such stories as "Town to Have New Tree-Cutting Policy" and "Woman Honored for Founding Orphanage." No journalist worth his word processor wants to write about chicken-dinner news when he could be chasing corruption at city hall.

The Orange County Register has invented the ultimate suburban beat: the mall. Reporter Jennifer Lowe has written about mothers and daughters shopping together, people who hate malls, teenage shopping power and a shortage of mall bathrooms. "We're trying to reach people in their everyday lives," she says.

The California paper runs daily reader polls and invites people to submit "life letters" about a loved one who recently died. "We'll have 700 to 1,500 people a day calling us, faxing us," says editor Tonnie Katz. "It blows my mind."

Other papers are also pushing the traditional boundaries. The *Minneapolis Star Tribune* has a reporter covering two-career families. The *Rocky Mountain News* has started a gambling beat. The *Plattsburgh* (New York) *Press-Republican* has a reporter work a different job each week and write a first-person account. The *Portland* (Maine) *Press-Herald* invites average folks to its editorial-board meetings. *Florida Today* has an eighteen-year-old advice columnist for teens. *The Orlando Sentinel* has a singles columnist. ("Attention, men: What kind of kisser are you?")

Some editors have revived their women's sections in an effort to lure working women and young mothers who have no time to waste on newspapers that don't speak to their concerns. The *Chicago Tribune*'s "Womannews" section is relentlessly relevant, featuring such topics as women in the military, self-defense for schoolgirls, sexual chemistry, pregnant television anchors, premenstrual syndrome, infertility and office gossip.

Even *The Wall Street Journal* has added new subjects, from legal affairs to Madison Avenue, in an effort to become more user-friendly. "A lot of our readers read us more out of fear than love," Norman Pearlstine said before stepping down as editor. "I'd like to see us become a wanna-read instead of a must-read."

The Washington Post has added sections called Health, Weekend, Washington Business and Washington Home since the late '70s. A new Style Plus page has tackled such sensitive subjects as stress, barhopping, discussing sex with children, divorce, alcoholism and lesbian couples. In recent years the *Post* has added beats on race relations, lobbying, family issues and immigration. The change is noticeable. In 1986, nearly all the *Post*'s front-page stories were of the hard-news variety. In 1991, there were page-one stories on suburban traffic jams, innovative schools, kids left motherless by crime, drivers who run red lights, food labeling, teenage boredom, middle-class renters who can't afford homes and the frustrations of layoff victims. Still, old habits were hard to shed. According to a summary of a 1993 newsroom survey, many staffers still believed the paper "concentrates too much on incremental government, institutional and policy stories at the expense of news about 'real people,' social trends and change." "Traditionally, American journalism was intimately tied to politics and government," Bob Kaiser says. "I think we're trying to break that relationship, partly because politics has departed from real life."

Nearly all newspapers indulge themselves with long investigative series on weighty issues that hold little appeal for ordinary citizens. Ron Martin, the Atlanta *Constitution* editor, recalled a 1990 series on poverty and health care in the South. "It was wonderful, groundbreaking reporting," he says. But despite a splash that began with four full pages on Sunday, the stories didn't get much response.

"We put together a number of focus groups," Martin says. "We said, 'Did anybody read this?' The bottom line was really no. That to me was a tragedy. I thought we as editors had failed them. It's simplistic to say, are you doing 'serious journalism'? Are you doing investigative reporting? The question is, how do you get into the heads of readers? Or are you making yourself feel warm all over because you've done your job, and the readers are just too dumb to get it?"

That, in a nutshell, is the dilemma. We know how to produce serious newspapers like *The New York Times.* We know how to produce pastel-colored fluff like the Boca Raton *News.* We know how to produce youth-oriented sections like the *Syracuse Herald-Journal.* But can we produce a single newspaper that will combine the strengths of all three? That will appeal to readers of *The Washington Post, Fortune* and *Rolling Stone?*

The signs of change are long overdue, but we are just scratching the surface. Newspapers are still too homogeneous, too predictable, too weighted down by incremental news. What we need is fewer pink flamingos and more old-fashioned hell-raising.

16

Reclaiming the Franchise

The newspaper business, battered and bloodied, has come to resemble the steel industry of the late 1970s. Its practitioners, who once felt immune from the shifting economic winds they charted, now find themselves buffeted like so many assembly-line welders.

The papers that have vanished, from Little Rock to Los Angeles, have dumped thousands of talented journalists on the street. They have been joined by thousands more layoff victims around the country. Virtually every large newspaper in America, from *The New York Times* to the *Los Angeles Times,* has trimmed its staff. When the Baltimore *Sun* offered buyouts in late 1991, nearly three hundred employees, a quarter of the eligible staff, chose to take the money and run.

The result has been a sort of communal midlife crisis for every scribe who ever harbored doubts about the business: Should I take the severance pay and find a good PR job? Will my paper still be around in five years? And if it is, will it be the kind of newspaper I want to work for?

Some of the best and the brightest of a generation, those who joined the fraternity in the '60s and '70s and became chroniclers of an era, are finding that it isn't much fun anymore. In the new corporate culture of the newsroom, editors hold endless meetings and cook up prefabricated story ideas. Prose is squeezed through more and more hands into ever-smaller receptacles. Controversial ideas are pasteurized and homogenized until most of the flavor has been drained. For many, the craft of Hemingway, Mencken and Reston now has all the romance of a fast-food kitchen stamping out Big Macs.

Even Hollywood has come to see the newspaper business in a harsher light. More than fifteen years after *All the President's Men,* Robert Redford agreed to star in another newspaper movie. This time he would play Bill Kovach, the former Atlanta *Journal* and *Constitution* editor, in a film about the corporatization of American journalism.

In this depressing atmosphere, it's hardly surprising that some fine people are drifting away from the business. "I belong to an entire generation of burned-out, fed-up, pissed-off reporters," says Bill Walker, who quit to join Greenpeace after working for the *Sacramento Bee, Denver Post* and *Fort Worth Star-Telegram.* "I could not spend the rest of my life producing the shallow, sensational, trumped-up trivia that passes for news today."

I have heard similar laments from reporters in newsroom after newsroom. They are tired of the old cliché formulas, tired of racial frictions, tired of hired guns who engage in drive-by editing, tired of the fascination with shorter-is-better, tired of producing pale imitations of what readers have already seen on television. A 1993 survey by the Associated Press Managing Editors found that nearly one-fifth of the newspaper journalists canvassed want to quit the business. I often hear colleagues say, only half-jokingly, that we are in a dying business. The number of journalism school graduates pursuing a career in newspapers has already declined. Richard Kipling, a hiring editor at the *Los Angeles Times,* calls it "the wholesale squandering of a generation of talent."

This sense of malaise has already eroded the franchise. Perhaps it is no coincidence that such larger-than-life figures as Ben Bradlee, Abe Rosenthal, Gene Roberts and Norm Pearlstine have been succeeded over the last several years by steady and competent but much less colorful men. At a time when newspapers need to take more chances than ever before—to get into "some pretty hefty shit," as Mac Borg put it—caution seems to be the watchword.

Still, there may be a silver lining amid the dark clouds. During heavy news periods, such as the Persian Gulf war or the Soviet coup, newspaper circulation has shot up dramatically. *USA Today* sold an extra 600,000 copies the day after Magic Johnson revealed he had the AIDS virus. When people are hungry for news, television rarely satisfies their appetite. The long 1992 strike against the Pittsburgh papers underscored a dozen ways in which people need their newspapers, from declining business among florists (because people were missing the obituaries of friends) to a sharp drop in game-day ticket sales at Pirates games. Without a newspaper to keep score, even being in first place isn't enough.

The collapse of communism and the painful lurching toward democracy around the globe produced some of the best daily journalism in decades. From the fall of the Berlin Wall to the liberation of Eastern Europe to the disintegration of the Soviet Union, print reporters have helped us sort out the jumble of televised images and showed us how average Germans, Poles and Russians were coping with the dramatic upheavals. And it was a *Newsday* reporter, Roy Gutman, who uncovered the Serbian "death camps" in Bosnia, a story that stunned the world when the television cameras got there.

Those who believe that CNN has made the print press obsolete are missing the larger point. To be sure, Ted Turner's network excels at blanketing fast-moving events—wars, trials, press conferences—with a speed that no competitor can match. But CNN covers what unfolds on the public stage, before the camera's eye. It is a video wire service. When there is no breaking story to command our attention, it can be deadly dull. Far from replacing newspapers, CNN's ubiquitous presence may well liberate them from their stenographic role, allowing them to dig deeper and range more widely than ever before.

On the one day when people have time to read and relax, newspapers have become a fixture in more and more homes. Sunday circulation, the one bright spot in newspaper sales, has jumped 25 percent over the last two decades. Sunday also happens to be the day when newspapers are most like magazines—with well-written features, special sections, provocative opinion pieces—and least dependent on incremental government news.

Therein lies the challenge: to raise the quality of daily journalism to Sunday levels; to grab people's attention on subjects they care about, even when the country is not racked by war or scandal, and to deliver this unwieldy package more efficiently for busy readers. A very tall order, to be sure.

One popular school of thought holds that the salvation of newspapers lies in modern technology. In the not-too-distant future, proponents say, most people will receive their news from electronic newspapers, and the ink-on-paper version will go the way of vinyl record albums.

Mark me down as a skeptic. While advanced gadgetry is obviously changing the business—everyone was still banging away on typewriters when I started working in the mid-'70s—the message is ultimately more important than the medium. If our stories and subjects aren't compelling, it won't matter much whether people access them by slipping off a rubber band or tapping on a computer keyboard.

Electronic newspapers are already here—dozens of papers are coming on line, and hackers can talk back to editors at the *San Jose Mercury News* and other papers—but not everyone is enough of a news junkie to start downloading the headlines. News has been available by fax and computer for a decade now and the concept hasn't exactly taken off. The *Chicago Tribune* dropped its fax edition after four months for lack of interest. Reading a computerized newspaper is a bit laborious— waiting for the phone connection, scanning the story titles, punching one up, scrolling from top to bottom, then moving on to the next title. There's no big headline to suggest that this story is more important than that one, no dramatic photo to catch your eye, no easy way to browse through the day's offerings. You can't clip out articles or take it on the bus. The *Fort Worth Star-Telegram,* a leader in the field, offers two to three times as much information by computer as in the daily paper, yet the service has only 3,600 subscribers. Knight-Ridder lost more than $50 million on a similar venture called Viewtron. I've seen some awesome technology on the drawing boards: from photos that come alive with videotape and sound (including instant replays) to interactive ads that allow you to order baseball tickets or make restaurant reservations at the click of a mouse. These innovations are helping to turn newspapers into twenty-four-hour data banks, but they remain a supplement to the basic paper product.

While electronic newspapers may never replace the Gutenberg variety, technology can help us better calibrate our product. The central paradox of newspapers today is that they deliver more news more efficiently than ever before at a time when readers are drowning in information. Newspapers have many audiences, and it has become increasingly difficult to cater to one segment without driving away the rest.

On the one hand, the newspaper remains a mass medium, read by bureaucrats, housewives, teachers, cops, college students and congressmen, all with varied interests and obsessions. At the same time, newspapers cannot survive without making themselves indispensable to a sophisticated elite that demands detailed coverage of public policy issues.

We have built these newsgathering machines that assemble a great mass of fact and opinion and use it just once, in a format that becomes fish wrap a few days later. Technology is allowing us to recycle this information at little additional cost. More than 1,200 papers now have 900 numbers that provide up-to-the-minute sports, weather and stock information. The Atlanta *Journal* and *Constitution* have received 1.5 million calls a month to their various phone services, some of which carry paid advertising messages. On PostHaste, *The Washington Post*'s phone service, kids can hear a sound bite from the latest Axl Rose album, soap-opera addicts can get summaries of "General Hospital" and executives can check the price of minor stocks no longer carried on the business pages. This may be the tip of an information-age iceberg. Scientists at MIT are experimenting with a custom-built newspaper whose offerings are tailored to the individual subscriber: medical news for doctors, concert information for rock fans, plane schedules for frequent fliers, and so on.

Such specialized services could help democratize daily journalism. For too long, we have catered to the insiders at the expense of the average reader. Editors instinctively care most about the movers and shakers, the pillars of the local establishment, the men and women with whom they share a special sense of responsibility for doing the public's business. The reporter who covers Congress or the city council quickly becomes engrossed in this world, gossiping about each twist and turn with a small group of players who find the power struggles fascinating. These are the people who call to compliment them on their work or run into the publisher at the charity fund-raiser. Put them all together and they would barely fill a high school gym. To write for them is to publish a newsletter for decision makers, and by implication to exclude everyone else. Some newspapers already "zone" editions by geography; the next step is a kind of intellectual zoning, serving up a Chinese menu of news for readers with different interests.

Technology may have an even more far-reaching effect on our ability to uncover the news. Computer data bases have already transformed the nature of reporting. With a touch of a button, a diligent journalist can now research the background of a Cabinet nominee, compare a senator's rhetoric with his record or find links between seemingly unrelated people. Even small papers can undertake sweeping investigations without exorbitant costs. The gatekeepers have taken note: All the Pulitzers for investigative reporting from 1989 through 1992 were awarded for computer-assisted stories.

In the old days—before the mid-'80s—most newsrooms relied on a morgue filled with tattered clippings that were often missing or incomplete. Now the range of electronic information is so massive—the Nexis/Lexis service alone records 55,000 news stories and legal cases a day—that we have barely begun to grasp its potential. A reporter can quickly search for all *New York Times* stories that mention Mario Cuomo and the presidency, or Mario Cuomo and a campaign contributor, or Mario Cuomo and his mother. Or check specialized publications from *Architectural Digest* to *Aviation Week*. Or examine the files of the Securities and Exchange Commission and Bureau of Labor Statistics. Or look at local real estate transactions, Supreme Court rulings and pending federal legislation.

Computer wizardry helped *The Philadelphia Inquirer*'s investigative team, Donald Barlett and James Steele, crack a key mystery when they were examining how congressional tax writers had earmarked huge benefits for certain companies without naming the firms. One company in the tax bill was identified only by the size of three of its loans—$975 million, $400 million and $225 million, and the years they were due, 1994, 1998 and 2001. Steele fed these numbers to a computer researcher, who checked the Dow Jones data base. Up popped the name of FMC Corporation of Chicago, which had gotten a $975 million loan due in 1994. "The whole thing literally took about ten or fifteen minutes," Steele says.

Computer research has opened the door for newspapers to master the kind of ambitious, complicated, paper-trail investigations that are rarely attempted by television. It is another way to expand the frontiers of print journalism, rather than merely mimicking TV's breezy style.

There is no magic formula, no all-purpose panacea for revitalizing newspapers. But we seem to have lost sight of the basics that once put the press at the center of our political and cultural life.

Jon Katz has written in *Rolling Stone* about pop culture's New News, delivered by the likes of Spike Lee and Guns n' Roses, usurping the function of mainstream journalism. "Bart Simpson's critique of society seems more trenchant than that of most newspaper columnists," Katz says. "Movies like *Boyz 'n the Hood* and *Straight Out of Brooklyn* and rappers like Public Enemy and Ice Cube deal with race more squarely than 'Nightline.' " Lost in the entertaining din, of course, is any notion of accuracy or balance.

It is time for newspapers to reclaim their heritage. We must go back to the future, to a time when papers spoke the language of the streets and were not yet seen as part of an arrogant, ivory-tower elite. Unfortunately, the rigid architecture of newspapers does not reflect much of the outside world. Our beats are based on buildings (the statehouse, the courthouse, the White House) and issues (transportation, health care); news that is sociological or simply unorthodox often slips through our net. It's often said that the press slept through one of the biggest domestic stories of the century—the great migration of blacks from the rural south to the industrial north—because no one called a press conference to announce it.

What if newspapers wrote about life with the same passion we bring to sports? Think of all the elements in a sports section. Money. Injuries. Strategy. Drug abuse. Trades. Competition. Strikes. Statistics. Winning and losing. Big-mouth writers calling the manager a bum. Where else in a newspaper do you find that kind of passion? No wonder fans devour the sports section long after they've watched the main event on television. Even *The New York Times* now takes sports very seriously.

Do sports reporters know something that other journalists don't? In the cable era, after all, a devoted fan can watch a half-dozen baseball games on a good night and all manner of athletics on ESPN, the CNN of the jock world. Why bother to read about it the next day? Perhaps it's because sportswriters are so much more opinionated, hailing the heroes and kicking the goats with reckless abandon. Perhaps it's that they have such freedom to second-guess and analyze whether the sacrifice bunt was a blunder or the starting pitcher should've been lifted earlier. Perhaps it's their ability to soak up locker-room color, or translate the most arcane strategy into the language of the casual fan. Winners and losers are never quite so clear in the real world, of course, but surely journalists have much to learn about bringing everyday drama alive.

Here, then, is a sampling of what newspapers need to do more of:

• **Make people mad.** Write about outrages and injustice. Don't be afraid to get folks riled up; it's better to be controversial than ignored. A good newspaper should be like the feisty columnist that readers love to hate but would never dream of missing. When the president tells an obvious fib, let's call him out on strikes. When the mayor blows a big decision, why not holler: Throw the bum out! If a big corporation is giving some poor soul the shaft, let's blow the whistle. The New York tabloids, for all their bluster, have a healthy sense of crusading for the little guy, but most newspapers rarely deviate from their studied, above-the-fray posture.

•   **Tell us things the authorities don't want us to know.** We've become so obsessed with the latest middle-class comforts that we've drifted from our original mission of afflicting the comfortable. There is no shortage of malfeasance and misfeasance in public life, and even small examples—the Pentagon's $640 toilet seat, or John Sununu's frequent flying—have symbolic value. Perhaps the press should have focused on the pampered life-styles of members of Congress long before the House Bank furor forced the issue onto the front pages. Let's wean ourselves from our addiction to inside baseball and start questioning the rules of the game.

•   **Make us laugh.** Newspapers take themselves much too seriously. Let's pay less attention to the public-policy nerds and explore the lighter side of the human condition. There's no reason to grant Dave Barry a monopoly in this area; surely we can find more comic relief amid the depressing headlines.

•   **Touch readers in their daily lives.** Too much journalism, like government, exists on an abstract plane that has little meaning for most readers. Let's sink our teeth into subjects that people care about—schools, housing, crime, day care, traffic, hospitals—in ways that get their juices flowing. We need to spend less time at city hall and more time in the neighborhoods. The great popularity of traffic columns in some major papers—"Road Warrior" in the Bergen *Record,* "Dr. Grid-lock" in *The Washington Post*—shows that there is a thriving market for pothole-level journalism. Unglamorous stories about appealing a property tax bill or evaluating local doctors might not win any Pulitzers, but they could win over some disaffected readers.

•   **Break the shackles of mindless objectivity.** One reason the press was unable to sound the alarm on the S&L debacle is that we have become the prisoner of experts. Had more reporters trusted their instincts and made the case that the industry was collapsing, many billions of dollars might have been saved. Fairness and balance are essential, but hiding behind the old he said/she said formulas is a convenient copout. When *The Seattle Times* reported the charges of eight women who said they had been sexually harassed by Senator Brock Adams, it was, in effect, taking a stand against such conduct. *The Des Moines Register*'s powerful series on the rape of Nancy Ziegenmeyer fueled a national debate on how the courts and the media treat rape victims. If that amounts to activist journalism, so be it.

• **Turn the writers loose.** Serve up one magazine-quality piece each day that soars above the pedestrian. Let individual voices emerge from the bland chorus of daily journalism. We are a writer's medium; let's exploit that to the fullest. Why should magazines corner the market on terrific prose? When Maureen Dowd cast her spotlight on sexual harassment during the Clarence Thomas hearings, it was an event that had everyone buzzing. When Mike Barnicle or Mike Royko takes aim at a juicy target, it's the talk of the town. The era when all news stories affected the same Olympian tone is over; we need to cultivate more writers who can peel the onion of multilayered subjects.

• **Set the agenda.** With few exceptions, the press remains a reactive instrument with a toddler's attention span. We spend millions of dollars following the president around the globe and recording his every burp. We get wrapped up in campaign photo ops and attack ads. We swarm like bees into an agency like HUD after the place has been looted, then buzz off in search of the next calamity. It's time to stop prospecting for official leaks and start digging up more news off the beaten path. In 1992, Charles Shepard of *The Washington Post* reported on the lavish spending habits of United Way's $463,000-a-year president, William Aramony, including his chauffeured car service, Concorde flights and expensive condominiums. The story not only led to Aramony's resignation but sparked a widespread reappraisal of how charities spend their money.

• **Make it a picture medium.** Newspapers must make better use of photographs to tell the story, particularly as we drag ourselves into the color era. Too many papers still publish too many pages of gray type. We need more arresting, more artistic photography that captures the moment, and fewer pictures of diplomats shaking hands. If the wordsmiths must sacrifice a few words to accommodate more pictures, so be it.

• **Satisfy the specialists.** Newspapers should offer regular features and columns for folks vitally interested in law, computers, publishing, science, religion, health care, personal finance and so on. These should be accessible to the layman, but sophisticated enough to interest the aficionados. Such pieces won't appeal to everyone, but they help make the newspaper more like a modern supermarket and less like an old five-and-dime.

• **Liberate the op-ed pages.** The stuffed-shirt opinions proffered on these pages often run the gamut from A to B. While there are several provocative columnists around, we need to restrict the soporific lectures of the Henry Kissingers and Jeane Kirkpatricks and throw open the gates to new, vibrant, even radical voices. The *Los Angeles Times'* new "Voices" section, launched after the 1992 riots, is one such step forward.

• **Connect with the community.** Anyone who's ever dialed a newsroom and listened to the phone ring twenty times, or been bounced from one voice-mail recording to another, knows how remote the local paper can seem. We need to give people a sense that we're listening—by making it easier for readers to register complaints, get errors corrected, publish letters to the editor, track down old stories or rectify subscription problems. More publishers should follow the example of the *Boston Globe, Washington Post, Chicago Tribune* and twenty-five other papers that have hired an ombudsman to field complaints and criticize the paper. Editors should get out in the community, and every paper should have a senior editor who uses the opinion pages to explain its inner workings. We must lift the curtain of secrecy from the editorial process and do a better job of illuminating what we do.

Some of the best newspapers are already moving in this direction. The proliferation of special sections, from the *Chicago Tribune*'s Womannews to the *Fresno Bee*'s Teen Tempo, shows that we are reaching out to a fragmented audience. When *The New York Times* runs a front-page series on suburban shopping malls, it is clear that the old definitions of news are melting away. But we need to weave these threads into the fabric of daily journalism, rather than presenting them as occasional frills.

Critics undoubtedly will suggest that my prescription for more in-depth, serious reporting flies in the face of economic reality. Obviously, the first responsibility of any publisher is to stay afloat; we don't need any more dead newspapers sacrificed on the altar of high-minded journalism. And investing in better reporting and writing is hardly a quick fix of the kind so many corporate chieftains have come to favor. Instead, it presumes that strong and substantive newspapers prosper over the long haul. There is, however, some historical evidence for this assertion. Knight-Ridder spent considerable sums in the '70s and early '80s to improve *The Philadelphia Inquirer,* now a prosperous paper that has outlasted its competition. *The New York Times* thrived financially after Abe Rosenthal decided to "put more tomatoes in the soup" in the mid-'70s. But *USA Today,* despite its recent improvement, has yet to turn a profit.

To be sure, a newspaper's revenue rests on variety of factors, from labor costs to retail advertising, that have little to do with the quality of reporting. But if better journalism is not a surefire formula for profitability, neither does it ignore marketplace realities. The plain fact is, in a world where news is delivered at 186,000 miles per second, there is no reason for people to buy newspapers unless they provide detailed, compelling material that can't be found elsewhere. And that means more than eight-inch stories and computer-generated charts. It means a willingness to tackle such controversial subjects as race and homosexuality with new honesty. It means taking risks and offending people. And it means tossing out much of the incremental pseudo-news that makes newspapers seem dull and irrelevant.

Our dismal performance over the past decade contains some important lessons, if we are smart enough to heed them. How can we avoid being dazzled by the next Donald Trump? Missing the next S&L scandal? Falling for the next Stuart murder hoax? Hyping the next Kitty Kelley book? Losing our cool over the next Palm Beach rape case? Shying away from the next Norplant editorial? Getting snookered in the next war? The press is in deep, deep trouble. We need to spend more time thinking about our shortcomings rather than chasing after the next fire truck.

This book has, by necessity, focused on those shortcomings, but there have been a number of hopeful signs as well. The *Inquirer*'s Barlett and Steele struck a nerve with a nine-part series on how Washington rulemakers and corporate power brokers created an economic structure "rigged against the middle class." Based on two years of research, the provocative series ranged from how a factory relocation eliminated the job of a woman earning $7.91 an hour to a 2,184 percent increase in millionaires' salaries during the '80s. Each piece ran at least three full pages, far outstripping the supposed attention span of today's readers. Yet the *Inquirer* filled requests for 400,000 reprints, the paper received 20,000 letters and the series became a best-selling book. The authors did precisely what newspapers are supposed to do: They sparked a real debate.

Other examples abound. Martin Gottlieb and Dean Baquet of *The New York Times* took the time between racial disturbances to produce an honest portrait of Al Sharpton as an "impresario of an abrasive floating street theater involving demonstrations of rarely more than a few hundred people." Lynne Duke of *The Washington Post* has written candidly about blacks who have doubts about affirmative action, and whites who think that blacks "have a chip on their shoulder" and "do not seem to want to work." *USA Today* ran a vivid series on why "many of our beliefs about sports are based on classic racial stereotypes," such as that "black athletes are fast runners, and white athletes are slow." If we can finally begin to write intelligently about race, then no subject should be off-limits.

The problem is that in-depth journalism—the kind of writing that probes and presses and pushes the edge of the envelope—costs money. At a time when editors and publishers are struggling with profits far below the giddy levels of the late '80s, spending money is not a popular prescription. It is cheaper, and undoubtedly safer, to crank out what-happened-yesterday stories, toss in some canned life-style features and spruce up the package with fancy graphics. But that is no longer enough.

Newspapers have no God-given right to exist; they must compel people's attention in a cacophonous world of a thousand media distractions. We must make television eat our dust, not by winning the headline race but through breadth and vision and a willingness to face hard truths.

Less than twenty years ago, print reporters were on top of the world, hailed by Hollywood as the disheveled icons of a rogue profession. Now, in the blink of an eye, we are obsolete, ridiculed, fighting for survival. It is a time for boldness, for risk-taking, for once again reinventing the daily newspaper. Otherwise, we are history.

Sources

All interviews were conducted by the author, unless otherwise noted.

Introduction

3 "a leading candidate": Tom Kenworthy, *The Washington Post*, June 5, 1993.

4 "a leading contender": Thomas L. Friedman, *The New York Times*, June 8, 1993.

4 "the clear front-runner": Jeffrey H. Birnbaum and Joe Davidson, *The Wall Street Journal*, June 7, 1993.

4 "the odds-on favorite": Bill Nichols, *USA Today*, June 9, 1993.

4 "officials . . . expected . . .": Richard L. Berke, *The New York Times*, June 12, 1993.

4 "appeared imminent": Paul Richter, *Los Angeles Times*, June 12, 1993.

4 "some top aides . . .": Richard L. Berke, *The New York Times*, June 14, 1993.

1.
Trump: The Decade

15 "He is tall . . .": Judy Klemesrud, *The New York Times*, Nov. 1, 1976.

19 "Bad publicity is . . .": Donald J. Trump, *The Art of the Deal* (Random House, 1987).

19 "Combining a huckster's flair . . .": Randall Smith, *The Wall Street Journal*, Jan. 14, 1982.

19 "obscenely condescending": Sydney Schanberg, *The New York Times*, Aug. 2, 1983.

391

20 "Donald J. Trump is . . .": William E. Geist, *The New York Times Magazine,* Apr. 4, 1984.

21 "Trump, who believes . . .": George F. Will, *Newsweek,* Dec. 23, 1985.

21 "I hate to . . .": Lois Romano, *The Washington Post,* Nov. 15, 1984.

21 "He just dresses . . .": *New York Post,* Dec. 31, 1985.

22 "a modern-day Gatsby": Haynes Johnson, *The Washington Post,* Nov. 27, 1987. The *Newsweek* article was also cited by Johnson.

22 "It should be . . .": The *Newsweek* spokeswoman was quoted by Laura Landro and Laurie P. Cohen, *The Wall Street Journal,* Nov. 30, 1987.

23 "Insisting that he is not . . .": Fox Butterfield, *The New York Times,* Oct. 23, 1987.

23 "Donald Trump insisted yesterday . . .": Maralyn Matlick, *New York Post,* June 16, 1987.

25 "the nation's royal couple . . .": Robert Lenzner, *The Boston Globe,* July 8, 1988.

27 Even Smith complained that: James Barron, *The New York Times,* Feb. 17, 1990.

28 He demanded that the *News*: Bill Hoffmann, *New York Post,* Feb. 19, 1990.

29 "It's over! The scandalous . . .": Bill Hoffmann and Esther Pessin, *New York Post,* Mar. 22, 1990.

30 "How Much Is Donald . . .": Richard Stern, *Forbes,* May 14, 1990.

32 "At last, all of us . . .": Robert Reno, *Newsday,* June 6, 1990.

32 "used to kiss my ass . . .": Donald J. Trump, *Trump: Surviving at the Top* (Random House, 1990).

33 "Trump is obviously . . .": Carla Bruni's quote was cited by Bill Hoffmann, *New York Post,* Sept. 12, 1991.

33 "Who gets the ring? . . .": Ann Trebbe, *USA Today,* Sept. 25, 1991.

34 In 1991, he announced: Leo Standora, *New York Post,* Aug. 8, 1991.

34 "Donald and Marla are calling it . . .": Cindy Adams, *New York Post,* Oct. 14, 1992.

34 "Donald Trump's love child": Bill Hoffman, Cathy Burke and Hal Davis, *New York Post,* Apr. 8, 1993.

34 "the world's tiniest . . .": Malcolm Balfour, *New York Post,* Oct. 14, 1993.

35 "Tacky. Overblown.": Amy Pagnozzi, New York *Daily News,* Dec. 18, 1993.

35   "our P. T. Barnum": Graydon Carter was quoted by Jane Furse, New York *Daily News,* Dec. 21, 1993.

2.
The Agency Nobody Covered

44   In Camden, New Jersey: The Camden scam was reported by Tim Weiner in a series of articles appearing in *The Philadelphia Inquirer* beginning in June 1983.

48   "some funding decisions . . .": Andre Shashaty, *Multi-Housing News,* July 1988.

49   Watt, who made $120,000: The HUD report on consultants and the James Watt quote were recounted by Gwen Ifill, *The Washington Post,* June 10 and June 21, 1989.

49   "Thanks!": Watt's letter to Samuel Pierce was reported by Gwen Ifill, *The Washington Post,* June 10 and Aug. 4, 1989.

50   "I've kicked myself . . .": Bill Kovach was quoted by Martin Schram, *Columbia Journalism Review,* Sept.–Oct. 1989.

52   Pierce made sure his harshest critic: DuBois Gilliam's account was reported by Gwen Ifill, *The Washington Post,* May 1, 1990.

52   "a confidential report . . .": Guy Gugliotta, *The Washington Post,* Mar. 10, 1993.

52   "Another HUD scandal . . .": Jason DeParle, *The New York Times,* Mar. 11, 1993.

3.
Bank Job

56   "since the Depression": The thrift president was quoted by G. Christian Hill, *The Wall Street Journal,* Mar. 26, 1980.

56   "hemorrhaging": G. Christian Hill, *The Wall Street Journal,* Feb. 20, 1981.

56   "Throughout the country . . .": *The Washington Post,* July 3, 1985.

56   "Looming insolvencies . . .": Bert Ely, *The Wall Street Journal,* July 17, 1986.

57   "The failure rate . . .": Janet Novack, *Forbes,* May 4, 1987.

57   "Disposing of the carcass . . .": William Greider, *Rolling Stone,* Aug. 11, 1988.

58   Mike Binstein wrote a column . . . : Jack Anderson and Dale Van Atta, *The Washington Post,* Nov. 6, 1986.

58 Anderson's libel lawyer: Details of the David Branson–Jack Anderson situation were first reported by Jill Abramson, *Manhattan Lawyer,* Oct. 27, 1987. (In the interest of full disclosure, it should be noted that I worked for Anderson in the late 1970s and that Branson once represented me in a lawsuit.)

59 "Mr. Keating has transformed . . .": Richard W. Stevenson, *The New York Times,* May 25, 1987.

59 "a crude attempt to intimidate": Michael Binstein, *Regardie's,* July 1987.

60 "were illegally obtained . . .": Charles Bowden, *Smart* magazine, Mar. 1990.

61 The most dramatic collapse: Details on Empire Savings & Loan were drawn from Rick Atkinson and David Maraniss, *The Washington Post,* June 12, 1989.

64 "walked away from . . .": Michael Dukakis was quoted by Jerry Knight, *The Washington Post,* Sept. 30, 1988.

65 "federal fiasco": Jeff Bailey and G. Christian Hill, *The Wall Street Journal,* Mar. 25, 1988.

65 "The sad shape . . .": Gerald F. Seib and Robert E. Taylor, *The Wall Street Journal,* Oct. 25, 1988.

66 "Many in the industry . . .": Nathaniel Nash, *The New York Times,* June 28, 1988.

67 "big, big, black bottomless pit . . .": James O'Shea, *Chicago Tribune,* Sept. 25, 1988.

68 "S&L Rescue Could Cost . . .": Tom Furlong, *Los Angeles Times,* Jan. 27, 1989.

68 "Brace yourself . . .": Paulette Thomas and Paul Duke Jr., *The Wall Street Journal,* Jan. 13, 1989.

68 "S&L Hell": Kathleen Day, *The New Republic,* Mar. 20, 1989.

69 In the fall of 1986: Gregory Gordon, UPI, Oct. 28 and Nov. 1, 1986.

70 There was Glenn saying . . . : Mike Binstein, *The Washington Post,* May 15, 1988.

70 "an unprecedented display . . .": Stephen Kleege and Stan Strachan, *National Thrift News,* Sept. 28, 1987.

72 While Don Riegle was being pilloried: The Riegle letter was reported by Eleanor Randolph, *The Washington Post,* Dec. 14, 1989.

73 The lawsuit also: Dale Keiger, *Cincinnati* magazine, Feb. 1990.

4.
The Fire This Time

75 "Los Angeles, you broke . . .": George Ramos, *Los Angeles Times,* May 4, 1992.

76 "did not take police brutality . . .": Andrea Ford was quoted by David Shaw, *Los Angeles Times,* May 26, 1992.

81 When Tawana Brawley crawled out: Valuable information on the Brawley case was provided by *Outrage: The Story Behind the Tawana Brawley Hoax,* by Robert D. McFadden, Ralph Blumenthal, M. A. Farber, E. R. Shipp, Charles Strum and Craig Wolff (Bantam Books, 1990).

88 "the election transformed , , ,"; Mark Kriegel, *New York Post,* Mar. 9, 1993.

88 "I haven't changed . . .": Al Sharpton was quoted by Todd S. Purdum, *The New York Times,* July 27, 1992.

95 "covered themselves with glory": Mike Barnicle's column was quoted by Christopher Lydon, *Washington Journalism Review,* Mar. 1990.

97 "coercion and intimidation . . .": The U.S. attorney's report was cited by Christopher B. Daly, *The Washington Post,* July 12, 1991.

98 One night in August 1991: The Linda Bennett case was reported by Mike Barnicle, *The Boston Globe,* Aug. 15, 1991.

100 "busing minority journalists . . .": Linda Williams was quoted by Ron LaBrecque, *Washington Journalism Review,* July–Aug. 1992.

5.
A House Divided

101 "Dare we mention . . .": *The Philadelphia Inquirer,* Dec. 12, 1990.

103 "Marauders from . . .": The *L.A. Times* headline was cited by David Shaw, *Los Angeles Times,* Dec. 12, 1990.

104 "the core issues . . .": Joe Klein, *New York* magazine, Nov. 13, 1989.

105 When a 1991 fire: Paul Taylor, *The Washington Post,* Sept. 6, 1991.

105 "bizarre": Scott Shuger, *The Washington Monthly,* Feb. 1990.

105 a *New York Times*/CBS poll: Jason DeParle, *The New York Times,* Aug. 11, 1991.

106 "that I shouldn't have been born": Garry Howard was quoted by Thomas B. Rosenstiel, *Los Angeles Times,* Dec. 20, 1990.

106 "Nordic arrogance": Chuck Stone, *The Philadelphia Daily News,* Dec. 18, 1990.

107 "What we have . . .": Steve Lopez, *The Philadelphia Inquirer,* Dec. 16, 1990.

108 "suffers from the notion . . .": Claude Lewis, *The Philadelphia Inquirer,* Dec. 21, 1990.

108 "impoverished, unmarried . . .": *The Philadelphia Inquirer,* Nov. 1, 1990.

109 "running a macho newsroom": Muriel Cohen was quoted by Mark Jurkowitz, *Boston Phoenix,* Oct. 11, 1991.

110 "an unofficial little quota system": Ken Auletta, *The New Yorker,* June 28, 1993.

110 "up in arms": Howie Carr, *Boston Herald,* Nov. 17 and Nov. 24, 1991.

111 ". . . worst racial incident . . .": Renee Graham was quoted by Brian McGrory, *The Boston Globe,* Nov. 28, 1991.

114 "is still an overwhelmingly white . . .": David Shaw, *Los Angeles Times,* Dec. 14, 1990.

115 "The 'victims' are . . .": Art Carey, *The Philadelphia Inquirer,* June 30, 1991.

116 "a militant conservative . . .": Fasaha Traylor, *The Philadelphia Inquirer,* June 30, 1991.

118 "a strong sense of defensiveness . . .": Juan Williams, *The Washington Monthly,* July–Aug. 1986.

119 "For the rest of my life . . .": Milton Coleman, *The Washington Post,* Apr. 8, 1984.

119 "I'm with the store owners . . .": Richard Cohen, *The Washington Post* Magazine, Sept. 7, 1986.

120 "It is difficult to explain . . .": Len Downie was quoted by Marcia Slacum Greene, *The Washington Post,* Dec. 8, 1986.

122 "We love this city . . .": Marion Barry was quoted by Tom Sherwood and Eric Pianin, Dec. 30, 1988.

122 "Color Barry white . . .": Richard Cohen, *The Washington Post,* Jan. 1, 1989.

123 "an especially hypocritical . . .": *The Washington Post,* Jan. 20, 1990.

123 The *Afro-American*: The black newspaper coverage was described by Paul Ruffins, *The Washington Post,* July 8, 1990.

124 "conspiracy" against Barry: Jill Nelson, *Volunteer Slavery: My Authentic Negro Experience* (Noble Press, 1993).

124 "It was a black thing . . .": Jill Nelson, *The Washington Post,* Aug. 11, 1990.

6.
The Glass House Gang

125 *The Boston Globe* reported: Anthony Flint and Muriel Cohen, *The Boston Globe,* July 2, 1991.

125 The *Times* had chased: Fox Butterfield, *The New York Times,* July 3, 1991.

126 "I knew what I was doing . . .": R. Foster Winans, *Trading Secrets: Seduction and Scandal at the Wall Street Journal* (St. Martin's, 1986).

127 "There's a mythology . . . : Bill Green, *The Washington Post,* Apr. 19, 1981.

127 "air kisses all around": Maureen Orth, *Vanity Fair,* Jan. 1992.

127 ". . . class of its own": John Russell, *The New York Times,* Jan. 22, 1991.

128 journalists have posed as: The list of journalistic impersonations was recounted by Tom Goldstein, *The News at Any Cost* (Simon and Schuster, 1985). Information on publishers' outside interests and Goldstein's own experience with fabricating stories was also drawn from Goldstein's book.

130 In a 1984 series: David Shaw, *Los Angeles Times,* July 5 and July 6, 1984.

131 "It was done in broad daylight": Eleanor Clift, *Newsweek,* Apr. 16, 1991.

132 "a heist in broad daylight": Thomas J. Brazaitis, Cleveland *Plain Dealer,* Mar. 31, 1991.

132 "Letter from the Mosquito Peninsula": Laura Parker, *The Washington Post,* July 7, 1991.

133 "On a very dark day in 1980 . . .": Gregg Easterbrook, *The Washington Monthly,* Oct. 1986.

133 "On a dark day in 1980 . . .": Richard Tanner Pascale, *Managing on the Edge* (Simon and Schuster, 1990).

134 "There has been an accident . . .": William Booth, *The Washington Post,* Dec. 13, 1990.

134 "Last year, there was an accident . . .": Katie Sherrod, *Fort Worth Star-Telegram,* June 19, 1991.

135 They invite their news sources: The Evans and Novak seminars were described by Eleanor Randolph, *The Washington Post,* Apr. 18, 1987.

135 They pull in lecture fees: Eleanor Randolph, *The Washington Post,* Apr. 14, 1989.

136 The *Chicago Tribune* has even: Thomas B. Rosenstiel, *Los Angeles Times,* Apr. 26, 1989.

137 "has created his first book-jacket . . .": Ken Jackson, *Tulsa World,* Aug. 25, 1991.

138 Al Hunt of *The Wall Street Journal*: Hunt's fund-raising was reported by Eleanor Randolph, *The Washington Post,* Nov. 1, 1989.

140 ". . . doing an exposé . . .": Dennis Washburn was quoted by Steve Singer, *Washington Journalism Review,* Sept. 1991.

140 The Portland *Oregonian* has: G. Pascal Zachary, *The Wall Street Journal,* Feb. 6, 1992.

141 "a chilling mix . . .": Anne E. Murray, Don Broderick and Marsha Kranes, *New York Post,* July 17, 1991.

142 "Confessions of a Fallen Schoolboy": Phil Donahue, *The Washington Post,* June 27, 1991.

143 "presented the case for . . .": Santa Fe *New Mexican,* Mar. 10, 1991.

144 But Richard Nixon reached: Nixon's view was reported by Jason DeParle, *The New York Times,* Feb. 7, 1992.

145 "an amorphous amalgamation . . .": Richard Harwood, *The Washington Post,* Aug. 9, 1987.

146 "either in content, tone . . .": David Shaw, *Los Angeles Times,* July 1–4, 1990. Len Downie's "embarrassed" comment was quoted by Shaw.

147 "She now acknowledges . . .": Howell Raines was quoted by Alex S. Jones, *The New York Times,* Apr. 16, 1989.

7.
Fit to Print?

151 In 1940, the press: Wendell Willkie's affair with Irita Van Doren was reported by Dick Kluger, *The Paper* (Random House, 1986).

152 "mother superior . . .": Margaret Carlson was quoted by George F. Will, *The Washington Post,* Aug. 15, 1991.

153 "Madonna & AIDS . . .": *Entertainment Weekly,* Dec. 20, 1991.

155 Lynn Armandt: The sale of the *Enquirer* photos was recounted by Larry J. Sabato, *Feeding Frenzy* (Macmillan, 1991).

156 Hart withdrew: Paul Taylor, *The Washington Post,* May 8, 1987.

156   the Cleveland *Plain Dealer* reported: William Woestendiek was quoted by Paul Taylor, *See How They Run* (Knopf, 1990).

157   The debate erupted: Susan Gilmore, Eric Nadler, Eric Pryne and David Boardman, *The Seattle Times,* Mar. 1, 1992.

158   "Nancy Reagan was . . .": Dick Sheridan, New York *Daily News,* Apr. 7, 1991.

159   "could shatter forever": Maureen Dowd, *The New York Times,* Apr. 7, 1991.

159   *USA Today* questioned: Deirdre Donahue, *USA Today,* Apr. 8, 1991.

159   *The Washington Post* described: David Streitfeld and Donnie Radcliffe, *The Washington Post,* Apr. 8, 1991.

160   "essentially compromising position": Charles Robb was quoted by Donald P. Baker, *The Washington Post,* Apr. 26, 1991.

165   Overholser overruled: David Margolick, *The New York Times,* Mar. 25, 1990.

166   The front-page piece: Fox Butterfield and Mary B. W. Tabor, *The New York Times,* Apr. 17, 1991.

167   "it is sexual harassment . . .": A. M. Rosenthal, *The New York Times,* Oct. 15, 1991.

168   "The article drew no . . .": *The New York Times,* Apr. 26, 1991.

168   "This is a crisis . . .": Max Frankel was quoted by William Glaberson, *The New York Times,* Apr. 26, 1991.

169   "rumors and gossip column . . .": Felicity Barringer and Michael Wines, *The New York Times,* May 11, 1991.

169   ". . . Others say that when . . .": Mary Jordan, *The Washington Post,* May 10, 1991.

170   Florida prosecutors later: Mary Jordan, *The Washington Post,* July 24, 1991.

171   But Williamson would not allow: Steve Duin, *The Oregonian,* Mar. 8, 1992.

173   "Our decision was based . . ." Len Downie was quoted by Foster Church, *The Oregonian,* Dec. 1, 1992.

8.
Out of the Closet

175   "lavender fascism": Randy Shilts's first remark was quoted by David Shaw, *Los Angeles Times,* June 28, 1992.

176   In 1963, the front page: Michelangelo Signorile, the *Advocate,* May 5 and May 19, 1992.

177 ". . . every form of intimidation and threats . . .": The Wisconsin politician was quoted by Doug Mell, Eau Claire, Wisconsin, *Leader-Telegram*, July 19, 1991.

178 In 1990, ACT UP pasted: This and other outing incidents were recounted by Eleanor Randolph, *The Washington Post*, July 13, 1990.

178 "homosexual thought police": *New York Post*, June 9, 1992.

178 John Schlafly confirmed: Larry Bush and Lance Williams, *San Francisco Examiner*, Sept. 18, 1992.

179 "We commit ourselves . . .": Richard Rouilard, the *Advocate*, Aug. 27, 1991.

181 "To bring the hypocrisy . . .": James Ledbetter, *The Village Voice*, Aug. 13, 1991.

181 "To my mind . . .": Howell Raines, Robert Giles and Richard Harwood were quoted by Gary Blonston and Fred Tasker, *The Miami Herald*, Aug. 7, 1991.

182 "Born in rage . . .": C. Carr was quoted by Rita Giordano, *Newsday*, Aug. 9, 1991.

183 A similar fate: Terry Dolan's homosexuality was reported by Elizabeth Kastor, *The Washington Post*, May 11, 1987.

183 John Robinson's story: John Robinson, *The Boston Globe*, May 30, 1987.

185 "The humiliation . . .": Wesley Pruden, *The Washington Times*, June 9, 1989.

185 "because I believed . . .": Reverend Moon's comments were made in a full-page *Washington Times* ad, May 22, 1992.

185 "Moonie newspaper": James Whelan was quoted by Michael Isikoff, *The Washington Post*, July 22, 1984.

186 "trumped-up," "shameful": Gene Grabowski, *Washington Journalism Review*, Dec. 1988.

186 "a nest of homosexuals": The *Washington Times* call boy stories were recounted by Eleanor Randolph, *The Washington Post*, Aug. 1, 1989.

186 "much like Watergate": Arnaud de Borchgrave was quoted by Eleanor Randolph, *The Washington Post*, Aug. 1, 1989.

186 "Sex Sold . . .": Paul Rodriguez and George Archibald, *The Washington Times*, Aug. 25, 1989.

188 "a modern version . . .": Thomas Oliphant, *The Boston Globe*, Sept. 15, 1989.

188 "Barney, it won't wash . . .": Ellen Goodman, *The Boston Globe*, Sept. 21, 1989.

188 "mindless pursuit . . .": David Nyhan, *The Boston Globe*, Sept. 17 and Oct. 8, 1989.

189 "a sicko . . .": Howie Carr, *Boston Herald,* Aug. 26, 1989.

190 "The virus seemed . . .": Kim Foltz, *The New York Times Magazine,* Jan. 5, 1992.

192 "Bullshit. I know what it's like . . .": *The New Yorker,* Oct. 5, 1992.

192 "out of the shadows of American politics": Jeffrey Schmalz, *The New York Times Magazine,* Oct. 11, 1992.

192 "witch hunt": John Lancaster, *The Washington Post,* June 4, 1992.

193 "Some editors no doubt . . .": Wes Pruden was quoted by Rowan Scarborough, *The Washington Times,* Jan. 11, 1993.

193 Larry Kramer had told the crowd: Rene Sanchez and Linda Wheeler, *The Washington Post,* Apr. 26, 1993.

9.
A Question of Harassment

196 One reporter who clearly: The Arch Parsons incident was disclosed by Timothy Phelps and Helen Winternitz, *Capitol Games* (Hyperion, 1992).

198 Bush administration officials: The Clarence Thomas marijuana story was reported by Ann Devroy, *The Washington Post,* July 11, 1991.

199 The Wyoming senator quickly: Nina Totenberg and Alan Simpson debated on ABC's "Nightline," Oct. 7, 1991.

200 "the hysterical feminists . . .": Wesley Pruden, *The Washington Times,* Oct. 9, 1991.

203 "The capital has always . . .": Maureen Dowd, *The New York Times,* May 29, 1991.

203 "The Senate and Sexism": Maureen Dowd, *The New York Times,* Oct. 8, 1991.

204 "Women make these calculations . . .": Marjorie Williams, *The Washington Post,* Oct. 11, 1991.

204 "There's a world of men . . .": Donna Britt, *The Washington Post,* June 2, 1991.

204 "It's a hell of a thing . . .": Donna Britt, *The Washington Post,* Oct. 10, 1991.

204 "appeared unlikely . . .": *The Wall Street Journal,* Oct. 7, 1991.

206 ". . . the frustration of many middle-class blacks . . .": Juan Williams, *The Atlantic,* Feb. 1987.

206 hate mail: Juan Williams, *The Washington Post,* Mar. 6, 1988.

206 "Even as I struggle . . .": Juan Williams, *The Washington Post,* July 16, 1989.

206 "The entire Clarence Thomas . . .": Juan Williams, *The Washington Post,* Sept. 15, 1991.

207 ". . . Hill and the Senate staffers . . .": Juan Williams, *The Washington Post,* Oct. 10, 1991.

210 "I love *The Washington Post* . . .": Alex S. Jones, *The New York Times,* Oct. 16, 1991.

211 Pruden attacked the coverage: Wesley Pruden, *The Washington Times,* Oct. 11, 1991.

211 On the first day: Dawn Ceol, *The Washington Times,* Oct. 12, 1991.

211 Ceol wrote her lead: Dawn Ceol, *The Washington Times,* Oct. 14, 1991.

213 "Politically Correct Newsrooms": *The Wall Street Journal,* Oct. 17, 1991.

213 "the growing influence . . .": Robert Lichter, *The Wall Street Journal,* Nov. 13, 1991.

214 "left the impression that . . .": Albert Hunt, Jr., *The Wall Street Journal,* Oct. 17, 1991.

215 "gag order": *Richmond Times-Dispatch,* Oct. 22, 1991.

215 "chose to shut him up": *The Washington Times,* Oct. 16, 1991.

215 "are guilty of . . .": Richard Harwood, *The Washington Post,* Oct. 27, 1991.

215 "self-serving ineptitude": *Columbia Journalism Review,* Nov.–Dec. 1991.

215 "a serious screw-up": Mark Jurkowitz, *Boston Phoenix,* Oct. 18, 1991.

215 ". . . angry women reporters . . .": Jonathan Alter, *Newsweek,* Oct. 28, 1991.

215 " 'She used to fantasize . . .' ": John Elvin, *The Washington Times,* Oct. 11, 1991.

216 "Senate Judiciary Committee members . . .": Paul M. Rodriguez and George Archibald, *The Washington Times,* Oct. 23, 1991.

217 Then Williams minimized: James Cox, *USA Today,* Oct. 30, 1991.

10.
Outflanked

222 "The Persian Gulf press briefings . . .": Henry Allen, *The Washington Post,* Feb. 21, 1991.

224 Perhaps the greatest indignity: NBC's "Saturday Night Live," Feb. 9, 1991.

226   "There was just a safer . . .": Michael Cox was quoted by Jason DeParle, *The New York Times,* May 5, 1991.

227   "the *Mirabella* problem": John J. Fialka, *Hotel Warriors* (Woodrow Wilson Center Press, 1992).

228   A senior administration official: The Grenada incident was reported by Lou Cannon, *The Washington Post,* Nov. 28, 1983.

228   During the 1989 invasion: Matt Mendelsohn, *The Washington Post,* Jan. 7, 1990.

236   Officers had told Browne: Malcolm W. Browne, *The New York Times Magazine,* Mar. 3, 1991.

236   "We were essentially . . .": Malcolm Browne testimony before the Senate Governmental Affairs Committee, Feb. 20, 1991

237   When Stephanie Glass: Stephanie Glass and Doug Jehl were quoted in a June 24, 1991, letter from seventeen news organizations to Defense Secretary Dick Cheney.

238   Other attempts at manipulation: James LeMoyne, *The New York Times,* Feb. 17, 1991.

238   after Schwarzkopf was interviewed: Fialka, *Hotel Warriors.*

240   "They looked like ghostly . . .": John Balzar's dispatch was quoted by Christopher Hanson, *Columbia Journalism Review,* May–June 1991.

244   "Having given up their birthright . . .": Sydney Schanberg, *New York Newsday,* June 7, 1991.

11.
The Media Primary

247   "If Cuomo doesn't run . . .": Richard Reeves, *The Philadelphia Inquirer,* Nov. 2, 1991.

248   "rumor-mongers and wimps": John Brummett, *Arkansas Democrat,* July 23, 1991.

248   "The five-term governor insists . . .": Hugh Aynesworth, *The Washington Times,* July 30, 1991.

248   "extramarital affairs . . .": George F. Will, *The Washington Post,* Aug. 15, 1991.

248   "in part because of nervousness . . .": Walter V. Robinson, *The Boston Globe,* Sept. 27, 1991.

248   "been forced to deal . . .": Robin Toner, *The New York Times,* Oct. 4, 1991.

249   the Bush White House started leaking: Some of the Bush headlines

were cited by John E. Yang and Thomas W. Lippman, *The Washington Post,* Jan. 25, 1992.

250   "economic recovery plan . . .": Robert Pear, *The New York Times,* Jan. 26, 1992.

251   "sickening . . .": Jim Gannon, *Detroit News,* Jan. 28, 1992.

252   "the degradation of democracy": David S. Broder, *The Washington Post,* Jan. 28, 1992.

252   "the Geraldo-ization . . .": *The Philadelphia Inquirer,* Jan. 28, 1992.

252   "grab-your-crotch journalism": David Nyhan, *The Boston Globe,* Jan. 28, 1992.

252   "Big Media": Thomas Oliphant, *The Boston Globe,* Jan. 29, 1992.

253   "became front-page news . . .": Kevin Sack, *The New York Times,* Jan. 30, 1992.

254   "trying to expatiate . . .": Wesley Pruden, *The Washington Times,* Feb. 3, 1992.

254   On February 6: Jeffrey Birnbaum, *The Wall Street Journal,* Feb. 6, 1992.

257   questionable Ozarks land deal: Jeff Gerth, *The New York Times,* Mar. 8, 1992.

258   "slander" and "intentional falsehoods": Thomas Oliphant, *The Boston Globe,* Mar. 18, 1992.

262   "startlingly regressive": Peter Gosselin, *The Boston Globe,* Mar. 19, 1992.

262   "snake oil": Jodie T. Allen, *The Washington Post,* Mar. 22, 1992.

262   "the single greatest rip-off . . .": Lars-Erik Nelson, New York *Daily News,* Mar. 25, 1992.

262   "shown reporters a statement . . .": Gwen Ifill, *The New York Times,* Mar. 19, 1992.

262   "an alien . . .": Lars-Erik Nelson, New York *Daily News,* Mar. 27, 1992.

263   "fraud" and "Liar Bill": Mike McAlary, *New York Post,* Mar. 20, 1992.

263   "buffoon" and "radical feminist": Ray Kerrison, *New York Post,* Mar. 20, 1992.

263   Arkansas ethics law: Jeff Gerth, *The New York Times,* Mar. 27, 1992.

264   man who denounced big money: Jerry Roberts and Susan Yoachum, *San Francisco Chronicle,* Mar. 13, 1992.

264   Brown had been a director: David S. Broder and David S. Hilzenrath, *The Washington Post,* Mar. 29, 1992.

265   The first hint that the adultery issue: Jack Nelson, *Los Angeles Times,* Mar. 26, 1992.

265   Even Hillary Clinton: Gail Sheehy, *Vanity Fair,* May 1992.

266   "the Jennifer question": Deborah Orin, *New York Post,* Apr. 13, 1992.

266   "long-denied rumors . . .": Andrew Rosenthal, *The New York Times,* Apr. 13, 1992.

12.
The Talk Show Campaign

268   FDR gave fireside chats: Dirk Smillie, *An Uncertain Season* (Freedom Forum Media Studies Center, 1992).

268   "don't matter" . . . "what happens on TV . . . ": Ross Perot was quoted by Michael Kelly, *The New York Times,* May 26, 1992.

269   "The elfin, crewcut . . .": Steven A. Holmes and Doron P. Levin, *The New York Times,* Apr. 13, 1992.

269   "Computer tycoon . . .": David Shribman, *The Wall Street Journal,* Apr. 9, 1992.

269   "a crewcut billionaire . . .": Walter V. Robinson, *The Boston Globe,* May 10, 1992.

270   During a routine interview: David Remnick, *The Washington Post,* Mar. 29, 1992.

271   "This country does have . . .": Jack Newfield, *New York Post,* May 19, 1992.

271   "Are Perot's supporters . . .": Donald Kimclman, *The Philadelphia Inquirer,* June 3, 1992.

271   "Millions of blind mice . . .": Derrick Z. Jackson, *The Boston Globe,* June 3, 1992.

272   Perot told Woodward: Bob Woodward and John Mintz, *The Washington Post,* June 21, 1992.

273   "patsy" . . . "confessed": William Safire, *The New York Times,* June 29, 1992.

273   he disputes Woodward's contention: James Squires' explanation was cited by Joann Byrd, *The Washington Post,* Sept. 20, 1992.

274   "a Mafia hit . . .": Richard Cohen, *The Washington Post,* July 19, 1992.

275   "I mean, if black people . . .": Sister Souljah was quoted by David Mills, *The Washington Post,* May 13, 1992.

275   "raw race hatred": Richard Cohen, *The Washington Post,* May 15, 1992.

276   "He Cheats on . . .": Joe Conason, *Spy,* July–Aug. 1992.

276 "right into the sewer . . .": Deirdre Donahue, *USA Today,* June 17, 1992.

276 "The Bush Affair": Jim Nolan, *New York Post,* Aug. 11, 1992.

276 The "evidence" consisted: Susan Trento, *The Power House* (St. Martin's Press, 1992).

277 "There is, quite simply . . .": Joe Klein, *Newsweek,* July 13, 1992.

278 "New Heartthrobs of the Heartland": Joel Achenbach, *The Washington Post,* July 22, 1992.

278 choice of Gore "magical": Hendrik Hertzberg, *The New Republic,* Aug. 10, 1992.

278 "Bill and Al are back . . .": David Maraniss, *The Washington Post,* Aug. 6, 1992.

279 "what is likely to be conspicuously absent . . .": Sam Fulwood III, *Los Angeles Times,* Aug. 6, 1992.

279 "Once the rumor game . . .": David Lauter and Douglas Jehl, *Los Angeles Times,* July 24, 1992.

279 "almost certainly will lose . . .": George F. Will, *The Washington Post,* July 29, 1992.

280 "dominated by hate-mongering . . .": Molly Ivins, *Newsweek,* Aug. 31, 1992.

281 "the Republicans have perfected . . .": Richard L. Berke, *The New York Times,* Aug. 20, 1992.

281 Michael Kinsley exposed: Michael Kinsley, *The Washington Post,* Aug. 11, 1992.

282 "it works": Scot Lehigh and Michael Kranish, *The Boston Globe,* Aug. 28, 1992.

283 The Clinton rebuttal hit: John Harwood, *The Wall Street Journal,* Oct. 2, 1992.

283 "aides to Governor Clinton say . . .": Elizabeth Kolbert, *The New York Times,* Oct. 22, 1992.

284 His period of press coddling ended: William C. Rempel, *Los Angeles Times,* Sept. 2, 1992.

284 79 percent of those questioned: Robin Toner, *The New York Times,* Sept. 16, 1992.

284 "many of the people . . .": Wesley Pruden, *The Washington Times,* Sept. 23, 1992.

285 "eerie replay": Kenneth H. Bacon and Alan Murray, *The Wall Street Journal,* Sept. 25, 1992.

285 "promising hundreds of billions of dollars . . .": Alan Murray, *The Wall Street Journal,* Sept. 15, 1992.

286   "The Bush-man is toast": David Nyhan, *The Boston Globe,* Nov. 4, 1992.

286   "a landslide on the order . . .": Richard Harwood, *The Washington Post,* Sept. 27, 1992.

286   "liar". . ."bozo": Steve Lopez, *The Philadelphia Inquirer,* Sept. 27, 1992.

286   "charade": Jack Cheevers and John M. Broder, *Los Angeles Times,* Oct. 1, 1992.

286   "head case": Pete Hamill, *New York Post,* Sept. 30, 1992.

287   Clinton had "quietly" turned up: Jerry Seper and George Archibald, *The Washington Times,* Oct. 5, 1992.

287   "with an Anna to stroke . . .": Wesley Pruden, *The Washington Times,* Oct. 11, 1992.

288   The red-baiting tactics . . . ': Curtis Wilkie, *The Boston Globe,* Oct. 9, 1992.

288   "A new low . . .": Lars-Erik Nelson, New York *Daily News,* Oct. 9, 1992.

288   "Slime": Anthony Lewis, *The New York Times,* Oct. 12, 1992.

288   "A GOP dirt-bomb": Baltimore *Sun,* Oct. 9, 1992.

288   Tom Oliphant recounted: Thomas Oliphant, *The Boston Globe,* Oct. 11, 1992.

288   " 'political chameleon' ": *The Washington Post,* Oct. 15, 1992.

289   a senior State Department official: Michael Isikoff and Eugene Robinson, *The Washington Post,* Oct. 14, 1992.

289   Flowers had sold new details: Art Harris, *Penthouse,* Dec. 1992.

289   "Most of the article . . . is devoted . . .": Ralph Z. Hallow, *The Washington Times,* Oct. 17, 1992.

290   "jerks" and "teenage boys": Perot was quoted by Debbie Howlett, *USA Today,* Oct. 20, 1992.

13.
White House Warfare

298   "Bill Clinton is preparing . . .": David Wessel, *The Wall Street Journal,* Jan. 8, 1993.

298   "with more amorphous 'goals' ": Chris Black, *The Boston Globe,* Jan. 13, 1993.

299   "the privileged ninety or so . . .": R. W. Apple, Jr., *The New York Times,* Nov. 21, 1992.

299   "Kay introduced us . . .": William Safire, *The New York Times,* Dec. 14, 1992.

299   "For the first time . . .": Walter Shapiro, *Time,* Nov. 16, 1992.

299   "under increasingly serious consideration" Jack Nelson, *Los Angeles Times,* Dec. 10, 1992.

299   "confidential word": Rowland Evans and Robert Novak, *New York Post,* Nov. 21, 1992.

300   Baird had acknowledged: David Johnston, *The New York Times,* Jan. 14, 1993.

300   "Baird's Hiring Disclosure . . .": Michael Isikoff, *The Washington Post,* Jan. 15, 1993.

300   "an almost sure thing": David Lightman, *The Hartford Courant,* Jan. 15, 1993.

300   "have sometimes hired the person . . .": Anna Quindlen, *The New York Times,* Jan. 20, 1993.

302   "Men Need Not Apply": Lars-Erik Nelson, New York *Daily News,* Dec. 23, 1992.

302   "Hope is rapidly turning . . .": Karen Tumulty and Michael Ross, *Los Angeles Times,* Jan. 29, 1993.

302   "The new president . . .": R. W. Apple, Jr., *The New York Times,* Feb. 6, 1993.

303   In 1908: The Kaiser Wilhelm interview was recounted by Meyer Berger, *The Story of the New York Times* (Simon and Schuster, 1951).

303   In a private chat: James Reston, *Deadline* (Random House, 1991).

309   1,865 questions: James Bennet, *The Washington Monthly,* Nov. 1991.

310   "one person familiar . . .": Robert D. McFadden, *The New York Times,* Feb. 7, 1993.

311   "Mr. Clinton is proving . . .": Jeffrey H. Birnbaum, *The Wall Street Journal,* Mar. 9, 1993.

311   "a president who is tireless . . ." David Shribman, *The Boston Globe,* Mar. 21, 1993.

312   "dazzled" the capital: David Von Drehle, *The Washington Post,* Mar. 26, 1993.

312   "Almost everyone in town . . .": Joel Achenbach, *The Washington Post,* May 27, 1993.

312   "It doesn't get much . . .": Thomas B. Rosenstiel, *Los Angeles Times,* May 28, 1993.

313   "spurned lovers": Mickey Kaus, *The New Republic,* June 21, 1993.

314   "young Capitol Hill wizard . . .": David Maraniss, *The Washington Post,* Nov. 23, 1992.

314   "a symbol of everything . . .": Lloyd Grove, *The Washington Post,* June 1, 1993.

317   "the icon . . .": Margaret Carlson, *Time,* May 10, 1993.

317   ". . . leading cult figure": Martha Sherill, *The Washington Post,* May 6, 1993.

318   "the press' fault": Jann S. Wenner and William Greider, *Rolling Stone,* Dec. 9, 1993.

318   "Picking up . . .": Ruth Marcus' report was quoted by Christopher Hanson, *Columbia Journalism Review,* Nov.–Dec. 1993.

319   "Contradicting the assertions . . .": David Johnston, *The New York Times,* Aug. 14, 1993.

319   "rife with rumors": Thomas L. Friedman, *The New York Times,* July 22, 1993.

319   "salacious rumor" which "suggested . . .": James Adams, *The Sunday Times* (London), July 25, 1993.

320   "suicide over a sizzling affair . . .": Mel Juffe, *New York Post,* Aug. 6, 1993.

320   "Near the end . . .": Gerald F. Seib, *The Wall Street Journal,* Sept. 22, 1993.

320   "Government activism was . . .": R. W. Apple, Jr., *The New York Times,* Sept. 22, 1993.

321   "feminism's first mainstream icon": Tamar Lewin, *The New York Times,* Oct. 3, 1993.

321   "may be the stronger . . .": David S. Broder, *The Washington Post,* Sept. 24, 1993.

321   "riding a wave . . .": Carl Cannon, Baltimore *Sun,* Sept. 24, 1993.

321   ". . . new, slimmer haircut . . .": R. W. Apple, Jr., *The New York Times,* Sept. 24, 1993.

322   "may have come into his own": Bill Nichols and Adam Nagourney, *USA Today,* Nov. 18, 1993.

322   "relentless and resourceful": R. W. Apple, Jr., *The New York Times,* Nov. 18, 1993.

322   "a bit nutty": David Brock, *The American Spectator,* March 1992.

322   "sexual predator": David Brock, *The American Spectator,* January 1994.

14.
The Smell of Death

325 Dustin Hoffman sat: The filming of *All the President's Men* was recounted by Tom Shales, Tom Zito and Jeanette Smyth, *The Washington Post,* Apr. 11, 1975.

331 When Cox Enterprises: Details of the Miami JOA were reported by
Jerry Knight, *The Washington Post,* Oct. 18, 1988.

333 Soon Gannett asked Michael Gartner: The Gartner-Patterson
memos were reported by Karl Cates, *Arkansas Democrat,* Apr. 28,
1991.

336 "the women of this state . . .": Keith Moyer, *Arkansas Gazette,* Apr.
21, 1991.

342 "I can't take the paper . . .": Ali Nejeli was quoted by John Kifner,
The New York Times, Oct. 30, 1990.

343 "His bustling, baroque . . .": Alessandra Stanley, *The New York
Times,* Mar. 17, 1991.

343 A British government agency: The 1971 finding on Robert Maxwell
was recounted by Paul Farhi, *The Washington Post,* Dec. 13, 1991.

351 Time used the *Star*: Gregg Easterbrook, *The Washington Monthly,*
May 1981. Easterbrook provided details on Time's self-promotion,
the Thomas Watson editorials and the Goody Solomon incident.

353 Seventy thousand people were dropping: Dale Russakoff, Ron Shaf-
fer and Ben Weiser, *The Washington Post,* Aug. 18, 1981.

15.
Pink Flamingo Journalism

356 "So much of what we do . . .": Christian Anderson was quoted by
David Shaw, *Los Angeles Times,* Mar. 15, 1989.

358 Few marketing tricks: The history of newspapers is drawn in part
from Peter Stoler, *The War Against the Press* (Dodd Mead & Co.,
1986), Michael Schudson, *Discovering the News* (Basic Books, 1978),
and Meyer Berger, *The Story of The New York Times* (Simon and
Schuster, 1951).

360 *USA Today* was: Valuable background information on *USA Today*'s
history was provided by Peter Prichard, *McPaper* (Andrews, McMeel
& Parker, 1987).

361 ". . . Who Say They Sleep Nude": The poll is from *USA Today,* Oct.
7, 1991.

364 "When *USA Today* first began . . .": Linda Ellerbee, *News Inc.* magazine, Feb. 1991.

365 "I prefer to tell . . .": Stephanie Murphy was quoted by Elizabeth Lesly, *Washington Journalism Review,* Nov. 1991.

372 "There is a single woman . . .": Jane Gross, *The New York Times,* Apr. 28, 1987.

16.
Reclaiming the Franchise

380 "I belong to an entire . . .": Bill Walker, *San Francisco Bay Guardian,* July 18, 1990.

380 the wholesale squandering . . .": Richard Kipling, *Columbia Journalism Review,* Oct. 1991.

383 The Atlanta *Journal:* The Atlanta phone service and other new technology was well described by David Shaw, *Los Angeles Times,* June 3, 1991.

384 "Bart Simpson's critique . . .": Jon Katz, *Rolling Stone,* Mar. 5, 1992.

387 the lavish spending habits: Charles Shepard, *The Washington Post,* Feb. 16, 1992.

389 Barlett and Steele struck a nerve: Donald Barlett and James Steele, *The Philadelphia Inquirer,* Oct. 20, 1991.

390 "impresario of an abrasive floating . . .": Martin Gottlieb and Dean Baquet, *The New York Times,* Dec. 19, 1991.

390 "have a chip . . .": Lynne Duke, *The Washington Post,* Dec. 24, 1991.

390 "many of our beliefs . . .": Christopher John Farley, *USA Today,* Dec. 16, 1991.

Index

About the Author

Howard Kurtz is the media reporter for *The Washington Post,* where he has worked since 1981. He is a veteran of the Bergen *Record* and now-deceased *Washington Star,* and his work has appeared in *The New Republic, Columbia Journalism Review, The Washington Monthly* and *New York* magazine. He lives in Washington, D.C., with his wife and two daughters.